AF413094

Civil War Photo Forensics

Civil War Photo Forensics

INVESTIGATING BATTLEFIELD PHOTOGRAPHS THROUGH A CRITICAL LENS   SCOTT HIPPENSTEEL

THE UNIVERSITY OF TENNESSEE PRESS | KNOXVILLE

Library of Congress Cataloging-in-Publication Data

Names: Hippensteel, Scott, 1969- author
Title: Civil War photo forensics : investigating battlefield photographs through a critical lens / Scott Hippensteel.
Description: First edition. | Knoxville : The University of Tennessee Press, [2026] | Includes index. | Summary: "Author Scott Hippensteel reconsiders iconic photographs from the American Civil War in a completely new light, questioning everything we have been taught about the images and their significance. Employing new scientific techniques to investigate the timing, location, and authenticity of photographs taken by Alexander Gardner, Mathew Brady, Timothy O'Sullivan, and their contemporaries, Hippensteel provides fresh insights into the motivations behind these pioneers in battlefield photography"—Provided by publisher.
Identifiers: LCCN 2025045287 (print) | LCCN 2025045288 (ebook) | ISBN 9798895270875 hardcover | ISBN 9798895273227 epub | ISBN 9798895273173 adobe pdf
Subjects: LCSH: United States—History—Civil War, 1861–1865—Photography—Historiography | Photography in historiography | War photography—United States—History—19th century | Image analysis | Gardner, Alexander, 1821–1882 | Brady, Mathew B., approximately 1823–1896 | O'Sullivan, Timothy H., 1840–1882 | LCGFT: Case studies
Classification: LCC E468.9 .H67 2026 (print) | LCC E468.9 (ebook) | DDC 973.70022/2—dc23/eng/20260128
LC record available at https://lccn.loc.gov/2025045287
LC ebook record available at https://lccn.loc.gov/2025045288

In loving memory of Emma Mains Tritt and Monette Eissen Redslob

CONTENTS

PREFACE

A few years ago, the University of Tennessee Press published an award-winning book about the photographic history of the Port Hudson campaign.[1] Before delving into the fascinating and mostly never-before-seen collection of photographs, the author, Lawrence Lee Hewitt, briefly explored the historical relevance of Civil War photographs. His discussion was not limited to the photographs from Port Hudson, as he also broadened the dialogue to explore how a historian's crafting of a narrative of an event might be supported, or occasionally diminished, by the inclusion of these negatives.

The author also discussed several broad and confusing debates among Civil War photographic aficionados pertaining to the "importance" of one particular image when compared to others of a specific genre, and, for example, the exact criteria a photograph must meet in order to be classified as having been "taken in action." His description of the most *significant* photographs, and collections of photographs, from the war included descriptors such as "quantity," "diversity," "rarity," and "uniqueness."[2]

A few years before the publication of *Port Hudson: The Most Significant Battlefield Photographs of the Civil War*, another volume took on a similar task. When J. Matthew Gallman and Gary W. Gallagher published *Lens of War: Exploring Iconic Photographs of the Civil War* in 2015, they asked twenty-six historians to select and write an essay about their favorite photograph. Many of their selected "iconic" photographs are well known and several can be found in this very book, but none can be found in Hewitt's book about Port Hudson and "The Most Significant Battlefield Photographs of the Civil War." This raises an interesting question about how historians can look at a collective group of photographs from the war and argue that the "iconic" and "significant" groups are entirely mutually exclusive.[3]

This book is about this continuum spanning between iconography and significance. The text starts with an entirely novel approach to determining the most *iconic*—by this measure, best known and most republished—photograph from the last one hundred years and ends with a discussion and argument for the war's most *historically important* photograph and photographer. Along the way, there are multiple investigations that are reminiscent of the skeptical debunking of William Frassanito and the photographs of Gettysburg, and a few chapters that include scientific analysis and critical reasoning applied to the photographic process and resulting compositions.

In short, this book is about the historical significance of the best-known photographs that emerged from the Civil War, and not always in a positive way. Critical and scientific analysis of these photographs demonstrates that much of what we think we know about history, as portrayed in these negatives, is incorrect or, at best, misleading. The photographs of Brady and Gardner appear to show us where men died, how they were killed, and the weapons they were carrying, but not really. Bodies were moved, photographs were staged, and props were added, repeatedly. After this fraudulent behavior is thoroughly documented, then, the question to be addressed is whether a photograph can truly be iconic, significant, or historically important if the subject matter has also been manipulated.

Hewitt wrote that "Historical events are never black and white, but historians, ironically, have done a better job of interpreting them than black-and-white photographs."[4] The goal of this book is to provide context to the photographs of the Civil War from a methodically critical perspective. In doing so, we'll take a fresh look at these photographs through a lens that recognizes the photographers' manipulation, motive, and artistic license. Hopefully, the reader will be rewarded by applying these new scientifically oriented perspectives on these old stereo views, and the result will be a better contextual understanding of the photographs and of the role of the Civil War photographer as a "photojournalist."

ACKNOWLEDGMENTS

Thirty-three years ago my parents, Phil and Jane Hippensteel, gave me an unusual gift for my birthday: They paid for my tuition for a one-day short-course offered by the college where they both taught. This book is the result of that class, because what I learned that Saturday promoted a lifelong fascination with science—specifically geology—and the photographs from the Civil War. The professor for the course was a familiar name, William Frassanito, and during the afternoon portion of the seminar we walked the battlefield of Gettysburg, completing a spellbinding "then and now" exploration of the black-and-white photographs in real life.

This book is dedicated to two grandmothers, Emma, my mom's mother, and Monette, my wife's grandmother. I miss my conversations with them both and wish they had had a chance to read some of my books. Speaking of family members who will never read my books, I'd like to thank my wife, Kyra, and my daughter, Tenley, for their support and willingness to tolerate innumerable battlefield visits and history lessons at the dinner table. Finally, I'd like to thank my friend of twenty-five years, Walter Martin, for his support and encouragement, both with my writing and in the classroom.

PART 1

PHOTOGRAPHERS AND HISTORIANS

CHAPTER 1

The Photographers and Their Photocraft

When Alexander Gardner's grisly images of the dead of Antietam were first displayed in Mathew Brady's gallery in New York City they reframed the general public's perception of what combat could yield. Gone forever were the unblemished visions of glorious charges by brave men and gallant defensive stands. Instead, the aftermath on the battlefield delivered bloated and mangled corpses, often gathered for a massed, undignified, and anonymous burial.

For the next three years Brady and Gardner and their colleagues, competitors, and employees produced tens of thousands of additional priceless images. The contrast between these two prolific photographers, and their approach to documenting the war, is both fascinating and illuminating. Brady, for example, is seen by historians as "the father of photojournalism,"[1] his camera representing "the eye of history."[2] Gardner, though slightly less famous in most Civil War circles, produced images that were disturbingly graphic, and the first to be clearly identified as greatly manipulated—the opposite of photojournalism.[3] By the end of the war this terrific collection of historical artifacts, so treasured by amateur and professional historians, would be reproduced as woodcarvings in national newspapers and later reprinted in hundreds of history books over the years. Also, by the finish of the fighting, nearly all of the most important photographers, and their teams, would be demonstrated to be guilty of manipulating their subject matter to some degree. This book is about these photographers, their photographs, and their tendency to blur the concept of photographer as journalist. These pages contain discussions of which artists are the most iconic and most popular, having their work reprinted in the most texts over the decades; at the same time, the most important individual pictures from the era can be established, based on opinions from both historians and publishers. Of course, this demands an interpretation of the term *important*, from either a historical or aesthetic perspective. And this, in turn, leads logically to an interpretation of the photographs with respect to authenticity: Can a documentary picture be both important and, at the same time, completely fraudulent? Here the hierarchy of manipulation is discussed, with many war images used to demonstrate the gauntlet of alteration from the posing of subjects to the addition of props, to the inclusion of false captions, to the wholesale posing of the living as the dead.[4] At what point does the "eye of history" lose all focus? Can a photograph document history that didn't happen? And what value is a photograph that is unaltered in any way if the photographer provides a false or misleading caption? Can you trust what you are seeing in a Civil War negative? Are you positive?

Outline of an Argument

The first part of this book deals with mid-nineteenth-century photography, the men who took the pictures, and the future historians who studied their work in magnificent detail. Here the artists' journeys from battleground to battleground are tracked and the products of their efforts are analyzed with respect to their popularity in contemporary history books. Also discussed is the early work of the father of photo-forensics, historian William Frassanito, and his fifty-year-old methodology for detecting Alexander Gardner's "creativity" at Gettysburg.

The second portion of the book delves into controversy: Were these men journalists or artists? If the latter, of what value are their images to historians? How does their work compare to the contemporaneous sketch artists who were patrolling the same battlefields, and who could at least capture moving subject matter on their paper?

Even before scrutinizing these photographs from a critical or scientific perspective, the degree of bias present is obvious. Keith Davis points out in "A Terrible Distinctness," "It must be emphasized that the great bulk of Civil War images are records of Union activities and personnel. . . . Clearly, the surviving photographic documentation of the war is grossly one-sided from a political and military point of view."[5]

The third part of the book spans the gauntlet between the incredibly silly and disturbingly grotesque. Here history is explored by analyzing the subtle details found in the photographs, and what these (often disquieting) details reveal about the motivations of the photographers. Why, exactly, was a particular subject chosen for permanent fixture on glass? Pets and silly poses humanized combatants and helped to sell photographs (figs. 1.1 and 1.2).[6] So did the shock of viewing dismembered or disemboweled dead soldiers. What had intrigued the photographer, and what made him think the images would be popular?[7] From puppies to spilled innards, the details of a photograph have stories to tell about the people on both sides of the lens.

I've been an avid photographer my entire life. In high school I had my

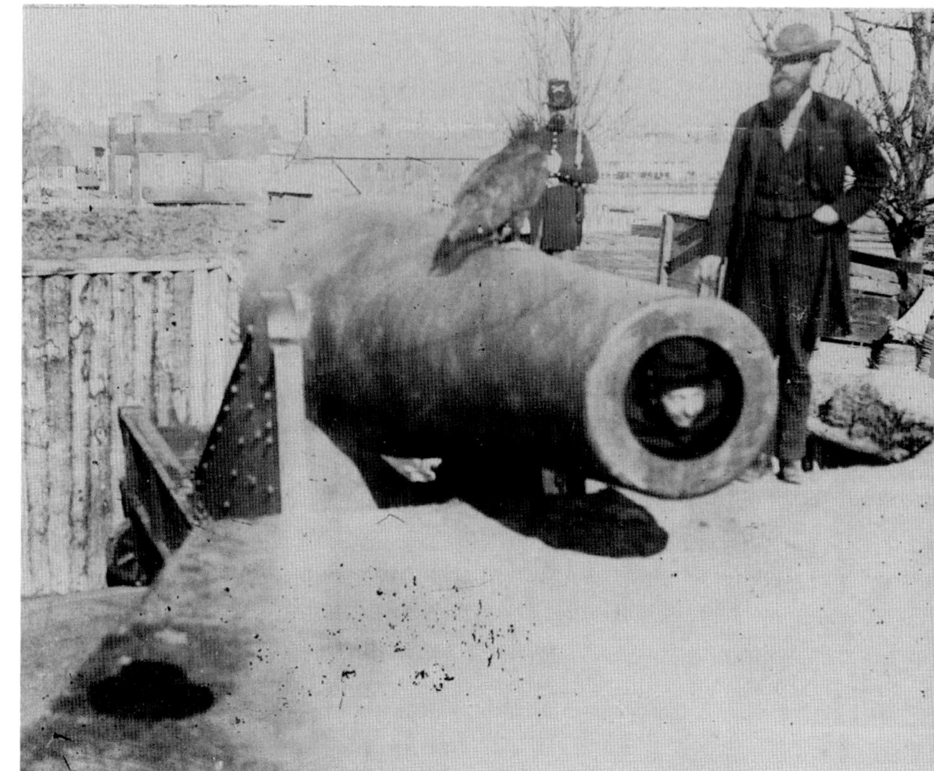

FIGURE 1.1. One of the sillier photographs from the Civil War: A soldier inside a fifteen-inch Rodman cannon at Battery Rodgers in Alexandria poses under a large bird on the barrel. Such a strange composition raises questions as to the motivation of the photographer. Library of Congress.

own darkroom, and in college I managed a photography store. Twenty years ago, I exclusively shot two types of film: Kodachrome 64-color slides and black-and-white Kodak Tri-X 400. Taking pictures was expensive and I was conservative with my shot selection. If I went on vacation, often to a battlefield or two, I might bring three rolls of film. Today, like everyone else, I shoot high-resolution digital images. If I see something of interest, I take thirty shots of it, waiting to pick out the best for later. That's the equivalent of a roll of film *per subject*. A typical visit to Gettysburg or Antietam might yield more than 500 images. With this comparison in mind, imagine a Civil War photographer and his assistants arriving on a battlefield soon after combat, knowing that each image would take, at a minimum, at least ten minutes to produce and they had a highly constrained number of glass plates to complete their work. Imagine Gardner in 1862 at Antietam, surrounded by combat casualties, with the equivalent of a single roll of film for the day. For certain scenes the selection of subject matter is obvious, but for others, the choice of subjects is found in the (often obscure) details. This section of the text explores this selectivity.

The final part of the book explains what new insights about the war can be gleaned from critical analysis of the sepia images. How much, for example, did the choice of weaponry change between 1862 and 1865? Why didn't Gardner or Brady or anyone else capture a true photograph of men in combat? And why did the photographers take dozens of photographs of Devil's Den at Gettysburg but nary an image of the fields of Pickett's Charge? The role of photography as a tool for historians is further discussed. A photograph from Devil's Den that lacks any historical context—unknown photographer, date, and precise location—can still be identified using science, and specifically geology. The boulders of the outcrops and their natural and anthropogenic weathering and deterioration can be used to both identify the locality of the postbellum photograph and provide an approximate estimate of the time it was taken, to within a decade or so.[8]

All four sections of this book carry a common theme: Civil War history as interpreted though the lens of science and critical reasoning.[9] Careful analysis and consideration of the details in the sepia images can elucidate what is true and false in the photographs and what contributions these pictures really offer about the realities of the war and the era. In other words, what insights can critical reasoning and scientific analysis provide to the question of whether Civil War photographers were acting more as journalists or artists?

Hundreds and hundreds of books have been published that include photographs from the Civil War and dozens of texts have been written about

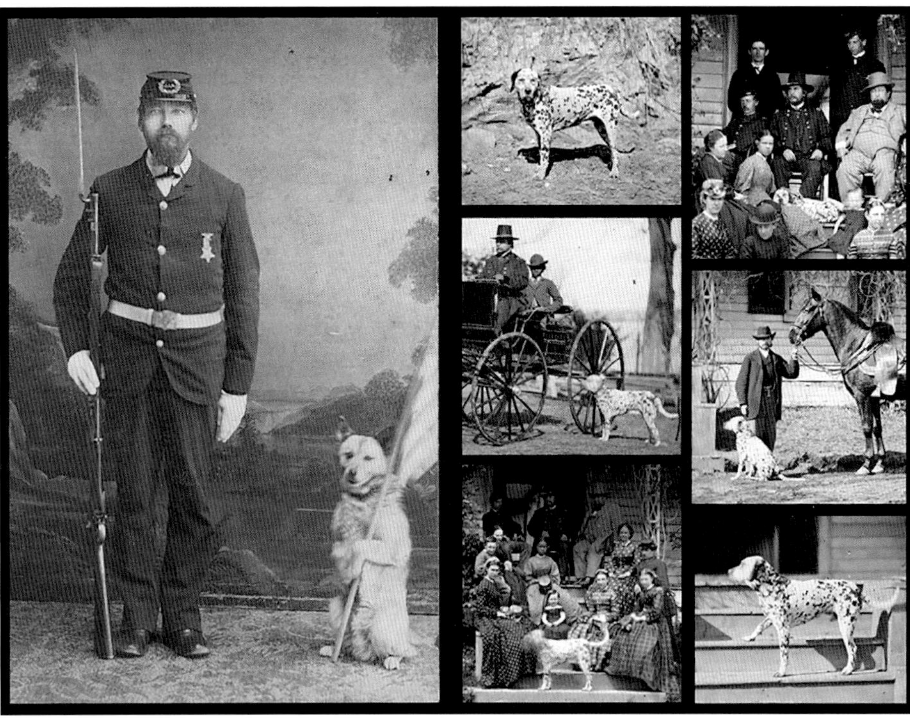

FIGURE 1.2. The most patriotic dog from the Civil War, as photographed by William Cass (*left*) and the most photographed dog of the war (*right*), a dalmatian owned by Maj. Gen. Rufus Ingalls. While campaigning against Petersburg, Ingalls oversaw supplying the army commanded by his friend and West Point classmate Ulysses Grant. The dog was very popular at City Point and the breed was relatively rare in the United States at the time. Library of Congress.

the photographs themselves. None have explored, in detail, the true historical value of these images *after* the degree of alteration and manipulation has been assessed. Historians have long credited Mathew Brady as being the most prolific and important of the photographers of the time. Nevertheless, it is easily demonstrated that he, himself, took few of the negatives produced by "Brady & Co." After all, you can't take a photo and appear in the same image—cameras with self-timers didn't exist in 1863.

Additionally, Brady & Co. produced at least a few fraudulent images. So, we are left with a seminal photojournalist who rarely operated a camera in the field and, acting as a visual correspondent, didn't always practice the very basic tenets of journalism.

At a time when modern journalism and news reporting have come under fire like never before, perhaps it is useful to also reconsider what we know and don't know about the infancy of the craft. Careful inspection and critical consideration of the images of the Civil War can provide a better understanding of how and why a photograph was created, as well as the truth about what was purported to be occurring at that time and place. All too often in the past those who publish and pass on these images have given only cursory consideration of the pictures themselves, trusting first impressions and captions to represent reality. Civil War photographs are incredibly valuable artifacts, our only high-resolution, bias-free images of the time period. However, this is only true if these artifacts are viewed through a critical filter: identifying manipulation or fabrication introduced by their creators.[10] Only after this has been accomplished can the true value of the photographs be appreciated, and the search for that context is what this book is about.

The Photographers

MATHEW BRADY

The best-known photographer from the Civil War is certainly Mathew Brady, although, in reality, he took only a fraction of the actual negatives in the field that have been attributed to him as a cameraman. Instead, Brady worked with a number of talented assistants, who operated his cameras and mobile equipment when traveling to the front or a specific battleground. He also often remained in his galleries in either New York City or Washington, DC, sending his teams with well-stocked wagons into the field to represent the interests of "Brady & Co." Proof that Brady's (usually uncredited) assistants took most of the images produced by Brady & Co. from Gettysburg or Harper's Ferry or Petersburg can be found in the subject matter: Brady himself is often featured in the scenes, proving both his presence at a historic site and his willingness to face danger along the front lines.[11]

Brady was born around 1822 in upstate New York. Early in life he trained under the portrait painter William Page. Page had been a student of the famous inventor Samuel F.B. Morse, who, along with originating his famous method of communication, also pioneered the art of daguerreotype portraiture in America. Brady soon began to study under Morse's tutelage as well, and when Morse opened a studio in New York and began offering lessons on the daguerreotype methodology, Brady joined as one of his first photographic pupils.

While only in his twenties Brady made a bold and independent move when he opened his own photography studio on Broadway Street in New York. Here he photographed all types of celebrities, from poets to presidents. Success led him to open a second gallery five years later in the national capital, where he met his future wife Juliet (Julia) Handy. Over the next decade Brady's galleries would transition from expensive metallic daguerreotypes to ambrotypes, the form of glass positives that were so famous from the Civil War.

In the early 1860s, as war loomed, Brady's business boomed. Thousands of young men, anticipating facing combat for the first time, created a large market and terrific demand for immediate portraiture and hopeful remembrance. Brady the businessman took full advantage of the situation, taking out an advertisement in the *New York Daily Tribune* morbidly reminding families and friends, "You cannot tell how soon it may be too late."[12] Brady realized around this time that the war might provide a second opportunity to sell many photographs—potential images of future calamitous battles might prove highly saleable and historically significant. Nothing like this had ever been presented to the American public before. He didn't want to "be too late" to arrive on the field of battle for this opportunity, so he assembled a team of assistants, (semi) portable cameras, and a mobile darkroom in early 1861.

Two things were needed for Brady and his men to successfully photograph a battle and its immediate aftermath: a northern victory in the fight so the territory being photographed was in friendly hands and permission from the commanders of the victorious army. Brady obtained the second of these requirements from two of his former studio patrons, General Winfield Scott and Abraham Lincoln. The first requirement proved much more problematic, which Brady soon realized as he fled back to Washington from Manassas along with the routed Federal army.

Over the next several years, Brady employed more than twenty talented photographers and provided his mobile teams with stereographic and large-plate cameras to go with their mobile darkrooms.[13] Two of these assistants, Alexander Gardner and James Gibson, forever changed the public's perception of warfare when they found themselves on the farm fields surrounding Sharpsburg, Maryland, the day after the great battle. When Brady displayed their gruesome images of rows of fallen Confederates along the Hagerstown Pike, in the Sunken Road, and gathered for mass burial, they created a sensation around his studio in New York City. These photographs were not credited directly to the photographers, instead carrying the label "Brady's Album Gallery."[14]

Brady and Company's contributions to history are certainly significant—his team of photographers were responsible for thousands of Civil War–era images from the camps and battlefields of the great conflict. What is less easily demonstrated is the role of Brady himself in the composition and creation of these important images. For example, historian William Frassanito explained that Brady gave up operating his camera because of deteriorating eyesight, switching instead to a more managerial position.[15] Ron Fields (*Silent Witness*) argues that Brady's eyesight was fine (if corrected) and that he simply let his assistants capture the actual negatives. Perhaps Brady's experience at the fiasco that was the First Battle of Manassas convinced him that subordinates would be more capable of chasing the armies with their cameras.[16]

Brady had invested a huge sum of money in financing his company and their field operations, as well as running his two galleries. By 1865, he and his men created more than 10,000 glass negatives. Brady & Co. also photographed Abraham Lincoln many times, as well as more than 90 percent of the presidents who were still alive during the Civil War. It is also hard to think of a high-ranking officer in the US army that did not appear before Brady's lens.

Brady had expected to be rewarded for all his hard work, organizational skills, and personal investments after the war ended. He anticipated that the Federal government would be eager to pay him for his important documentary treasures, archiving his work as a new way to capture for posterity the visual record of this great national strife. The citizens of the republic had been fascinated by his collections, and certainly Congress would provide a great deal of money to acquire and preserve these negatives for future generations of Americans. Instead, it was clear in the aftermath of the war that the general public was ready to move on; no one wanted to be re-reminded of *The Dead of Antietam*. With the lack of interest from public collectors greatly diminished, and little clamor from administration officials to preserve his fragile plates, the deeply in debt Brady had no financial choice but to sell his entire collection to the government, with Congress approving a paltry $25,000 in 1875 for the acquisition of his negatives.[17] A decade later, Brady's beloved wife died, leaving him alone, and a decade after that Brady would pass tragically without a dollar to his name after being badly injured in a streetcar accident.

ALEXANDER GARDNER

Although Mathew Brady is the best-known photographer from the Civil War—and the "father of photojournalism"—a convincing argument can be made that his former assistant, Alexander Gardner, took or produced significantly more historically important photographs and made a greater contribution to the early growth of battlefield photography.[18]

Gardner was born in southeastern Scotland in October of 1821. As a teenager he apprenticed under a jeweler before deciding on a journalism career. At the age of thirty, he purchased his own newspaper, *The Glasgow Sentinel* and took over as editor. That same year he visited *The Great Exhibition* in London, where he gazed for the first time at Brady's photographic prints. During the next five years Gardner's experiences from earlier in life—from the imaginative (jewelry artisan), the journalistic (newspaper), and technical (Brady's photography) merged into a desire to leave his birth country and travel to New York City where he hoped to combine all these trades. This amalgamation seemed a possibility if he were to contact Brady, optimistically wishing to join him as a new employee of the great photographer. Brady saw potential in Gardner and put him to work using his large-format camera and huge glass negatives, producing what at the time were deemed "Imperial Prints."[19]

Brady's hiring instincts proved correct, and when he decided to expand his business by opening a second gallery in the nation's capital, Gardner was the obvious choice for manager. In Washington, Gardner continued to flourish as a portrait photographer. As the war inevitably approached and business increased, Brady and Gardner plotted how best to document and profit from the inevitable fighting in the field. By the very early 1860s, Gardner had developed a relationship with Allan Pinkerton, who Lincoln had appointed the head of Intelligence Operations. This gave Brady, through Gardner, a path to present his ideas to the president. Pinkerton recommended Gardner work with the US Topographical Engineers, and by 1862 Brady's top assistant was working as the staff photographer under George B. McClellan. By this point he was no longer managing Brady's Washington studio, instead traveling and camping with the massive Army of the Potomac. Thus, on September 17, Gardner and his assistant James Gibson and their mobile darkroom were behind Federal lines at Sharpsburg.

In the two days that followed the great bloody battle, Gardner and Gibson traversed the battlefield, capturing grisly images of the dead around the Dunker Church, on the Cornfield, in the Sunken Road, and along the fences of the Hagerstown Pike. Two weeks later, Brady printed and displayed these images in his New York gallery, with the only attribution to himself, and with no mention of the actual photographers.[20] The prints garnered Brady a phenomenal amount of attention from the public and press, but they garnered Gardner nothing.

In late fall and early winter, several circumstances collided to help sever the working relationship between Brady and Gardner. Gardner was working more independently from Brady, traveling almost exclusively with the Federal army. However, with McClellan's dismissal by Lincoln after Antietam, Gardner lost some degree of access to the Federal camps. This circumstance doubtless decreased his importance as a field assistant to Brady. Additionally, the amount of credit Brady had given to Gardner and Gibson for the sensational Antietam series—none—no doubt irked the field photographers, creating another source of tension. The exact reason for the parting was complicated and may never be completely understood, and historians continue to debate the magnitude of the "Photographed by Brady" label in causing the rift between the men.[21] Unfortunately, misattributions of Gardner's fieldwork to Brady continue to the present day.

When Gardner left Brady's employment, he took more than a collection of glass-plate negatives. Also joining Gardner were several experienced field photographers who would later capture many of the most important images to emerge from the war, including Timothy O'Sullivan, James Gibson, John Reekie, and David Knox.

With his new independence, Gardner hoped to gain fame (and finance) of his own by duplicating the "success" he had at Antietam on another battlefield. To his misfortune, he fell into a situation similar to that of his former mentor and employer after the first battle at Manassas. As Gardner followed Burnside to Fredericksburg, then later Hooker to Chancellorsville, he and his team never had an opportunity to photograph the immediate aftermath of battle. The reason was simple—they could not gain access to a battleground held by the enemy, and the winter and spring of 1862/1863 was a dark time for the Army of the Potomac.

Gardner and his men would have to wait until July of 1863 for their next opportunity. Their timing was fortuitous, as a month earlier Alexander and his brother James had opened a new gallery in Washington, where they proceeded to raid Brady's gallery for personnel to populate their staff.

Gardner, O'Sullivan, and Gibson were the first photographers to arrive at Gettysburg, reaching the battlefield in the days immediately after the fighting ceased. They arrived in time to find corpses spread across the fields and among the boulders on the southern portion of the battleground. Brady & Co. arrived ten days later to tour Gettysburg, long after the dead had been buried.

In the early fall, after the tremendous battle, Gardner issued a catalog listing more than 500 images for sale, including scenes of the dead on the battlefield. Seven-by-nine-inch prints sold for $1.50, and smaller album prints and stereographs sold for twenty-five cents and fifty cents.[22]

During 1864 and 1865 Gardner photographed the siege lines at Petersburg and visited a devastated and scorched Richmond. His brother James and colleague O'Sullivan were also busy, sending back negatives from Spotsylvania, Brandy Station, Belle Plain, and Fredericksburg. The well-traveled O'Sullivan even trekked from Petersburg to Fort Fisher on the Cape Fear River in North Carolina, before returning to photographs the events at Appomattox.

Competition between Brady and Gardner continued on all fronts: Brady is best known as the portrait photographer of Abraham Lincoln (look at a five-dollar bill), but Gardner took a number of photographs of the great president as well, including the last one before his assassination. And, unlike Brady, he captured Lincoln's conspirators on glass, documenting both their unhappy portraits in confinement and their executions.

Within a decade after the war Gardner had given up photography, pursuing a career selling insurance. Before he switched professions, he made one final attempt to profit from his battlefield photography, and this production, while financially not a terrific success, made an important contribution to Civil War history and the art world. *Gardner's Photographic Sketch Book of the Civil War* (volume 1) consisted of fifty high-resolution, hand-mounted prints, each accompanied by a poetic, if fanciful, description that was written by Gardner.[23] The two-volume set contained one hundred photographs and was quite expensive when it arrived in 1866, as many Americans were trying to move on from the recent unpleasantness.[24] As a result, sales were paltry.[25] Despite the lack of financial reward, this artistic contribution was well summarized by the Metropolitan Museum of Art, who stated the *Sketch Book* "Still serves as a salutary model for photographic volumes."[26]

One interesting aspect of Gardner's two volumes is the choice of work he chose to include. In a general sense, Gardner's opinion of his colleagues' photographic skill can be broadly assessed by the number of images he selected from each photographer for inclusion among his one-hundred images (Table 1.1).

When the one-hundred-total images are broken down by artist, it is clearly apparent whose work most pleased Gardner's eye. Timothy O'Sullivan created almost half of the negatives recorded by the volumes, and he was, of course, credited by Gardner. Gardner himself and his brother were responsible for another quarter of the photographs in the books, while George Barnard and James Gibson, working together, and John Reekie, credited alone, are responsible for another seventeen prints.

TIMOTHY H. O'SULLIVAN

While Brady is the most famous photographer from the war, and Gardner is the most notorious, Timothy O'Sullivan might be the most interesting. O'Sullivan worked under the tutelage of both Brady and Gardner, and by the end of the war he likely traveled to more battlefields, camps, and depots than both men combined.

TABLE 1.1 Which photographers did Alexander Gardner hold in the highest respect? Of the one hundred prints included in his famous *Sketch Book*, Timothy O'Sullivan created the negative for nearly half.

Photographer(s)	Number of Negatives in Sketch Book
Timothy O'Sullivan	44
Alexander Gardner	15
James Gardner	10
George Barnard and James Gibson	9
John Reekie	8
John Wood and James Gibson	5
David Knox	4
William Pywell	3
David Woodbury	1
W. Morris Smith	1
TOTAL	100

O'Sullivan originally worked for Mathew Brady in his gallery in New York City. At the start of the Civil War, the twenty-one-year-old photographer moved south to join Gardner in Brady's District of Columbia shop. When Gardner joined McClellan's command as an official photographer, O'Sullivan followed along, specializing in reproducing maps using his skills with the large-format camera. In early 1862 he moved south, photographing the coastal campaigns in the Carolinas and Georgia. Here he captured on glass the famous photographs of the shell-torn rubble of Fort Pulaski.

By the summer of that year, O'Sullivan was back in Virginia, following Major General John Pope's confusingly named Army of Virginia as it plodded towards destruction at Second Manassas. It was during this interval that he visited the battlefield of Cedar Mountain, soon after the fighting ended.

Toward the final months of 1862, Gardner split from Brady, and O'Sullivan went with him. Gardner, O'Sullivan, and James Gibson traveled to Gettysburg during the first week of July 1863, where they took a series of ghastly photographs of the dead that surpassed the earlier Antietam series in terms of brutality, melancholy, and (especially) gore. This was the location where O'Sullivan photographed Gardner's famous *A Harvest of Death*.

After Gettysburg, O'Sullivan had free reign to travel from battlefield to battlefield, sending negatives back to Gardner in the capital. His travels took him across Virginia to Spotsylvania Court House, Petersburg, Appomattox, and south again to coastal North Carolina (Fort Fisher). His photographic technique also showed great improvement, with much clearer and well-defined negatives captured at Fort Fisher when compared to the set published two years earlier from Fort Pulaski.[27]

After the war, O'Sullivan continued his photographic pursuits, joining the United States Geological Exploration of the Fortieth Parallel as their official photographer. This expedition was jointly led by a Civil War field officer, Andrew Humphreys, and a field geologist, Clarence King. Fieldwork for the survey lasted from 1867 until 1872, with O'Sullivan photographing landscapes, rock formations, mines, and Native American ruins. Around this same time, he also left the country to photograph the survey team that was looking for the best path across the Isthmus of Panama. He also spent three years in the early 1870s with Lieutenant George Wheeler and his survey of the 100th Meridian.

During his travels, and unbeknownst to O'Sullivan, he had pioneered the field of geophotography. Many of his works found their way into the United States Geological Survey's photographic archive, where they compare favorably to the work of another later and more famous black-and-white specialist, Ansel Adams. Unfortunately, many of O'Sullivan's fragile negatives were destroyed during the demanding trip and in transit east back to Washington.

During his first twenty-one years, O'Sullivan learned to become a great photographer. During his second twenty-one years, he used these skills as a master photographer of both battlefield carnage and landscape beauty. He died at age forty-two of tuberculosis.

ANDREW J. RUSSELL

Russell took the most "technical" or documentarian photographs from the Civil War, often concentrating on railroads, supply depots, and bridges.[28] Nevertheless, Russell was more than a technician; he was a true artist, painting landscapes and portraits prior to the war.

Russell worked for the US army from almost the beginning of the war, but not as a photographer. Instead, he painted dramatic dioramas that were intended to capture the attention of potential young recruits. During the summer of 1862 he volunteered to join the fight and mustered in as a Captain in the 141st New York Volunteer Regiment.

The next winter the soldier/artist met Egbert Guy Fowx, a photographer who had worked for both Mathew Brady and the War Department. Russell hired Fowx to teach him how to create negatives using the collodion wet-plate process. Soon after mastering this technique, Russell's photographs began appearing in the *Official Reports* of Colonel Herman Haupt. Haupt was a civil engineer with a particular talent for railroad construction. Impressed with Russell's work, he arranged to have the photographer transferred from the infantry to work on documenting the progress of the United States Military Railroad and the Quartermasters Corps.

In this position Russell could travel across the Eastern Theater of war, and in early May 1863, less than two months after learning the basics of photography, he found himself along the infamous Stone Wall at Fredericksburg, with newly fallen Confederate soldiers lying before his camera.

Russell stayed with the army until after the war, remaining the only "official" military officer who produced photographs. After the war, he would continue photographing railroads, operating as the official photographer of the Union Pacific Railroad in 1868. The next year he photographed the construction and completion of the first transcontinental railroad, including the driving of the golden spike on May 10, 1869. In many ways, Russell's post-bellum career mirrored that of Timothy O'Sullivan.

After these adventures in the war and in the west, Russell settled down in New York City, working as a photojournalist for *Frank Leslie's Illustrated Newspaper*. Russell was the longest-lived of the major Civil War photographers, surviving into the twentieth century.

GEORGE N. BARNARD

Barnard, like Brady and Russell, was a New Englander, and all three photographers were born within three years of each other. Early in life he dabbled in the hotel business in Oswego, New York. Here he began to study photography and in 1853 he captured images of a massive fire consuming several local grain elevators. Many historians of photography consider this picture to be the first authentic contribution to the field of popular photojournalism.

After photographing Lincoln's 1861 inauguration on March 4, Barnard started a career in the military that was similar to that of Gardner, Brady, or, more formally, Russell—except Barnard was in the Western Theater of the war. He was named official photographer of the Military Division of the Mississippi and in this role he photographed the campaigning around Nashville and Knoxville, eventually following Sherman to Atlanta and then across the south to Savannah.[29]

Barnard is known to have struggled with cold weather during his efforts to photograph the fortifications in Tennessee.[30] When the weather cooperated, he successfully took detailed and remarkable photographs, including an important series documenting the fortifications surrounding Atlanta.

At the end of the war, Barnard produced a volume of his collected photographs comparable to Alexander Gardner's *Sketch Book*.[31] This book of sixty-one high-resolution albumen prints illustrated convincingly the chaos Sherman's Campaign for Atlanta brought to the south.[32]

After the war Barnard continued his photographic practice, opening studios in several cities, and losing one of them to the Great Chicago Fire of 1871. In one small way he contributed to the broadening of the practice of photography for the non-specialist. Later in life he worked briefly with a young inventor/entrepreneur named George Eastman, the man who held the patent for roll film and the Kodak camera. Barnard died in 1902, just a few months before his colleague Andrew Russell.

THOMAS C. ROCHE

When Henry and Edward Anthony needed a photographer for their New York City chemical company in the late 1850s they hired Thomas Roche. The E. & H.T. Anthony Company specialized in manufacturing and distributing the chemicals and supplies necessary for capturing images on glass negatives.

When the war broke out the company sent Roche south to continue his photography, but instead of taking pictures of buildings and New York harbor, he was in the field following the Army of the James. As a result, he sent back hundreds of stereoviews and ten-inch-by-twelve-inch negatives of City Point, Dutch Gap Canal, and eventually, the dead in the trenches of Petersburg (fig. 1.3). These were divided between government use (large format prints) and public sale by the Anthony company (primarily stereoviews).[33] After the war he published a book on photography like Gardner and Barnard, although his volume was more of a technical manual than an artistic work.[34] This text, co-authored with Henry Anthony, was part instruction manual, part sales catalog.

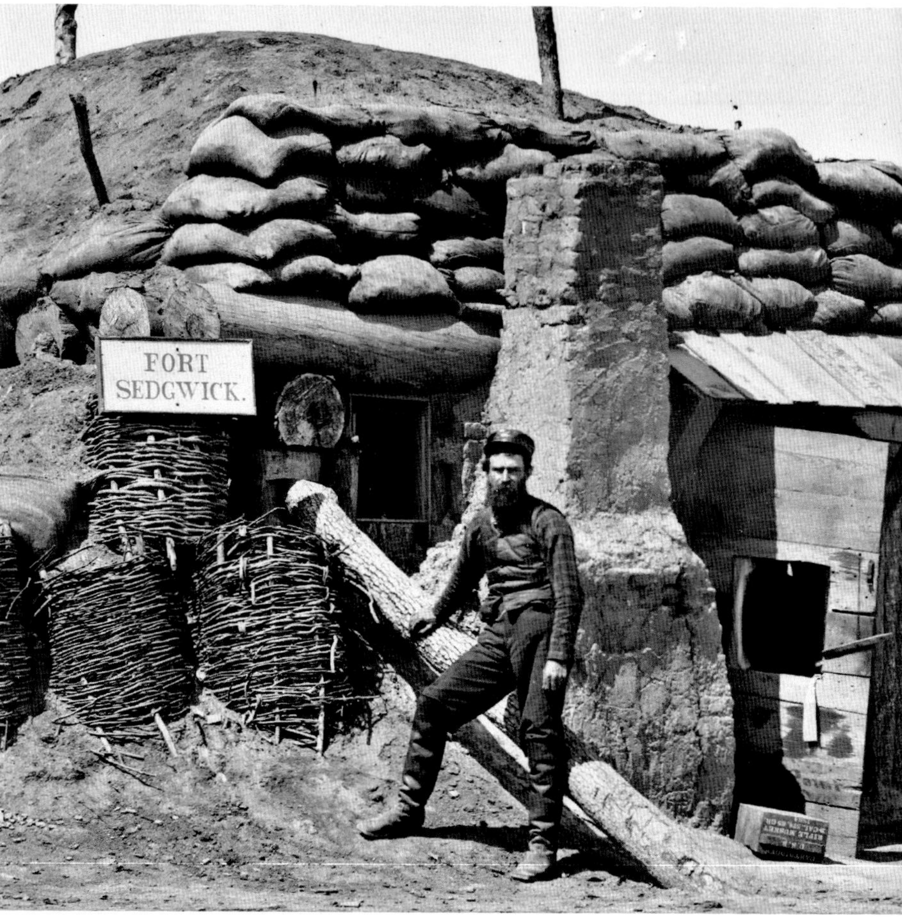

FIGURE 1.3. Thomas Roche on the Petersburg line in April 1865. The headquarters in Fort Sedgwick was dubbed by the soldiers "Fort Hell." Library of Congress.

Other Photographers of Note

JAMES F. GIBSON

Gibson's background is a bit of a mystery, but he may have migrated to America from Scotland with Alexander Gardner. Gibson worked for Brady in Washington and joined Alexander Gardner in the field to capture the two most important collections of photographs of dead soldiers on the battlefield at Antietam and Gettysburg. Gibson had also worked with Barnard earlier in the war in central Virginia around Manassas and Centreville (fig. 1.4). He also secured some moving and stark photographs of the wounded during the Peninsula campaign. Gibson started his work on the Peninsula after collaborating with John Wood at Yorktown and then taking a series of important shots of the famous *Monitor*, complete with fresh battle scars from her contest with the CSS *Virginia* at Hampton Roads.[35] All of these images were sold, of course, as belonging to "Brady's Album Gallery."

In the fall of 1864 Gibson purchased half ownership in Brady's Washington studio.[36] After the war, he sued both Gardner and Brady before taking out a mortgage on the DC studio. Cash newly in hand, he traveled (or perhaps fled) to Kansas, where he remained. His later life, much like his early life, remains a mystery.

GEORGE S. COOK

Cook was born in 1814 and spent his life in the south, operating galleries in New Orleans and Charleston. After the war, Cook moved to Richmond where he ran another studio. Both of his sons followed him into the business and after his father moved to Virginia, George Lagrange Cook kept his Charleston studio operational. Here, in early September 1886, he photographed the devastation sustained by the city's brick and stone buildings by the Great Charleston Earthquake.

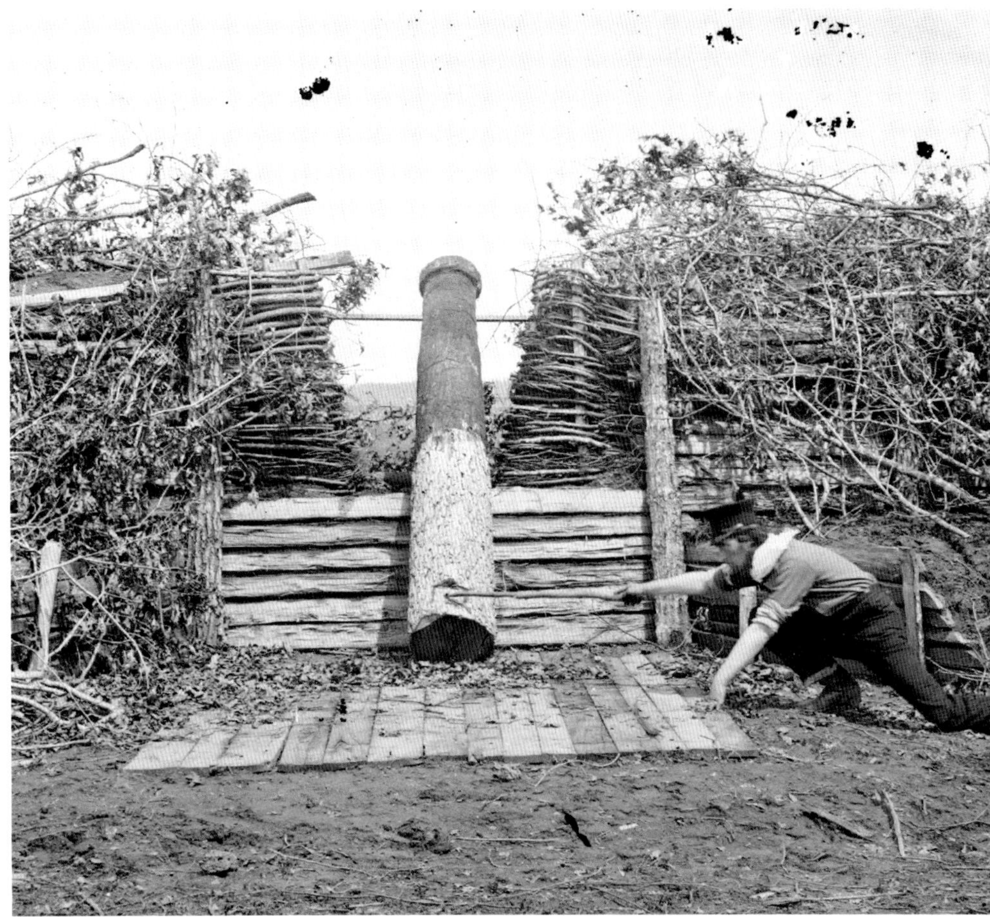

FIGURE 1.4. At least we know some of the photographers from the Civil War had a sense of humor. Here, in a photograph by George Barnard, the artilleryman is almost certainly James Gibson. Library of Congress.

George Cook is best known for capturing the first "true combat" photograph (fig. 1.5). Note that the definition of the term "combat," with respect to photography, is ill-defined. Are Gardner's famous images of the dead at Antietam truly "combat photography" if they were taken a day or more after the actual fighting occurred? Or, rather, are they photographs of the aftermath of combat? These awful images are certainly the result of combat, but the term "combat photography" suggests more immediacy. Regardless, on September 8, 1863, Cook climbed to the top of the pile of brick rubble that had been Fort Sumter and positioned his camera to photograph Federal monitors bombarding Fort Moultrie across the harbor. In doing so, he encased on a negative, men in the heat of battle for the first time, undoubtably in combat. Note that the great distance from which he took the picture did more that impart a degree of safety for the photographer—it also assured that the ships and action was taking place far enough away that the relative movement of the combatants was very small, reducing the amount of blurring that would be produced in the image. Had Cook been significantly closer the ships would have presumably been moving too fast to capture using the wet-plate/slow "shutter speed" of the time.

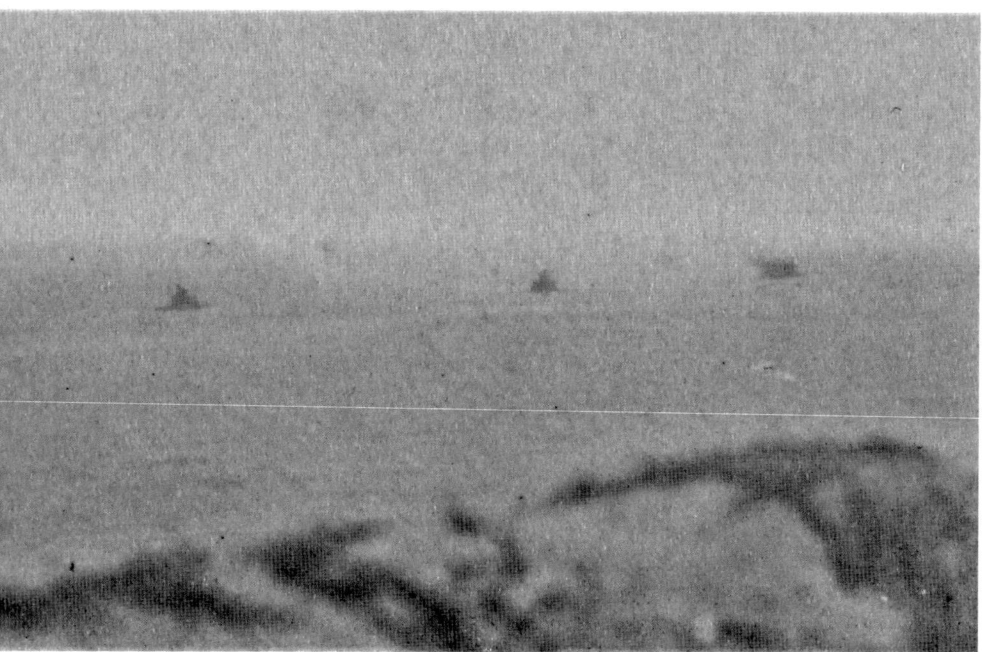

FIGURE 1.5. An enlarged and cropped version of George Cook's photograph from the top of an obliterated Fort Sumter, showing US ironclads exchanging gunfire with Fort Moultrie (*left, out of view*). Library of Congress.

JOHN REEKIE

Reekie worked for both Mathew Brady and Alexander Gardner, although only the latter, of course, credited his work. Eight of his images appear in Gardner's *Sketch Book*, all taken in Virginia. The most famous of these, and the most horrid, depicts an African American burial party gathering skeletal remains on the Cold Harbor battlefield.

Not much is known about Reekie's early life. He was a member of the Federal Quartermaster's Corp, which is where he was working when hired by Gardner. While operating a camera for the fellow Scot, Reekie visited Gaines' Mill, Cold Harbor, Dutch Gap, City Point, and Richmond.

SAMUEL A. COOLEY

Cooley was born and died in Hartford, Connecticut, but spent much of his life in the Carolinas. When the Federal navy came to Port Royal, South Carolina, Cooley traveled the short distance from his home in Beaufort to capture the events on glass. With this success, he was named as the official photographer of the US Army's Department of the South. In this position, he trailed the Federal X Corps and eventually produced coastal images of St. Augustine, Charleston, and Savannah. Particularly noteworthy were his collection of pictures taken after the fall of Fort McAllister to Sherman's invading infantry in Georgia.

After the war, Cooley continued to sell his photographs, but also branched into other areas of interest, becoming both an auctioneer and a sheriff. In 1869 he moved back to his hometown where he spent the final thirty years of his life.

WILLIAM D. MCPHERSON

William McPherson was born in 1833 and was another New Englander. McPherson's career early in the Civil War mirrors that of Andrew Russell, as he joined the fighting ranks before finding his calling as a field photographer. McPherson recruited seventy enlistees for the 2nd US Sharpshooters, where he was appointed as a captain of Company G. He fought at Second Manassas, South Mountain, and Antietam before he was discharged.

After his service in uniform, he returned to photography and traveled to New Orleans to join the Federal Department of the Gulf. He opened a studio in Baton Rouge after the Confederates abandoned the city, always hoping to stay near his customers, US soldiers. McPherson took on a partner, A. J. Oliver, and soon after this the duo recorded a photograph of a formerly enslaved person that was both heartbreaking and enraging. "Whipped Peter" depicted the gruesome reality of slavery, as the recently escaped slave's back was covered with scarred and tortured flesh left behind by his owner's lash.[37] This photograph was soon in the hands of abolitionists in the North and was reprinted, under Brady's name, across New England.

Later that year McPherson and Oliver left Baton Rouge and followed Major General Nathaniel Bank's army as it moved toward Port Hudson. Here they photographed the Federal lines during the siege, including a distant image of US sharpshooters apparently engaged with the enemy, and even managed to capture the only photograph of an army in the process of surrendering.[38] Their collection is not known for this photograph, but rather, as historian Lawrence Hewitt commented, McPherson and Oliver seemed fixated on "Lots and lots of cannons."[39]

JACOB F. COONLEY

Jacob "Jay" Coonley was a protégé of George Barnard. Early in his career, Coonley concentrated on landscape painting before Barnard taught him how to take and process glass negatives. During the first two years of the war, he bounced around between New York, Washington, and Philadelphia taking portraits and occasionally working for Edward Anthony's stereographic print shop.

In 1864, his photographic skills earned him a commission resembling that obtained by Andrew Russell: Quartermaster General Montgomery Meigs assigned him to photograph the rail lines of the Western Theater of the war (primarily Eastern Tennessee, Alabama, and Georgia). While conducting these operations Coonley continued to take photographs for Edward Anthony, including an important historical series from Nashville.

Coonley traveled between major cities in the west on a specially outfitted boxcar with darkroom facilities along with sleeping and cooking quarters. On his many journeys, he was hindered by frequent encounters with Confederate cavalry units and recently destroyed tracks and bridges.[40]

Towards the end of the war, he relocated to Charleston, South Carolina, where he (probably) photographed the Federal flag-raising ceremony at Fort Sumter.[41] After the war the photographer operated the gallery of G.J. Quinby in Charleston, where in 1868 he gained a managerial partner, George Barnard. Late in life Coonley spent a great deal of time traveling, primarily between his home in New York and his adopted home in the Bahamas, before dying by his own hand in 1915.

DAVID KNOX

Knox was, like Alexander Gardner and James Gibson, Scottish. He spent his early years operating as a machinist, a trade he continued after emigrating to America in 1849. How Knox gained his photographic training is a mystery, but he was probably taught to use the large-format camera by Gardner. Knox joined Mathew Brady's Washington gallery sometime during the first half of 1862. Later, when the two great photographers split, he followed his countryman.

Knox has several images that were included in Gardner's *Sketch Book*, with the most recognizable taken of the thirteen-inch mortar *Dictator* at Petersburg. [42] After the war, Knox joined Gardner in the west for a brief time to capture events in the Dakota Territory, after which he returned to original trade, operating machine tools instead of cameras.

DAVID B. WOODBURY

Woodbury was one of the youngest photographers to take to the field during the Civil War, being only twenty-three years old when, in 1862, Mathew Brady sent him and Edward Whitney to Manassas. Woodbury was Brady's most loyal employee, producing negatives for him until 1865. Woodbury expeditions brought him to the Peninsula and Gettysburg, and he traveled with Grant's command in Virginia. His most famous photograph was captured with the help of Jacob Coonley on the steps of the Treasury Building, photographing the Grand Review of the Union Army in May 1865.

At the end of the war the young photographer was suffering from tuberculosis and sought a more suitable climate for his affliction, so he moved to Gibraltar. He died a year later.

More Obscure Cameramen

This brief summary of the dozen or so most famous, productive, or noteworthy photographers from the Civil War is not exhaustive; many other men working behind the camera produced a significant number of the more than 10,000 images to emerge from the war (Table 1.2). Some of these men worked for the more famous studios, while others remained more local photographers, taking only pictures of battlefields close to their small studios. Photographers from across south-central Pennsylvania, for example, flocked

to Gettysburg in the decades after the battle to photograph the landscape and, occasionally, recreate rather imaginative "after-battle" photographs.

Who Was Where and When?

Two general trends emerge from the travel of the field photographers from the Civil War. The first trend is that gallery owners like Brady and Gardner ventured into the field earlier in the war but remained at their studios in New York and Washington more often as the war dragged on. Both supplied subordinates with cameras and equipment for the hard task of following the Federal armies (fig. 1.6). Their teams of photographers also concentrated on the Eastern Theater of the war. [43] When they did travel to the front, their behavior was markedly different: Gardner *almost* never appeared in his photographs, while Brady seemed determined to prove his "field" photojournalist *bona fides*, demonstrating his presence among the combat troops by appearing in his own negatives. [44]

The second trend to emerge from the travel records is one of mobility: Timothy O'Sullivan, for example, was everywhere. He worked for both of the most important gallery owners during the war, and their separation in late 1862 allowed him, and many other photographers, new opportunities to travel to the front lines. He photographed Fairfax, Virginia, outside the national capital, the coast of South Carolina and Georgia, and Manassas Junction. He captured on glass the dead at Gettysburg with Gardner and the dead at Petersburg with Knox. His camera visited Spotsylvania, North Anna, Cold Harbor, and Appomattox. He followed the armies of McClellan, Pope, Gillmore, and Grant.

O'Sullivan's photographs are abundant in popular illustrated histories of the war, although pictures of their creator are rarer. Brady's are also common, of course, and a little scrutiny reveals that he is present in more of the illustrations than one might suspect (figs. 1.7 and 1.8). O'Sullivan is not known to have appeared in any of the photographs

Table 1.2 Less well-known photographers from 1861 to 1865 and their most notable accomplishments.

Photographer	Working for	Most Famous Work	Notes
Abraham I. Blauvelt (and William Brooks)	Independent	Photos of US Colored Troops at Port Hudson	Took several photographs of the headquarters of the "Corps D/Afrique" in late 1863 and early 1864.
William F. Browne	Independent/ Gardner	Photos of Custer / James River batteries	Like several other photographers, he died of consumption (tuberculosis) soon after the war ended.
James Gardner	Brady / Gardner	Ruins of the Norfolk Naval Yard / Harpers Ferry	Younger brother of Alexander, they worked together for Brady in 1862.
Frederick Gutekunst	Independent	Gettysburg (Chambersburg Pike and John Brown)	Philadelphia photographer also notable for his portrait of Grant.
Philip Haas (and Washington Peele, his assistant)	Independent	Gillmore's siege of Morris Island and Union ironclads in action against Forts Sumter and Moultrie	Recorded Union operations against Charleston in spring/summer of 1863, then resigned position because of poor health.
Robert "Royan" Linn	Independent	Hundreds of photographs of Union officers and soldiers at Point Lookout (Chattanooga)	Worked on Lookout Mountain from 1863 to 1886. He is the primary reason this location was probably the most photographed spot from the Civil War.
William R. Pywell	Brady / Gardner	Slave pens at Alexandria	Photographed in the east and west; joined Gardner on the Kansas-Pacific Railroad Survey after the war.
William Morris Smith	Gardner	Forts around Washington, DC	Mostly photographed scenes around the national capital (Georgetown, Manassas).
Isaac and Charles Tyson	Independent	Lincoln at Gettysburg	Studio in Gettysburg; William H. Tipton was an apprentice.
Edward T. Whitney	Brady	Peninsula Campaign (Yorktown)	Took many of the "Brady & Co." images.

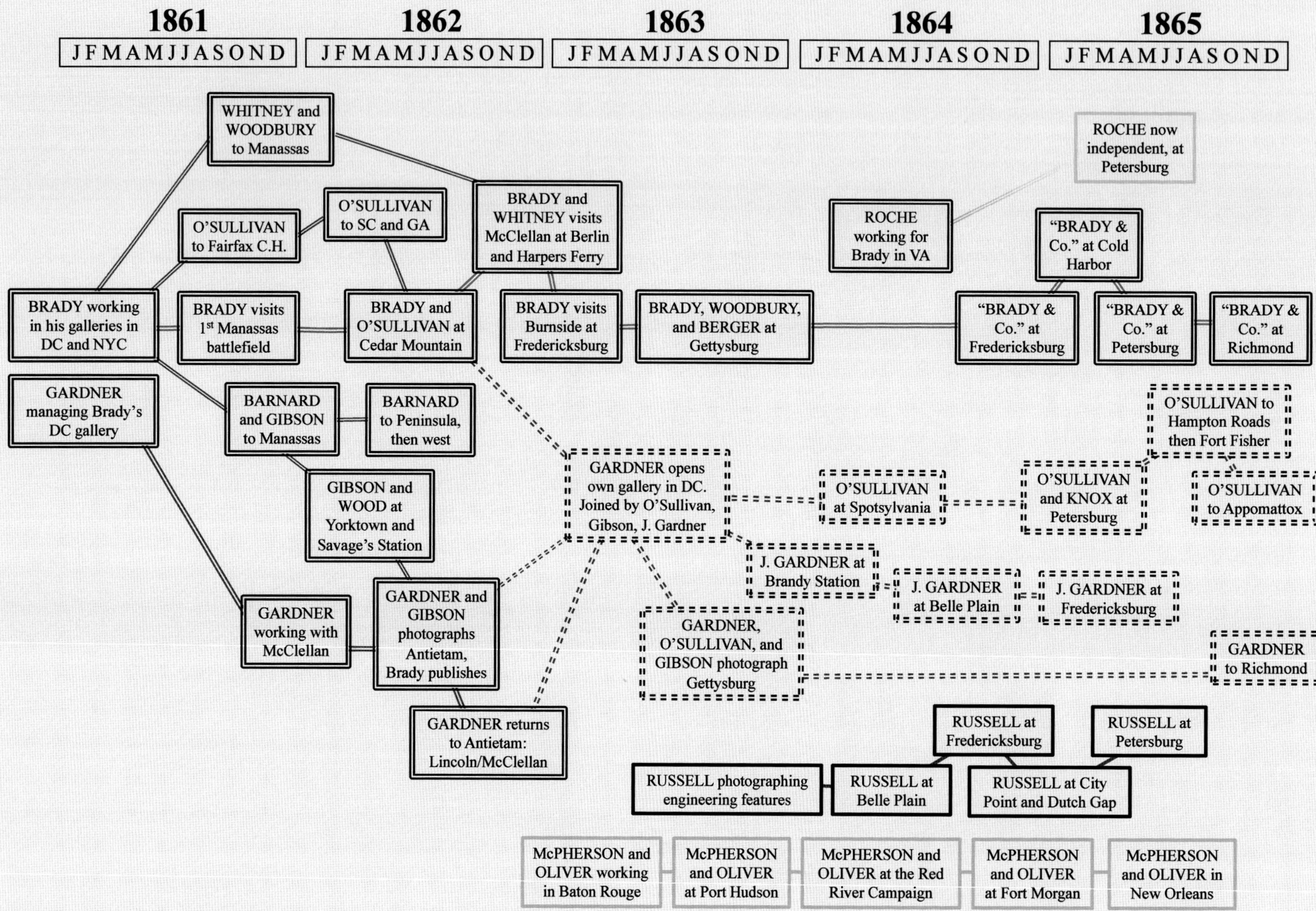

1861 JFMAMJJASOND
1862 JFMAMJJASOND
1863 JFMAMJJASOND
1864 JFMAMJJASOND
1865 JFMAMJJASOND
WHITNEY and WOODBURY to Manassas
ROCHE now independent, at Petersburg
O'SULLIVAN to Fairfax C.H.
O'SULLIVAN to SC and GA
BRADY and WHITNEY visits McClellan at Berlin and Harpers Ferry
ROCHE working for Brady in VA
"BRADY & Co." at Cold Harbor
BRADY working in his galleries in DC and NYC
BRADY visits 1st Manassas battlefield
BRADY and O'SULLIVAN at Cedar Mountain
BRADY visits Burnside at Fredericksburg
BRADY, WOODBURY, and BERGER at Gettysburg
"BRADY & Co." at Fredericksburg
"BRADY & Co." at Petersburg
"BRADY & Co." at Richmond
GARDNER managing Brady's DC gallery
BARNARD and GIBSON to Manassas
BARNARD to Peninsula, then west
O'SULLIVAN to Hampton Roads then Fort Fisher
GIBSON and WOOD at Yorktown and Savage's Station
GARDNER opens own gallery in DC. Joined by O'Sullivan, Gibson, J. Gardner
O'SULLIVAN at Spotsylvania
O'SULLIVAN and KNOX at Petersburg
O'SULLIVAN to Appomattox
J. GARDNER at Brandy Station
GARDNER working with McClellan
GARDNER and GIBSON photographs Antietam, Brady publishes
GARDNER, O'SULLIVAN, and GIBSON photograph Gettysburg
J. GARDNER at Belle Plain
J. GARDNER at Fredericksburg
GARDNER to Richmond
GARDNER returns to Antietam: Lincoln/McClellan
RUSSELL at Fredericksburg
RUSSELL at Petersburg
RUSSELL photographing engineering features
RUSSELL at Belle Plain
RUSSELL at City Point and Dutch Gap
McPHERSON and OLIVER working in Baton Rouge
McPHERSON and OLIVER at Port Hudson
McPHERSON and OLIVER at the Red River Campaign
McPHERSON and OLIVER at Fort Morgan
McPHERSON and OLIVER in New Orleans

for which he is credited (although Brady often failed to credit anyone, including the young photographer). In contrast, Brady is often credited as being the cameraman for a photograph in which he actually makes an appearance.

In the next chapter we revisit these photographers from a different perspective: Which of their images have made the largest impact on how Americans remember the war? Which of these photographers captured the most evocative pictures, images that have illustrated history books with the highest frequency? After evaluating their popularity, we will turn a more critical eye towards their composition and creation to determine if their contributions to history and memory are commensurate with their apparent acceptance, and even admiration.

Opposite:
FIGURE 1.6. Field travels of Civil War photographers. Those working for the Brady studio are connected by a solid double line. Those working for Gardner's team are related with a dashed double line. Note how much easier it is to trace the movements of Gardner's employees than those of Brady & Co. This is primarily because Gardner was careful to provide attribution for the negatives.

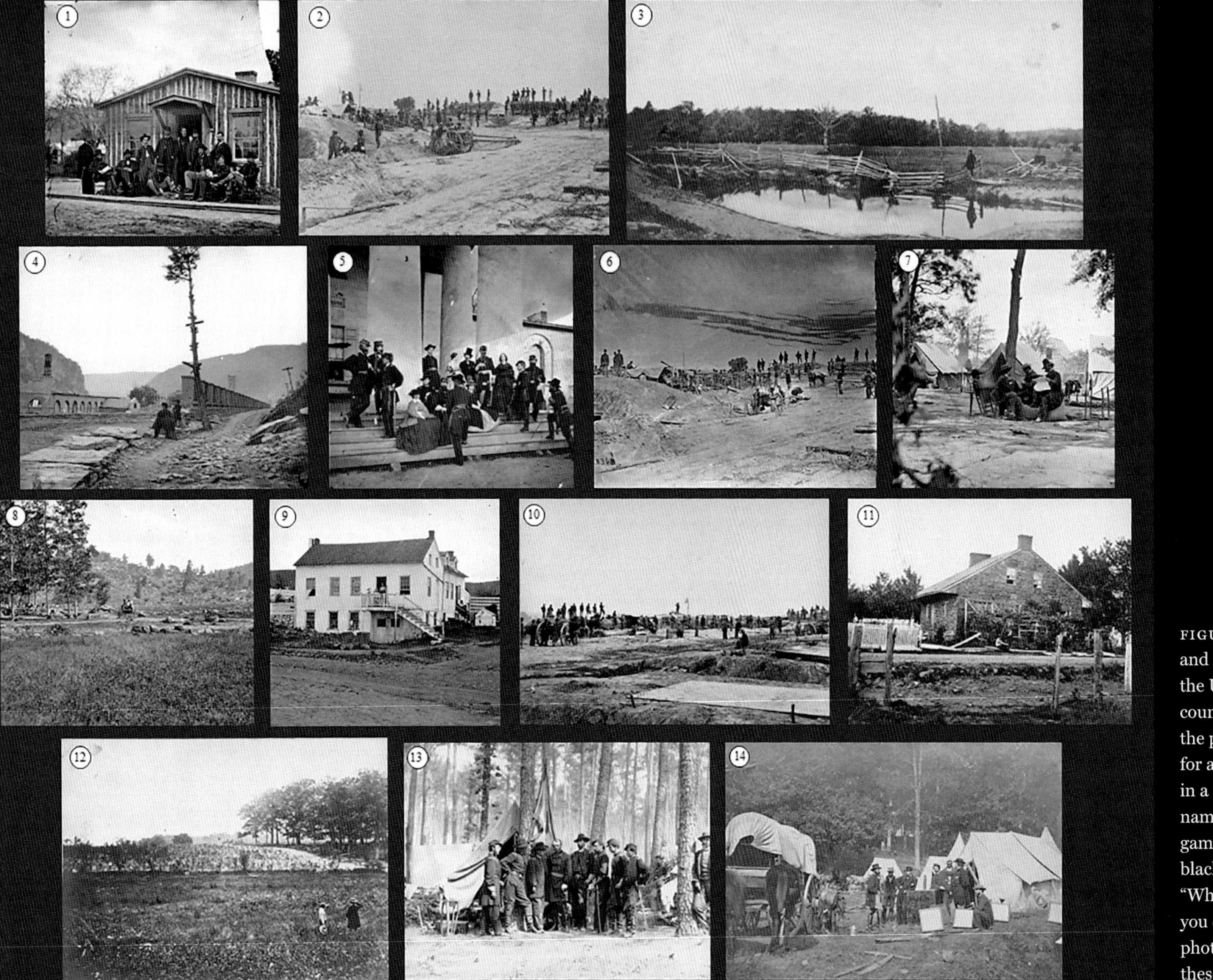

FIGURE 1.7. In the 1980s and 1990s children in the United States spent countless hours searching the pages of a colorful book for a bespectacled chap in a red-and-white shirt named Waldo. A similar game can be played in black and white called "Where's Mathew?" See if you can identify the famous photographer in each of these Civil War prints.

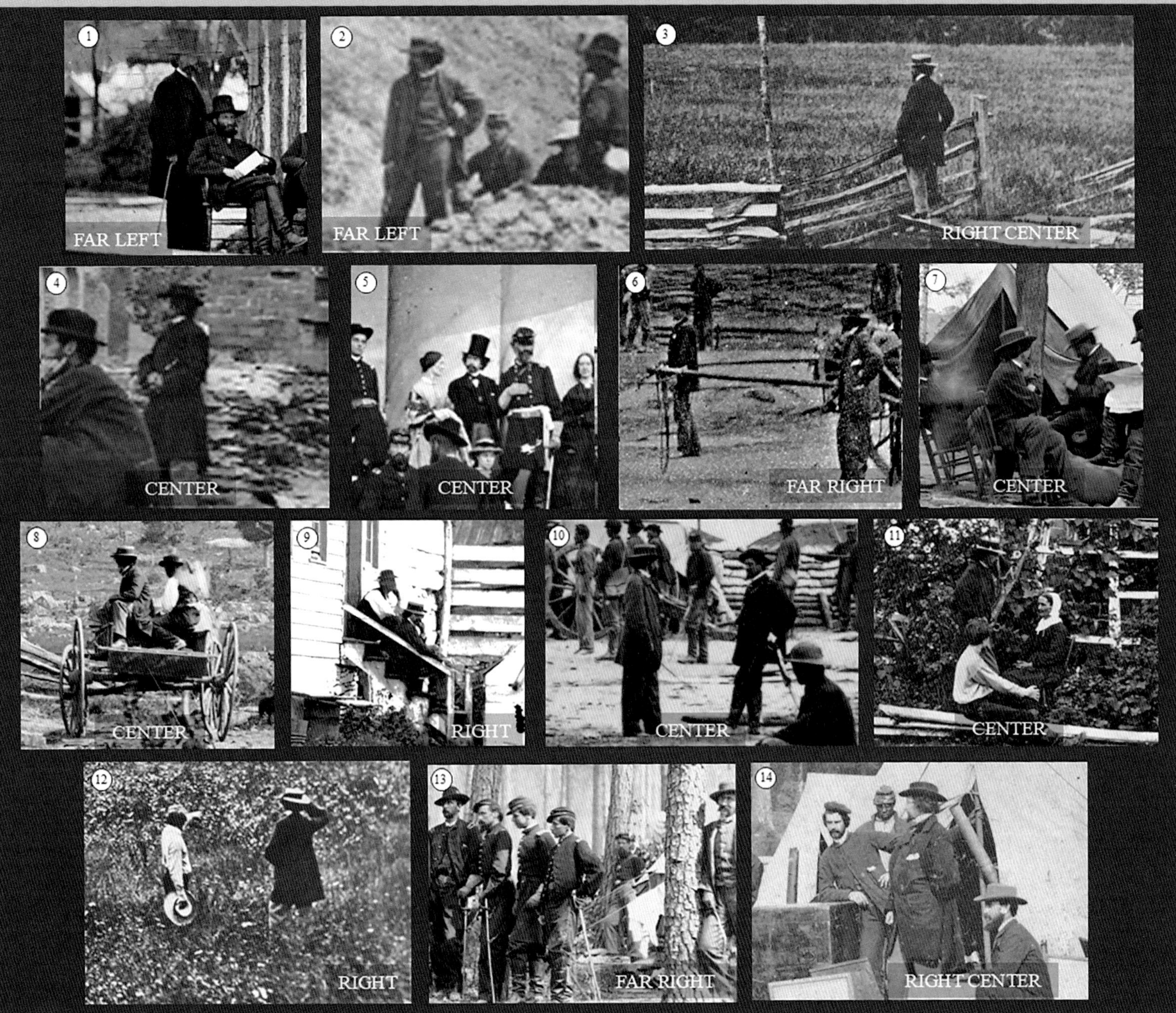

FIGURE 1.8. There he is! Enlargement of each photograph in figure 1.7 reveals the famous photographer's location. Text included on each photograph provides orientation of Brady in the original, uncropped version.

CHAPTER 2

The Hierarchy of Historical Preeminence

Who took the most popular photograph from the Civil War and who, on the whole, was the most popular photographer? This chapter is targeted at answering both questions and the answers may surprise you.

Before a discussion of the historical significance of the contributions made by Gardner, Brady, and others can commence, the exact strictures of this exercise need to be defined. This chapter, and frankly, this book, focus on Civil War photography as it pertains to the lives (and deaths) of the soldiers in camp and on the front lines. Nearly entirely absent are images captured in studios that represent personal portraits of individual soldiers, or any portraits of generals or politicians. Almost all textbooks and general pictorial histories of the Civil War era will include a photograph of Lincoln and Lee, or McClellan or Grant, in studio or camp. These common images are not considered in this chapter dedicated to popularity; instead, we focus on images of soldiers on the march or on the battlefield, or the destruction that their fighting wrought. The rationale behind this selection process is simple. This book is about combat photography, not portraits. Lee, as an example, appears in almost all illustrated compilations, but the dead along the Hagerstown Pike at Sharpsburg are shown in only a fraction of books. If an image has appeared in your wallet, it isn't discussed here—those images are, quite simply, too commonly reproduced and have

little to tell us about the nature of Civil War warfare or how these photographs were used to interpret history. If, on the other hand, the image contains men in fortifications, ready for battle, or the dead on the battlefield after the fight, or even comrades simply passing the time in camp, it is evaluated herein.

So, of all the images captured around the battlefronts, which should be considered the most significant or popular from a historiographical perspective? Which single photograph has had the largest influence on how authors, editors, historians, and the general public remember the events of 1861–1865? Note that this chapter concentrates on the popularity of photographs through time as a measure of importance, a question that can be definitively answered through the collection of data. The final chapter of this book revisits the idea of importance, but not from a popularity study but from a more historical and, frankly, opinionated perspective. This chapter investigates the popularity of photographs by considering how often they have been reprinted in books and magazines or appeared on websites, *regardless* of their historical value. Later in the book, after discussion of the manipulation and artistic license employed by many photographers is investigated, the same question of "importance" can be revisited from a more subjective, and educated, and perhaps even critical perspective.

Metrics and Methodology

The definition of "most historically significant" is complicated, with lay-people and professional scholars having a myriad of qualifications. Steven Berry, Gregory Professor of the Civil War Era at the University of Georgia, wrote a wonderful article in *Lens of War* about a photograph of an African American soldier sitting outside a bookstore in Atlanta.[1] The soldier is re-laxing with his Springfield rifle musket leaning against the storefront while he is engrossed in the pages of a newly discovered tome. Nevertheless, this thought-provoking and powerful image has only been seen by a fraction of the readers of Civil War nonfiction, who are vastly more likely to recognize Gardner's (staged) photograph of a dead Confederate "sharpshooter" in Devil's Den. Why is this so?

Lawrence Lee Hewitt recently contributed a fascinating new book on the photographs of Port Hudson, to which he added the subtitle "*The Most Significant Battlefield Photographs from the Civil War.*"[2] Apparently, his original working title for the book was "Port Hudson: The Most Photographed Battlefield of the Civil War," which led to a discussion among Civil War photographic aficionados about whether the statement about "most photographed" was entirely correct. At the end of the debate, Port Hudson finished third, far behind Chattanooga.[3] Brandy Station was probably the second most photographed battleground.

Hewitt's definition of "significant" is based on several criteria. He states, "Quality counts, but so does diversity of subject matter and uniqueness of the photograph."[4] After reviewing the collection in Hewitt's book, the differences between "significant" or "important" in this chapter, based on *popularity*, and those in the final chapter, based on *historical importance* becomes clearer. Hewitt's photographs from Port Hudson are highly sig-nificant with respect to shaping historical perspectives, but they are far from the most popular—in many cases they were only discovered recently, "That the most significant collection of photography relating to a single battlefield remained undiscovered until the Civil War's sesquicentennial should not surprise anyone reasonably knowledgeable of the conflict."[5]

This chapter is dedicated to popularity, not necessarily quality. As such, the "most significant" designation goes to the photograph that has appeared in the most history books. Soldiers in camp, on the march, or preparing for a fight have been photographed during most campaigns from the war. The dead on the battlefield were photographed on several battlegrounds, including Antietam, Corinth, Fredericksburg, Gettysburg, Spotsylvania, and Petersburg.[6] Which of these grisly images has appeared in the most general history books about the Civil War? Which photograph has been reproduced the most times during the last one hundred years, the dead along the Hagerstown Pike or in the Sunken Road at Antietam? How do these morbid shots compare, with respect to popularity, to Russell's photograph of dead Confederate infantrymen behind Fredericksburg's fa-mous Stone Wall?

To quantify the popularity of this collection of images, a rather simple methodology was employed. Fifty common and randomly selected Civil War books, all intended for a general audience, were analyzed from cover to cover to discovery which photographs were included or omitted in the highest frequency. These books, all published between 1912 and 2022, would be familiar to any Civil War enthusiast: *The American Heritage Picture History of the Civil War* or William C. Davis's and Russ Prichard's *The Battlefields of the Civil War*, for example.[7] For obvious reasons related to selection bias, no books on particular battles or campaigns were in-cluded in this compilation of works—only full breadth popular histories of the war. Along the same line of reasoning, no biographies were included in the data set. Comprehensive illustrated atlases of the Civil War, on the other hand, make up about 10 percent of the books in the collection. A few other titles from the collection make it clear that they are intended to be authoritative as to their inclusion of the most important images of the time-period (e.g., Time-Life's *The Civil War in 500 Photographs*).

After pouring endlessly through every page of these texts, twenty-eight photographs were determined to appear with the highest frequency—these represent the collection of images that will be ranked by popularity. Nearly all these books were published after the centennial of the war, and more than half were published after 1985. All in all, these twenty-eight photos appear exactly 300 times in the fifty-book data set, an average of six famous photographs per book. All images appeared in at least 10 percent of the books. Many of the books were significantly above average in terms of the number of photographs included: the *American Heritage* volume contained seventeen of the twenty-eight, while *The Civil War: A Complete Photographic History* seems to live up to its all-inclusive title by portraying more than half of the collection. Many other books, in contrast, have only one or two of the photographs found between their covers.

In the next subsection of the book, the rank-order of the photographs is presented with a brief commentary about the history and background of each photograph, and why later authors and publishers might have deemed it worthy of inclusion in their work. A discussion of the qualities of the images that are common to all of the photographs is also included. This breakdown of popularity, quality, and composition will establish the foundation for later analysis and investigation regarding forensics, fraud, and photojournalism.

Finally, a similar survey of the most popular photographs was conducted for Civil War magazines and journals, websites, and online videos. The methodology was essentially the same for all types of media: Fifty Civil War history-related publications were randomly selected and surveyed to see which of the photographs from the popularity contest were present. All the magazines and journals were titles that related, in some way, to military or Civil War history (e.g., *The Civil War Monitor*, *America's Civil War*, *Military History*). The same is true with websites—they all had a broad connection to the Civil War. For the online videos, all clips were between two minutes and one hour long. Most were found on YouTube, although some were associated with the *Civil War Trust* digital collection. A complete breakdown of the analysis can be found in Appendices A and B, and a summary of the popularity in each type of medium will be included in the discussion of the top five most popular images.

The Popularity Contest

The twenty-five most commonly reproduced Civil War photographs (non-portrait edition) are presented in figure 2.1, scaled in size according to their popularity.[8] For example, Brady's photograph of three Confederate prisoners-of-war at Gettysburg (fig. 2.2) is approximately 120 percent larger than most of Gardner's photographs from Antietam, because it appeared in 42 percent of all books, while most of the Antietam photographs did not appear in more than 20 percent.

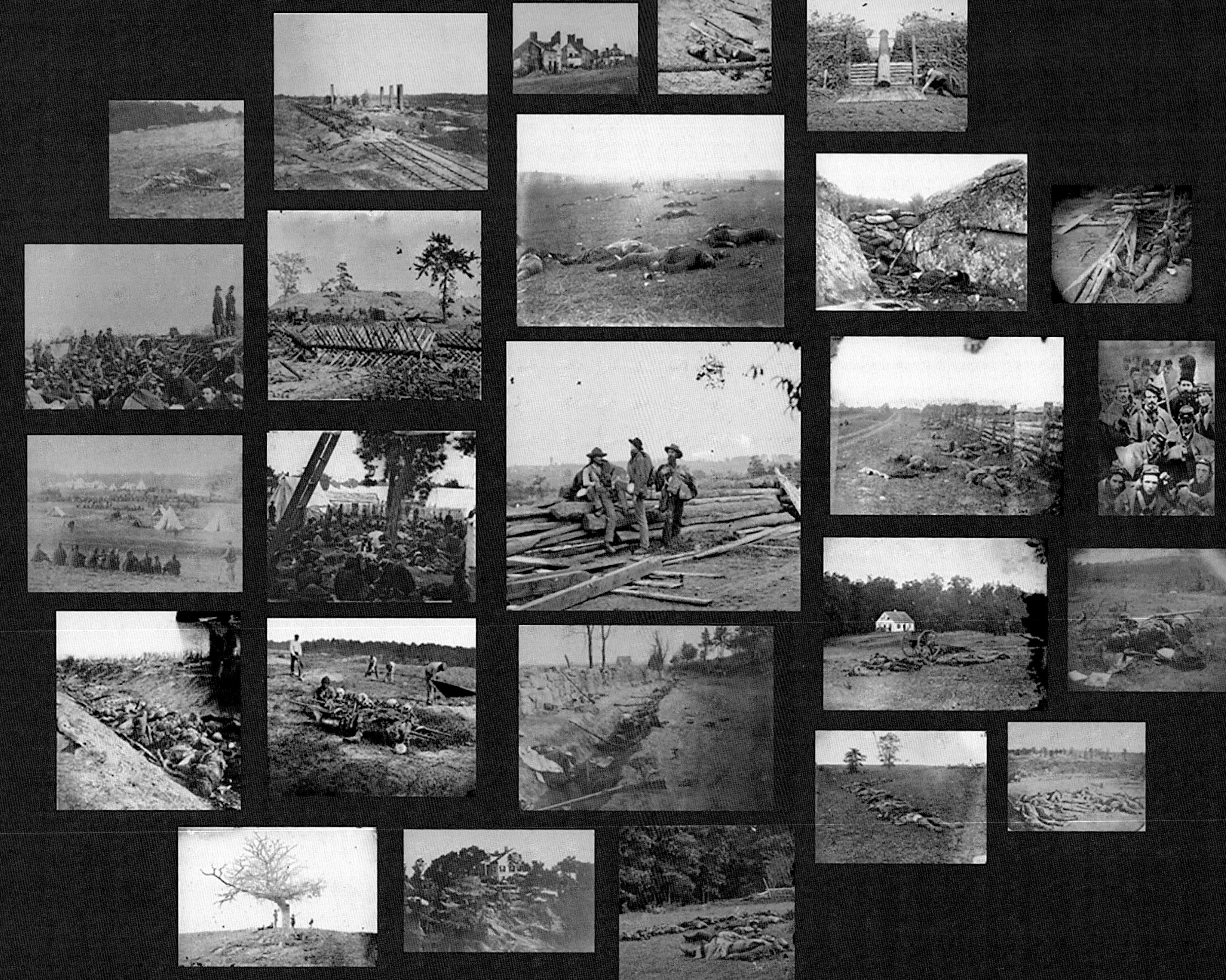

FIGURE 2.1. The twenty-five most popular photographs in Civil War history books, scaled according to popularity. Mathew Brady's photographs of three Confederate prisoners at Gettysburg narrowly edges out Alexander Gardner's image of the dead at Antietam and Gettysburg and Andrew Russell's photograph of the dead along the Stone Wall at Fredericksburg.

Results

RANK #1 (MOST POPULAR): FIGURE 2.2

CAPTION: Gettysburg, Pa. Three Confederate prisoners.

PHOTOGRAPHER: Brady & Co.

Details of Analysis (appearances)

Books: 42 percent

Magazines: 2 percent

Websites: 16 percent

Videos: 12 percent

Average Appearances: 18 percent

7 percent more common in print than online

Background

The original stereograph caption provided by Brady's National Photographic Art Gallery for this image, the most iconic picture in the survey, was "Three 'Johnnie Reb' Prisoners." The general consensus is that Brady's camera captured these three Confederates on July 15, 1863.[9] It remains a mystery as to what these three soldiers were doing during the eleven days between when Lee began his retreat south and when they posed before Brady's camera on the northern end of Seminary Ridge across the street from Lee's former headquarters. Presumably, they were stragglers who were picked up somewhere in southcentral Pennsylvania and brought back to the great battlefield along with 2,500 other prisoners of war. On July 16, all these men would have been dispersed, traveling to one of a variety of different prisoner-of-war camps.[10]

Analysis

What elements of this photograph make it so compelling, to the point that almost half of all Civil War illustrated histories include the image? Brooks Simpson, a historian at Arizona State University, writes that these are "perhaps the three most recognizable Confederate soldiers of the American Civil War."[11]

This photograph is a fine study of the dress and equipment used by the typical Confederate soldier. We see here three apparently adequately fed and clothed infantrymen, all wearing acceptable footwear. Interestingly, many of the first rebels to enter Gettysburg proper would have marched within a few feet of the location of this picture, although the breastworks wouldn't have been constructed yet.

One little-noted aspect of this photograph is the massive tree on the horizon, to the left of the seated soldier. This hardwood is located on Cemetery Hill, so the relative position and distance between both armies during the great battle can be appreciated. This huge tree is also visible on several other landscape photographs taken by Brady and his crew in mid-July 1863, providing a useful reference point for location analysis.

Careful inspection of the photograph also reveals some interesting aspects about the nature of Civil War defensive fortification. A plaque along the stone wall that currently occupies this site identifies the rocks as breastworks "constructed by Rode's Division C.S.A. July 4, 1863," presumably in anticipation of a Federal counterattack after the disaster of Pickett's Charge. The photograph, of course, demonstrates that the breastworks were not originally sandstone, as they are today, but instead rough-hewn timber and fence rails. Additionally, the original breastworks were actually stronger than they might initially appear. The earthen fronting of the works, which faced to the east/southeast and the Army of the Potomac, is just visible to the left of the sitting soldier. This artillery-resistant sod facing is still intact with the more recent and permanent stone wall replacement, where the slope of the soil covers most of the rock face on the eastern side of the wall, but very little on the rocks to the west. Clearly, the timbers were not deemed strong enough to survive a bombardment by the Federals, and soil was piled along the breastwork front during the lull in the fighting on July 4.

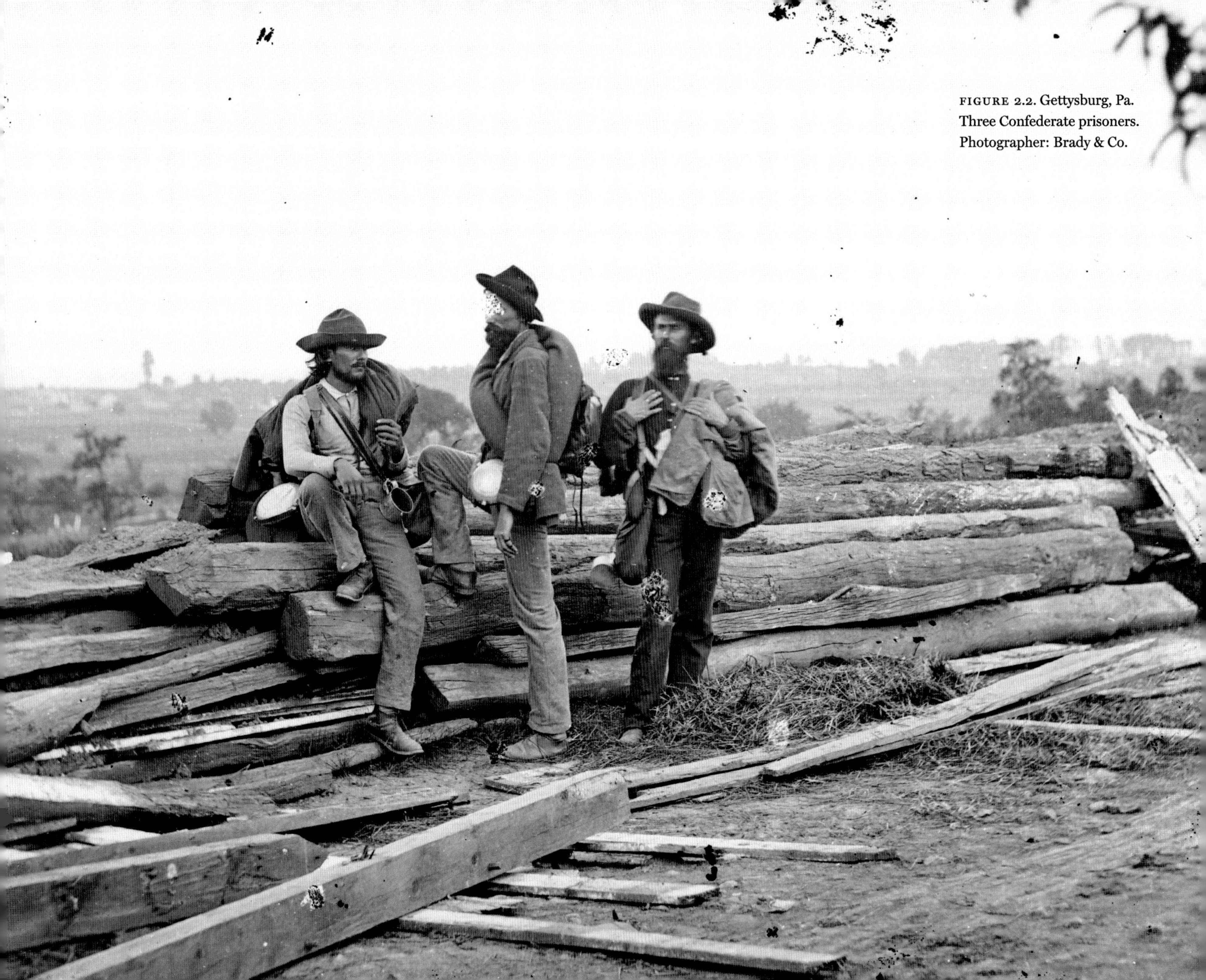

FIGURE 2.2. Gettysburg, Pa.
Three Confederate prisoners.
Photographer: Brady & Co.

Brady's photograph is much more popular in books than it is in magazines and online. This might be a combination of the picture's very high-resolution and "printability," but also the nature of the photograph itself: of all the photographs included in this analysis of the most popular images, it has the least "shock-value." Instead, it is an interesting study of the dress and equipment of the Army of Northern Virginia, sans gore, misery, bloating or bloodshed. Contrast this image with the grisly scenes that represent the rest of the top five most reproduced "combat" photographs, and one can imagine a publisher being more amenable to including these three rebels in a book intended for a broad, general audience, rather than one of the other more sensational and disturbing scenes that complete the popularity grouping.

RANK #2: FIGURE 2.3

CAPTION: A Harvest of Death.
PHOTOGRAPHER: Timothy O'Sullivan under the direction of
Alexander Gardner.

Details of Analysis (appearances)

Books: 38%
Magazines: 6%
Websites: 28%
Videos: 32%
Average Appearances: 26%
8% more common online than in print

Background

Alexander Gardner, James Gibson, and Timothy O'Sullivan captured a total of five negatives of this ghastly scene of Federal dead. The photographers used both plate and stereo cameras for these shots, and photographed the men from two different camera positions, angled about 135 degrees apart.[12] The exact location on the battlefield remains a mystery, confused in part by the wild variety of captions and descriptions Gardner provided for the prints.[13]

Analysis

In his 1995 extensive volume *Early Photography at Gettysburg*, the original master of battlefield photo-forensics, William Frassanito, discussed his attempts to locate the site of these fallen soldiers on the modern battlefield. He also discussed his frustrating lack of success, and of learning of "12 different 'discoveries' for the scene," all of which he dismissed as unconvincing.[14]

There are two primary challenges to determining the precise location where these photographs were taken. The first is related to geology and terrain. Unlike Gardner's images from the Rose Farm, where durable and distinctive igneous boulders are abundant natural tracers through time, no outcropping and fractured rocks are visible in these shots. This, combined with natural weathering and land use change (shifting wood lines, for example), makes geolocation difficult.

Second, Gardner did historians no favor with his fraudulent picture captions, describing the dead soldiers in various shots as belonging to different armies and haven been killed during the fighting on July 1st or 2nd. Frassanito points out that after Gettysburg the US army buried their own fallen first, so these rarer, uninterred Federal casualties were probably the first subject the Gardner team chose to photograph upon reaching the battlefield, even as the burial parties closed in. Later, they were able to capture more negatives of dead Confederates in the nearby fields and boulders on the southern part of the battleground.

As discussed in the previous chapter, Mathew Brady often appeared as a subject in his own compositions; Gardner did not. Nevertheless, he may have inadvertently been caught on the very edge of one of these stereoviews. A bearded man, holding a notebook, is dressed in a manner similar to Gardner's usual attire, complete with the type of hat he was known to wear in the field (fig. 2.4).

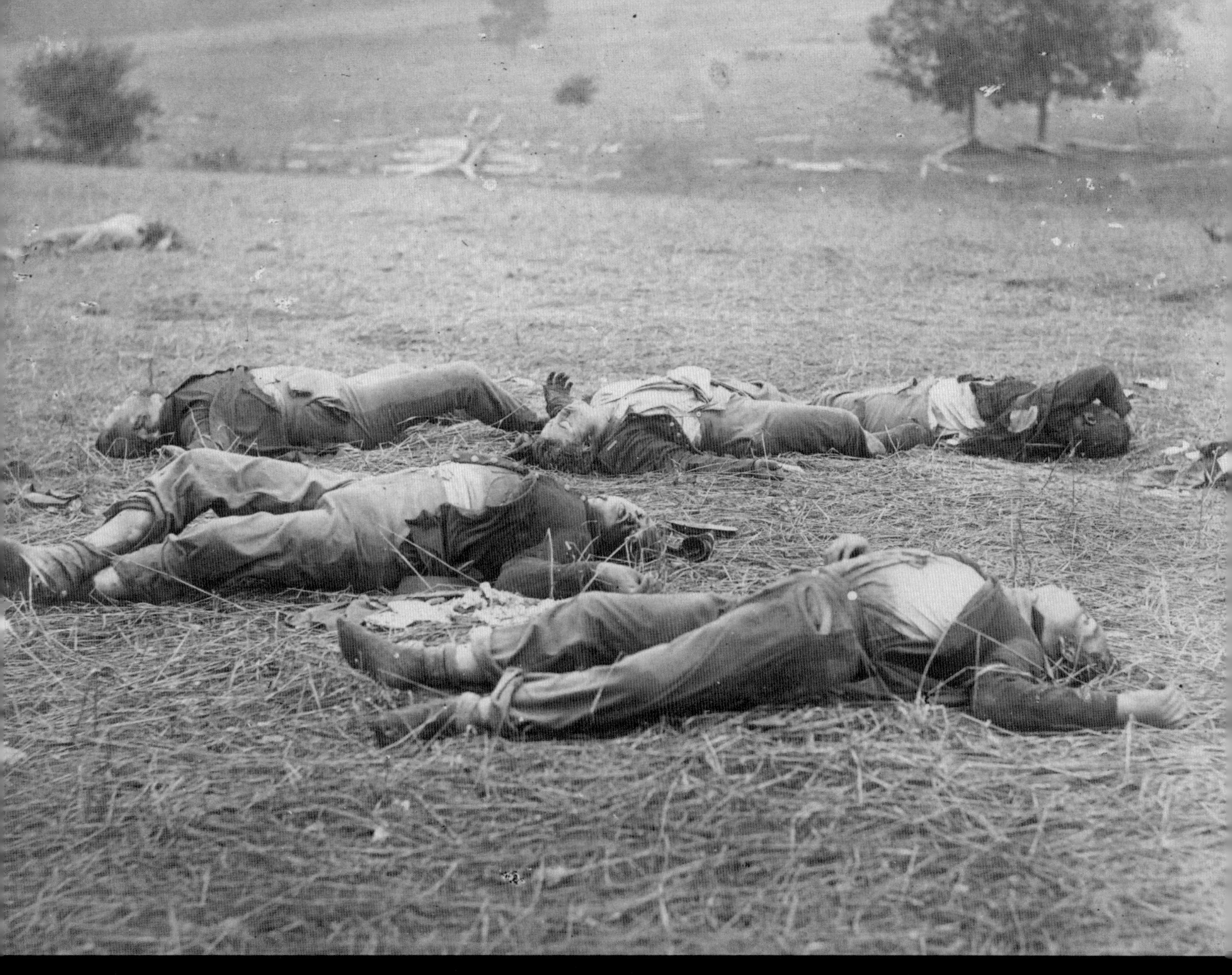

FIGURE 2.2. A Harvest of Death. Photographer: Timothy O'Sullivan under the direction of Alexander Gardner.

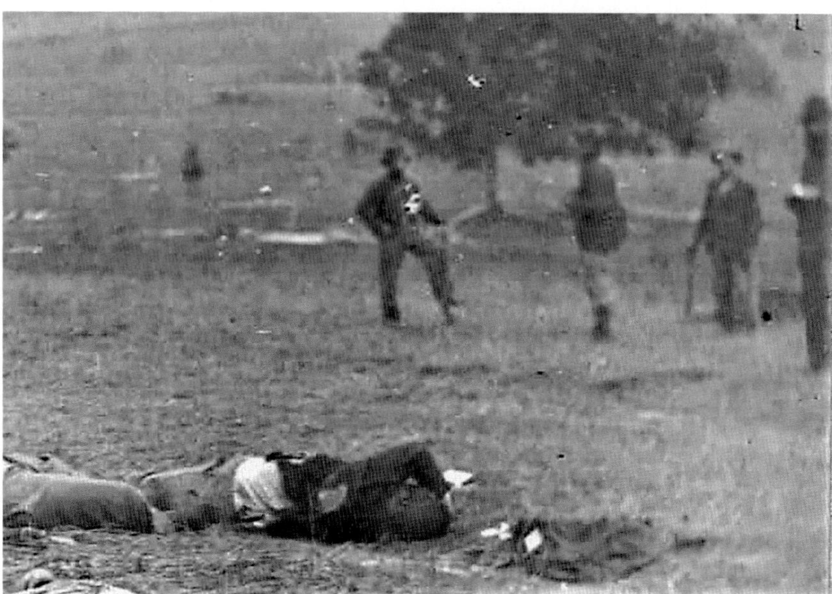

FIGURE 2.4. Detail of Alexander Gardner's stereoview. The bearded man on the far right standing with the burial crew appears to be Gardner himself. "Bodies of Confederate Soldiers, Round top, Left of Union Line, Gettysburg, Pennsylvania," 1863, Military Order of the Loyal Legion of the United States [MOLLUS] Massachusetts Civil War Photograph Collection, U.S. Army Heritage and Education Center, Carlisle, PA.

Of all the photographs in this popularity contest, this one has certainly caused the most debate among historians and the most controversy surrounding who these men were and where they died. To date, more than twenty sites have been suggested and debated, with absolutely no consensus developing over the years. Later in this book we'll look at some of these hypothesized locations and make a few suggestions of our own.

CAPTION: Stone wall, rear of Fredericksburg with rebel dead, May 3d, 1864 Capt. Russell, photo.
PHOTOGRAPHER: Andrew J. Russell.

Details of Analysis (appearances)

Books: 36%
Magazines: 0%
Websites: 12%
Videos: 14%
Average Appearances: 16%
5% more common in print than online

Background

Alexander Gardner's morbid photographs at Antietam and Gettysburg were all taken more than a day after the local fighting had ceased. This delay resulted in images of bloated corpses, often collected and arranged into a "V" shape for their imminent and largely anonymous mass burial. Andrew Russell's photographs behind Fredericksburg's infamous Stone Wall captured during the Battle of Chancellorsville is different, as Russell took the photograph only a few hours after the Federal lines had swept up and over Marye's Heights.[15]

This Confederate position proved unconquerable during the earlier Battle of Fredericksburg, even after repeated catastrophic assaults by Burnside's army. However, in late May, the Federals possessed a four-to-one advantage in manpower, allowing their attack to overcome the strong defensive position held by Jubal Early's infantry.

Analysis

This book contains numerous descriptions of the manipulation of subject matter by photographers of the era—moving bodies, the addition of props, even the inclusion of live soldiers who were pretending to be dead. This

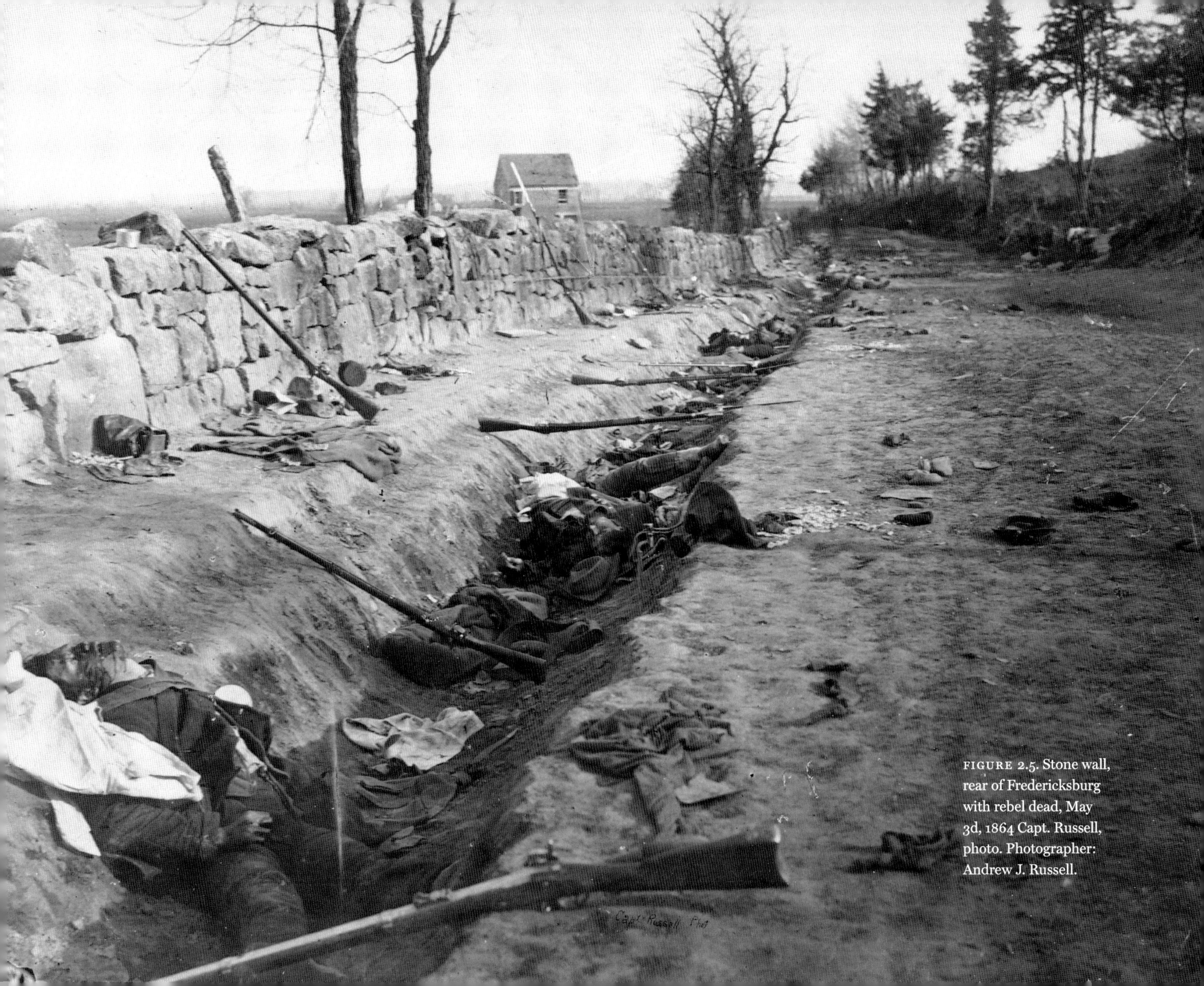

FIGURE 2.5. Stone wall, rear of Fredericksburg with rebel dead, May 3d, 1864 Capt. Russell, photo. Photographer: Andrew J. Russell.

photograph has not escaped this type of scrutiny. Prolific historian Earl Hess, in his essay on this photograph for the compendium *Lens of War*, points to the contrast between the few crumpled bodies and the neatly arranged rifle muskets as evidence that Russell staged at least one aspect of the dramatic shot, "There are simply too many muskets in this view that seem to be neatly laid across the ditch or leaning up against the stone wall to be circumstantial" (p. 164).

An alternate explanation might point to a more authentic reason for the arrangement and alignment of the rifles: Perhaps they were placed in a convenient location for salvage, freed from the torn bodies and surrounding battlefield detritus. Note that there are no wounded soldiers present in the photograph, only men killed very recently. For every dead body at this location, we would expect around three or four wounded to also be present, but they have already been rescued from the scene. In between the time of the evacuation of the wounded and the burial of the dead, any functional weapons would have been collected, especially in territory that might soon be relinquished to the enemy. Even the presence of a bayonet, stuck into the ground on the edge of ditch, blade-side down, could also indicate that it has been placed for rapid collection. Russell might have happened upon this scene after the Federal line had shifted towards the Salem Church to the west, at the perfect time when no moving soldiers were present, and corpses and weapons of war remained *in situ* on (temporarily) friendly ground.

A second interesting aspect of the layout of the subjects in this photograph, corpses and guns, is the location of the fallen soldiers. While it has traditionally been accepted that the Confederate infantrymen were sheltering behind and adjacent to this waist or chest-high wall, ducking before rising to fire over the breastwork and being resupplied with loaded muskets from the rear, might it also be possible that the men were standing upright and shooting from the drainage ditch? During the first Battle of Fredericksburg, the soldiers behind this wall had enough strength (reinforcements) that one soldier might crouch behind the wall while others reloaded muskets for him, presumably standing out of enemy sight farther from the wall or in the ditch. Keeping in mind that it is much easier to rapidly reload a muzzle-loading rifle while standing upright, the shooters could remain adjacent to the wall while the re-loaders could stand in the ditch, with the wall protecting everyone.

During the second Battle of Fredericksburg, the Confederate strength was a fraction as great as it was in December. As a result, every shooter possible was required for the defense. Perhaps these men, needing to re-load for themselves and in great peril because of the overwhelming strength of the enemy, choose to stand and shoot from the ditch, maximizing their firepower while upright to quickly manipulate their ramrods. Note the presence of a small bench, or banquette step on the left side of the ditch—the direction they were shooting—but not the right. This would have been a convenient place to rest a left foot while aiming over the wall.[16]

Had the men been adjacent to the wall when shooting, wouldn't we expect that at least one of them would have slumped against the wall or on the road between the wall and the ditch? This whole argument is complicated, of course, by the small data set (four bodies) and the fact that there was reportedly hand-to-hand combat behind the wall as the Federal infantry pushed through the men from Mississippi.

RANK #4: FIGURE 2.6

CAPTION: Antietam, MD. Confederate dead by a fence on the Hagerstown Road.

PHOTOGRAPHER: Alexander Gardner.

Details of Analysis (appearances)

Books: 34%
Magazines: 6%
Websites: 18%
Videos: 22%
Average Appearances: 20%
Found equally online and on paper.

Background

There are many similarities between the images Gardner captured of dead Confederates along the Hagerstown Pike north of Sharpsburg and the photographs he took of dead infantry nine months later at his *A Harvest of Death* at Gettysburg. He spent an unusual amount of time at both locations, producing five negatives of each—requiring the equivalent of around an hour and a half to compose and process the photographs. He also repositioned his camera at both locations along a 135-degree arc, searching for the most compelling aspect of the arrangement of the dead.[17] For both series, he and his crew were photographing men who had been killed between twenty-four and seventy-two hours before they arrived.

Gardner recorded these dead men as belonging to a brigade from Louisiana. He took these photographs with the help of James Gibson on September 19, 1862. The fighting had subsided on the evening of the seventeenth, and both armies sat stagnant, stunned, and immobile on the eighteenth. McClellan had planned on attacking on the nineteenth, but Lee had decided to terminate his Maryland Campaign the previous afternoon and left Sharpsburg that evening. Thus, on the morning of the planned attack, the photographers had access to the recent carnage strewn across a battlefield that was now in Federal possession.

Analysis

One of the more unusual aspects of this series of photographs, once one absorbs the presence of the grossly contorted bodies, is the durability of the rail fences along the pike. Bullets, canister and shot, and troops alike swept back and forth across the road, yet the rails remain 97 percent intact.[18] The fence offered only minimal protection against incoming projectiles, with the rails only adequately thick to stop or deflect around half of the approaching Minié balls, but its sturdiness assured that a charging enemy would need to slow to climb over the obstacle. Unlike most split-rail fences, these fences couldn't be quickly dismantled by skirmishers to form low breastworks. In some ways these fences are reminiscent of another set of obstacles that hindered the Confederate attack along the Emmitsburg Road during Pickett's infamous assault on the third day at Gettysburg.

One other interesting aspect of the durability of this set of fences is found when analyzing all of Gardner's five photographs from this general location: while the rails of the fence to the west of the Hagerstown Pike are, in total, 98 percent intact, those from the fence on the eastern border of the lane are in poorer condition. Only approximately 80 percent are still in place.[19]

Regarding the fences and the fighting, note that the majority of the fallen soldiers are located around the one significant breach in the western fence, just to the right of the dead soldier with his arm curled to the right in the air (above and to the right in the center of the group of dead in the background). Not all rebels were killed behind and west of the fence, however. One often overlooked aspect of this series of photographs is that one corpse remains on the roadside of the fence, largely hidden by his fellow dead compatriots (fig. 2.7).[20]

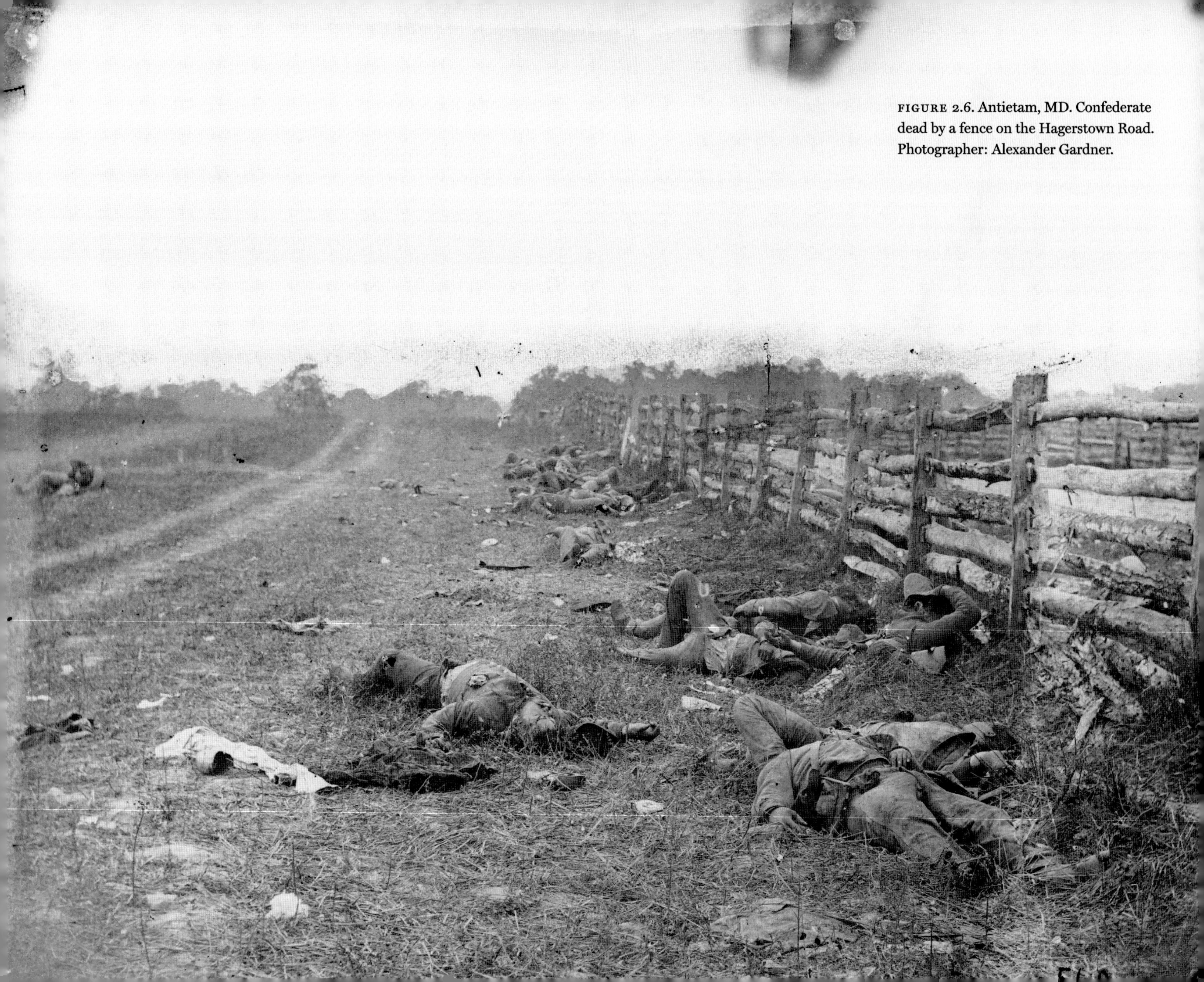

FIGURE 2.6. Antietam, MD. Confederate dead by a fence on the Hagerstown Road. Photographer: Alexander Gardner.

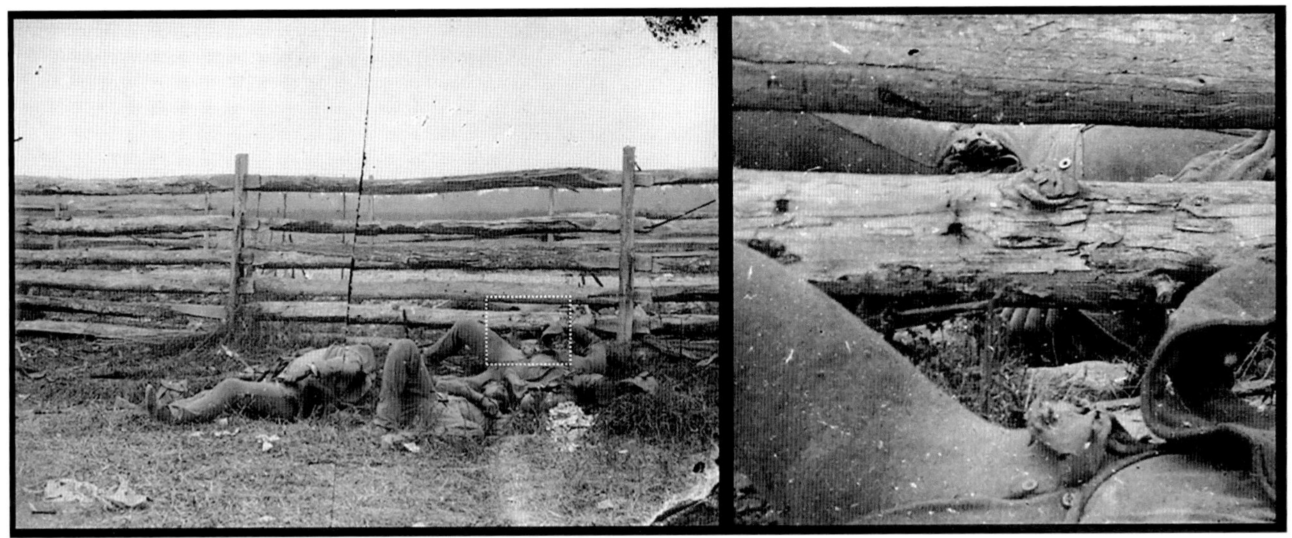

FIGURE 2.7. Another view of the dead along the Hagerstown Pike. Details in the callout box show the fingers, pocket, and button of a dead soldier who is visible through the rails on the other side of the fence. Nearly all historical texts describe this photograph as containing three dead soldiers, while four are present.

RANK #5A: FIGURE 2.8

CAPTION: Antietam, MD. Bodies in Front of the Dunker Church.
PHOTOGRAPHER: Alexander Gardner.

Details of Analysis (appearances)

Books: 32%
Magazines: 10%
Websites: 24%
Videos: 18%
Average Appearances: 21%
Found almost equally online and on paper.

Background

Gardner's image of the dead in front of the Dunker Church edges out his other morbid photograph of the dead in the Sunken Road because of the higher average of digital appearances (the number of appearances in paper books, 32 percent, is the same for each photograph—the average in all media was used as a tiebreaker).

Gardner and Gibson captured this photograph several hundred yards to the south of the five terrible images of the dead along the Hagerstown Pike. According to photographic historian William Frassanito, these photographs are "among the best known of Gardner's Antietam photographs." This quote, published in 1978, presages the popularity of this image almost fifty years later where it is found in more than one in five books, magazines, videos, and web pages about the Civil War.

This image is also captivating and popular, no doubt, because of the inclusion of the battle-damaged church. The southern face of the building contains numerous impact structures, almost certainly fired by Confederate artillery and infantry aiming at Federal men who had penetrated the West Woods. The church, nine years old at the time of the battle, was being used as a convenient field hospital when Gardner took this photograph. It was destroyed in a storm in the 1920s, only to be rebuilt on the original foundation for the centennial of the battle.

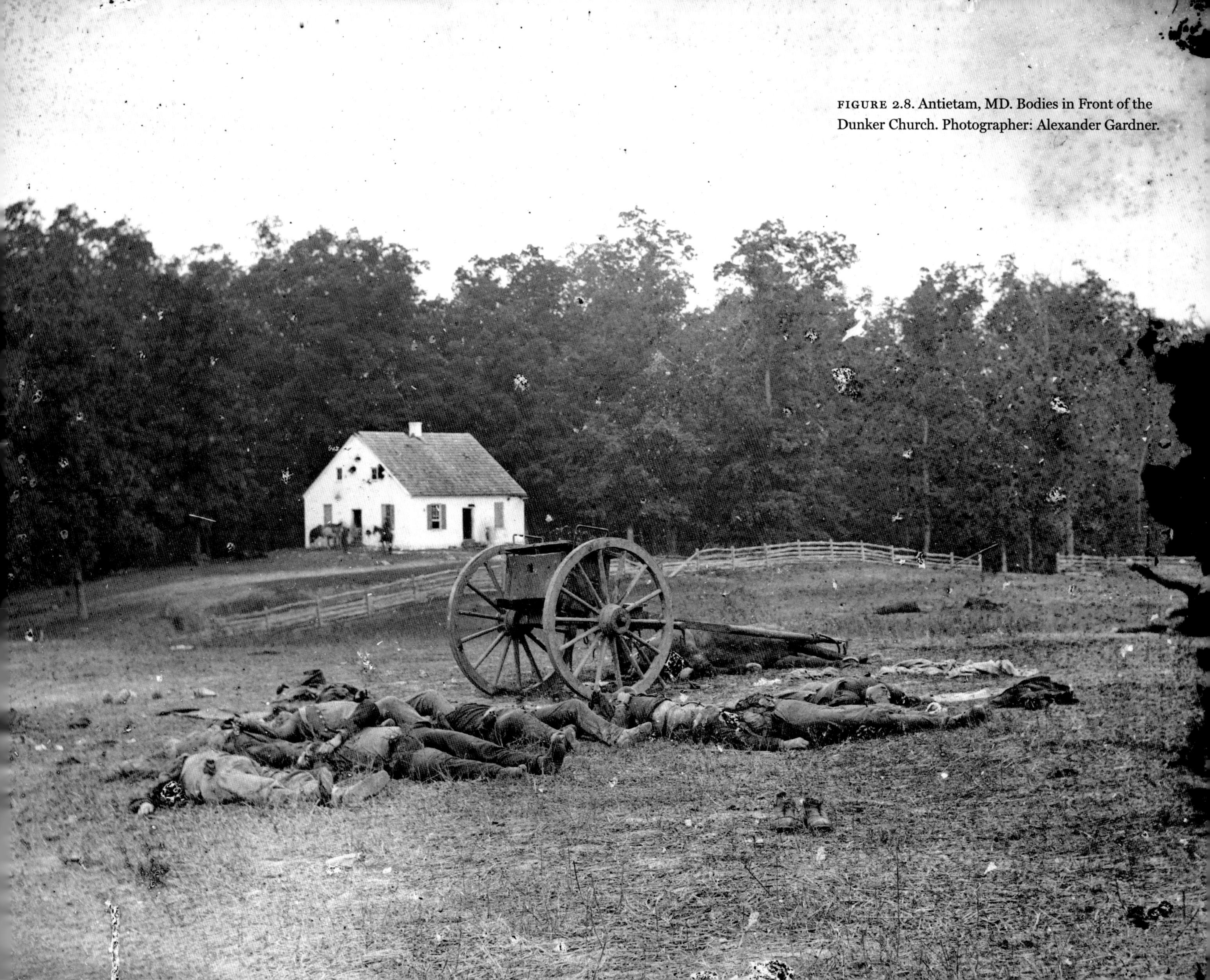

FIGURE 2.8. Antietam, MD. Bodies in Front of the
Dunker Church. Photographer: Alexander Gardner.

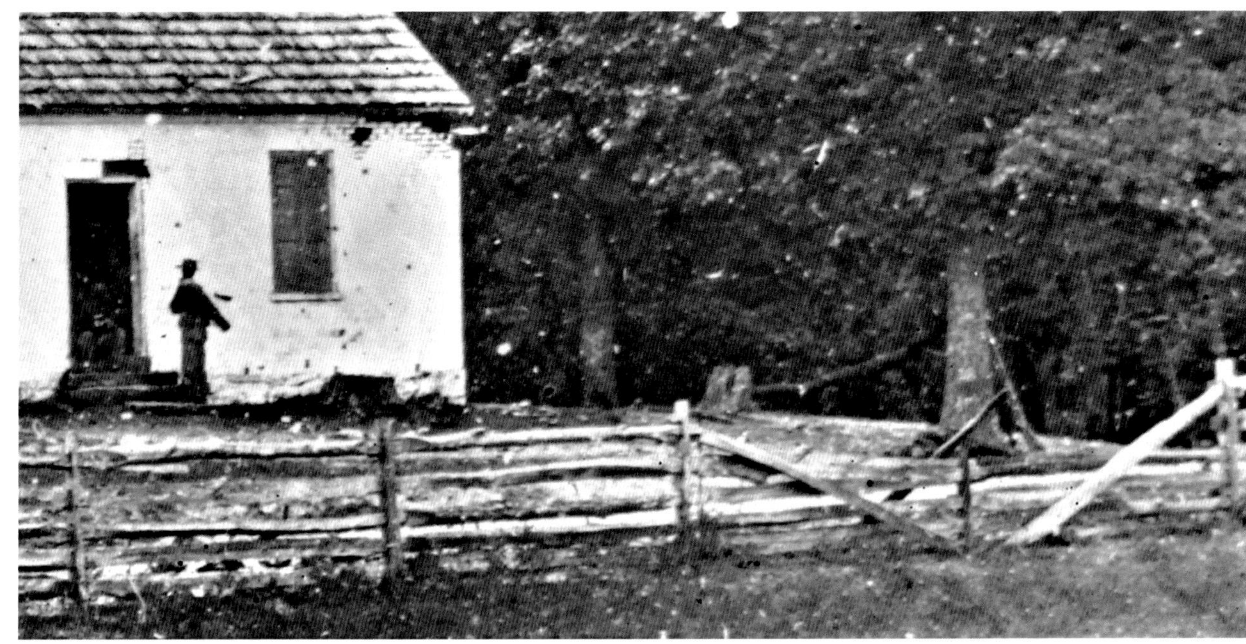

FIGURE 2.9. A rifle musket rests against the right side of a tree, framed by the damaged portion of the fence line.

Analysis

There are two aspects of this photograph that have always provoked contemplation—the first concerned footwear; the second, animal cruelty. A pair of shoes has been collected from this carnage, probably from the dead around the caisson—more than one dead soldier here now wears only socks. The second curiosity referenced the dead horses. At least five are found on this small section of the battleground. There are nearly as many dead equines as humans. One is clearly associated with the caisson, and a second, clearer in a different view, is nearby. A third lies adjacent to the left side of the church, perhaps cut down by wild rebel artillery fire. Two more lie behind the caisson and closer to the church. Gardner would use another glass negative to photograph one of these two horses, and the church, in another image where dead soldiers are absent. He may have taken this photo while moving between the dead along the turnpike and the corpses strewn around the damaged caisson.

One final detail of note: In the photograph of the church sans caisson, Gardner's image captured a rifle musket that can be spotted resting against a tree (fig. 2.9). Gardner would later use a similar weapon as a prop in many of his photographs from Gettysburg, placing a ramrod-less musket beside multiple corpses in Devil's Den and on the Rose Farm, perhaps to increase a sense of immediacy.

CAPTION: View of Ditch: Which has been used for a rifle pit
at the Battle of Antietam.

PHOTOGRAPHER: Alexander Gardner.

Details of Analysis (appearances)

Books: 32%

Magazines: 0%

Websites: 6%

Videos: 28%

Average Appearances: 17%

Found almost equally online and on paper.

Background

The infamous Sunken Road, later Blood Lane, was used as a natural trench by men belonging to G.B. Anderson's North Carolina brigade and Rodes' Alabama brigade. They were attacked by Federals from French's division, who were approaching the rebel line from over the crest of harder rock to the north.

As the fighting dragged on during the late morning phase of the battle, both sides committed reinforcements to the struggle. For nearly three hours the casualty count climbed until finally, two US regiments from New York managed to gain a foothold in the center of the lane, providing an enfilading position for the Federals into the rest of the remaining southerners.

Three views of this famous site were captured by Gardner and Gibson as the burial parties waited nearby. This one is the more commonly reproduced view, and it contains more dead bodies.

Analysis

The 130th Pennsylvania Volunteers were tasked with removing the bodies from the lane for burial in trenches on the nearby farm fields. They began working while Gardner was still occupied along the Hagerstown Pike and reported removing 138 corpses in total.[21] By the time Gardner discovered this gruesome location, it was late in the afternoon and many bodies had likely already been removed from the lane. Several pieces of evidence support this conjecture: After taking a dozen images around the Hagerstown Pike and Dunker Church, Gardner only took three negatives of the dead in the Sunken Road, suggesting he may have been pressed for time and running out of sunlight. Close examination of the photograph, and especially the long shadow behind the man standing beside the road, suggests it was late in the afternoon.

One mysterious aspect of the three Bloody Lane photographs is the positioning of the dismantled split rail fencing. The sunken road has traditionally been presented in history books as a natural trench, ideal for conducting a defensive stand. In reality, it is a significantly flawed defensive position, both in terms of its depth and its location behind a ridge of higher ground to the immediate front.[22] The Confederates in the lane no doubt tore down local fencing and piled the rails along the top of the trench for added height and protection—a supplemental breastwork. In figure 2.11, the split rails lie where they would be expected, along the northern edge of the lane between the defenders in the lane and the field over which the Federals attacked.

However, Gardner's photograph of the southern side of the roadbed, figures 2.10 and 2.12, includes rails along the berm to the right, on the southern side of the trench.[23] This would mean that the rails had been piled between the Confederate defenders in the road and their second line of defense, located on the rise above and behind the lane. There are two explanations for the apparent location of these rails along the southern border of the road. The first is that this isn't, in fact, the southern edge of the lane but instead the northern side (the photograph was taken from the same side of the lane in both photographs, one looking towards the west "up" the lane and the other looking to the east "down" the lane). The second explanation of the rail positioning would be that the Federal infantry essentially

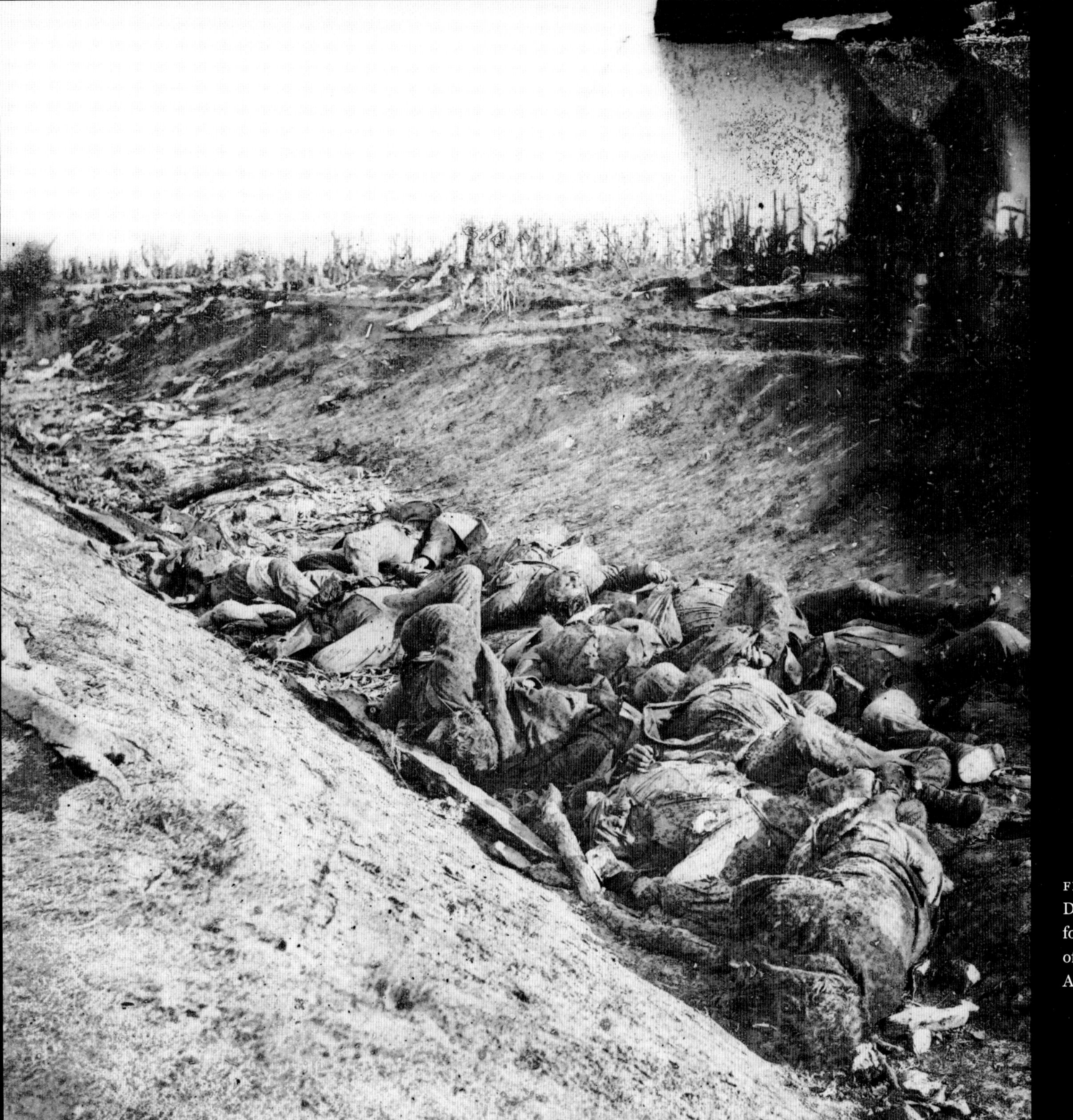

FIGURE 2.10. View of Ditch: Which has been used for a rifle pit at the Battle of Antietam. Photographer: Alexander Gardner.

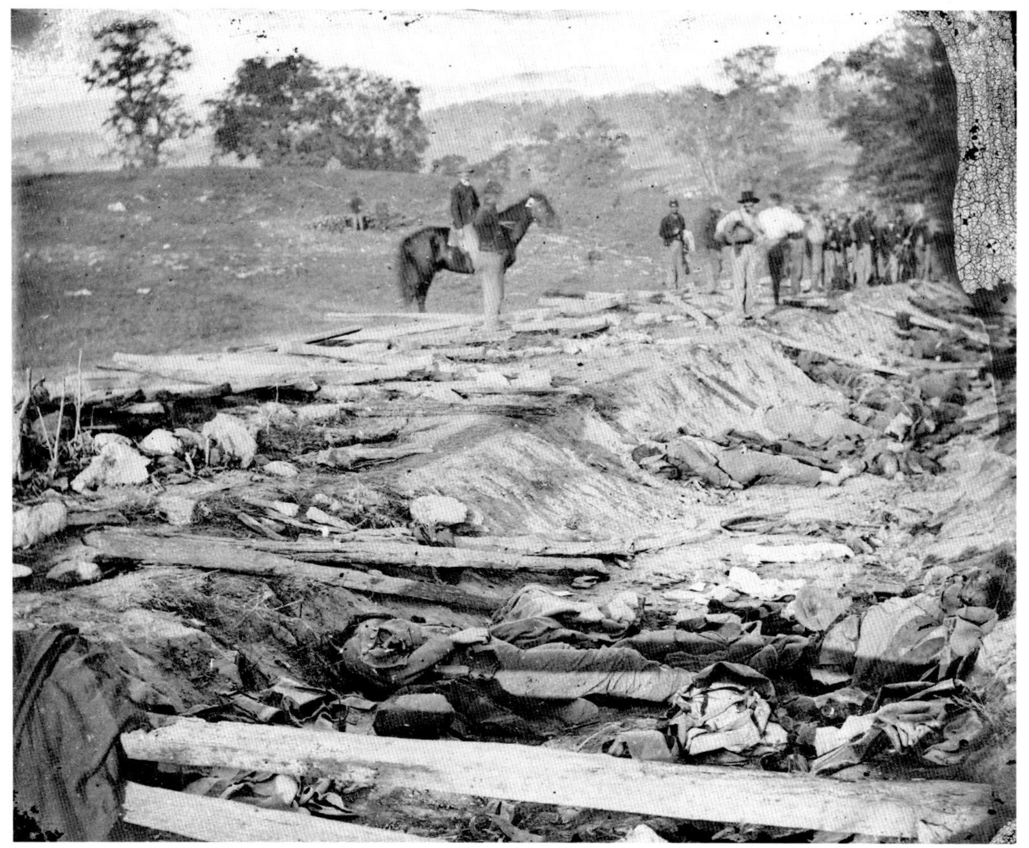

FIGURE 2.11. Alexander Gardner's photograph of the Sunken Lane likely includes members of the 130th Pennsylvania, standing on the northern edge of the berm, patiently waiting to continue their burial duties.

reversed the natural trench, shifting the rails from one side to the other after capturing the position. This would make perfect sense because the Confederates still held the high ground to the south of the Sunken Road even after the heaviest of the fighting had shifted elsewhere.

Both of Gardner's photographs appear to have captured members of the Federal burial crew who in most cases, paused, to allow the photographer to take his shot. Careful examination of figure 2.12 reveals several ghost figures—moving men who didn't stay still during the duration of the exposure and thus were captured as a ghostly, semitransparent blur.

On a final note, compare the density of the dead in the lane between the three photographs. Large sectors of the roadbed are free of dead bodies, perhaps because they had already been moved. In figure 2.10 the bodies are close enough together that a person could walk from one side of the road to the other without stepping on the soil. This may have been the scene, and photograph, that started the often-told story of a battleground so strewn with the dead that one could walk from one side of the field to the other without touching the ground. Later, eyewitnesses and historians erroneously transferred this density of death to the nearby infamous cornfield on

CHAPTER 2

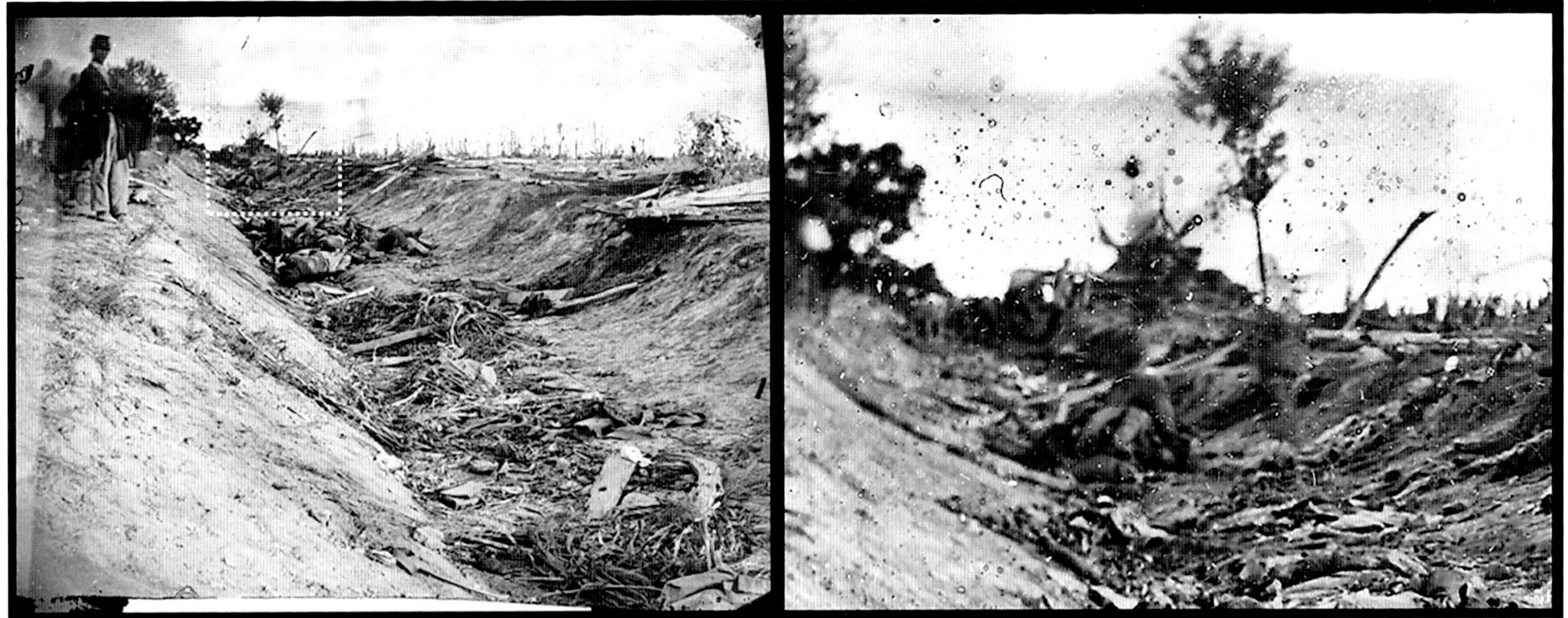

FIGURE 2.12. A third view of the Sunken Road taken by Gardner on September 19, 1862 (*left*).
Note position of the split rails on the right and "ghost" soldiers in detail (*right*).

David Miller's Farm.[24] One example of such a transposition is from Richard Clem of the *Washington Times*: "A witness to the aftermath of the morning encounter recorded, "One could cross the entire length of Miller's 40-acre cornfield without touching the ground by walking on the dead." Apparently, the density of the dead in the Sunken Road led others to describe a similar landscape for the cornfield, and still later the fields below Marye's Heights at Fredericksburg, the Carter house and grounds at Franklin, and the famous Wheatfield at Gettysburg. Even the vast fields of Pickett's Charge have not escaped this preposterous exaggeration through time, and Gardner's camera captured at Antietam the one place where the geography and density of the fallen may have accurately been captured by the claim.

In the next chapter we move away from popularity and explore some of the mysteries that surround these famous photographs. Despite their popularity, much of the background about exactly when and where these twenty-five photographs were taken has been lost through time. Forensic photographic analysis can help restore, or at least illuminate, the context in which these famous images were captured.

CHAPTER 3

Photographic Forensics

When I was in high school, just like many teenagers, I needed to have my wisdom teeth extracted. Anticipating the unpleasantness and monotony of the recovery process led my mother, an avid reader, to take me to a local bookstore where she told me to pick out a book to help pass the time. After visiting my two favorite subject areas at the time—history and sports—I pleaded for two selections: a Bill James *Baseball Abstract* and a book by a Civil War historian about photography at our nearby battlefield, Gettysburg. The selections shouldn't have been a surprise as I was a ballplayer who loved photography.

The disparate subjects were both engrossing in different ways; nevertheless, what really made an impression on me was the cross-disciplinary methodologies employed by both authors. Bill James famously studied the most common tropes of traditional baseball wisdom and shattered them with blunt critical reasoning and (rather) simple statistical analysis. Batting average was *not* the most important baseball statistic. Bunting and stolen bases are really *not* all that valuable or important—if you are going to try to steal a base, you had better be safe 70 percent of the time. Baseball players are *not* at their peak in their early thirties, they are at their prime when they are significantly younger. Don't believe what the "experts," whether commentators, newspaper writers, or former players, have been telling you.

William Frassanito would seem to be a strange comparison for James. Nevertheless, he accomplished for the field of Civil War photography what James did for baseball statistics: a distrust of the historians and skepticism about what experts have led us to believe. Frassanito's first book, *Gettysburg: A Journey in Time*, took many of the most iconic photographs of the Civil War and the dead on the battlefield and demonstrated that these images were not what the photographer and later historians claimed they were. These men were *not* killed in combat; they are pretending to be dead. These two different photographs do *not* show US and Confederate dead, killed on two different parts of the battlefield on different days, they are simply the same corpses photographed from different angles. This caption is wrong. That photograph is staged. That book is passing on misinformation.

What James the baseball historian, and Frassanito, the military historian, had in common was their interest in uncovering the truth and providing context about historical "facts." Although written to describe James, this passage from the Ben McGrath article in the *New Yorker* summarizes the goals of both men, "What set the writing apart . . . was the accessibility of the logic, the insistence on eliminating biases and ignoring illusions, the practical tone."[1]

Bill James would read and hear that Catfish Hunter was the best pitcher in the American League. Cy Young award and the Hall of Fame voters backed this claim. James used logic and creative analysis to efficiently disprove these assertions. William Frassanito would read that Alexander Gardner captured the most iconic and historically significant photograph from the Civil War when he found a lone dead sharpshooter among the picturesque boulders of Devil's Den. Books by famous historians, including the preeminent Bruce Catton, concurred. Frassanito used logic and creative analysis to undisputedly implode these claims, demonstrating that the photograph was not what it seemed or what the experts were proclaiming.

In this chapter we explore the interaction of historical skepticism and Civil War photography, documenting the multitude of forensic tools initially developed by Frassanito, and employed by others, to identify photographic fraud and manipulation. We'll also explore other aspects of the photographs to provide more context for the images:

Who was photographed (and *who* took the picture)?

Where were they photographed?

When were they photographed?

Why was this subject selected to be photographed?

One quote from each baseball/history scholar will shape our search for contextual clues in the sepia. James: "I'm sort of a baseball agnostic; I make it a point never to believe anything just because it is widely known to be so."[2] Frassanito: "History is like a vast puzzle from which most of the pieces will forever remain missing. . . . The historians must then evaluate all of these pieces, and develop a rational interpretation of the subject at hand."[3] So, we will start with a fresh look at each photograph, assuming almost nothing we know about it is definitive. We will then use the approach of James and the techniques of Frassanito to critically consider what is being shown to the viewer, and why the subject was deemed worthy of a glass plate negative.

Who: Details in the Silver Crystals

When asked to list the "Best books on photography and reality," Academy Award-winning filmmaker Errol Morris had thousands of books to choose from, and he selected Frassanito's *Gettysburg: A Journey in Time*.[4] What made the Civil War photo-historian's scholarship so remarkable was the employment of his two unusual skill sets: a seemingly limitless knowledge of the photographs taken during the Civil War and an intimate knowledge of the terrain of the Gettysburg battleground. Both of his volumes, *Gettysburg* (1975) and *Early Photography at Gettysburg* (1995) used a combination of different forensic techniques to tell the story of the photographs and the dead men captured in Gardner's discomforting negatives.

The first of these techniques involved detailed and greatly magnified analysis of the very high-resolution black-and-white images left behind by the photographers, including accessing the original large glass negatives. Civil War negatives have a resolution that exceeds the cellulose film and digital images that we are accustomed to, and the reason is fairly straightforward—the glass negatives are gigantic in comparison to the other media, capturing terrific quantities of visual information.[5] One of Brady or Garner's eight-inch by ten-inch glass negatives has *sixty-six times* the surface area of a 35-mm slide, for example. When converted to digital data, the files are enormous. Many of the Tag Image File Format (TIFF) images of Civil War photographs from the Library of Congress are files that exceed one hundred megabytes.

Frassanito took full advantage of the available resolution in each negative to search for details in the image that could provide clues about the identity of the fallen soldiers. Thus, "identification" can be broken down into two broad categories: 1) Demonstration of who, *relatively* speaking, the men were or which side they fought for; or that two dead men, or a group of fallen soldiers, appearing in two different pictures, are actually one in the same (despite what the caption tells the viewer); and, 2) The *absolute* identification of a specific army or unit for the fallen men; or, in rare cases, the actual name of the dead man (or men).

In the natural sciences phenomena are often broken down into "relative" and "absolute" categories. For example, in geology the age of the rock can be determined using relative dating (sequencing: this rock is older than that rock but younger than this rock) or absolute dating (radiometric dating: this rock is 450 million years old). For Civil War photographs, the first category of identification—are they the same men? —can be thought of as "relative" identification. We know they are the same men, but not who specifically they are or what unit, or even army, they fought with. The second category of identification, where details about the background of the men are pursued, can be through of as "absolute" identification (e.g., these men were killed while fighting with the government's III Corps on July 2, 1863).

The first of these types of identification, correlating the dead between photographs, involved the study of the orientation and body configurations of the dead. Perhaps, for example, two dead soldiers were lying next to each other head to toe, with one man having his left knee raised. Closer examination of the details of the clothing, or even battlefield detritus, vegetation, and rock outcrops, can demonstrate when the photographers were simply photographing the same men from different perspectives—despite what they stated in their captions.

The second category of identification, seeking the absolute insights about who the men were and which units they belonged to, requires even more detailed analysis in even higher resolution. For an example of Frassanito's methodology in this respect consider Alexander Gardner's *A Harvest of Death*. Timothy O'Sullivan captured this image on an eight-inch by ten-inch glass negative. Gardner provided all manner of misleading descriptions of the photograph's location and the identity of the men, including that the men were killed during the first day's fighting northwest of town; later he added "Field where General Reynold's fell" (also northwest of town). Frassanito pointed out, in contrast, that one barely noticed discarded article of clothing suggested an entirely different location and identity for the men. As he states, "Clearly visible against the dark coloring is what appears to be the diamond-shaped badge worn exclusively by soldiers of the Union Third Corps."[6]

Unfortunately, the exact geographic location where Timothy O'Sullivan took *A Harvest of Death* has never been satisfyingly documented (see chapter 4). The historical debate about the location of the photograph can be summarized as this: Gardner states that the men were cut down in the vicinity of the McPherson's barn during the fighting on July 1; Frassanito points to the fields around the Peach Orchard, where the fighting raged during the late afternoon the next day. These sites are two-and-a-half miles apart.

Where: Clues in the Mineral Crystals

One unusual aspect of the *Harvest* photograph is that the image reveals more about *who* the men were than it does *where* they were killed. For most of the other pictures that Gardner and his team created, the identification of the precise location of the shot could later be determined by one outstanding characteristic of the Gettysburg region: the geology.

The town and battlefield of Gettysburg are located in a physiographic region geologists call the Gettysburg Basin. This region is underlain by Triassic and Jurassic rocks that are around 200 million years old.[7] The older of the primary rock types are sedimentary in nature, representing dinosaur-age stream and lake deposits. Thick sequences of layered clays, siltstones, and sandstones are all interbedded across this wide basin. The second type of common rock in the region is slightly younger and completely different in nature. These rocks are an igneous variety, having cooled from molten magma and they are of primary interest here because of their great hardness. This durability means that they do not weather as

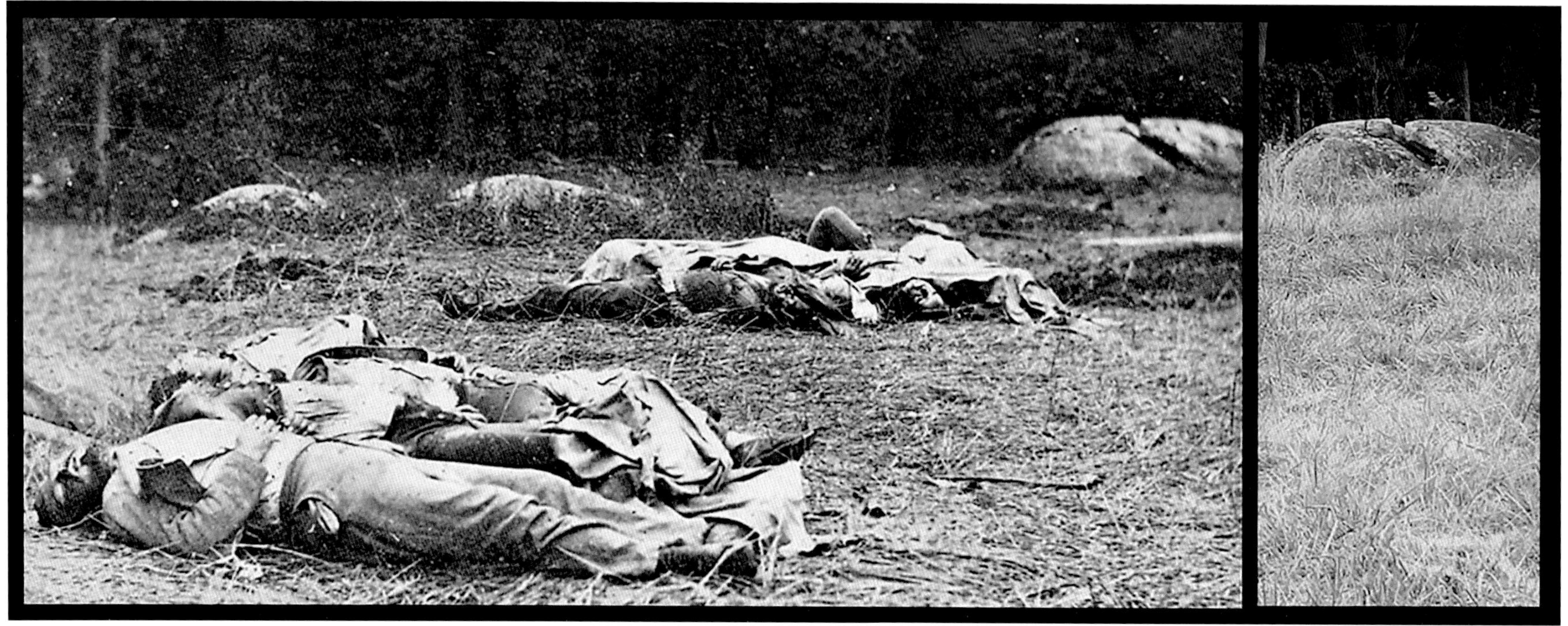

FIGURE 3.1 The key fractured diabase boulder that revealed the true location of the Confederate dead on the Rose Farm at Gettysburg. Photographed in 1863 and 2025. Library of Congress.

easily or quickly as the sedimentary rocks, and the results are higher ridges and giant rounded boulders composed of the igneous rock diabase. Over almost 200 million years of differential weathering and erosion between the softer sedimentary rocks and the harder diabase produced ridges like Cemetery or Seminary, or large hills, like Culp's or the Round Tops.[8]

The two key characteristics of the diabase outcrops at Gettysburg that make them so valuable to photographic historians are their strange weathering patterns, resulting in unusual spheroidal and occasionally fractured shapes, and their superior hardness, as they change appearance over geological, rather than historical, time spans.

The most important of these diabase boulders, at least to historians like Frassanito, was located on the Rose Farm. The photographic expert recognized the value of one of the cracked round boulders seen in the background of one of Gardner's more morbid photographs as a natural tracer through time. Everything else in the photograph might have changed after almost 150 years, but the dark gray boulder would remain intact, largely unchanged. The big stone was also particularly distinctive, showing both spheroidal weathering—rounded exfoliation patterns like the layers of an onion—and freeze-thaw fracturing, which split the rock in half (fig. 3.1). When Frassanito found the rock after a five-year search in the late 1960s,

CHAPTER 3

he had unlocked the mystery to where Gardner's largest collection of photographs of Confederate dead had been taken. Once he had established the location of this one particular photograph, he used the orientation and configuration of the cadavers and the other boulders present on the field to establish the relative locations of another ten photographs. Similar outcrops from other battlefields can also be used to identify the locations of camera positions on the modern landscape (fig. 3.2).

While the landscape has evolved tremendously over the last 160 years, including alterations to forests and trees, hillslopes, stream meanders, and roadways and fence lines, the hard-rock geology has not. For this method of geolocation to work, three factors must work in concert: 1) the region is underlain by lithified rock and not sediments; 2) the hard rock crops out so that it is visible on both the Civil War and modern landscape; and 3) the outcropping rock is distinctive in appearance, either through structure, shape, or weathering patterns.[9]

Battlefields located on the Piedmont and Valley and Ridge physiographic provinces often meet these three geological criteria. Those on the Coastal Plain or Mississippi River Valley never do (Table 3.1).

After evaluation of the geology and landscape features of the primary battlefields of the war, there should be little surprise that Antietam and Gettysburg were the two locations where the geosciences proved most valuable as a forensic tool. Both battlefields have hard rocks that crop out in abundance and unique forms, distinctive landscape features (Little Round Top, Sunken Road), and lasting anthropogenic landmarks (Lutheran Seminary, Dunker Church) that make the identification of the locations of so many battlefield scenes undeniable. Large battlegrounds like Petersburg, located primarily on the Coastal Plain, lack any such geological features and the location of many of the photographs of trenches or the dead in the field remain unrecognized.

The Civil War is not unique in with respect to the use of geology as a forensic tool for providing insights into the location and timing of early battlefield photography. Film director and documentarian Errol Morris,

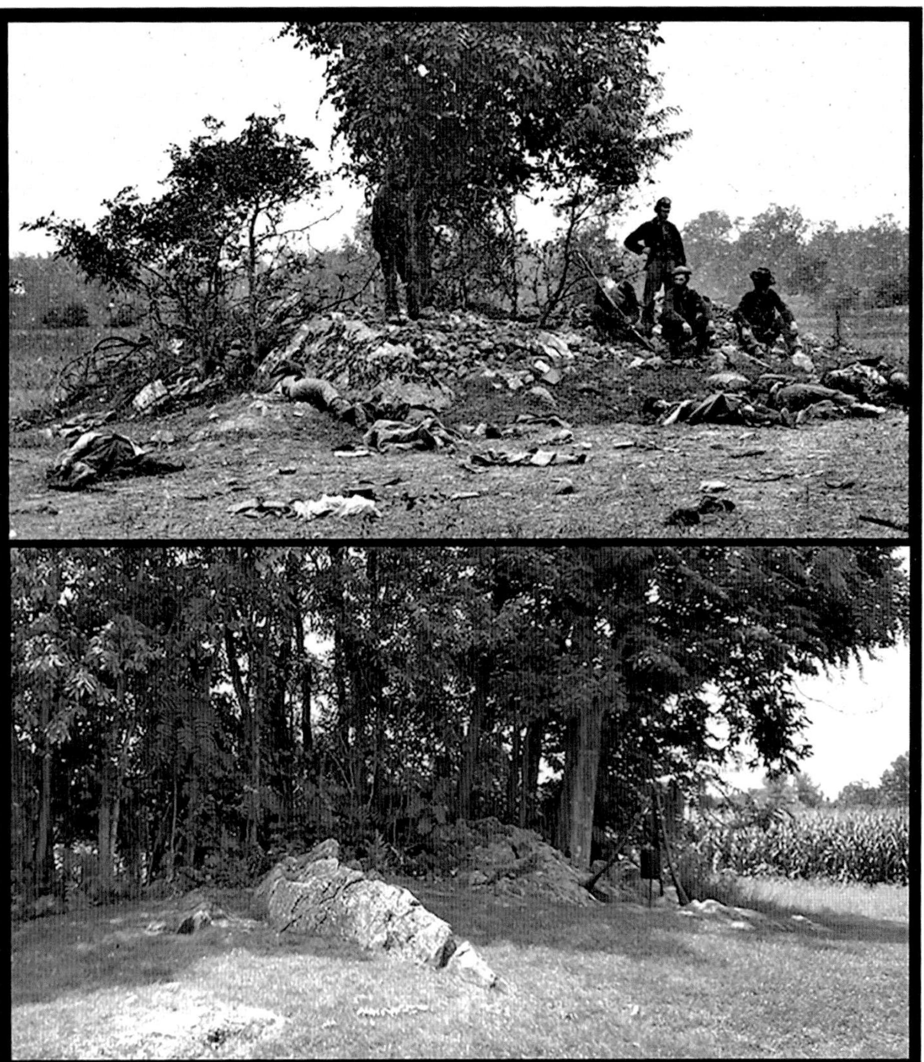

FIGURE 3.2. A Federal burial crew overlook scattered dead Confederates surrounding an outcrop of the Conococheague limestone on the Antietam Battlefield; and the same location today, clearly identified by the weathering pattern of the soft carbonate rock. Top image from the Library of Congress.

TABLE 3.1 Evaluation of Civil War battlefields and the criteria for using geology as a forensic photographic tool. Gettysburg and Antietam, although in different physiographic provinces, both have hard rocks and outcrops that are ideal for using geology as a tracer for photographic interpretation.

Campaign	Duration	Geologic Province	Secondary Geologic Province	Hard Rock	Rock Outcrops	Unusual Weathering	Bodies of Water	Distinctive Landscape Features	Enduring Anthropogenic Structures
First Manassas	July 1861	Piedmont (Mes. Basins)		✓✓✓	✓	✓	✓	✓	✓✓
Fort Henry/Donelson	Feb. 1862	Nashville Basin	Coastal Plain				✓✓✓	✓	✓✓
Mississippi River	Feb. 1862–July 1863	Coastal Plain	Nashville Basin				✓✓✓	✓	✓
Peninsula	Mar.–Aug. 1862	Coastal Plain					✓		✓
Shiloh	April 1862	Coastal Plain	Nashville Basin				✓	✓	✓
First Shenan. Valley	May–June 1862	Valley and Ridge		✓✓	✓	✓	✓	✓	✓
Second Manassas	Aug.–Sept. 1862	Piedmont (Mes. Basins)	Blue Ridge	✓✓✓	✓	✓	✓	✓	✓
Antietam	Sept. 1862	Valley and Ridge	Blue Ridge	✓✓✓	✓✓	✓✓	✓	✓✓	✓✓
Fredericksburg	Nov.–Dec. 1862	Coastal Plain	Piedmont				✓✓	✓	✓✓
Stones River	Dec. 1862 –Jan. 1863	Nashville Basin		✓✓✓	✓✓	✓✓	✓✓	✓✓	
Vicksburg	March–July 1863	Miss. River Valley					✓✓	✓	✓✓
Chancellorsville	April–May 1863	Piedmont	Coastal Plain	✓✓✓			✓		✓
Gettysburg	June–July 1863	Piedmont (Mes. Basin)	Val. and Ridge; B. Ridge	✓✓✓	✓✓✓	✓✓✓	✓	✓✓✓	✓✓
Chick. and Chattan.	Aug.–Nov. 1863	Valley and Ridge	Appalachian Plateau	✓✓	✓✓	✓	✓✓	✓✓	✓
Red River	Mar.–May 1864	Coastal Plain					✓✓	✓	
Overland	May–June 1864	Piedmont	Coastal Plain	✓✓✓	✓		✓	✓	✓
Atlanta (Tullahoma)	May–Sept. 1864	Piedmont	Val. and Ridge; B. Ridge	✓✓✓	✓✓	✓	✓	✓✓	✓
Petersburg	June 1864– Apr. 1865	Coastal Plain	Piedmont	✓			✓		✓
2nd Shenan. Valley	Aug.–Nov. 1864	Valley and Ridge	Blue Ridge	✓✓	✓	✓	✓	✓	✓
Franklin and Nash.	Nov.–Dec. 1864	Nashville Basin		✓✓			✓	✓	✓
Carolinas	Feb.–April 1865	Coastal Plain	Piedmont				✓	✓	
Appomattox	Apr. 1865	Piedmont		✓✓					✓

mentioned earlier, became fascinated with Roger Fenton's photographs from the Crimean War (1853–1856). Of particular interest was Fenton's two versions of *Valley of the Shadow of Death*. In one image, the viewer sees a road and footpath, separated by a ditch that contains approximately 200 cannon balls. In a second print, which was captured from the same camera position and perspective, abundant cannon balls remain in the ditch, but artillery rounds can also be observed that are spread dramatically all across and along the road (fig. 3.3). The traditional and most widespread historical interpretation of these contrasting views is that Fenton came across the scene with the road bereft of cannon balls, captured a negative, then for the sake of creating a more compelling image, he and his assistants tossed a bunch of the balls onto the road. He then took the more famous of the pictures.

Morris was skeptical of this convenient explanation for the timing and motivation for the photographic manipulation, and he pointed out that other plausible explanations exist for the discrepancies between the two shots. Perhaps, he argued, the order in which the photographs were captured has traditionally been reversed. For example, what if Fenton came upon the location where the rounds were scattered across the road, took a picture, and then watched salvage crews collect the rounds for later reuse against the Russians? What if the road had been cleared of ordnance to allow a column of soldiers or cavalry to pass by?

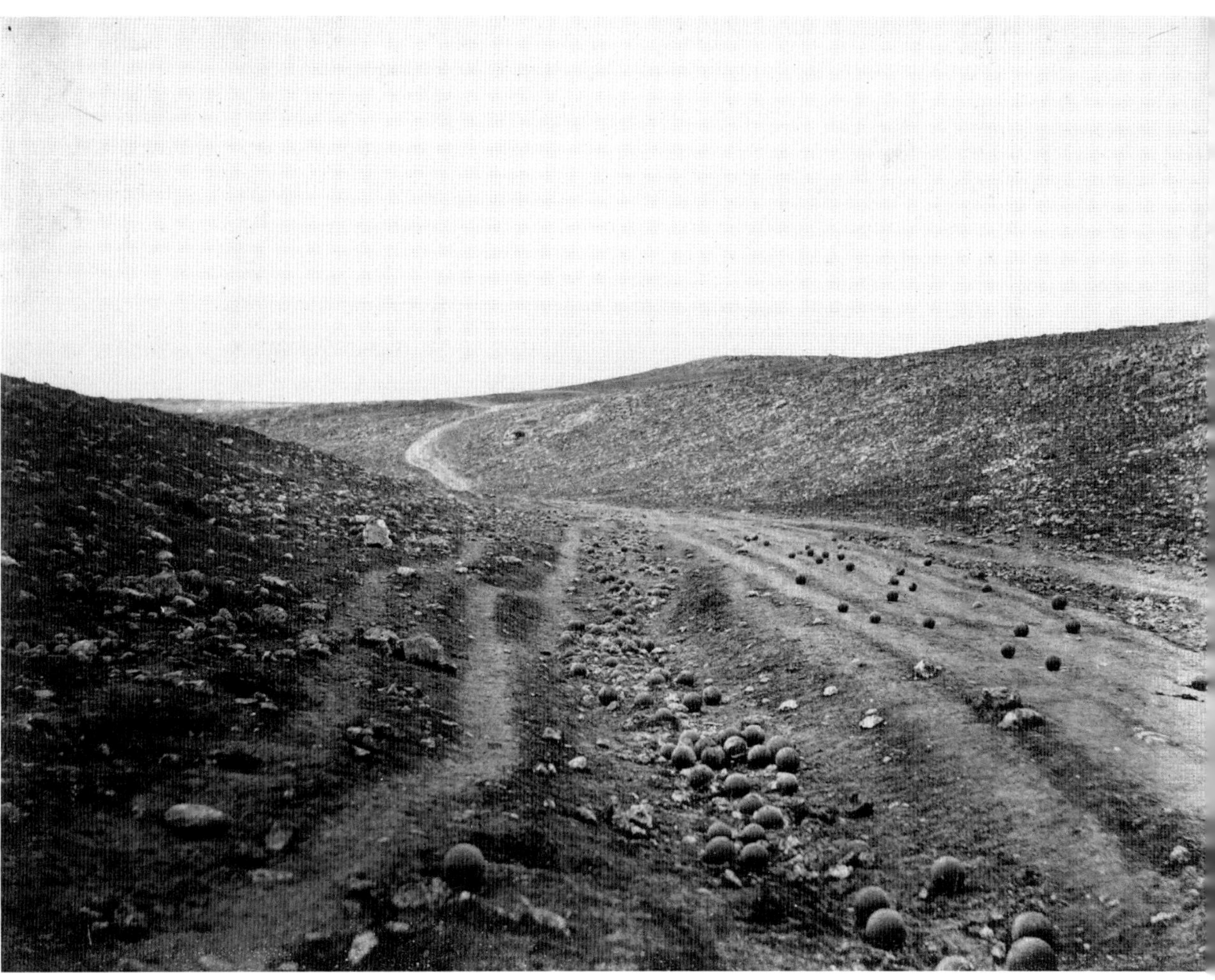

FIGURE 3.3. Roger Fenton's 1855 photograph *Valley of the Shadow of Death*. Library of Congress.

To investigate his suspicions, the filmmaker traveled to the site of the photograph, acquired an appropriate cannonball-sized sphere, and began to explore forensic methods for determining which photograph was taken first. These experiments with lighting and shadows in the afternoon sun and variations in exposures were confounded by the apparent lighting intensity or conditions between the original two shots (clouds versus clear sky) and, in the end, the exercise proved futile.

Nevertheless, one of the photographic experts that Morris had consulted pointed out that the geology of the scene changes in an incredibly subtle way: several small cobbles near the footpath change position between the two images. Rocks absolutely do move through time, especially if they have been kicked by walking soldiers, trampled by cavalry horses, or struck by wagon wheels. They also nearly always move downhill because of gravity and the cannonballs are all collected in a ditch for the same reason—they rolled there. Detailed inspection of the two images shows that in all the photographs where the road is free of artillery rounds, the disturbed cobbles are at a higher elevation; in the later, more dramatic shot, then they migrate downhill just a bit, making their way towards the cannonball-filled depression. In this particular case, traditional reasoning about the sequence, based on aesthetics, had been correct—but now there was scientific evidence found in the photographs to support the assumptions.

When: The Sun as a Forensic Tool

The historian Frassanito used geology to determine where photographs at Antietam and Gettysburg were taken; the filmmaker Morris used the lay of the land and terrain features to determine where the *Valley of the Shadow of Death* photographs had been imaged, before he used geological evidence to understand the sequencing of the photographs. Others who have studied early battlefield photographs have found additional forensic tools that proved useful for determining the timing of events that occurred far in the past.

One excellent, if subtle, example of this type of forensic chronological research can be found in Chris Fonvielle's photographic text about Fort Fisher, North Carolina.[10] While pouring over high-resolution 1865 images of the recently surrendered Gibraltar of the South, Fonvielle found that two photographs exist of the second gun chamber of Shepherd's Battery along the landface of the massive sand fortification (fig. 3.4).

When he arrived along the North Carolina coast, the first photograph Timothy O'Sullivan took was with his large format camera and the 7 × 9-inch glass negative he used was fractured either in processing or very soon after. The photographer then remounted the parapet, altered the position of his camera just slightly, and took a second photograph, this time with his stereoview camera.

How can we be certain that the stereoview was the second photograph to be captured of the captured fort? Isn't it possible that O'Sullivan simply wanted a photograph of this location with each type of camera and the more fragile glass negative was broken later?

The key clue for this sequencing is in the details proved by the very high-resolution of each image. US soldiers are busily working on repairing the timber palisade wall that separates the base of the rampart from the beach. These sharpened pine tree trunks were shattered and displaced by the repeated bombardments by the Federal navy during the previous two months. The repair crew appears to be working from east to west (progressing toward the camera position) as they add and repair or replace sections of the damaged wall. In the larger cracked negative, more large gaps remain in the timber barrier, while in the stereoview several of these openings have now been patched and repaired (fig. 3.5).

Meticulous study of one portion of the wall shows ~forty-nine trunks in the cracked negative view and ~sixty-five trunks in the stereoview, so unless the men were tearing the wall down, the larger format negative was taken first.[11] Also, analysis of both photographs indicates that the repair crew consisted of around fifteen to twenty men, although this is difficult to quantify because the men are working and moving, not posing for the slow,

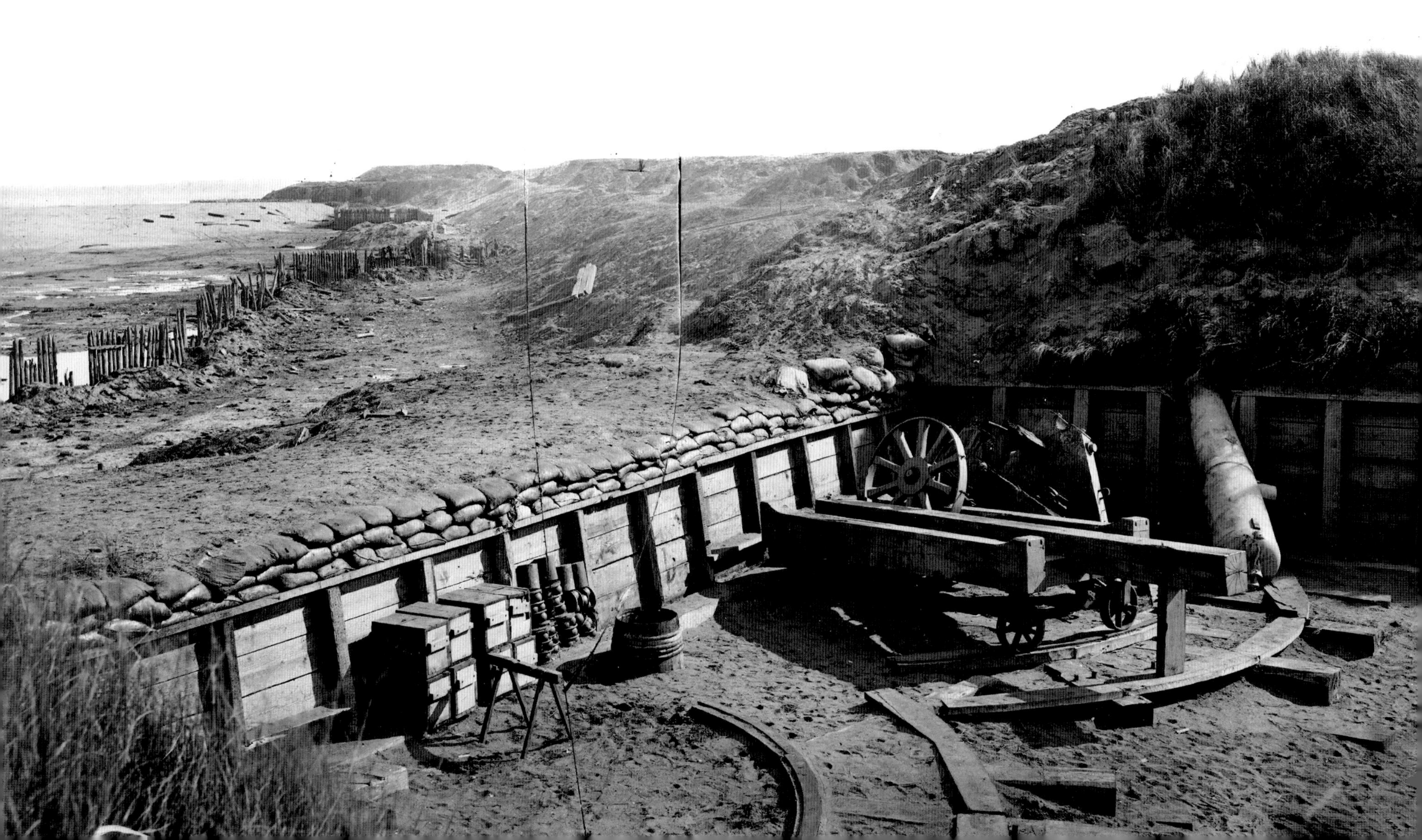

FIGURE 3.4. Timothy O'Sullivan's photograph of Shepherd's Battery of Fort Fisher. In the distance on the left, men can be seen repairing the timber palisade wall. Library of Congress.

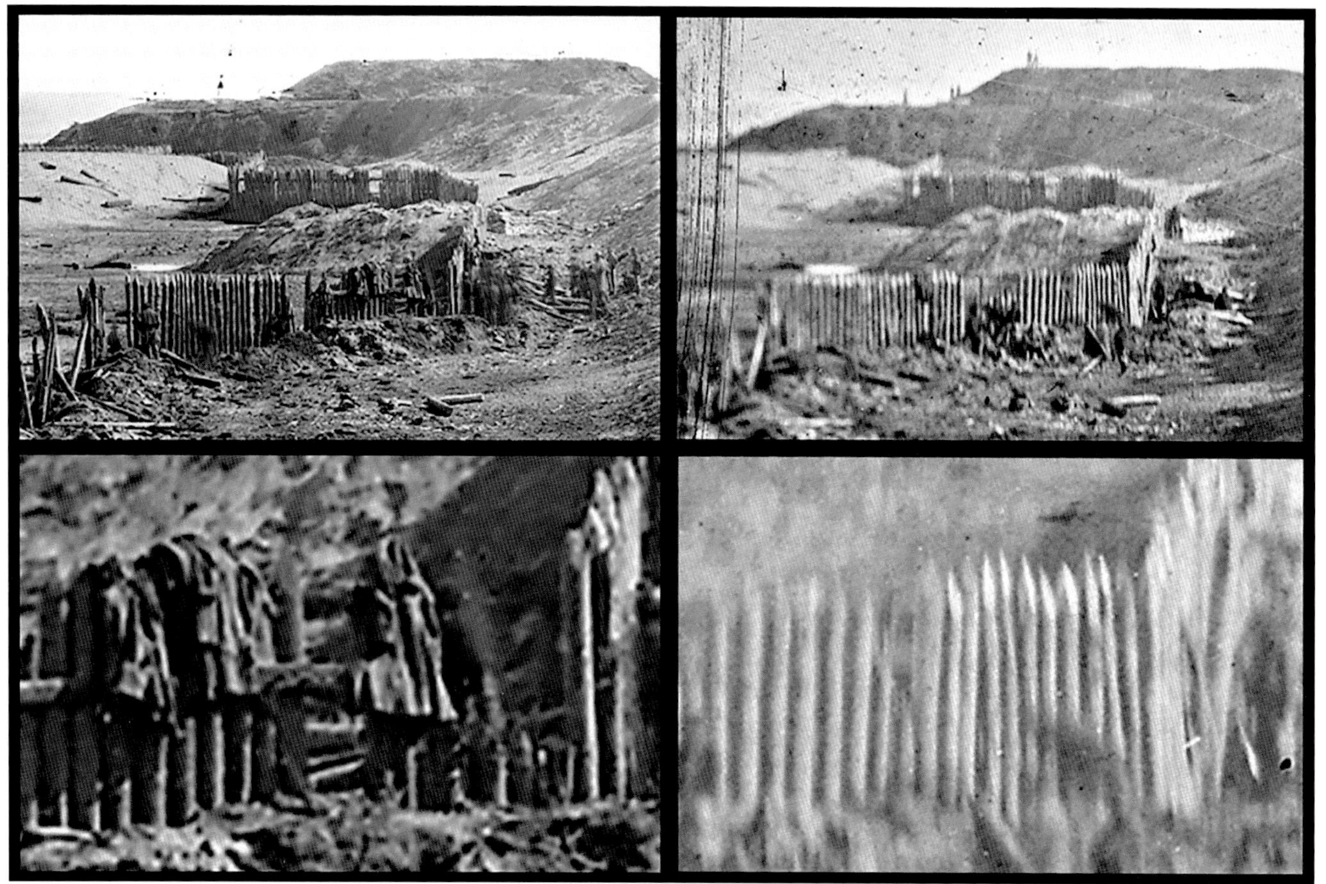

exposure-challenged camera. So how long would it take for this crew to re-pair somewhere around fifteen trunks in the wall? Perhaps an hour or so? Maybe less? This seems in line with the time it would take for O'Sullivan to process (and perhaps break) one negative, haul his other, smaller camera to the top of the parapet, prepare a new negative, and take a second shot.

A second forensic timekeeper can be found, figuratively, in the shadows. Again, only high-resolution negatives, which we have here, allow for the timing to be assessed using this methodology. Compare two sets of details:

an enlargement of the bolts used to attach the tires to the wagon wheel (fig. 3.6), and the shadow cast across the fractured axel (fig. 3.7).

As the sun moved across the North Carolina sky, the shadows of the bolts grew longer. In the fractured negative, the shadows of all three bolts are more vertical than in the stereo version because it was taken earlier in the day. Note that the shadow for most of the bolts are not very distinct, and the shadow is cast across a curved surface. This makes estimating an exact duration of time between the two shots difficult.[12]

Nevertheless, another nearby shadow doesn't have these complications, as the shadow of the broke axel is distinct and growing. Typically, in North Carolina at this time of day and year a shadow will move, or in this case grow, at approximately 15 degrees per hour. A comparison between the fractured negative and the stereoview shows the angle of the shadow increases by around 10 degrees; this would equate to around thirty to forty-five minutes, which seems like a perfectly reasonable estimate for the duration of time it might take O'Sullivan to prepare and create two wet emulsion negatives.[13] The timing also seems in line with the progress of the palisades repair crew.

In the end, photographic forensics has done more that tell us about the detail of the location and sequencing of O'Sullivan's priceless prints. Photographic processes that weren't recorded in 1865, including how difficult it was to record an image on a plate of fragile glass and how long the development of a negative might take, can better be understood using these techniques.[14]

This chapter focused on photographic forensics to explore the sequencing of photographs and to answer questions about *when* a photograph was taken. In the next chapter we attempt to answer a more lingering question about *where* a photograph was taken, and in later chapters we explore an equally compelling question, and one that is more difficult to answer conclusively: *Why* was this picture taken?

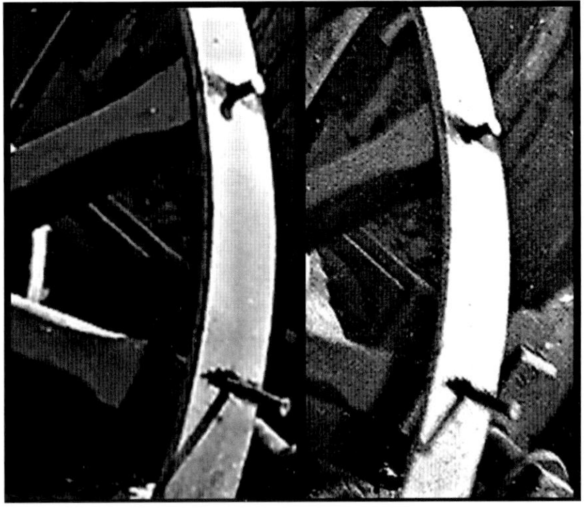

FIGURE 3.6. Two views of the extruding bolts used to fasten the steel tires to the carriage wheel: Left image is from the large-format camera, right is from the stereoview. Note the changing length of the shadow for the bolts between the images. Library of Congress.

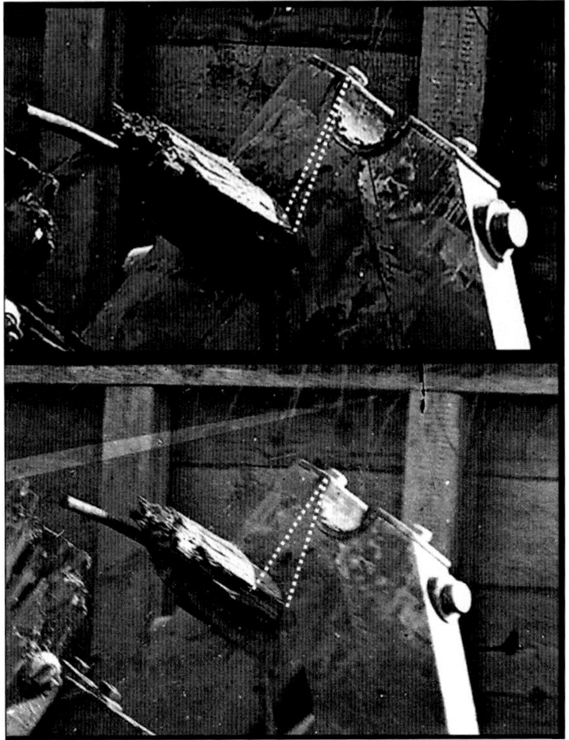

FIGURE 3.7. Two enlargements of the broken gun carriage from Shepherd's Battery: top image from large-format camera, bottom image from stereoview. The dashed lines indicate the growing shadow on the bottom image, pointing to the source of the shadow, the edge of the trunnion. Library of Congress.

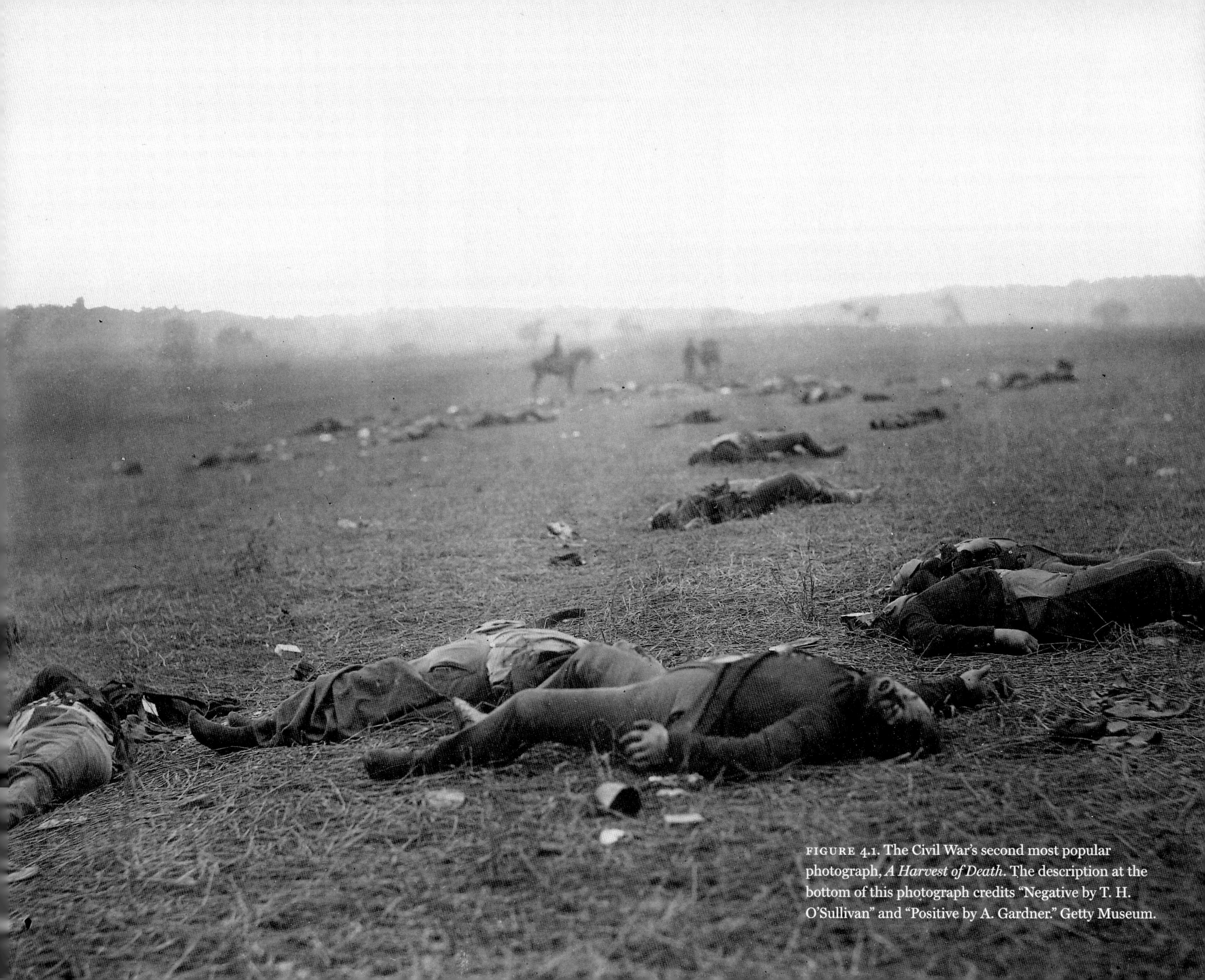

FIGURE 4.1. The Civil War's second most popular
photograph, *A Harvest of Death*. The description at the
bottom of this photograph credits "Negative by T. H.
O'Sullivan" and "Positive by A. Gardner." Getty Museum.

Harvest of Confusion

The Photographs

Timothy O'Sullivan might be the most underrated, and perhaps underappreciated, photographer from the mid-nineteenth century. Brady is better known, and Gardner is more controversial, but the young Scotsman took most the war's most compelling photographs. Included in the collection is the second most popular photograph to emerge from the war (fig. 4.1). This picture might also be the second most grisly photograph taken at Gettysburg, eclipsed in carnage only by O'Sullivan's other terrible photograph from the Rose Farm of a soldier who was disemboweled, presumably by an artillery bolt.[1]

Speaking of popularity, no book brought more attention to O'Sullivan's work than William Frassanito's *Gettysburg: A Journey in Time*. As discussed earlier, what made Frassanito's book so fascinating was his forensic approach to finding the definitive location where Gardner's negatives were actually created, with bodies scattered among boulders and strewn across farm fields—thus the "journey in time." *A Harvest of Death* remains even more compelling, because it confounded the photographic historian, forcing Frassanito to publish his groundbreaking book with the exact location of the shot left as an unknown.

Frassanito dedicated eight pages of analysis to the *Harvest* photographs at the end of his chapter discussing the Rose Farm collection, certainly suggesting the general location where he guessed the images had been captured. Additionally, while he couldn't document precisely where these photographs were taken, he certainly succeeded in proving that the series of photographs included the same group of dead men photographed from different angles and that Gardner had provided erroneous captions for the negatives in his 1863 catalogue.

Gardner, Gibson, and O'Sullivan took five photographs of these dead soldiers:

1) An 8 × 10-inch negative titled *View in the Field on the Right Wing where General Reynolds Fell.*

2) A stereoview identical to #1 titled *View on Field on Right Wing.*

3) A second stereoview identical to #1 titled *Federal Soldiers as They Fell.*

4) An 8 × 10-inch negative taken from an angle approximately 135 degrees from shots 1–3 titled *A Harvest of Death.*

5) A stereoview of the identical scene as #4 titled *Evidence of how Severe the Contest had been on the Right.*

These captions, considered collectively, make little sense. Gardner is suggesting that at least one of these negatives was produced on the fields of the first day's fighting, where General John Reynolds was killed. This location isn't really on the "Right Wing" of either army's position during the battle. And, *all* his other photographs of the dead were captured two-and-a-half miles away and far south of the town proper.

Frassanito (1975) thought the explanation for the confusing captions was fairly straightforward: When Gardner returned to his Washington studio, and after viewing Mathew Brady's less timely, but more geographically complete collection of photographs, he realized his team had missed the entirety of the July 1 battleground.[2] As a result, and "For the sake of competition," Gardner added four words to his original caption, letting everyone know Brady was not the sole photographer of the first day's battlefield: "View on Field on Right Wing" was modified by simply splicing on "Where General Reynold Fell" on one of the 8 × 10-inch negatives.[3]

Those four words changed the interpretation of this iconic photograph for the next century, misleading scholars and historians alike. It didn't help that three years later Gardner changed the title again in his 1866 *Sketch Book*, this time shortening it to *Field where General Reynolds Fell*.

Twenty years after publishing *Journey*, Frassanito published a more extensive study of the early photographs at Gettysburg.[4] The author again choose to include the *Harvest* image in his "The Rose Farm and Vicinity" chapter, this time at the beginning of the section. Here he described the primary problem most researchers who claim to have "identified" or "discovered" the site of the photographs encounter, "Several of these 'discoveries' have succeeded in closely matching one of the two camera perspectives to the terrain. Today, none has convincingly succeeded in matching both."[5]

The search for the location of the *Harvest* increased significantly in the 1980s, no doubt fueled by Frassanito's published frustration with locating the site. During the next several decades historians and amateurs amassed more than thirty proposed sites for the photographs.[6]

According to Frassanito and historian and photographic experts Tim Smith and Gary Adelman, none of these sites properly match both views of the dead in Gardner's images. They are also usually skeptical of proposed locations from the first day's battlefield. Frassanito, for example, is quick to point out the lack of evidence in the photographs for the Chambersburg Turnpike and the rail and post fences that parallel the important thorough-fare. Adelman frequently criticized the use of two-dimensional prints to match the proposed sites, when superior three-dimensional images are available; he is also effective at demonstrating what is missing from proposed locations, including landscape features that appear in other contemporaneous photographs.

The latest well-publicized "documentation" of the photographic site, which was immediately and credibly attacked by Adelman, is on the battleground of the July 1 fighting. This work comes from Patrick Brennan in a feature article (and cover story) from the widely circulated magazine *The Civil War Monitor* (Spring 2022 issue). The article begins thusly, "They're among the most iconic images of the Gettysburg Battlefield. But where were they shot? Modern technology may have helped figure this out." In this case, "modern technology" includes an "online coloring process based on artificial intelligence," Adobe Photoshop, an "open-source program called GIMP" (an image manipulation program), and the creation of a wire mesh reproduction of McPherson's Ridge.

The author then used the 1864 Simon Green Elliott burial map of Gettysburg and the 1868 Gouverneur Warren topographic map of the battlefield to narrow the location down to the fields south of Lee's headquarters and northwest of the Lutheran Seminary, between Seminary Ridge and McPherson's Ridge. Others had earlier proposed similar prospective sites nearby.

Problems abound with this methodology and, unfortunately, the final proposed location. First, the combination of colorizing and photoshopping the images to help differentiate the dead in blue and gray has the potential to introduce information into the images that doesn't really exist.[7] After Brennan established the ratio of fallen US and Confederate soldiers, he matched this distribution to the Elliott burial map, searching for plots of dead soldiers that match the distribution and demographics of the dead in the photographs. Having established a potential location, the terrain and landscape features were matched to the Warren topographic map. This then introduces two more potential errors based on cartography. Both the Elliott and Warren maps are known to contain errors, albeit mostly small in nature.[8] This leaves us with a set of altered, two-dimensional photographs to be matched with a wire mesh recreation based on a topographic map from 1868. When all this analysis is completed, the proposed site for the photographs doesn't really match the topography of the modern site. This leads the author to introduce a new round of what logisticians call "special pleading," a species of informal fallacy. The modern hillslopes do not match those in the Gardner photographs because "the ridge has changed dramatically since the 1860s, no doubt to create a level platform for both the roadway and many monuments planned there."[9]

Whether or not this claim is true, that the Corps of Engineers flattened this ridge to construct Reynold's Avenue and the adjacent monuments, renders the claimed site unfalsifiable. After all, if this ridge was flattened for the purposes of battlefield infrastructure, then certainly most of the fighting ground, which is littered with monuments and crossed by modern roads, has suffered a similar fate.[10]

Two other questions arise about these photographs that seem to suggest this proposed location is no better than any that proceeded it. First, Chambersburg Pike and the fences lining the road should be prominent in the image that contains the largest number of dead soldiers. Instead, the author points to a "dark line" that is "hard to spot at first." And the absence of the fences? "The fences are not present in the second image, but with good reason. The fences were subject to intense artillery fire from the Union line on Seminary Ridge. . . ."[11] Consider, however, the condition of the fences along the Hagerstown Pike at Antietam, where the fighting was equally intense (figs. 2.6 and 2.7). Even if all the rails had been knocked to the ground, at least some of the posts should remain upright and be visible in the photograph. These, Brennan argues, were completely removed by Ewell's men to construct "powerful breastworks" as evidenced by Mathew Brady's extra-popular photograph of the three captured rebels (fig. 2.2).

A second major problem involves the background in both sets of *Harvest* pictures. Several interesting buildings exist within one hundred yards of this proposed photographic site, including the landmark Lutheran Seminary and Lee's headquarters, the Thompson house. Even if Gardner was ignorant of the historical significance of Lee's headquarters and the imposing seminary building, why would the photographic team elect to intentionally omit these structures from their photographs? In fact, Gardner would need to select two of the *only* two angles available of this collection of corpses that would exclude these buildings in any of his shots. Why would the photographers do this? Perhaps the motivation was financial—to keep the exact location of the two sets of images a mystery so later they could be labeled as coming from different locations. Brennan explains that this was "A trick the canny businessman had learned earlier: make a number of photographs of the same corpses from different angles, thereby increasing his team's output (and commercial potential) with a minimum of effort."[12]

But when exactly is Brennan claiming that Gardner learned this "trick"? Gardner's lens was repositioned multiple time around a dead "sharpshooter" in Devil's Den, but these photographs certainly hadn't proven to be a commercial success because they were taken during the same battlefield visit as the *Harvest* series.[13] If the author is pointing to Gardner's famous work at Antietam nine months earlier, there is not clear evidence of manipulation by the photographer of any subject matter or captioning. Instead, Gardner included compelling anthropogenic structures like the Dunker Church in the background of many of his pictures of the dead.

In the end, we are left with a proposed site for the photographs which lacks many of the characteristics which would move it closer to a conclusive location. In making his burial map-based argument, the author even points to evidence of the interment crew beginning their grisly chore, "one of the soldiers actually broke ground just past the nearest corpse's head."[14] I've studied an extreme enlargement of this image and think that the "broken ground" sure looks like a pile of manure. Note that I'm not an expert on Civil War manure, but I feel better qualified to recognize it after analyzing this *Monitor* article in such detail.

A New Approach to an Old Problem

One aspect of the *Monitor's* article that reflects an uncommon approach to the search for the *Harvest* site is the use of "modern technology" (e.g., the use of an online, cloud-based colorization program with artificial intelligence). Perhaps a better approach would have employed "modern technology," but with a different variety of tools.

The fastest way to narrow down the location of Gardner's work would be to compile a list of what we know and do not know about the 1863 site, then turn this information into geographical data and eventually a series of digitized maps. For example, unlike many of Gardner's photographs of the dead, these bodies are not surrounded by distinctive boulders or trees, or steep ridges. That eliminates half of the battlefield from consideration, based on surficial geology alone. We also know that these men are dead, so that eliminates areas of the battleground that were not combat zones. Elliott's burial map gives us the approximate location where bodies were collected and interred, and it is probably safe to assume that the burial crews did not transport decomposing corpses a great distance prior to burial in the rushed days immediately after the fighting had stopped. That's another layer of geographical data.

All these different layers of data can be qualified based on probability of occurrence. For example, *Harvest* contains no outcropping boulders, so there is a very strong probability that the location today also doesn't have boulders (say, 90 percent or so); extreme erosion might have uncovered a few new rocks, but that would be an unusual circumstance in only 150 years of time. Outcrops are most common in areas of the battlefield that are underlain by igneous rock, like Devil's Den, Culp's Hill, and parts of Cemetery Ridge. The rest of the battlefield has sedimentary rock under it. "Most common" indicates some uncertainty, so it is probable—but not certain—that these photographs were taken on land underlain by sedimentary rock, otherwise there should be boulders visible cropping out somewhere across the terrain. Thus, the *Harvest* location was probably taken on sedimentary rock (say, 75 percent probability). The photographs contain dead bodies that do not appear to have been gathered for burial (see any of the several "top 20" photographs from the Rose Farm or Antietam where the corpses have been aligned in a "V" shape prior to burial). They appear to be *in situ*, not transported at all, so there is a 95 percent chance the photo was taken on a portion of the battlefield where there was intense fighting. Burial crews wouldn't have wanted to transport the group of putrefying corpses far before burying them, so we can use the Elliott map to estimate where the image was captured based on two sets of probabilities: Perhaps, a 90 percent chance the photograph was taken within one hundred yards of a mass grave of ten or more men and a 50 percent chance the shot was taken within fifty yards of the graves. Note that each of these variables, or layers of data, has a range of uncertainty that can be factored into the analysis; and, it matters little if we say 50 percent probability or 75 percent probability for a single geographic layer when a dozen layers of data are being compiled.

When we have completed our data set/geographic map for each of these site-specific variables, including forests (absent), proximity to forests (background: present), slope (based on LIDAR[15]), anthropogenic features (houses: absent), and bodies of water (stream/lake: absent), we have enough layers of data to begin to geographically and topographically eliminate much of the battlefield from the list of potential sites. Using a Geographic Information System (GIS), we can compile this data to create a map that superimposes all our layers and probabilities, producing a composite map that indicates where the photographs were most likely taken.

Testing the Approach

To test this probability-based GIS approach, let's analyze a photograph for which we already know the location (we'll pretend Frassanito failed to find the true location). Let's also select a photograph that has some, but not all, of the same characteristics as *Harvest*. Gardner's photograph of the dead on the Rose Farm is both popular (in the top ten), and in some books it is even mistaken or mislabeled as *A Harvest of Death* (fig. 4.2).

William Frassanito used the unusual weathering of the boulders on this portion of the battleground, along with the relative positioning and orientation of the groups of corpses, to identify the precise location where this image was made. Let's see what our new GPS-based model indicates about the most likely position for the photograph, and then we can compare this location (or locations) to Frassanito's well-documented site to test the methodology.

The parameters for each layer of data will be similar to those of the unknown location of *Harvest*, but not exactly:

Layer 1. 50% likely photograph taken within one hundred yards of another Gardner photograph[16]

Layer 2. 50% likely photograph taken within one hundred yards of where Gardner was known to travel while at Gettysburg

Layer 3. 90% likely there are modern outcrops of igneous rocks

Layer 4. 90% chance photograph was taken on land underlain by igneous rocks

Layer 5. 90% chance photograph was taken within one hundred yards of where men were killed

Layer 6: 90% chance photograph was taken within one hundred yards of a grave of ten or more men

Layer 7. 50% chance photograph as taken within fifty yards of a grave of ten or more men

Layer 8 90% chance photograph was taken of modern terrain with a moderate degree of relief based on LIDAR analysis (more rolling terrain vs. gently undulating)

Layer 9. 90% chance the photograph was taken on a portion of the battlefield with no historical anthropogenic structures

Layer 10. 90% chance the photograph was taken in an area that was not a forest (based on historical maps—the maps introduce the error)

Layer 11. 50% chance the photograph was taken where there is forest nearby (background)

Layer 12. 50% chance the photograph was taken on land held by the Confederate army on July 3 or in no-man's land (otherwise the dead may have been buried earlier)

Each of these layers of data was added to both the LIDAR image of the Gettysburg Battlefield and the Elliott burial map (figs. 4.3–4.5).

To give an example of two geographic layers that were added to the GIS base map, the location of outcrops and regions underlain by igneous rocks (fig. 4.4) are provided. Diabase is the hardest rock found on the Gettysburg battlefield, so it unsurprisingly tends to crop out more commonly than the slightly older and less durable sedimentary rocks.

The composite map, indicating the most likely and least likely locations for the photograph is figure 4.5 (same scale as the LIDAR and Elliott maps, but with no base map for reference). Lighter areas on this map indicate a lower probability (more eliminating factors), while darker shaded areas meet more of the criteria. One area of the southern portion of the battlefield stands apart as the most likely location, and this location is superimposed on an enlarged portion of the Elliott map.

The final location identified by the GIS analysis is precisely where Frassanito found his famous cracked boulder (fig. 3.1). Having demonstrated effectiveness at identifying the known "unknown" location, we will next use the same approach to search for the location of *A Harvest of Death*.

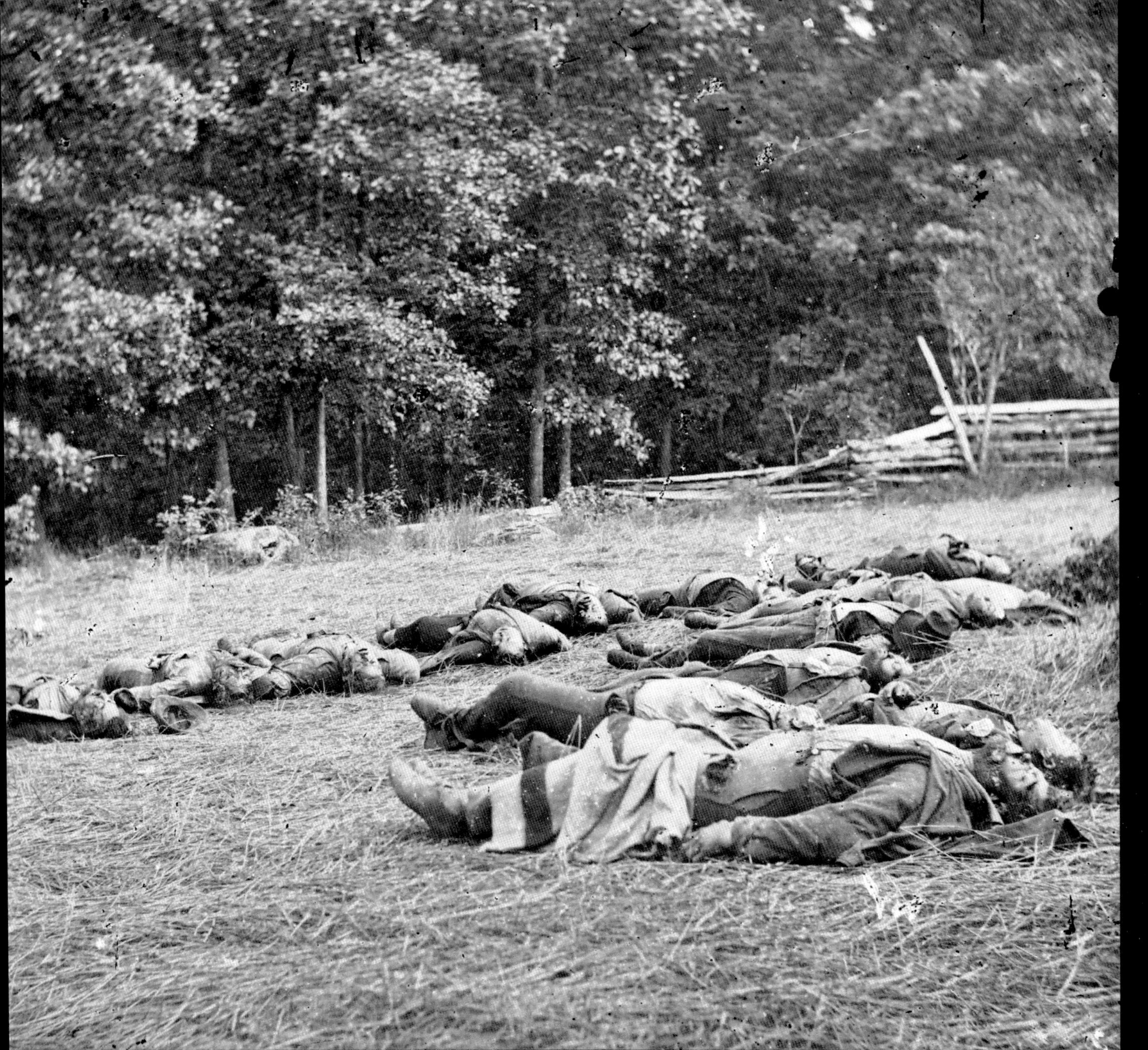

FIGURE 4.2. Timothy O'Sullivan's photograph of Confederate dead on the Rose Farm, gathered for burial. Library of Congress.

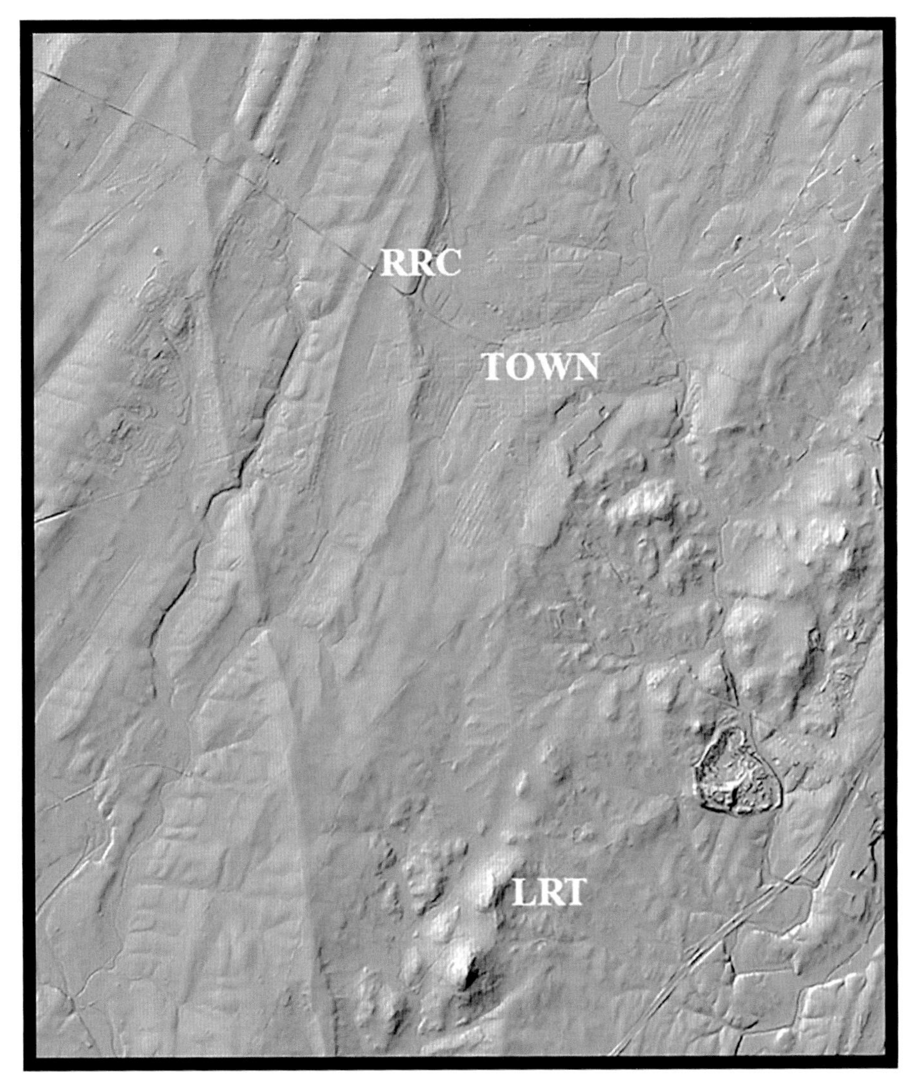

LIDAR

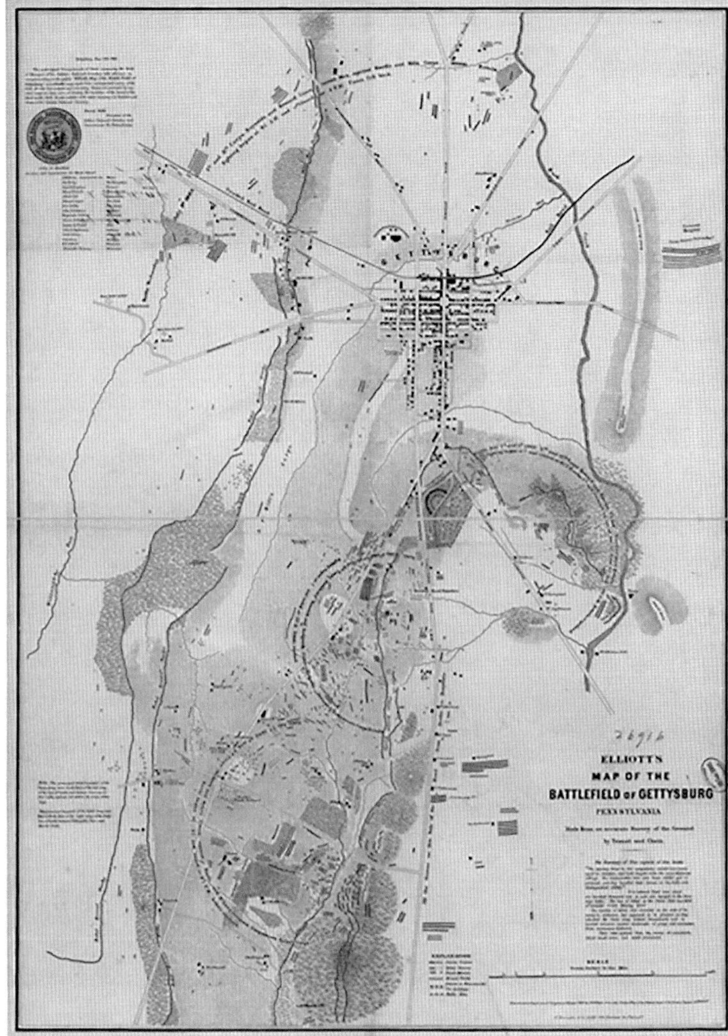

Elliott

FIGURE 4.3. LIDAR and burial maps of the Gettysburg Battlefield (base maps). Both maps are the same scale (*lower right on burial map*). On the LIDAR map, the town center, railroad cut (RRC), and Little Round Top (LRT) are labeled to provide orientation. LIDAR map from Pennsylvania Department of Conservation & Natural Resources (https://www.dcnr.pa.gov) and burial map from Library of Congress (http://hdl.loc.gov/loc.gmd/g3824g.cw0332000).

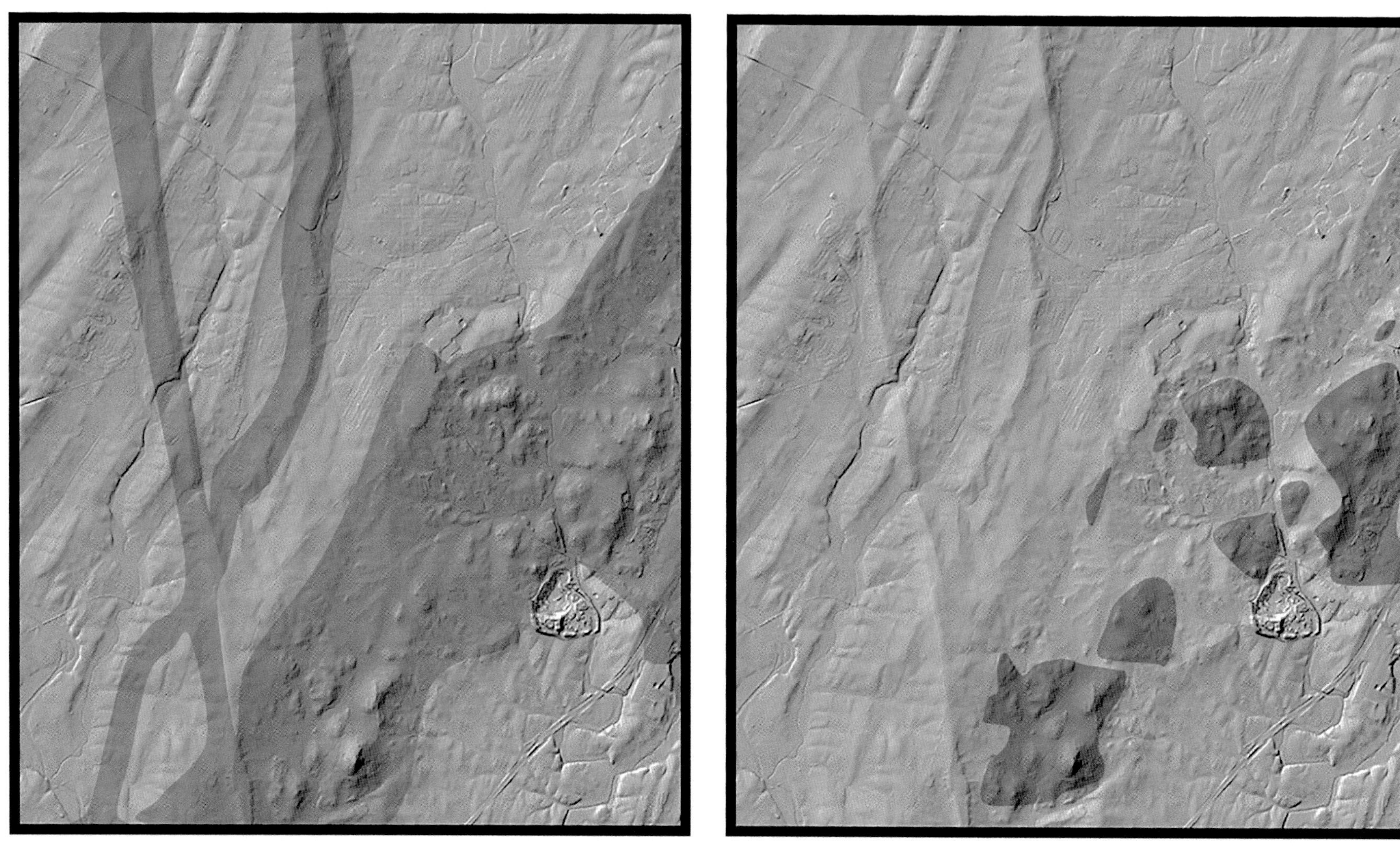

FIGURE 4.4. Regions of the battlefield underlain by igneous rocks and areas where diabase is cropping out, superimposed on the LIDAR image. Note that the outcrops are shaded slightly darker (less transparent), indicating a higher probability that the image in question came from an area with boulders present on the modern battlefield. The scar on the lower right of both images is a local diabase quarry.

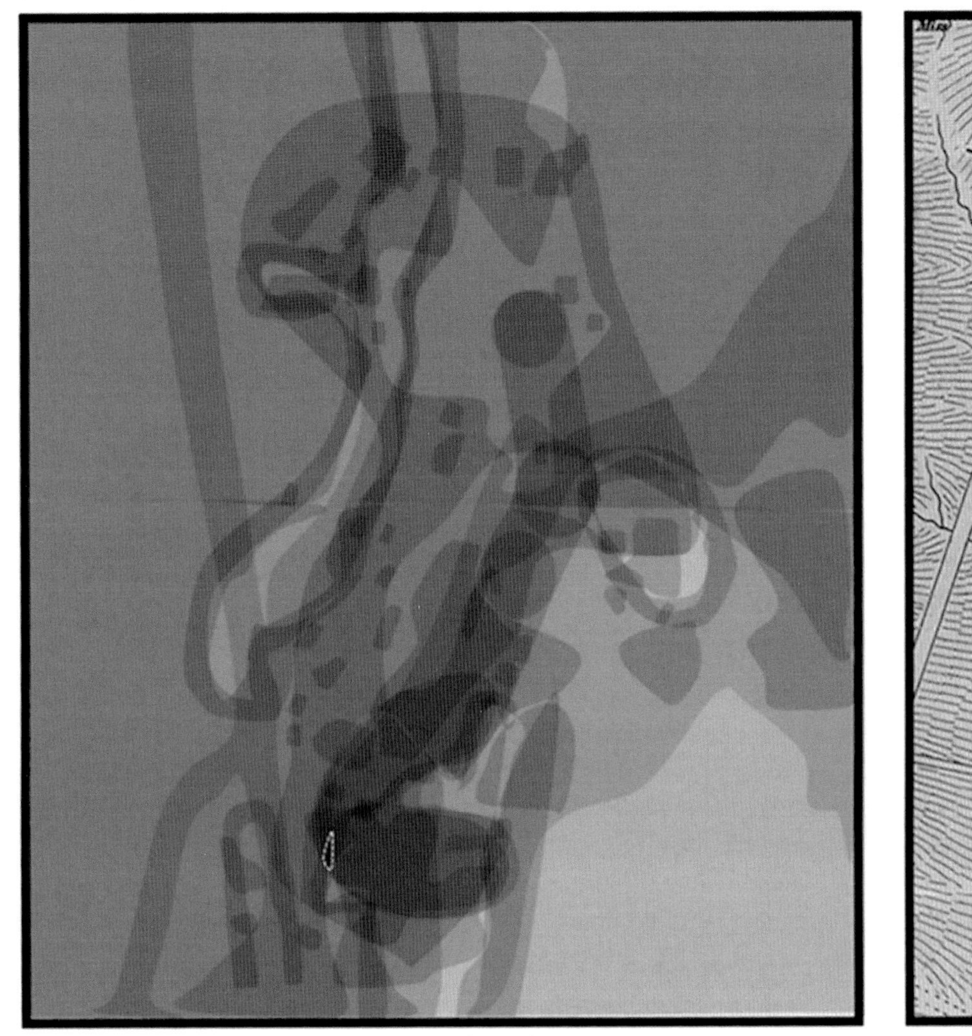

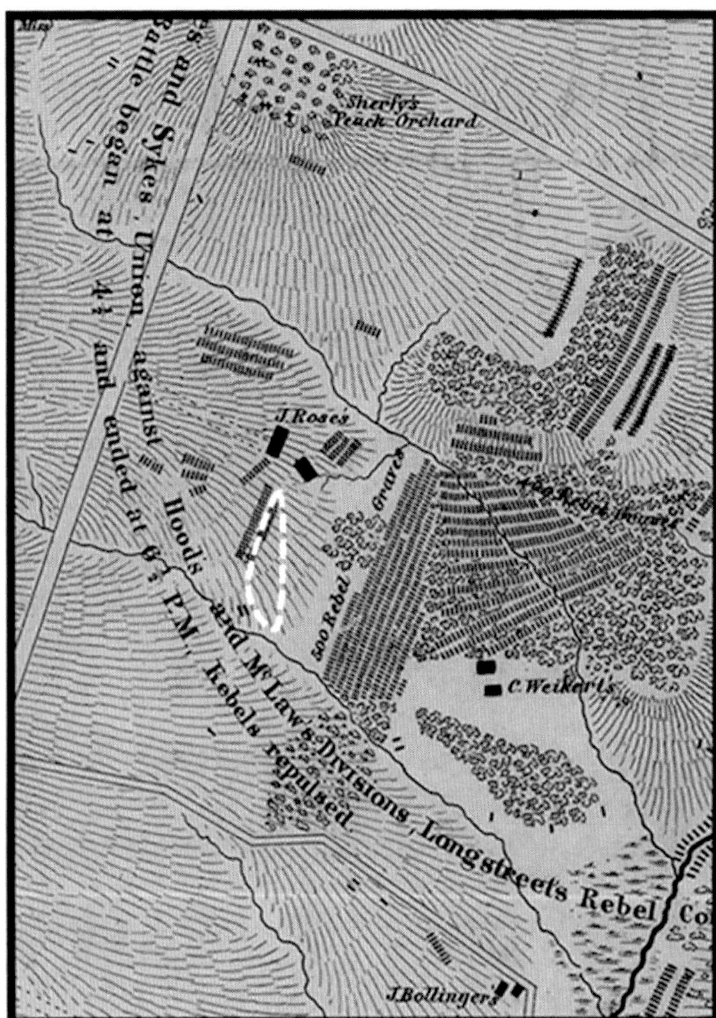

Most Probable Site

FIGURE 4.5. Composite map of the twelve layers of geographical data as compiled in the GIS (*left*). Darker areas indicate higher probability. One area had a slightly higher likelihood for the site of the photograph, outlined in white (all twelve layers matched). On the right, the same small area, only a few acres, is outlined on the Elliott burial map.

The Harvest

When identifying the location of *A Harvest of Death*, the parameters of probability change slightly, especially with respect to geology. All the layers pertaining to fighting, corpses, forests, water, and buildings remain largely the same. For the geology, rock outcrops become an eliminating factor, rather than something that should be present. Additionally, the landscape in the *Harvest* series is probably underlain by sedimentary, not igneous, rock. In total, there are thirteen different layers of geographic probability for the *Harvest* series.

One important note about the rating of probabilities in this analysis, which also pertains to the selection of GIS layers; some degree of critical reasoning is involved in the process. For example, the layers defining the location of "other photographs from Gardner" and "known path of travel for Gardner and his team" require the assumption that it is more likely that *Harvest* was taken somewhere near where Gardner, Gibson, and O'Sullivan had been working, rather than an area of the battlefield far from their journey across the battlefield. Nevertheless, we should not entirely eliminate many of the more distal localities (like the fields of the first day's fighting) simply because the photographers only took a few pictures there or nearby. It is certainly possible that the photographers found a site with the requisite dead bodies at an isolated location and recorded five negatives before moving on—it just isn't as likely as if they took all their images at a few stops after unlimbering all of their equipment. In other words, probability is scaled in the geographic elimination factors and these two factors, based on the known travels of the photographers, aren't especially strong. Conversely, there are no boulders in these pictures, so that almost certainly eliminates areas that today have boulders present above the diabase geology. Therefore, it is 90 percent probable that there will be no igneous boulders present at our modern site, and around 50 percent probable that the site will be located on sedimentary rock. The proximity to graves and areas that witnessed combat are also a stronger indicator in our GIS database than the proximity to other photographic localities.

The inclusion of artificial structures, roads, houses, bridges, or unusual terrain features like distinct hills, mountains, or well-documented forests, is also a bit more complicated because the photographers may have selected a camera angle to either purposely include or exclude these features. Just because a barn or seminary is not present in the photograph doesn't mean there isn't one nearby.

When all these GIS layers are superimposed, a largely unsurprising geographic location is indicated: the farm fields and pastureland on the southern portion of the battlefield that is bracketed by the Emmitsburg Road and Gardner's macabre Rose Farm-boulder location (fig. 4.6). This location differs from the well-established Rose Farm shots because of the underlying rock type—the *Harvest* is on rolling/undulating sedimentary strata while the cracked-rock series is definitely underlain by diabase.

The GIS analysis originally identified three potential sites for the *Harvest* photographs, including an area adjacent to the Rose house. The other two locations were located near the Peach Orchard on the Sherfy and Klingle farms. These locations can be eliminated for two reasons. First, both areas of highest probability are geographically exceedingly small, perhaps only covering an acre or two. Second, it would have been difficult for Gardner and his crew to capture the two photographs *without* also including at least one farm building or house. As a result, the much larger tract of land to the south is a more likely location for the photographs.

This is the area of the battlefield originally suspected by Frassanito and others, and it makes perfect sense. Gardner, drawn to the area by the many dead bodies on the field, photographed Devil's Den, Little Round Top, and the Rose Farm or *Harvest* collection (order indeterminate), then proceeded north, taking pictures of the dead horses at the Trostle Farm. The photographers skipped the fields of Pickett's Charge, perhaps because there was too little light to continue working or perhaps because all the bodies had already been buried and they remained ignorant of the

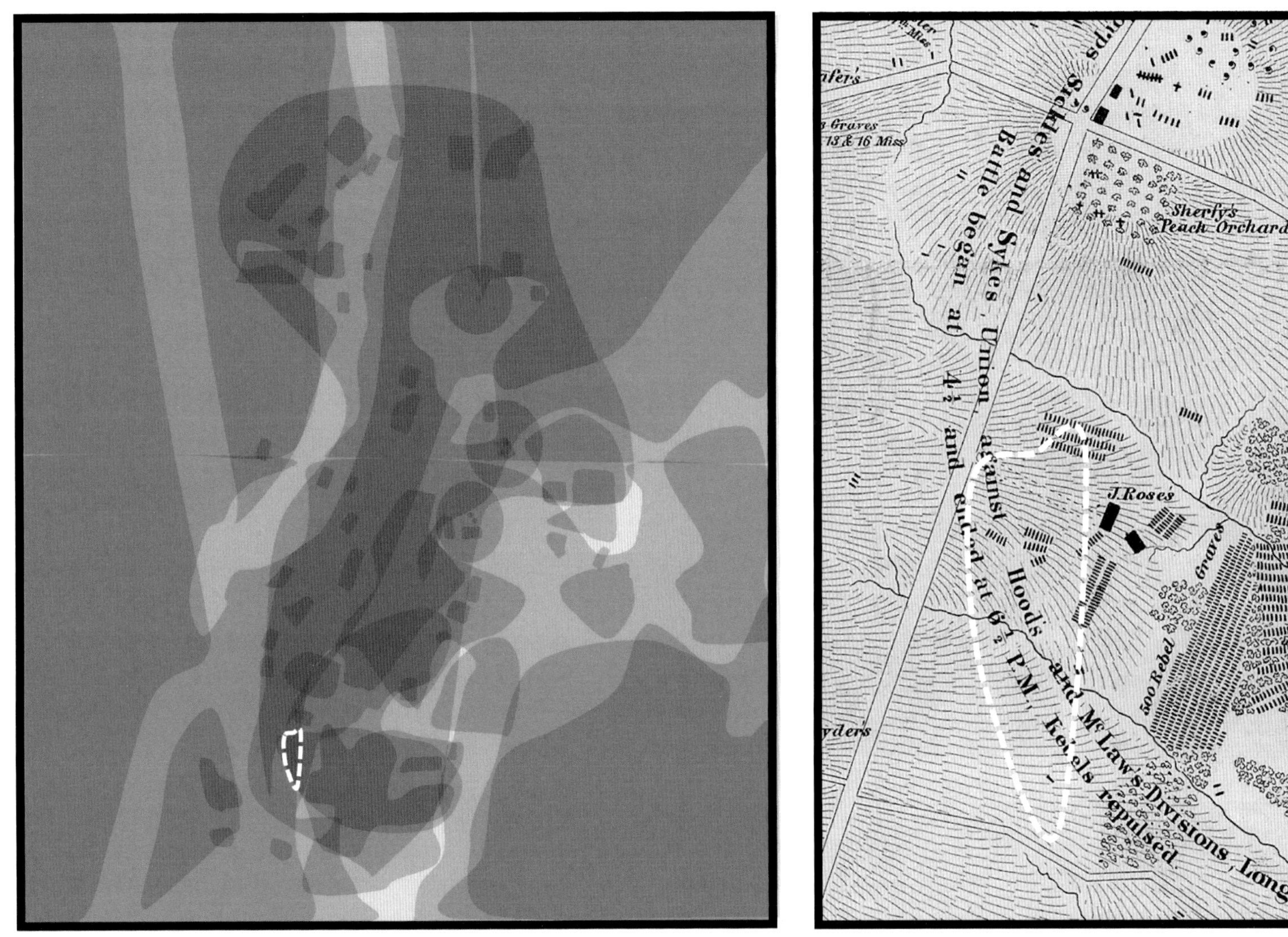

FIGURE 4.6. Region of the battlefield that best matches the GIS parameters for *A Harvest of Death*. This region of the battleground is just to the west of the contact between sedimentary and igneous rocks and we would not expect to find boulders strewn across this portion of the fields.

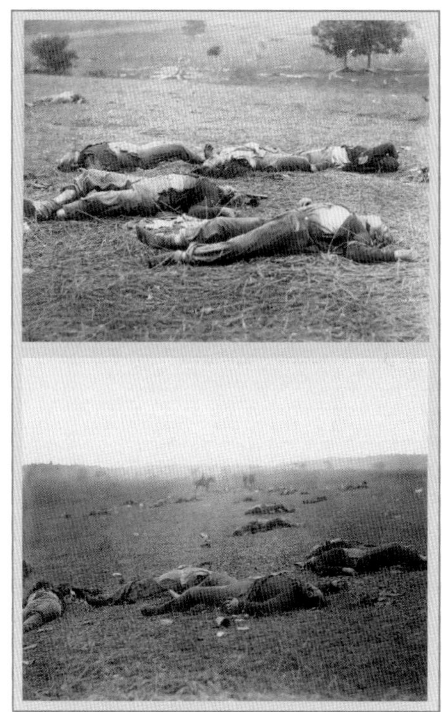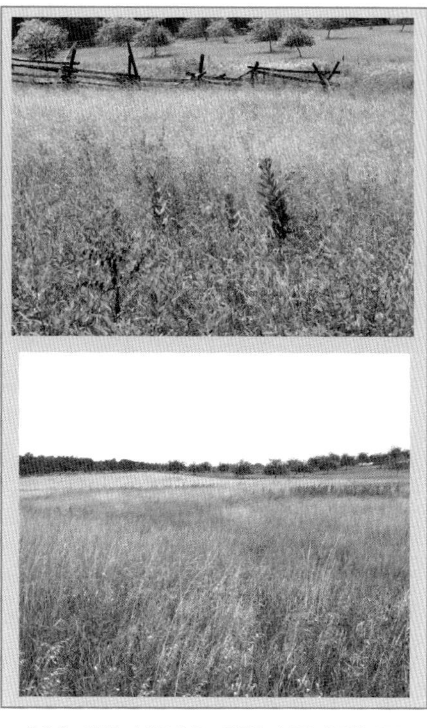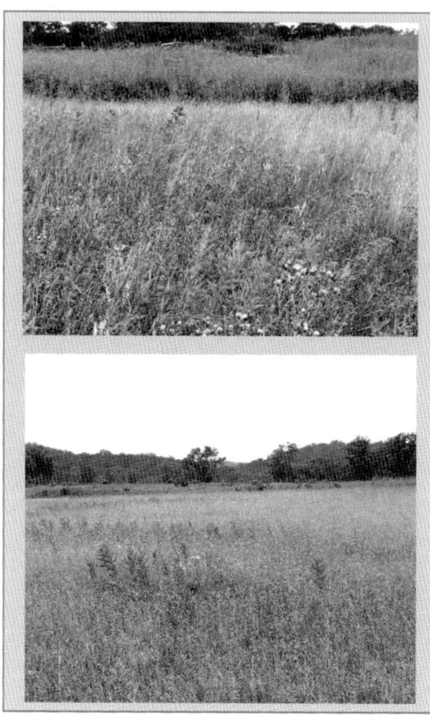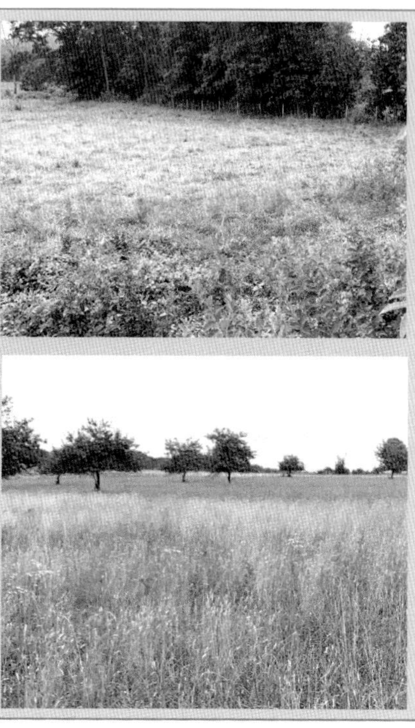

| Gardner Originals (135° apart) | 39° 47' 48" N; 77° 15' 02" W | 39° 47' 36" N; 77° 15' 07" W | 39° 47' 35" N; 77° 14' 59" W |

FIGURE 4.7. There are at least five locations within the geographical region outlined by the GIS probability map that match, to a good degree, the location where Gardner's *Harvest* collection was taken and three are presented here with their location coordinates. Each set of photographs represents two images, taken with the camera position rotated 135 degrees, and matched to each of Gardner's prints.

historical significance of the landscape, before traveling into Gettysburg proper (where they would take only a single picture during their stay). The next day they captured a few more negatives on East Cemetery Hill and the graveyard before heading back to Washington with their dreadful, fragile inventory.

Within the GIS-determined triangular target area, there are multiple locations that (apparently) match the landscape witnessed in the two different views (fig. 4.7). While none of these locations jump off the page as a perfect match for the *Harvest* location, all are certainly viable candidates. This demonstrates the difficulty of identifying the precise location after almost 175 years of landscape evolution. Based on field observations and consideration of the three-dimensional stereo images, and the fact that the group of photographs were taken after rotating the camera 135 degrees, the first location (fig. 4.7, leftmost) is the best fit for the photographic sites. It is also the location that is closest to the Rose farm barn and house and in close proximity to Gardner's other images of the dead on this part of the battleground.

The most important aspect of all three of these proposed locations is that they match both of Gardner's images—and there aren't any objects in any of the pictures (boulders, streams, buildings) that would eliminate any of the sites. Nevertheless, it is certain that none of these locations will be accepted as definitive, nor should they, and thus—despite the science— the mystery will remain.

Caveats, of Course

So why has the location of the *Harvest* images remained so difficult to definitively identify over time? Simply put, investigators have assumed a degree of stability for the landscape that may not be realistic, and the images themselves contain no indisputable tracer through time like the boulders on the Rose Farm or Devil's Den. Even the background of both angles of the *Harvest* images is blurry. The area where the photographs were taken is also probably underlain by sedimentary strata, rocks that are more susceptible to weathering and erosion over 150 years, especially when compared to the durable diabase.

Anthropogenic changes in this part of the battlefield should also not be discounted in rendering the landscape unrecognizable from how it appeared in 1863. Two houses that were built during the twentieth century marred the landscape in this region until they were demolished in September of 2010. Both were located along the eastern side of the Emmitsburg Road, and even after removal their former presence no doubt left a change in the appearance, or even relief, in the area.

The mid-twentieth-century "tourist boom" and centennial anniversary of the battle led to extensive commercial development of this region, including an invasion of businesses like a Stuckey's Pecan Shop, which opened near the Peach Orchard along the Emmitsburg Road. These structures were all later torn down, but their construction and mere presence hardly left the landscape unscathed.

These houses and business establishments were probably a minor scar on the landscape compared with earlier structures. In the 1930s the Lee-Meade Inn, complete with a lodge and eighteen cabins, intruded into this area. The owners sold the land to the Battlefield Park, no doubt increasing their asking price by threatening to construct a drive-in theater on the site![17] Visitors of the inn had the option to arrive by car, where there was a convenient service station nearby, or arrive at the Battlefield Airport.

This airport had, in turn, been used by the US Military when Camp Colt was operational in 1918 and 1919. Imagine what kind of military training center would be the very hardest on a local landscape and cause the largest change to the terrain; Camp Colt was a training center for tank drivers, where a young Dwight D. Eisenhower oversaw the development and refinement of America's first Tank Corps, largely by having them rip up the farm fields made famous by Longstreet's July 2 assault and Pickett's July 3 charge.

In recent years the National Park Service has made great efforts at returning the battlefield landscape to a visual status that is more similar to the appearance of the battlefield in 1863. Buildings and forests have both fallen in an effort to enhance historical interpretation. One coincidental, if not casual, outcome is an increased search effort to find the location of the *Harvest*. The precise location of the shots may, sadly, always elude us because of the mutilation of the topography and terrain on this part of the battlefield through time. Merely matching slopes and topography at 135 degree angles in "then-and-now" photographs may no longer be possible, because the "now" is simply too different from the "then."

PART 2

JOURNALISTS OR ARTISTS?

The Scale of Manipulation

Value versus Veracity

The value of a photograph from a historical, rather than an aesthetic, perspective is directly tied to context. The precise timing, location, and subject matter present in the photograph must be unambiguous for an image to accurately present information about the past. Mistakes regarding context abound in the literature, even when presented in books written by photographic experts.

Two photographic examples from Gettysburg make clear these contextual challenges. In his book *Historic Photos of Gettysburg*, John Salmon presents "hundreds of historical photographs" from the aftermath of the battle and the fiftieth and seventy-fifth reunions of the veterans.[1] In an online review of the book (3 stars out of 5!), fellow historian Scott Mingus pointed out several "glaring errors in these captions" including incorrect names, locations, and military units. He added, "The poorly researched captions are not enough of a distraction to prevent me from recommending this book, especially if corrected in a second edition." Nevertheless, for research purposes, these descriptive errors may lead future authors and researchers to repeat the misguided information, perhaps even solidifying the contextual problems in the collective literature.

Jennifer Murray published a thorough review of the creation and management of the Gettysburg National Military Park in her 2014 text.[2] Five years later she wrote a review of Brian Black's *Gettysburg Contested: 150 Years of Preserving America's Cherished Landscape* for Louisiana State University's *Civil War Book Review*. Murray spent about one-third of her 1,000- word critique criticizing one photographic "case-study" that was included in Black's work. "The Copse and National Reconciliation" includes six photographs from near the high-water mark along the center of the Federal line on Cemetery Hill. For the first photograph, Murray pointed out that the author's description of the production of the photograph, by William Tipton, is off by at least two decades. The third photograph in the collection is also misdated. Murray also had problems with the interpretation of the fourth image, before pointing out that the final image in the series was taken miles away from the famous Copse, when the Eternal Light Peace Memorial was dedicated in 1938. This leaves us with a 50 percent success rate for accuracy when describing photographs *of the author's own choosing*.

Even more mistakes regarding photographic context are easily found in wide-ranging Civil War history books intended for the general public. One of the most egregious examples can be found in *Bill O'Reilly's Legends and Lies: The Civil War*. On page thirty-three there is a picture of Federal officer in uniform with the caption "Before becoming president of the Confederacy, Jefferson Davis had served the United States as a soldier in the Mexican-American War. . ." (fig. 5.1, left). However, this isn't a picture

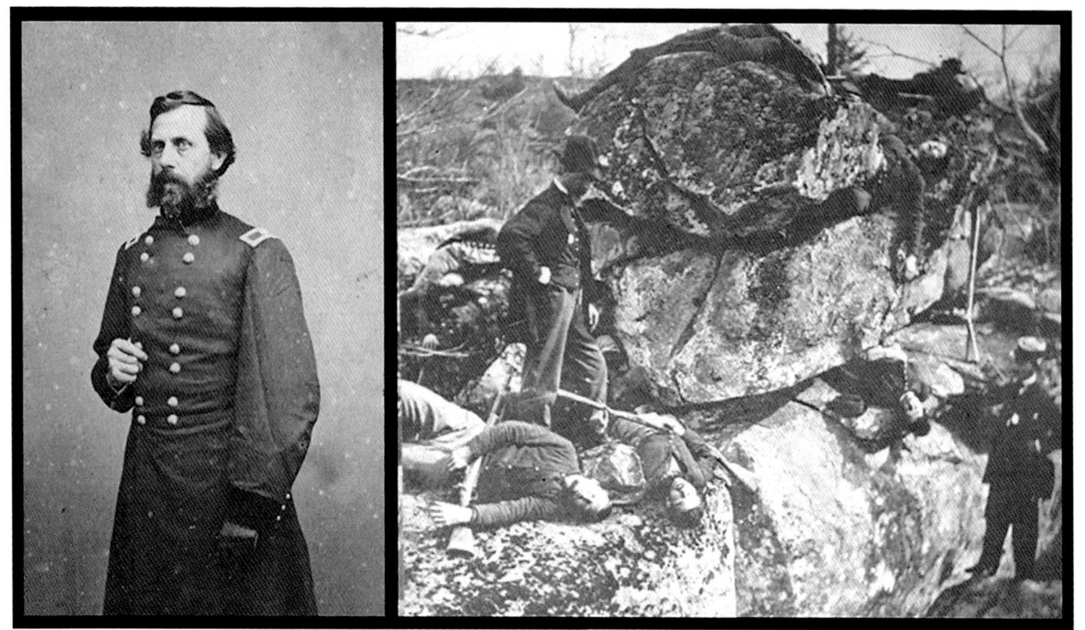

of Jefferson F. Davis, the president of the South; instead, this photograph is of Jefferson C. Davis, a US brigadier general who is probably best known for killing his superior officer.

On page 183 readers find an even more egregious mistake: an apparently gruesome photograph of eight dead US infantrymen scattered around a split diabase boulder in Devil's Den at Gettysburg (fig. 5.1, right). This caption ends with, "Here two doctors examine fallen men only hours after battle." In reality, this photograph was fabricated by Peter Weaver of nearby Hanover, Pennsylvania, more than five months after the battle. Weaver apparently convinced some Federal soldiers to take a pause from the national cemetery dedication to join him in the Den, where he whimsically posed them as combat victims. The caption in *Legends and Lies* is incorrect about the timing of the photograph (no one had a camera on the battlefield "only hours" after the battle—Gardner and his crew would not arrive for two days after Lee headed south), and even the basic subject matter (the men aren't dead, they are posing). Hints that this is a contrived scene are present throughout the image: healthy, non-bloated "corpses" strewn fancifully over, under, and even within the boulders, all surrounded by leafless trees—in July.

The point of describing these misidentified and mislabeled photographs is to demonstrate how common and simple it is for an author (or editor) to misconstrue what a historical image is actually presenting and what the context and significance of a photograph truly epitomizes. Additionally, it is important to remember that these factual errors are now introduced to a new audience and, perhaps, a new generation of non-skeptical historians. Now consider, among all this confusion and ambiguity of context, that even the original photographers themselves were introducing falsehoods and promoting obfuscation. This chapter concentrates on just this aspect of Civil War photography: the relationship between photographic authenticity and historical value.

The earlier two examples of misidentification at Gettysburg are simple errors that are easy to commit and relatively harmless (albeit mistakes that continue to frustrate professional historians). The third, in O'Reilly's book, is rather naïve and silly, and unlikely to be repeated by other students or historians of the conflict. The false caption and fake photography also represent the pinnacle of photographic inauthenticity: an event that didn't happen at a time it didn't occur—only the location is authentic. Only a complete fabrication or composite photograph would be of less value to historians. The rest of this chapter is dedicated to working through this scale of manipulation and how it relates to the historical value of a photograph.

Certainly we understand that all "combat" photographs were staged to some degree, unless they contain only the dead, because the subjects needed to remain motionless.[3] This represents only a small degree of manipulation. What, however, are we to think of photographs that have props added, dead bodies moved, or fake corpses included, from a photojournalism perspective?

Before working our way through this scale of manipulation, a few contextual caveats for all "action" or "combat" photographs need to be discussed.[4] First, traditional thinking is that no true photographs of men in the heat of battle exist for the simple reason that the cameras and wet negatives of the time required lengthy exposure times and prohibited movement by the subject matter.[5] As a result, any photograph of living humans that appears sharp and in-focus also indicates that the scene was staged to some degree. The slow "shutter speeds" or the length of time that a negative needed to be exposed to light required that the people in the frame needed to remain perfectly still—not something that happens in real life very often. The length of time for this posing has been a matter of debate among historians, but the general consensus is that at least several seconds of light were necessary to create an image.[6] For now, the simple matter that the subjects needed to remain motionless for some considerable period of time can represent one of the lowest levels of manipulation on our scale (fig. 5.2).[7]

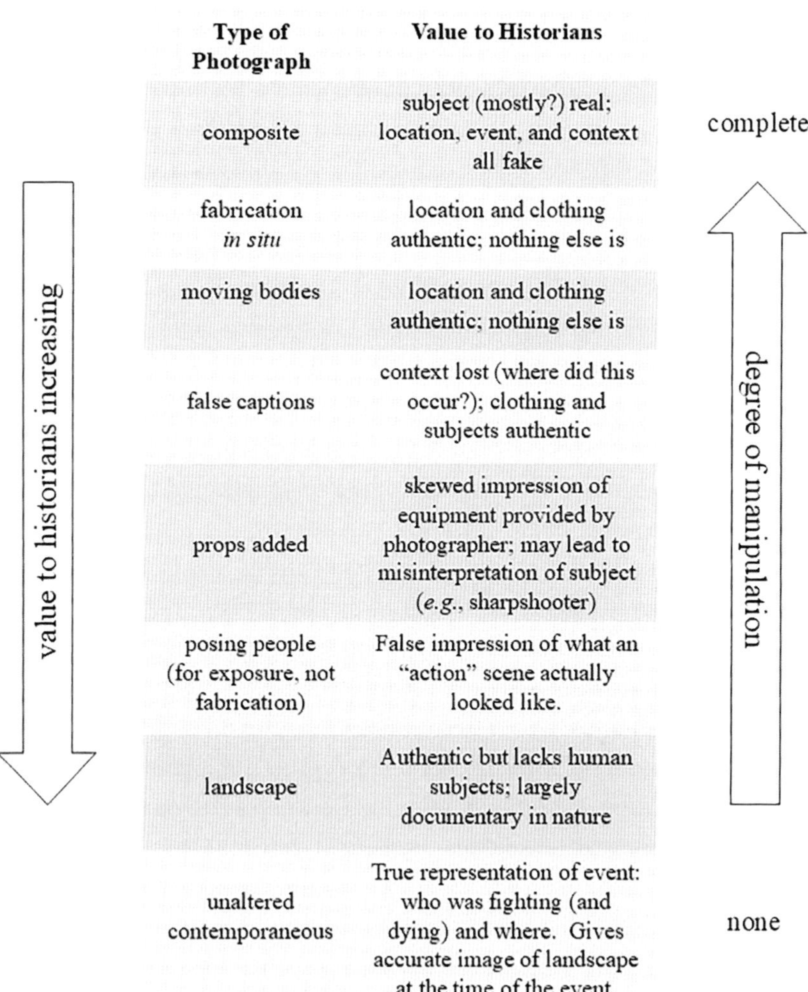

The Scale of Manipulation

Type of Photograph	Value to Historians
composite	subject (mostly?) real; location, event, and context all fake
fabrication *in situ*	location and clothing authentic; nothing else is
moving bodies	location and clothing authentic; nothing else is
false captions	context lost (where did this occur?); clothing and subjects authentic
props added	skewed impression of equipment provided by photographer; may lead to misinterpretation of subject (*e.g.*, sharpshooter)
posing people (for exposure, not fabrication)	False impression of what an "action" scene actually looked like.
landscape	Authentic but lacks human subjects; largely documentary in nature
unaltered contemporaneous	True representation of event: who was fighting (and dying) and where. Gives accurate image of landscape at the time of the event.

FIGURE 5.2. The scale of manipulation shows the inverse relationship between the degree of manipulation and the value of a photograph to historians. Unaltered negatives that were taken soon after battle are the most valuable, while composites are relatively useless with respect to subject matter or context.

The most valuable battlefield photographs to emerge from the Civil War are those that were captured soon after the fighting stopped and include details of the landscape where the fighting occurred.[8] For complete authenticity, they cannot include subjects who are posing. This means that for the photographs from our popularity study, most of Gardner's photographs of the dead at Antietam are slightly more authentic that his later photographs from Gettysburg (where burial crews paused to allow the photographers to collect their images or prisoners posed). Consider Gardner's photographs of the dead along the Hagerstown Pike at Antietam from a historical perspective: This photograph includes dead Confederate soldiers, as they appeared at the time of their killing, in the exact location where they were killed (with, presumably, no props added). The photograph is completely authentic and represents what actually happened where, precisely, it happened. Gardner's nearby photograph of the dead collected by burial crews is just as compelling, but slightly less valuable from a historical context: these men were all killed in the battle, but not at this exact location, as they have been gathered for burial. The same can be said for most of Gardner's collection of photographs from Gettysburg, although with this series there are often living humans posing in the frames.[9]

Brady & Co. didn't arrive at Gettysburg until after all bodies of the fallen had been interred. As a result, his team captured many landscape photographs which, while certainly valuable for interpretation, don't include the subject matter (dead soldiers, battlefield detritus) that would elevate them to the level of unaltered (nearly) contemporaneous shots. Brady often included a few living people, including himself, in the photographs to increase the human interest, and this posing decreased the genuineness of the photograph by a minute degree.

For the next lower level of value to historians, the addition of props to a scene, Gardner's work at Gettysburg stands out. Photographic historians have long suspected that Gardner and his crew had obtained a rifle musket sometime during their journey to the Gettysburg battlefield and that this rifle made its way into several of their photographs. However, few have commented on how obvious the prop is and how consistently it makes an appearance in this series of photographs.

Consider, for example, the probability that Gardner would find nine (!) dead Confederate soldiers, all armed with a similar model of rifle musket, *and all lacking a ramrod* (fig. 5.3). Which is more likely, that nine of the dead soldiers that Gardner encountered were all armed with utterly useless weapons, or that the photographer and his crew found a discarded weapon and added it to each of the photographs? Certainly a corpse with a rifle is more compelling than a body alone—the presence of the weapon adds a sense of immediacy and confirms the death occurred during the intensity of combat. Note also that the ramrod-less rifle also appears in two other of Gardner's compositions on Little Round Top, a circumstance that adds credence to the prop hypothesis (and that has never been presented before).[10]

Just to be certain that the ramrod was missing in all of these photographs, and not simply obscured by shadows, vegetation, or some other lack of resolution, consider several other photographs that include rifle muskets, whether carried by the living or lying next to the dead, on battlefields where the ramrod is present (fig. 5.4).[11]

For each of these six random photographs of soldiers with rifles, the ramrod is not only present, it is fairly easy to see.[12] That suggests the probability of Gardner finding soldier-after-soldier with nonfunctioning weapons more and more unlikely.[13]

So, in summary, the evidence—proof—that Gardner and his men were adding a prop can be summarized by these non-coincidental facts:

1) All the dead men were carrying a similar model Springfield rifle musket.
2) All the dead men were carrying a useless rifle musket because it lacked a ramrod for loading.
3) When more than one dead body was photographed, one man—*and consistently only one man*—was armed with a ramrod-less rifle.

The likelihood that all these criteria would be satisfied by each of the eleven photographs where the rifle appears demonstrates rather conclusively that

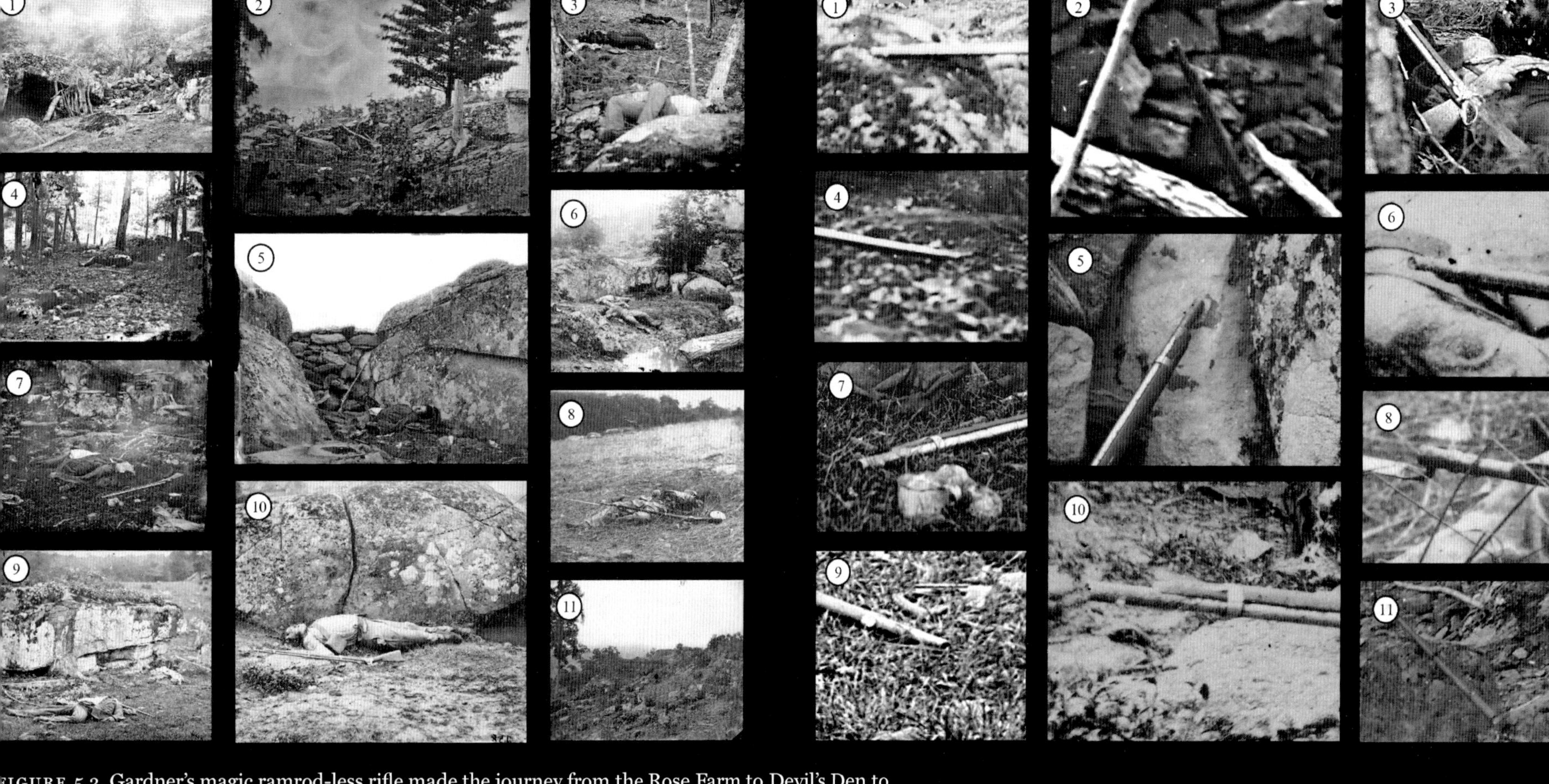

FIGURE 5.3. Gardner's magic ramrod-less rifle made the journey from the Rose Farm to Devil's Den to Little Round Top. Each photograph on the left includes a Springfield rifle musket (and only one single musket). Details of each picture (*right*) focus on the area of the image showing where the ramrod would have been found if present. Gardner's photographs of Little Round Top (#2 and #11) include this same nonoperational prop gun.

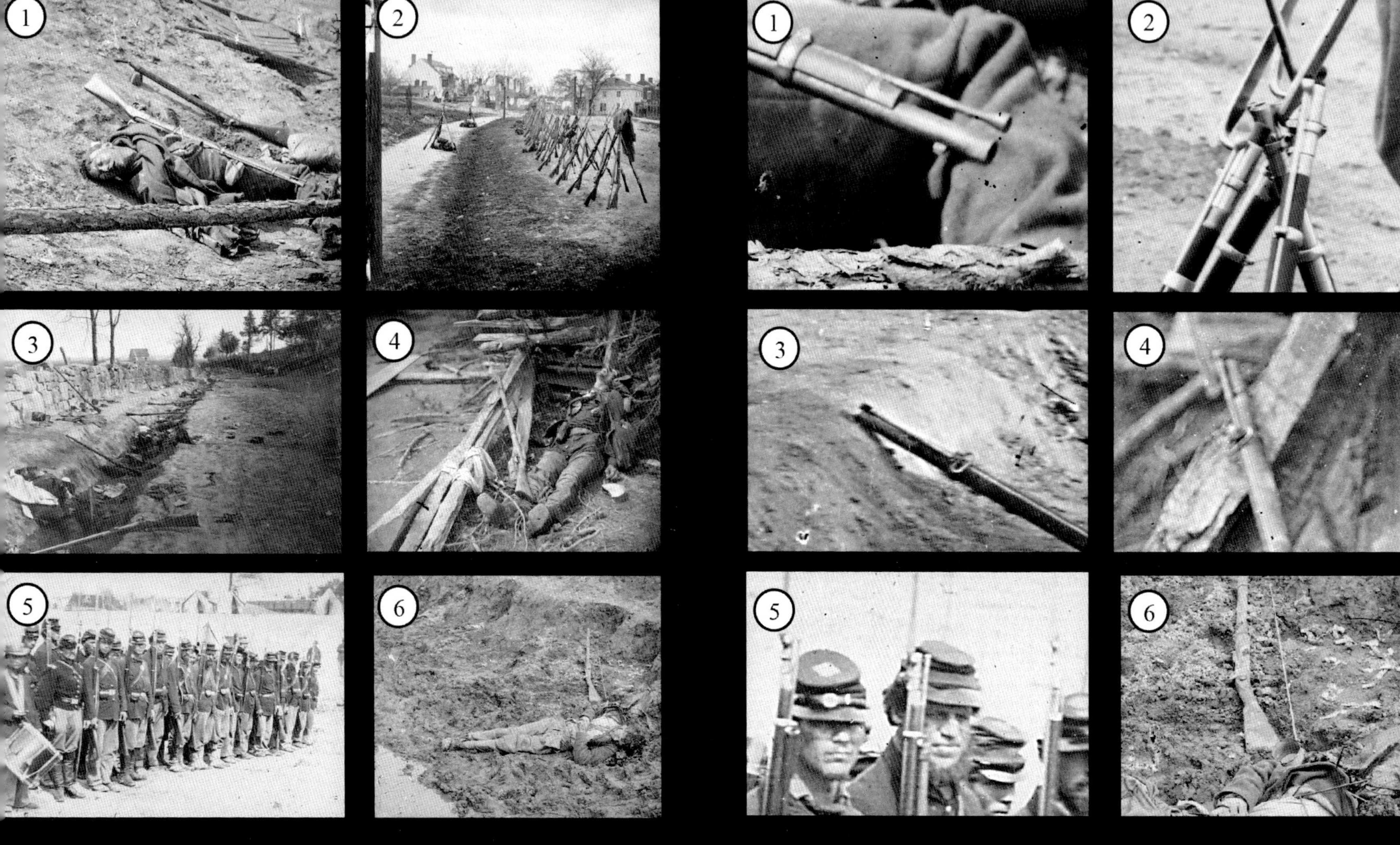

FIGURE 5.4. Each of the photos on the left contains either a Springfield or an Enfield rifle musket with a ramrod present. Detailed images on the right demonstrate how easily the ramrod is to identify if it is present. The poor dead Confederate soldier (#6) has two ramrods, one across his chest and another adjacent to his muddy rifle.

this gun was not present at any of these locations at the time the site was discovered. At best, the rifle was found beside one dead man and later added to the other ten compositions. The incredibly small chance that all of these solitary men were armed with a different rifle and the rifle was not a prop is further diminished by the photographs of groups of fallen comrades, with only a single gun present among them. Had the rifles truly been present at the time of the death, more than one rifle should have been seen in at least one of these other photographs.

This level of manipulation by Gardner and his team diminishes, at least to some degree, confidence in the authenticity of the photograph: The rifle is fake, but the soldier was actually killed in combat at (usually) the location where the negative was captured. The landscape, clothing, and condition of the body are all authentic, only the weapon is spurious. The next two levels of our scale of manipulation introduces even more falsehoods.

Maximum Manipulation

Of all the photographers to emerge from the Civil War, Alexander Gardner is most associated with the next two levels of manipulation, and in both cases, he purportedly committed these infractions at Gettysburg. His five *Harvest of Death* photographs represent the first of these falsehoods, as Gardner provided misleading and, in some cases, clearly incorrect or mutually exclusive captions for each of the images. As discussed earlier, these erroneous descriptions have confused and confounded scholars for a century and a half, which certainly diminished their historical value.[14] We can be fairly certain these photographs came from Gettysburg, but where on the battlefield they were captured, and who these men were, remains in doubt.

Gardner and his team were also famously responsible for moving a corpse in a (successful) attempt to compose a more compelling image. The resulting photograph, titled *Home of a Rebel Sharpshooter*, is today the most well-known example of a manipulated image to emerge from the

war. Nevertheless, it still finds its way into books with no mention that it was staged to this day.[15] The manipulation demonstrated in *Sharpshooter* is higher on the scale because the event, as depicted in the "truth-telling" photograph, never happened the way one might imagine. This dead man is authentic and the location is certainly real, but he wasn't killed here, and he wasn't carrying that rifle. He also almost certainly wasn't a sharpshooter, either.

In his 1866 *Photographic Sketch Book of the Civil War*, Gardner also provides a, frankly, preposterous story to accompany his dead rebel sharpshooter. This text, written by Gardner himself, tells the story of the photographer returning to Devil's Den in November 1863, almost five months later, to discover the body still lying in the sniper den accompanied by the now rusty musket. Keith Davis suggests that Gardner felt little guilt about their manipulation of the subject matter or story being sold:

> This "contrived" image was accompanied in the *Sketch Book* by text that was, in itself, a poetic fiction. Although Frassanito's discovery may have distressed historical purists, it is likely that Gardner created this image and story with a clear conscience. Indeed, by exercising aesthetic and compositional control over his subjects, Gardner achieved one of the most powerful visual/textual narratives of the war.[16]

Alan Trachtenberg in *Reading American Photographs* questions:

> But does the whole truth represented in the pictures lie in their literal content? They were received as 'true' because people believed in photographic 'truth.' What properly concerns us is that belief, and the more particular beliefs about the Civil War which governed the responses to the photographs.[17]

Both quotes drill down on the way these photographs were interpreted by their original audience, as true compositions by Gardner et al., without regard to whether the image's creator may have been exercising aesthetic control.

The final levels of manipulation, fabrication *in situ* and composites, offer the least value for historical interpretation. P. S. Weaver's posed scenes from Devil's Den (fig. 5.1) represent a good example of fabrication on a historically significant landscape. Only the location is authentic in this photograph—the events depicted never took place and the men are genuine soldiers, but not men who fought in or around Devil's Den. And, while the location was a part of the Gettysburg battleground that did see combat, it didn't really look like this because the photograph was taken in late fall, not during the heat of summer. From a historical or documentary perspective, this photograph would have more value had it been taken at a time closer to the battle and without the comically placed "corpses" strewn about. Weaver's creation falsely shows the audience how the landscape appeared after battle, instead of allowing the viewers to see the scene sans the dead and fake doctors and imagine how it might have looked.

Gardner wasn't alone in photographing fake dead soldiers. Brady & Co. posed the living to appear as battle casualties at least twice, as did T. C. Roche towards the end of the war at Petersburg (fig. 5.5). In each of these cases, the same "dead" soldiers can be spotted in other photographs, often posing or otherwise being alive.

The final, least historically valuable level of photographic manipulation is the composite. In these photographs and lithographs almost nothing is authentic, not the location, event, or subject matter. Take, for example, Levin Corbin Handy's photograph *General Ulysses Grant at City Point*. The only aspect of this image and title that is accurate is that this is the face of Ulysses Grant. That isn't his body, his horse, or City Point. Instead, it is Grant's head, cut from a photograph taken at Cold Harbor, spliced onto the body and horse of US Major General Alexander McDowell McCook, which in turn was dropped into a photograph of Confederate soldiers who had been captured at the Battle of Fisher's Hill in a completely different region of Virginia. And, this montage was put together twenty-five years after Grant died. Each separate photograph that was used to create this composite has its own authentic story to tell, but combined in this crude manner produces an assemblage that really only has one purpose—to sell and as it circulated, confuse the public.

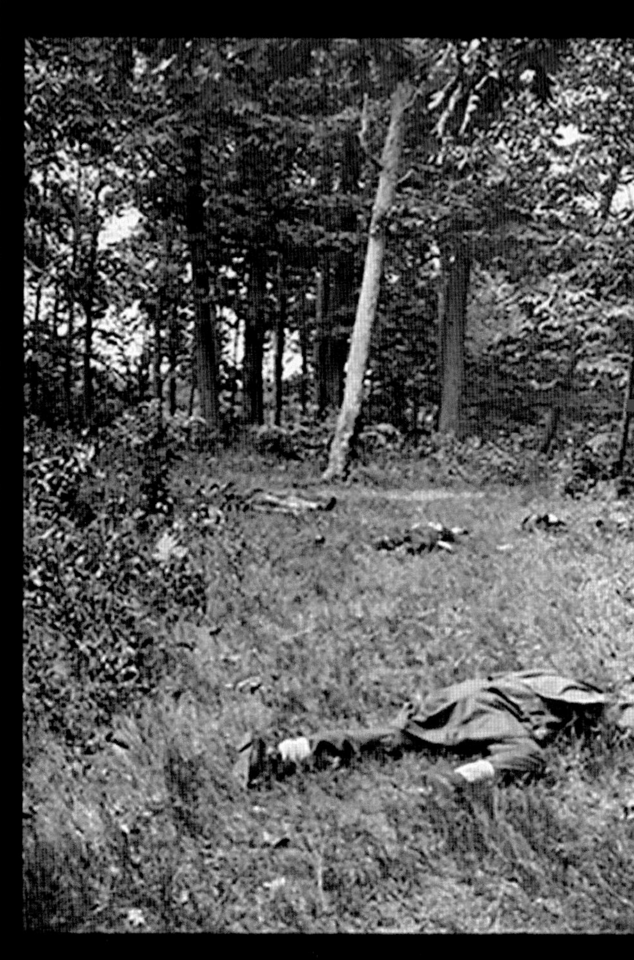

FIGURE 5.5. Six "dead" men are pictured in Brady and Roche's three photographs, but only one is really deceased (the man in the foreground on the far right). Note that in Roche's picture the artillery swab was added as a prop. Library of Congress.

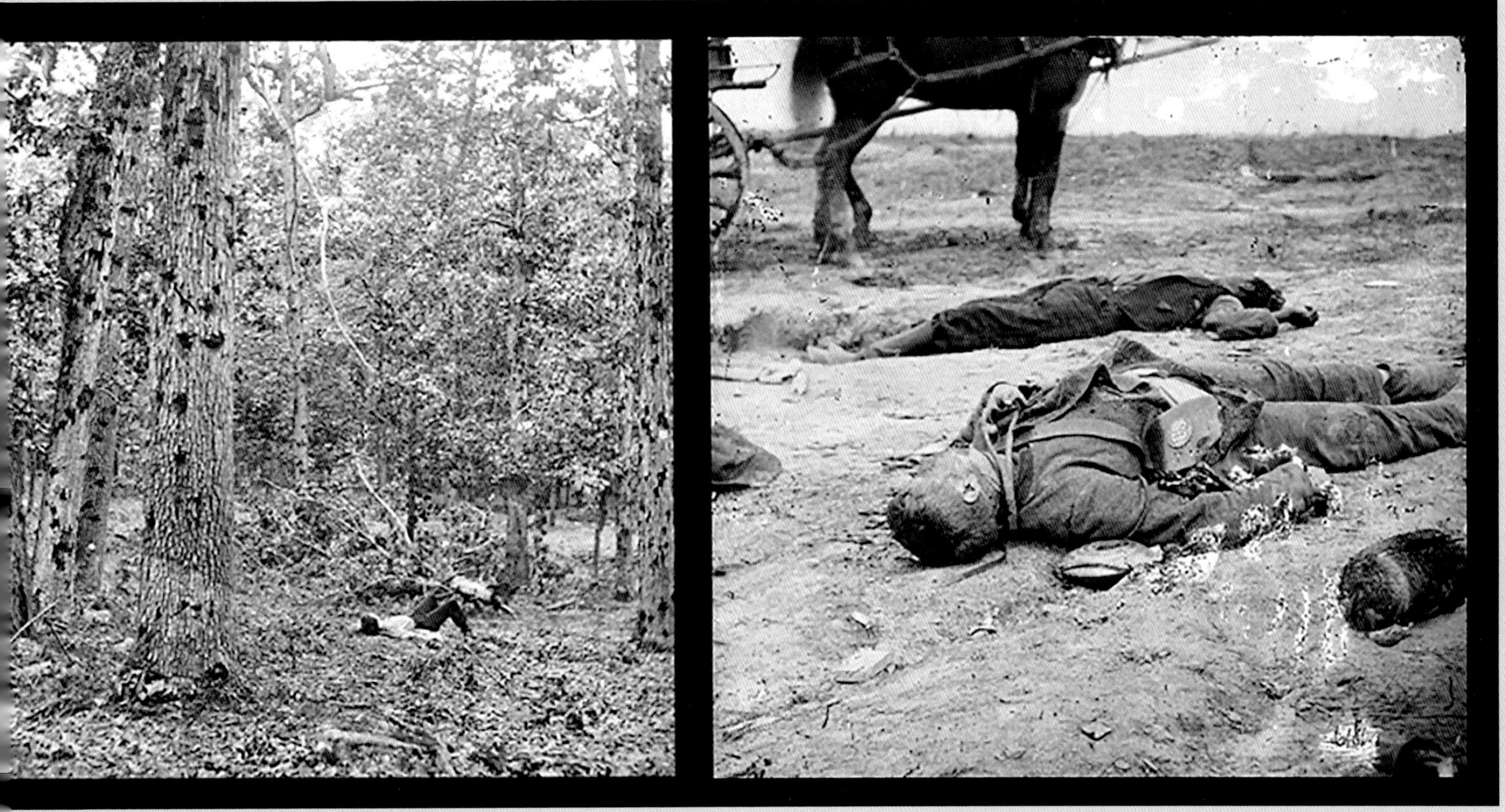

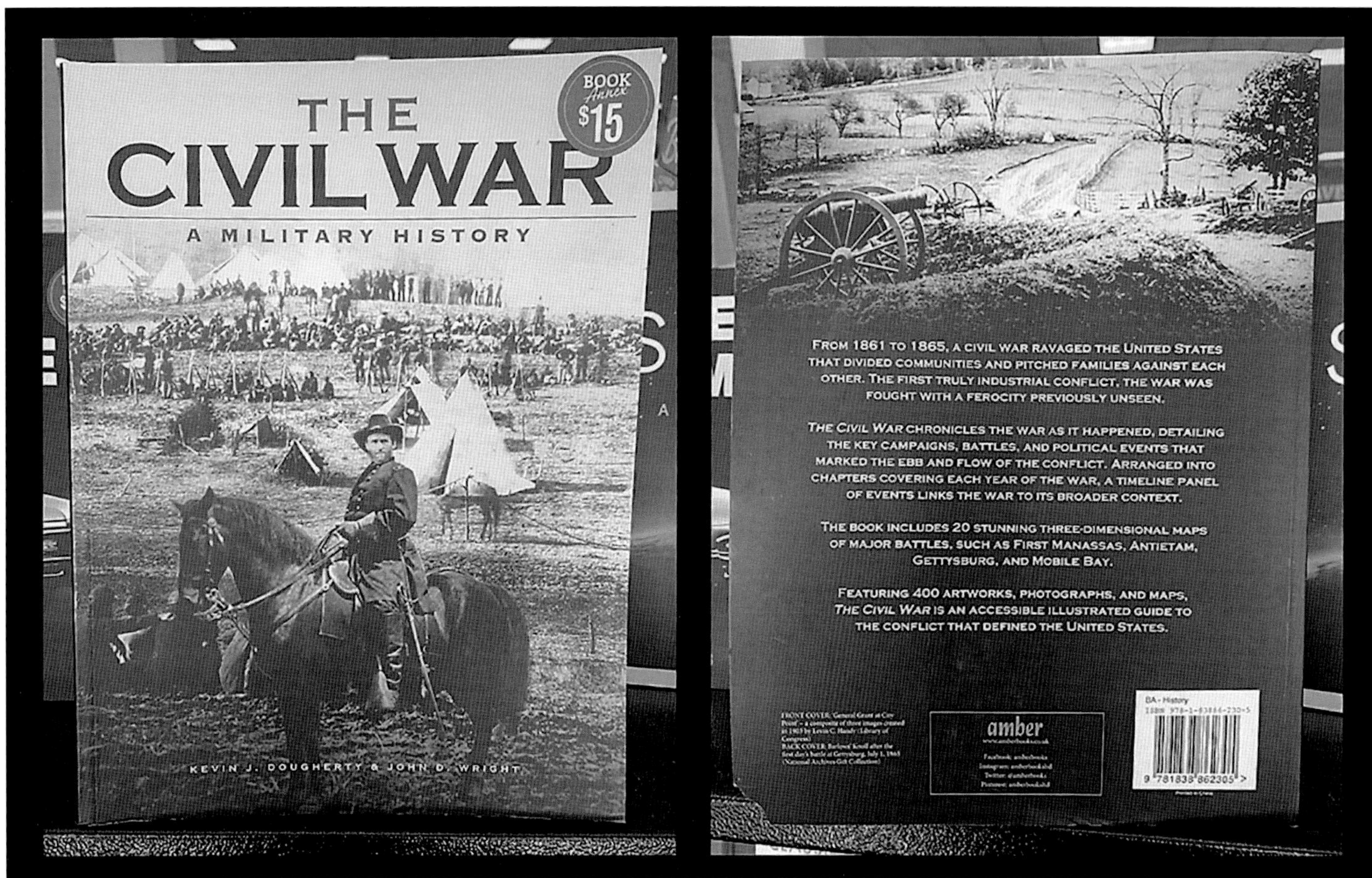

FIGURE 5.6. *The Civil War: A Military History* front and back cover, photographed on the shelf of a nationwide bookseller.

An image doesn't need to be genuine to sell, or sell books. Take, for example, a book that is currently on the shelf at my local nationwide bookseller: Kevin Dougherty and John Wright's *The Civil War: A Military History* (fig. 5.6). This book had previously been published under the titles *Battles of the American Civil War* and *The Timeline of the American Civil War*. The back cover assures a potential reader that the book covers the Civil War "as it happened."

Unfortunately, the rest of the cover, front and back, immediately fails on this promise. On the front we find Handy's montage of Grant (although the illustration is identified, in very small print on the back cover, as a composite). The back cover is dominated by a second large black-and-white photograph, identified as "Barlows' Knoll after the first day's battle at Gettysburg, July 1, 1863." There are a few problems with this documentation. First, this isn't Barlow's Knoll, it is Steven's Knoll. Barlow's Knoll,

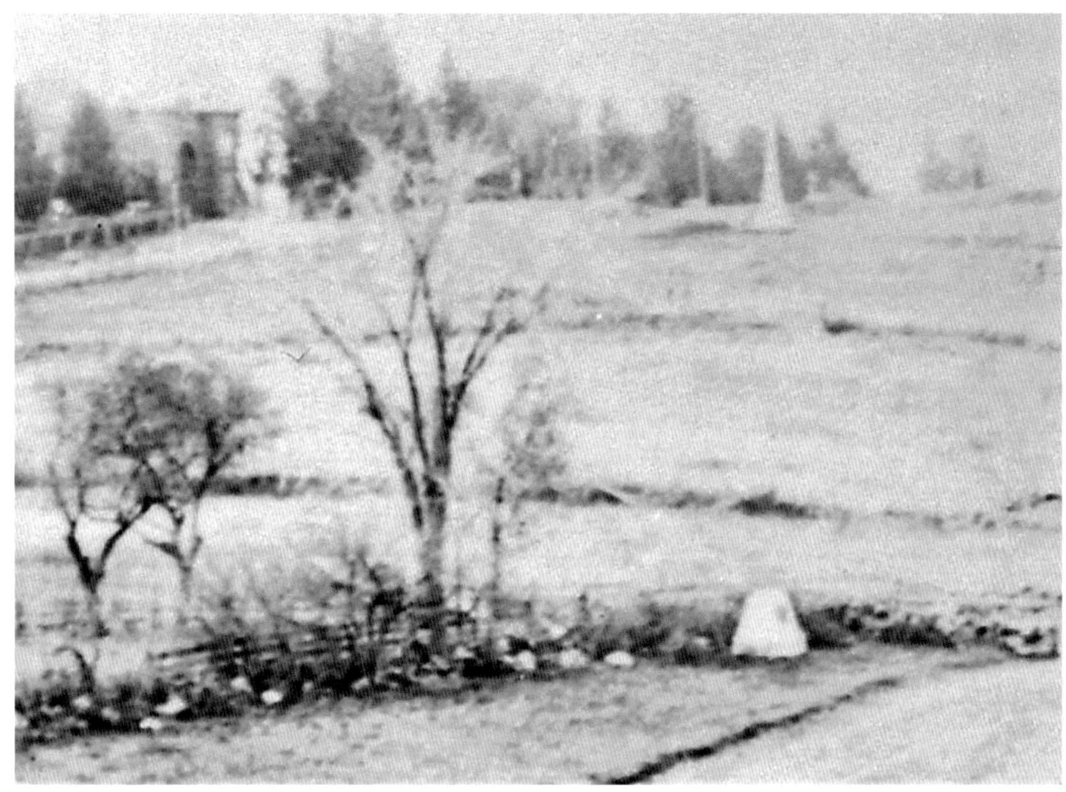

which is located more than a mile and a half to the north, was overrun by the Jubal Early's division on July 1. Steven's Knoll, which lies between Culp's Hill and East Cemetery Hill, was assaulted by Early's men on the evening of July 2. The Evergreen Cemetery gatehouse is visible at the top of the hill in the background, although in this rendering and cropping it is a little difficult to spot (fig. 5.7). Second, we are left to ponder how much "after" July 1 this photograph was purportedly taken. After all, a brief inspection reveals that there are monuments on the battleground in the background. The caption of the photograph leads the viewer to believe the photograph may have been taken in 1863 very soon after the fighting stopped, but in

reality, the presence of monuments that were dedicated more than twenty years later belies the fact.

So, in summary, of the more than 10,000 fascinating and compelling (and authentic) photographs to choose from for the latest reprinting of this book, the two selected for the covers include a composite image and a photograph accompanied by a caption with the wrong location and a date that is off by more than twenty years. At least in the text they have the right Jefferson Davis.

CHAPTER 6

Artistry and Authenticity

The Photographer versus the Sketch Artist

This portion of the book is centered around answering a deceptively challenging question. Which of the following groups of artists, collectively, contributed the most to our understanding and interpretation of Civil War history: photographers or sketch artists? In previous chapters we've looked at the fraught relationship between Civil War photojournalists and their unfortunate habit of manipulating their subject matter. For those photographs that were left untouched by these deceptive practices, like a Gardner's series at Antietam (presumably), the historical contribution is undeniable in importance.[1] Nevertheless, a "combat" photograph sans action of any form isn't really representative of the true nature of the fighting or the experiences of the soldiers.[2] Instead, the photograph represents the aftermath of conflict, which, in its own way, is engaging and abhorrent at the same time.[3]

Sketch artists, in contrast, were unfettered by ostensibly long exposure times or the need for a stationary (or dead) subject. Instead, they could record on paper any instantaneous scene that they could solidify in their short-term memory.[4] Their product differs from that of the photojournalist in one critical aspect: The sketch artist and their news outlet could promise authenticity, but the *perceived* vulnerability to a biased hand was clearly greater in a hand-drawn image than with a photo.[5] Manipulation and the inclusion of personal bias in a photographic negative must be knowing and deliberate, but with a sketch—who knows?

That leaves the critical question as to the historical contributions of photographers and sketch artists as this: How do sketch artists compare with photographers when it comes to authentically documenting historical events, as they happened, and how much did the advantage of being capable of capturing action on paper counterbalance the potential for embellishment or artistic license taken by the person who was sketching? In other words, with respect to authenticity, is there a way to tell when a sketch is becoming sketchy?

The "Special Artists"

Alfred Rudolph Waud and Edwin Austin Forbes are the two best-known sketch artists to emerge from the Civil War and their careers and works show some interesting contrasts. Waud spent most of the 1860s working as a "special artist" for the newspaper *Harper's Weekly*. Forbes worked of *Harper's* key competitor, *Frank Leslie's Illustrated Newspaper*. Both artists were present at most the key battles in the Eastern Theater, although for some critical events, like Pickett's tragic charge, Forbes was seeking shelter while Waud was drawing (fig. 6.1). Forbes tended to focus on camp scenes or images of soldiers on the march in all kinds of dreadful weather. Waud made many more illustrations of men in battle. In general, Forbes

Three sketches from Alfred Waud provide an opportunity to evaluate his eye for detail and attention to accuracy (figs. 6.2–6.4). Each of these sketches is matched to a similar photograph of the scene that was created within a year of the sketch, to see how well Waud matched the 'eye of history." The first of these comparisons is from Gettysburg, where Waud chose to draw the Lutheran Theological Seminary, a building with a cupola that was a critical observation point, especially during the first day of the battle. Figure 6.2 includes the artist's full sketch, which has been slightly enhanced for contrast and clarity, and a detail of the building matched with an 1863 Brady & Co. stereoview (detail) taken from a similar vantage point to the east.

Considering what a small portion of the overall landscape sketch the Seminary building represents in Waud's sketch, the artist's attention to detail is remarkable. The specifics of the roofline and aspect and dimension of the windows are quite genuine. Only the trees appear to have been altered in appearance and coverage to better reveal details of the architecture.

A second test of sketch accuracy involves one of Waud's favorite subjects, ships. Figure 6.3 includes a sketch and 1864 photograph of the sailing frigate USS *Sabine*. Waud may have chosen to complete a detailed sketch of the *Sabine* for a number of different reasons. The *Sabine* had a history to match its graceful lines, as it was one of the first US vessels to enter combat during the war and most of the crew of the famous ironclad USS *Monitor* were volunteers from the frigate.

A detail from the bowsprit and bobstay of the ship demonstrates, again, Waud's attention to detail (note that the photographic enlargement has been reversed to facilitate matching the minutiae of the rigging). Here a match can be made between individual ropes and the dolphin striker, the vertical bar that descends from the bowsprit about one-third of the way towards the very front of the vessel.

The third matched sketch/photograph set comes from Alexandria, Virginia, where Waud drew the Episcopal Seminary (fig. 6.4). This

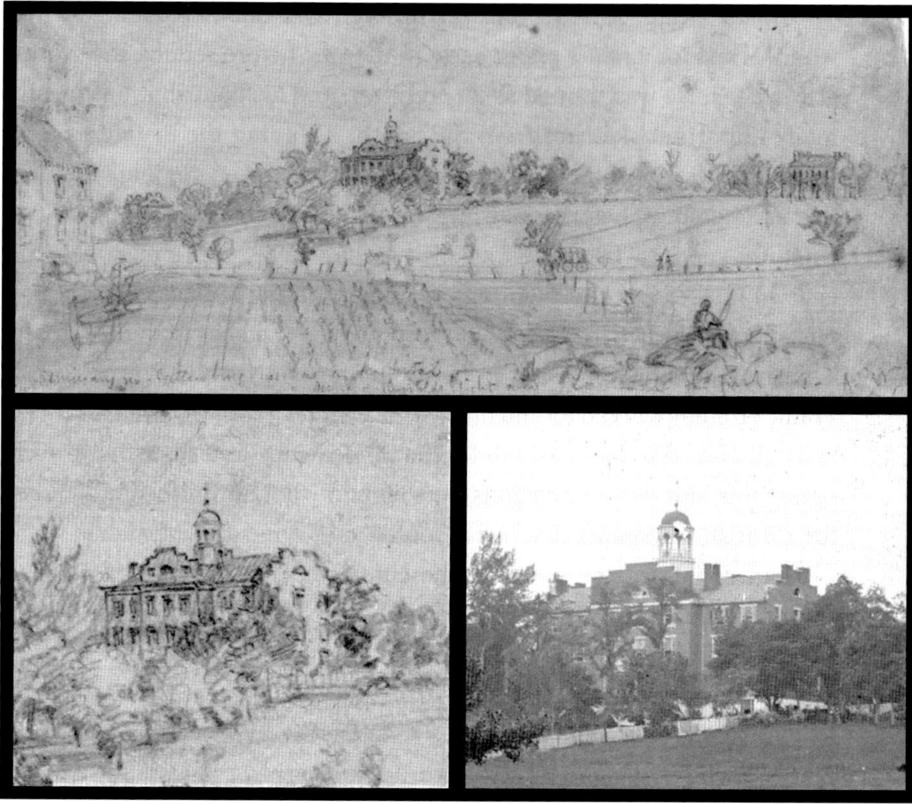

FIGURE 6.2. The Seminary Ridge, Gettysburg, and the Lutheran Theological Seminary as sketched by Alfred Waud (*top*). Detail of seminary building and enlargement of Brady & Co. photograph from July 1863, for comparison. The images were created within two weeks of each other. Library of Congress.

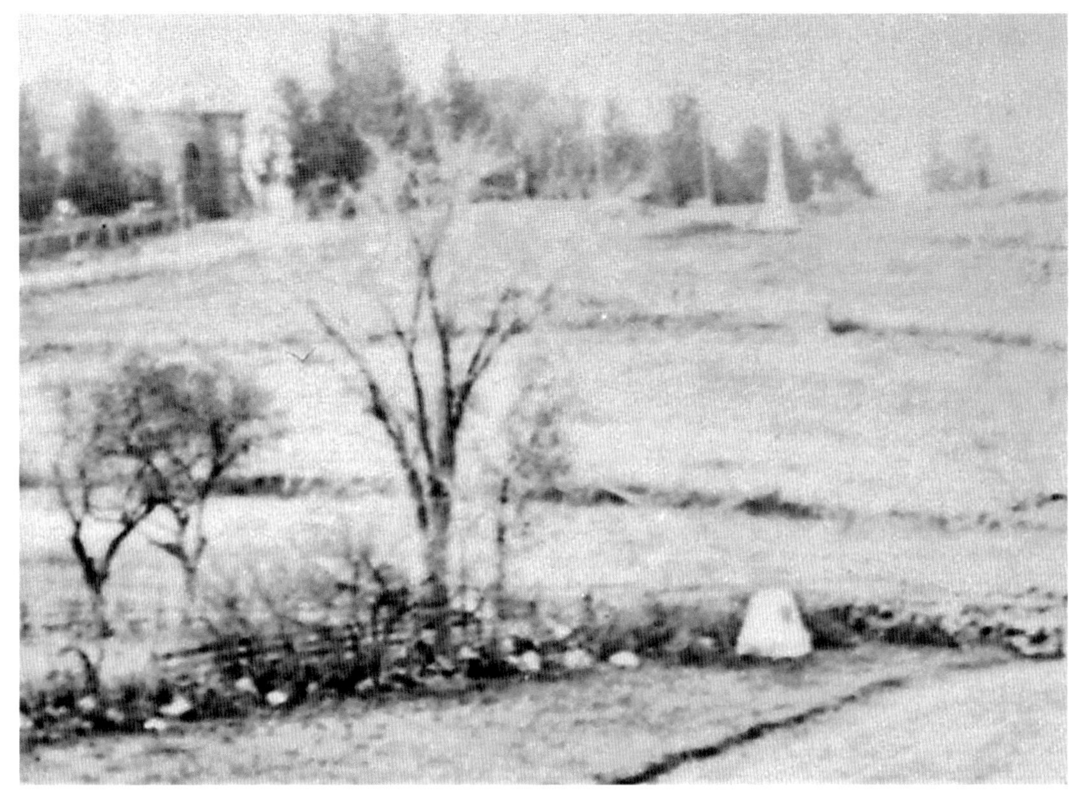

which is located more than a mile and a half to the north, was overrun by the Jubal Early's division on July 1. Steven's Knoll, which lies between Culp's Hill and East Cemetery Hill, was assaulted by Early's men on the evening of July 2. The Evergreen Cemetery gatehouse is visible at the top of the hill in the background, although in this rendering and cropping it is a little difficult to spot (fig. 5.7). Second, we are left to ponder how much "after" July 1 this photograph was purportedly taken. After all, a brief inspection reveals that there are monuments on the battleground in the background. The caption of the photograph leads the viewer to believe the photograph may have been taken in 1863 very soon after the fighting stopped, but in reality, the presence of monuments that were dedicated more than twenty years later belies the fact.

So, in summary, of the more than 10,000 fascinating and compelling (and authentic) photographs to choose from for the latest reprinting of this book, the two selected for the covers include a composite image and a photograph accompanied by a caption with the wrong location and a date that is off by more than twenty years. At least in the text they have the right Jefferson Davis.

CHAPTER 6

Artistry and Authenticity

The Photographer versus the Sketch Artist

This portion of the book is centered around answering a deceptively challenging question. Which of the following groups of artists, collectively, contributed the most to our understanding and interpretation of Civil War history: photographers or sketch artists? In previous chapters we've looked at the fraught relationship between Civil War photojournalists and their unfortunate habit of manipulating their subject matter. For those photographs that were left untouched by these deceptive practices, like Gardner's series at Antietam (presumably), the historical contribution is undeniable in importance.[1] Nevertheless, a "combat" photograph sans action of any form isn't really representative of the true nature of the fighting or the experiences of the soldiers.[2] Instead, the photograph represents the aftermath of conflict, which, in its own way, is engaging and abhorrent at the same time.[3]

Sketch artists, in contrast, were unfettered by ostensibly long exposure times or the need for a stationary (or dead) subject. Instead, they could record on paper any instantaneous scene that they could solidify in their short-term memory.[4] Their product differs from that of the photojournalist in one critical aspect: The sketch artist and their news outlet could promise authenticity, but the *perceived* vulnerability to a biased hand was clearly greater in a hand-drawn image than with a photo.[5] Manipulation and the inclusion of personal bias in a photographic negative must be knowing and deliberate, but with a sketch—who knows?

That leaves the critical question as to the historical contributions of photographers and sketch artists as this: How do sketch artists compare with photographers when it comes to authentically documenting historical events, as they happened, and how much did the advantage of being capable of capturing action on paper counterbalance the potential for embellishment or artistic license taken by the person who was sketching? In other words, with respect to authenticity, is there a way to tell when a sketch is becoming sketchy?

The "Special Artists"

Alfred Rudolph Waud and Edwin Austin Forbes are the two best-known sketch artists to emerge from the Civil War and their careers and works show some interesting contrasts. Waud spent most of the 1860s working as a "special artist" for the newspaper *Harper's Weekly*. Forbes worked of *Harper's* key competitor, *Frank Leslie's Illustrated Newspaper*. Both artists were present at most the key battles in the Eastern Theater, although for some critical events, like Pickett's tragic charge, Forbes was seeking shelter while Waud was drawing (fig. 6.1). Forbes tended to focus on camp scenes or images of soldiers on the march in all kinds of dreadful weather. Waud made many more illustrations of men in battle. In general, Forbes

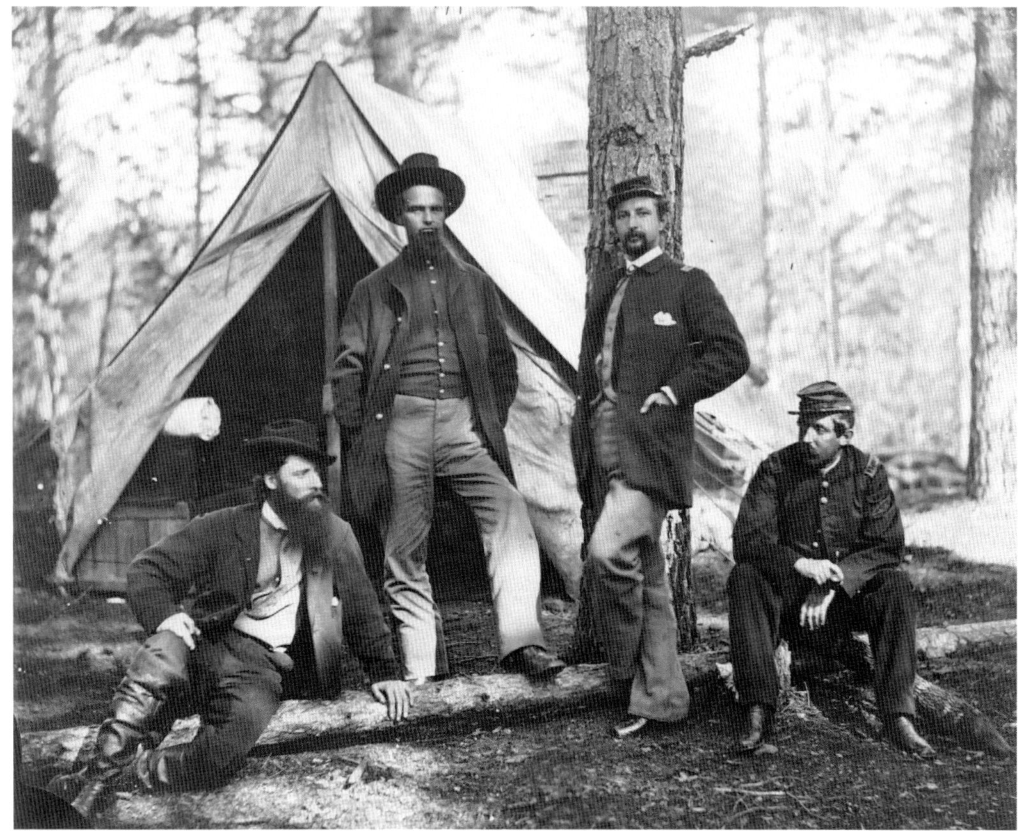

FIGURE 6.1. Alfred Waud was present at nearly all the significant battles in the East. Here he is (*seated left*) at Brandy Station with Captain J. Henry Sleeper (*seated right*) and other officers of the 10th Massachusetts Battery. Library of Congress.

was considered to be the more accomplished artist of human figures and animals, while Waud was best at drafting "short hand" action scenes.[6] In this respect the two famous special artists might be comparable to the two most famous photographers, with Forbes' artistic nature matching Brady's static landscapes, and Waud's action scenes matching Gardner's images of the gruesome aftermath of battle.[7]

Other artists of note included Theodore R. Davis, who submitted more than 250 illustrations to *Harper's Weekly*. He witnessed much of the action in the West and was notably injured several times while working. His proximity to danger is self-described in *How a Battle is Sketched*:

To really see a battle, however, one must accept the most dangerous situations, for in most cases this can not possibly be avoided. There have been occasions when some industrious sharp-shooter troubled me by a too personal direction of his bullets. No doubt the man regarded me as somebody on the other side, and considered he was there to shoot at anything or anybody on the other side. My most peculiar experience of this sort was having a sketch-book shot out of my hand and sent whirling over my shoulder.[8]

Another artist who was in even more peril during the war was Adolph Metzer, who was a Captain in the Federal army. He served in the Western Theater with the 32nd Indiana Regiment. While he did not publish with the newspapers of the day, his work did provide a glimpse of the life of a common soldier, whether in camp or battle.

William Waud, Alfred's younger brother, was another talented artist, who worked for *Leslie's* paper early in the war before joining his brother at *Harper's*. He was trained as an architect, and his contributions include many important sketches from the South, including the inauguration of Jefferson Davis and the bombardment of Fort Sumter. He joined his sibling at Petersburg before following Sherman's March to the Sea.

Other "specials" from the Civil War include Winslow Homer, who specialized in sketches and paintings of soldiers' (often tedious) life in camp. Henri Lovie worked for *Leslie's* and recorded 150 sketches from the Western Theater, including important scenes from Stones River and Wilson's Creek. Frank Vizetelly worked for the *Illustrated London News*. He is the first of the artist discussed so far to sketch for the Confederacy, and some of his works betray this bias. His motivations were certainly not diminished by working for a British newspaper that had a Confederate-sympathizing audience.

From a political perspective, the complete opposite of Vizetelly was Thomas Nast. Nast worked for *Harper's Weekly* for most of the Civil War as a staff illustrator. Many of his illustrations are so sentimental that they strike the viewer as completely unrealistic. He also gained great popularity as a caricaturist and cartoonist. Of all the Civil War newspaper artists, Nast's work is the most biased towards Northern soppiness, and Lincoln even referred to him as "our best recruiting sergeant."[9]

Arthur Lumley had almost 300 sketches reproduced by *Leslie's* and *New York Illustrated*. Some of his most well-known sketches came from the Battle of Bull Run, where he captured the initial Federal success before eventual collapse and panic.

William T. Crane worked exclusively for *Leslie's* newspaper and his sketches of Fort Sumter's reduction made it into the *Official Records*, where they were submitted to accompany General Quincy Gillmore's final report.

In total, these special artists contributed thousands of drawings that were eagerly received by the general public. Their popularity created in the newspapers of the day a new and invaluable tool for relating information from the front. Nevertheless, as with the photographs of the day, at least some degree of manipulation or embellishment can be found in these reproductions. The primary difference with this alteration is *when* it occurred—photographers mostly altered or enhanced the subject matter prior to capturing a negative, while with sketch artists the manipulation occurred during the engraving process, long after the artists had finished with their work.

Testing the Authenticity and Attention to Detail

Artists had no control over how their sketches were converted into newspaper images, and often some degree of inauthenticity and artistic enhancement was added to the work by the engravers. Later in the war this was true with photographs and on more than once occasion several of Gardner's and O'Sullivan's photographs were assembled into a composite to enhance the drama portrayed in a single engraving.

With the sketches, alterations during engraving take several forms. Details deemed superfluous were omitted, or sketches were combined to create a more compelling image (and, perhaps more judiciously, to save space). As a result, to be wholly impartial when evaluating the authenticity of a drawing, it is only proper to analyze the original sketch, not the final product after the image has proceeded through the engraving process. After all, the source of inauthenticity in a newspaper image may be completely at the hands of the engraver, having nothing to do with the original submitted work by the sketch artist.[10]

One useful tool for testing historical accuracy of a sketch would be a comparison of the original drawing with contemporary photographs of the same subject or scene. In other words, assuming a photograph of a building or landscape hasn't been altered or manipulated, this image would provide an authentic portrayal of a subject that might be used to analyze and evaluate the details of a sketch.[11]

Three sketches from Alfred Waud provide an opportunity to evaluate his eye for detail and attention to accuracy (figs. 6.2–6.4). Each of these sketches is matched to a similar photograph of the scene that was created within a year of the sketch, to see how well Waud matched the 'eye of history." The first of these comparisons is from Gettysburg, where Waud chose to draw the Lutheran Theological Seminary, a building with a cupola that was a critical observation point, especially during the first day of the battle. Figure 6.2 includes the artist's full sketch, which has been slightly enhanced for contrast and clarity, and a detail of the building matched with an 1863 Brady & Co. stereoview (detail) taken from a similar vantage point to the east.

Considering what a small portion of the overall landscape sketch the Seminary building represents in Waud's sketch, the artist's attention to detail is remarkable. The specifics of the roofline and aspect and dimension of the windows are quite genuine. Only the trees appear to have been altered in appearance and coverage to better reveal details of the architecture.

A second test of sketch accuracy involves one of Waud's favorite subjects, ships. Figure 6.3 includes a sketch and 1864 photograph of the sailing frigate USS *Sabine*. Waud may have chosen to complete a detailed sketch of the *Sabine* for a number of different reasons. The *Sabine* had a history to match its graceful lines, as it was one of the first US vessels to enter combat during the war and most of the crew of the famous ironclad USS *Monitor* were volunteers from the frigate.

A detail from the bowsprit and bobstay of the ship demonstrates, again, Waud's attention to detail (note that the photographic enlargement has been reversed to facilitate matching the minutiae of the rigging). Here a match can be made between individual ropes and the dolphin striker, the vertical bar that descends from the bowsprit about one-third of the way towards the very front of the vessel.

The third matched sketch/photograph set comes from Alexandria, Virginia, where Waud drew the Episcopal Seminary (fig. 6.4). This

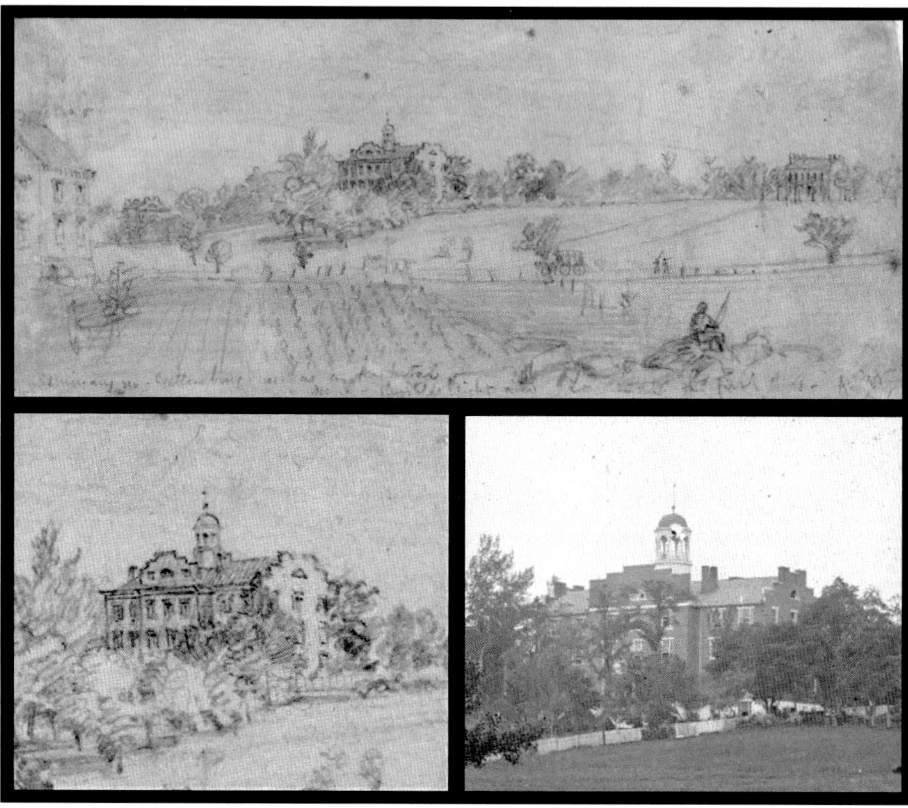

FIGURE 6.2. The Seminary Ridge, Gettysburg, and the Lutheran Theological Seminary as sketched by Alfred Waud (*top*). Detail of seminary building and enlargement of Brady & Co. photograph from July 1863, for comparison. The images were created within two weeks of each other. Library of Congress.

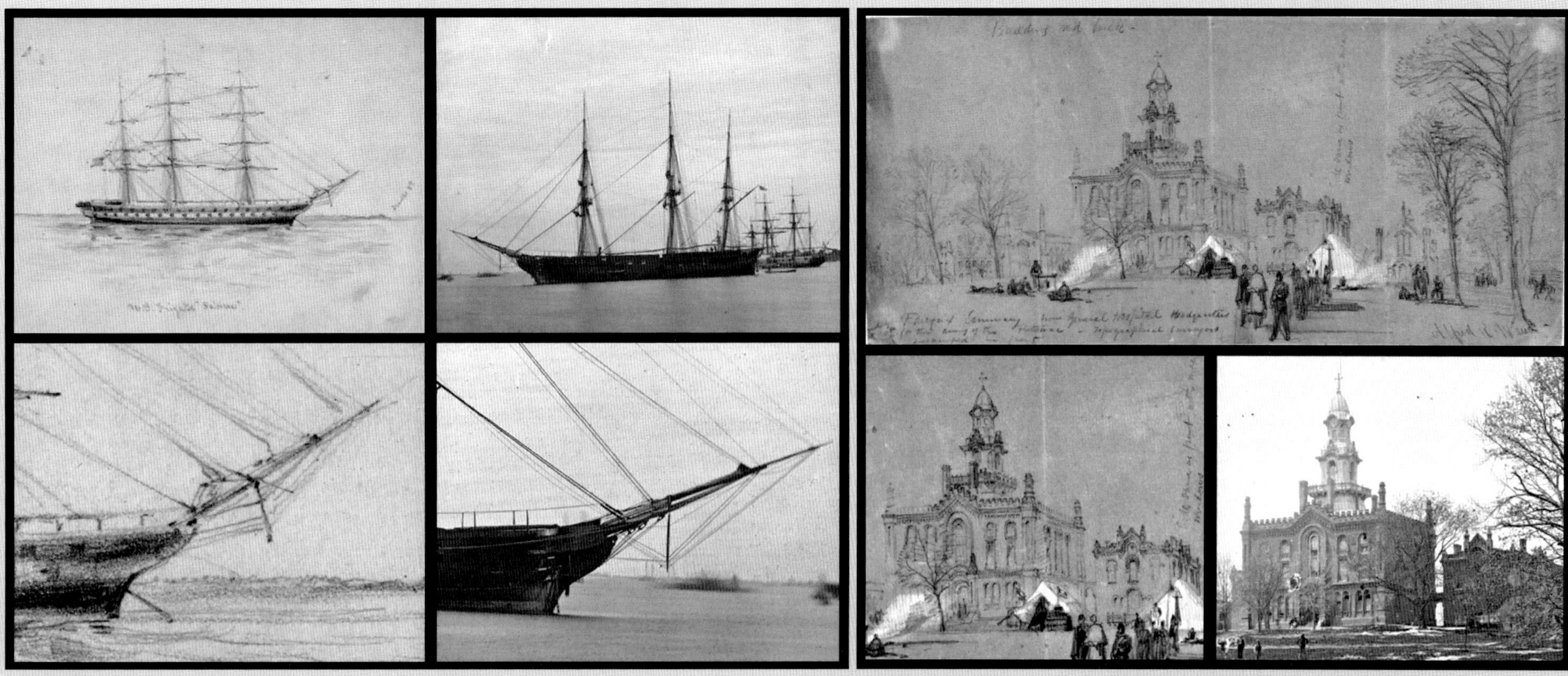

FIGURE 6.3. Alfred Waud's sketch of the USS *Sabine* and a backlit photograph of the same ship taken within a year of the drawing. Note in the detailed view of the bow just how well Waud represented every portion of the rigging. Library of Congress.

FIGURE 6.4. Alfred Waud's sketch of the Episcopal Seminary in Alexandria, Virginia, (*top*) and detail of the sketch compared with a contemporary photograph (*bottom*). Library of Congress.

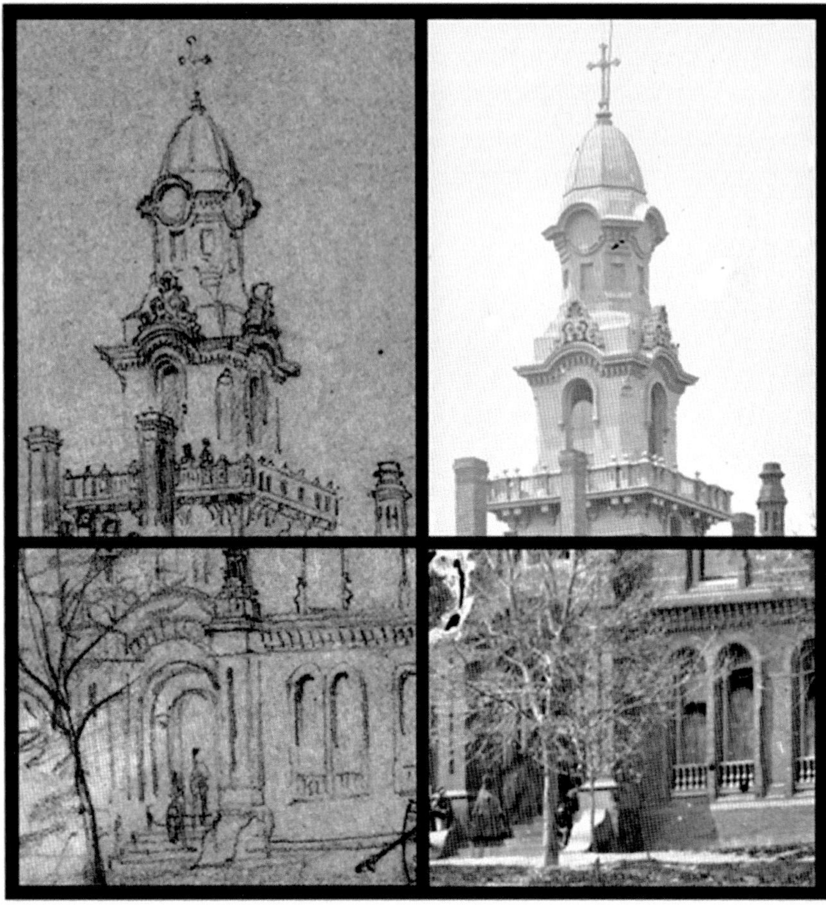

FIGURE 6.5. This enlargement from figure 6.4 demonstrates how well Waud's sketch matches reality, at all levels of detail, when compared to the same photographed structure. Library of Congress.

building later served as the general hospital headquarters for the Army of the Potomac. This sketch is compared with a contemporary stereographic photograph from a similar, but not quite identical, perspective.

Details of the ornamentation (spines, pinnacles, finials, modillions) and bell tower are faithfully represented by the drawing (fig. 6.5). The size of the windows on the first story do not match exactly, but they correctly show the shape and orientation. As with the seminary at Gettysburg, only the trees appear to have been altered in position and size. In the case of the Alexandria seminary, this may have been done to reveal the elaborately sculpted front entrance.

Waud's attention for detail and near-photographic sketching ability have been noted by other historians. For example, William Frassanito commented on this skill in *Early Photography at Gettysburg* (1995) when he described the artist's "almost obsessive concern for detail and accuracy in at least some of his landscape studies. Even down to the depiction of individual boulders in the Slaughter Pen. . . ."[12]

Other special artists, including Edwin Forbes, are not quite as precise when it came to representing details. Forbes' painting "View from the summit of Little Round Top at 7:30 PM on July 3rd" reproduces the boulders from the top of the hill in a rather artistic, as opposed to more authentic, manner (fig. 6.6).[13] A sketch from nearby looks down the Valley of Death towards the Round Tops (fig. 6.6, bottom). While this sketch certainly provides an impression of the Federal defensive position, details concerning the location of individual boulders and trees, as well as the general topography, certainly do not match the authenticity of a Waud sketch. This is especially apparent when compared with a contemporary photograph by Brady & Co.

For a second Forbes comparison, consider the Fredericksburg County Courthouse. Forbes sketched this impressive building while it was being used as a signal station and barracks by Federal troops (fig. 6.7). James Gardner photographed the building from several angles in May of 1864 as a stereoview.

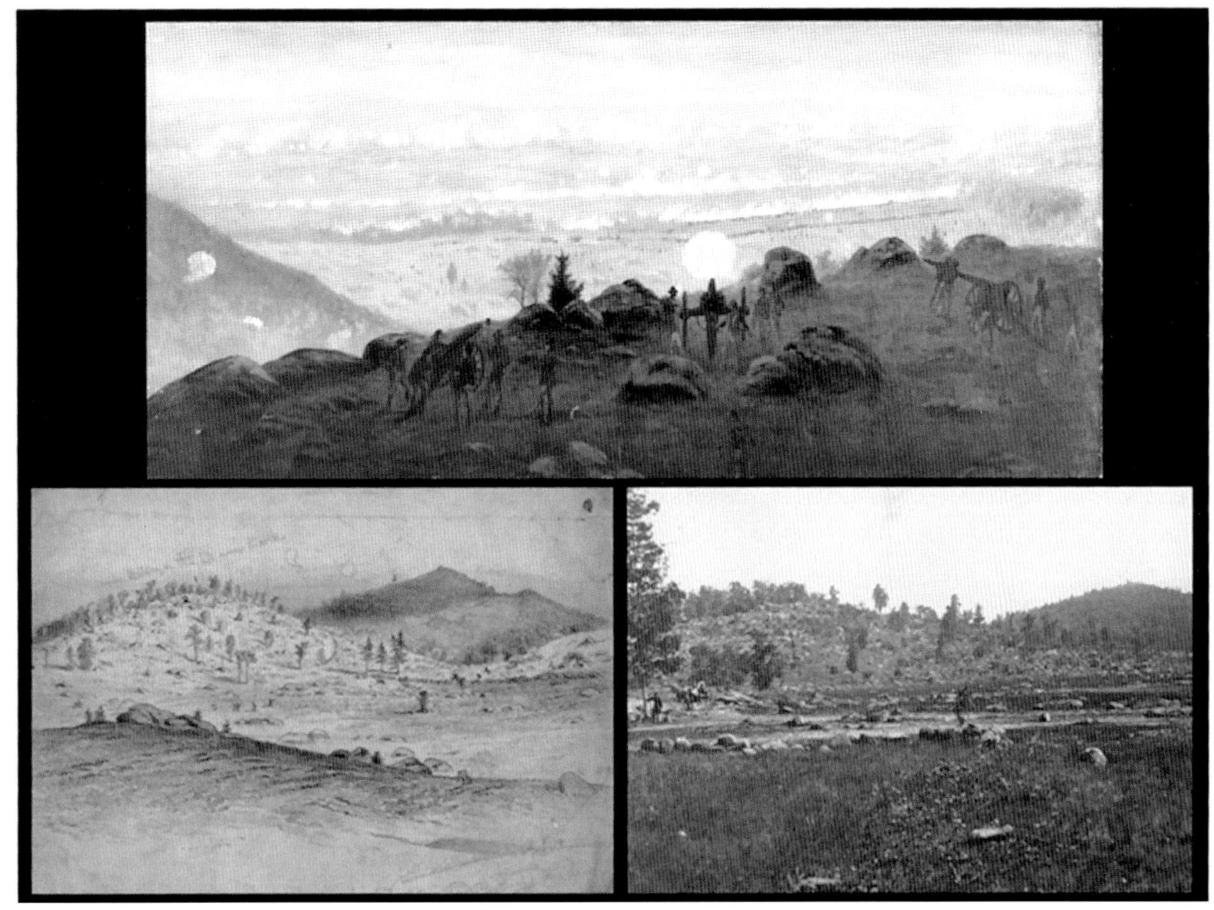

FIGURE 6.6. Edwin Forbes' painting of Federal artillery in action on the crest of Little Round Top (*top*) inaccurately depicts both the boulders and the topography of the hill. His sketch of the Round Tops (*bottom*) is compared with an 1863 photograph by Brady & Co. Note that Brady himself is standing under the tree on the far left of his photograph. Library of Congress.

Close examination of the sketch and photographs (and details of the bell tower) demonstrate that Forbes' sketch is for the most part accurate but lacks the attention to proportions and detail that Waud's best sketches exhibit. Consider, for example, the vertical spacing of the different levels of the bell tower—the sketch doesn't exactly match the two identical photographs, even if the latter were created from different perspectives.

Similar discrepancies between photographs and sketches can also be observed in the work of other special artists. In summary, Waud's sketches are just slightly better representations of physical objects—building and ships—compared to other sketch artists of the day. His work was more "photographic" in nature. The question then is, what about his action or combat scenes? How much attention to detail and photo-like quality do these scenes have?

The amount of time Alfred Waud spent on an individual sketch can only be roughly estimated. For detailed landscape or architecture studies he clearly spent a great amount of time. His attention to detail on battle

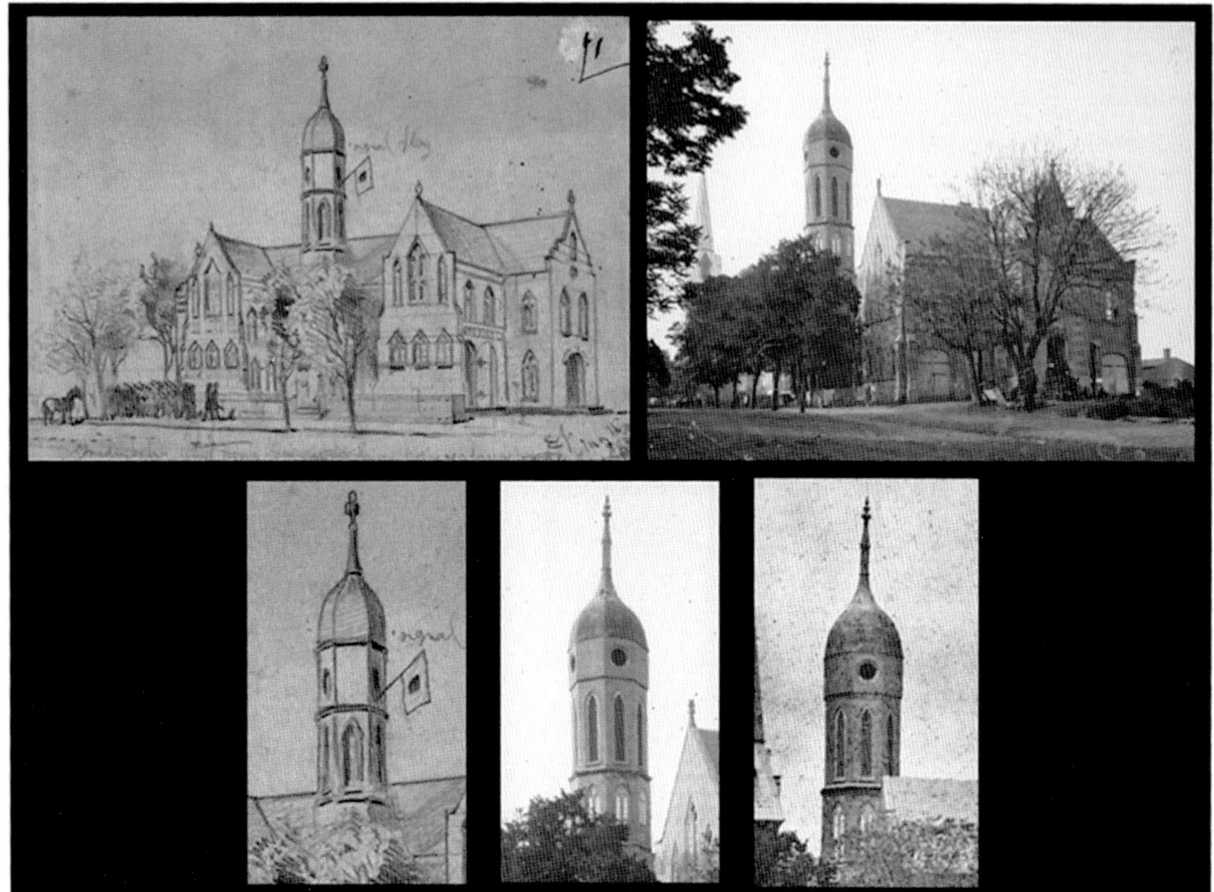

FIGURE 6.7. Edwin Forbes' drawing of the Fredericksburg County Courthouse matches photographs taken by Alexander and James Gardner during the Civil War; however, careful examination of details of the sketch (*bottom left*) and Gardner photographs (*bottom center and right*) reveals that some of the proportions and particulars are not perfectly represented in the drawing. Library of Congress.

scenes, and the amount of time he took to sketch an action shot, appears to vary greatly, with some sketches only providing a glimpse of what the drama entailed. For these images the artist was likely working as quickly as possible, hoping to convey a sense for the viewer of "being there," facing the danger and spectacle. For some sketches, the artist was probably in the process of drafting an image or quickly putting onto paper his recollection of an intense scene (fig. 6.8).

His impressions of the interplay between soldiers in combat and the harshness of the terrain can clearly be witnessed in these relatively rapidly sketched scenes from Atlanta and Gettysburg.

The process of creating a more detailed study and sketch, and the eventual engraving of the scene by other artists, can be observed in Waud's depiction of the death of John Reynolds at Gettysburg (fig. 6.9). This series of drawings documents one other aspect of Waud's contributions: He clearly

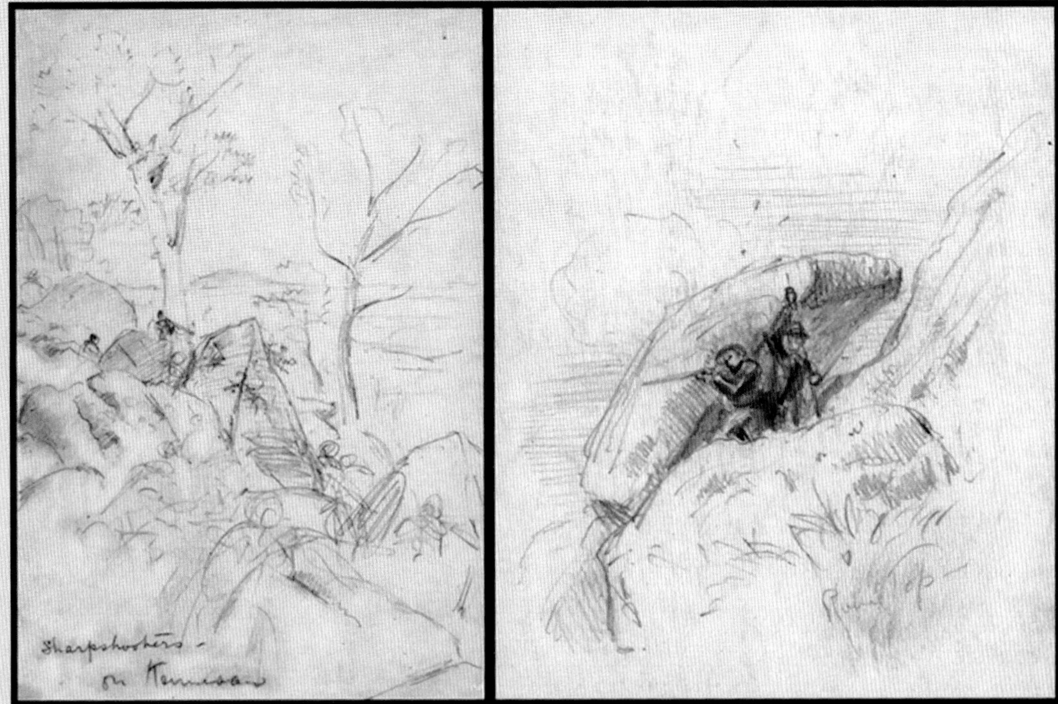

FIGURE 6.8. Waud's sketches of skirmishers or sharpshooters on Kennesaw Mountain (*left*) and Little Round Top (*right*). Although relatively crude in nature, both drawings give an impression of the ruggedness of the terrain and the interaction between soldiers and boulders. Waud may have sketched these quickly, intending to later add detail based on his memory. Library of Congress.

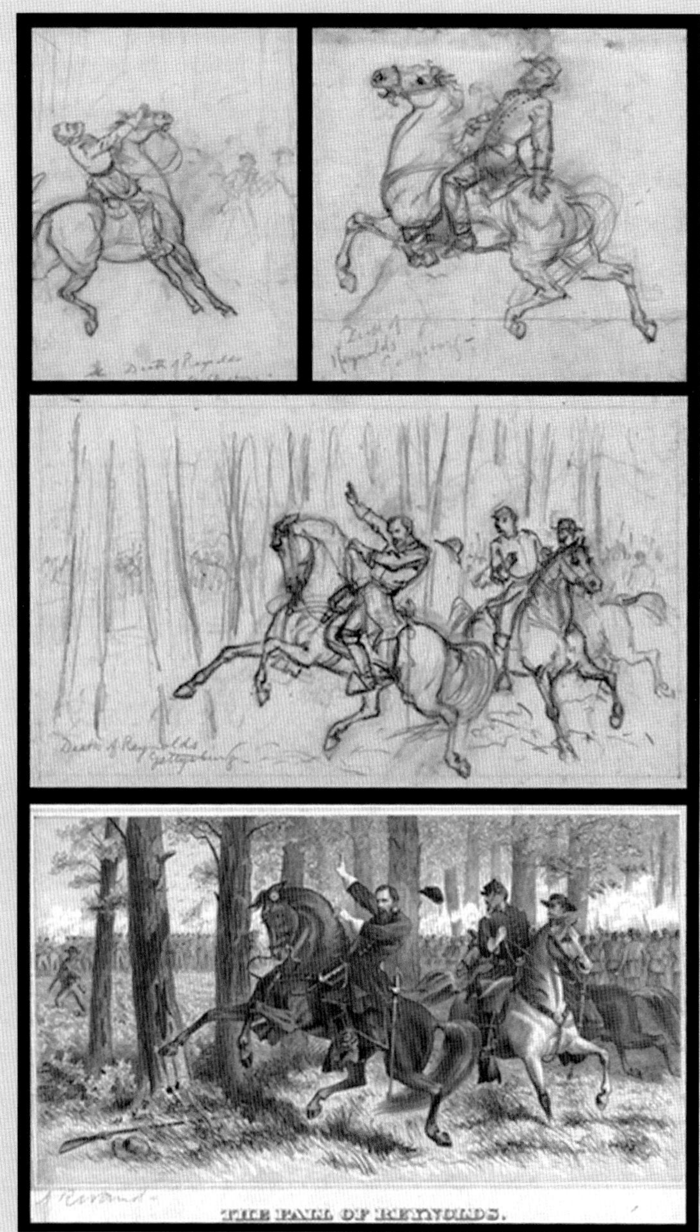

FIGURE 6.9. Waud's sketched three different studies of the moment John Reynolds was shot through the neck, but only one made it into the newspaper as an engraving (*bottom*). Library of Congress.

wasn't always sketching from the perspective of what he personally and directly observed. These three images, recorded from different viewpoints at slightly different times, document a scene as the artist perceived it, not how he actually witnessed it.

In the highly unlikely circumstance that the artist was standing within thirty or so yards of the general and looking directly at him at the instant the bullet struck home, it can't be determined where, relative to Reynolds, Waud was actually situated. After all, he could not have been behind and in front of the stricken officer at exactly the same time.

What is much more probable is that Waud was drawing based on the impressions of what he, or more likely, others had observed. Waud probably interviewed solders who witnessed the event or, even better, members of Reynolds' staff who were in the immediately proximity to the mortally wounded general and who even appear in his sketches.

The value of this piece of art, then, should be contrasted and evaluated relative to the best photograph involving the death of Reynolds: A Brady & Co. photograph showing the general location where Reynolds may or may not have fallen (fig. 6.10).[14] At best, this negative shows the vicinity of the mortal wounding two weeks after the event.

Alfred Waud was working for *Harper's Weekly* in July 1863, when he produced what might be his most important sketch (fig. 6.11). The importance of this work is magnified by the fact that no other sketch artists were present on the fields of Pickett's Charge and Gardner's and Brady's photographic teams largely ignored this area of the battlefield. As a result, Waud's sketch is the best representation of an "eye-witness"—whether human or camera lens—to the infamous attack.[15] While it is impossible, of course, to know just how accurate the details of Waud's sketch of the famous charge are, the earlier studies of the details of his sketches of buildings and ships provides at least some sense of confidence in his representation.

Waud was also present when the first photographers arrived on the great battlefield, and he can be placed in Devil's Den on July 6th—Timothy

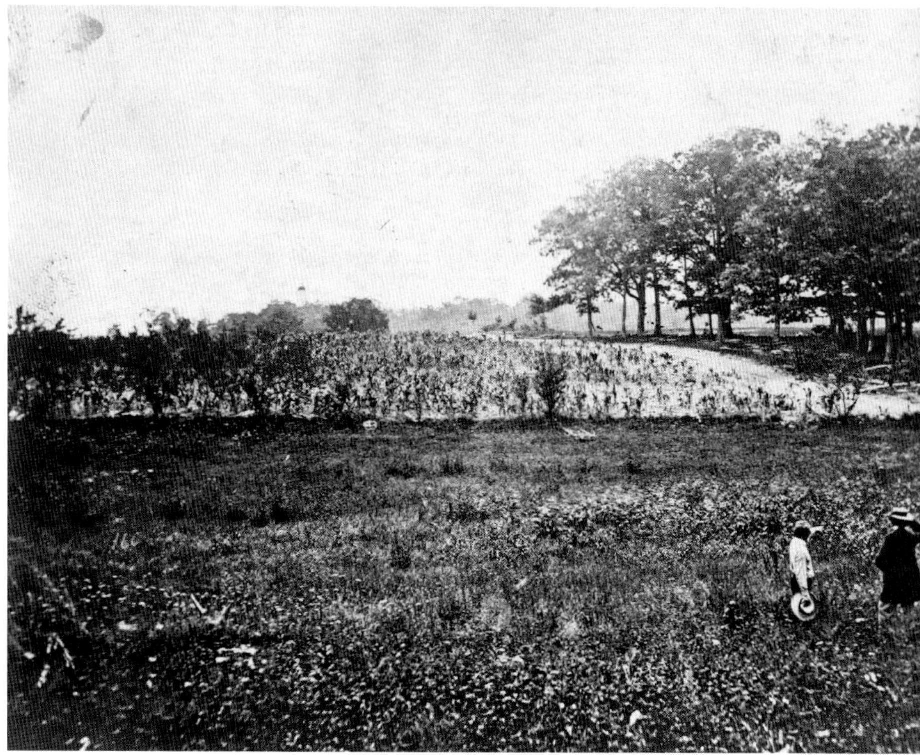

FIGURE 6.10. Brady & Co. photograph titled, "View of point of woods where General Reynolds was killed, July 1, 1863." The Seminary Cupola (fig. 6.2) faintly appears in the very distance on the left-center horizon. Brady himself appears in the far-right foreground. Library of Congress.

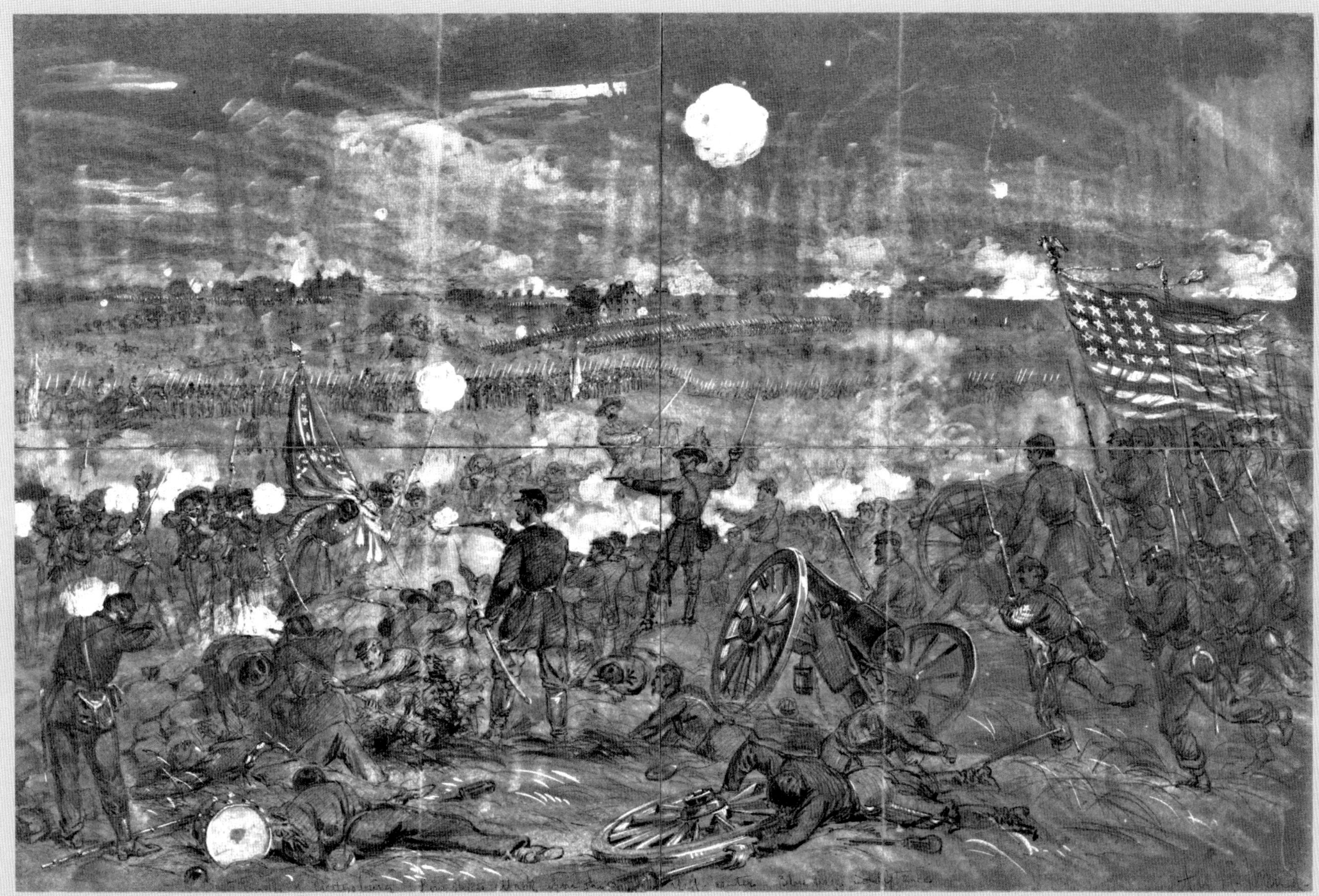

FIGURE 6.11. Alfred Waud's sketch of Pickett's Charge, the best in-person artistic representation of the catastrophic attack. Library of Congress.

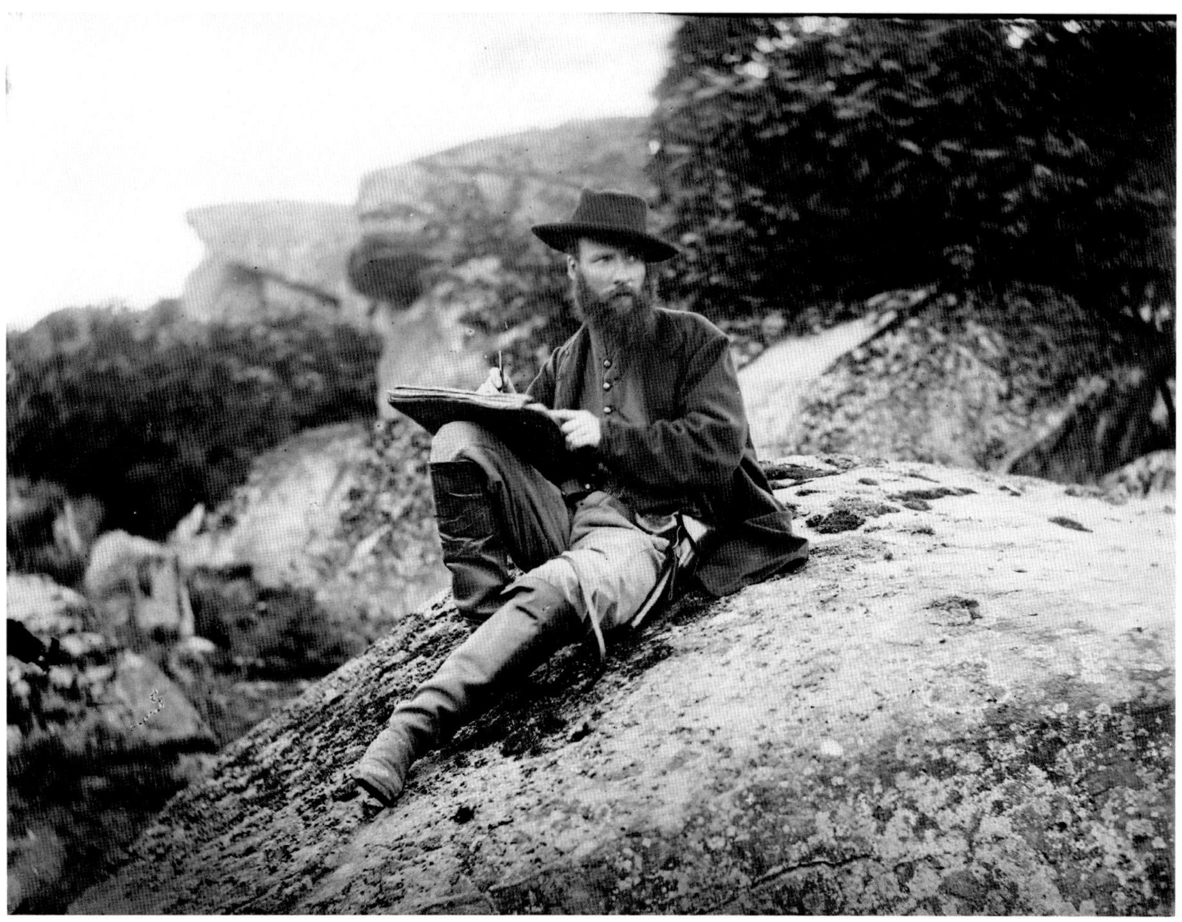

FIGURE 6.12. Alexander Gardner and Timothy O'Sullivan took time away from moving and photographing dead Confederates to take this stereoview of Alfred Waud perched upon a flat-topped boulder in Devil's Den. Library of Congress.

O'Sullivan photographed the artist with his sketchpad perched on a large, rounded, diabase boulder (fig. 6.12).

This would have meant that Gardner and his team took precious time (and sunlight) away from photographing the dead to capture the image of the living artist, an occurrence that certainly suggest a friendly and respectful relationship between the artistic and documentary competitors.[16] What is even more compelling is the sketch that Waud was composing at the time, "Hill where Genl. Weed was killed, called by the soldiers the Slaughter Pen and ravine from which the Rebels were driven by the 3rd Corps" (fig. 6.13).

The vantage point from the rock where Waud was posing for the photographers and the location from where he composed this sketch are not the same. The sketch's perspective was created around fifty to sixty yards to the west, along a direct path from the site of the famous posed dead

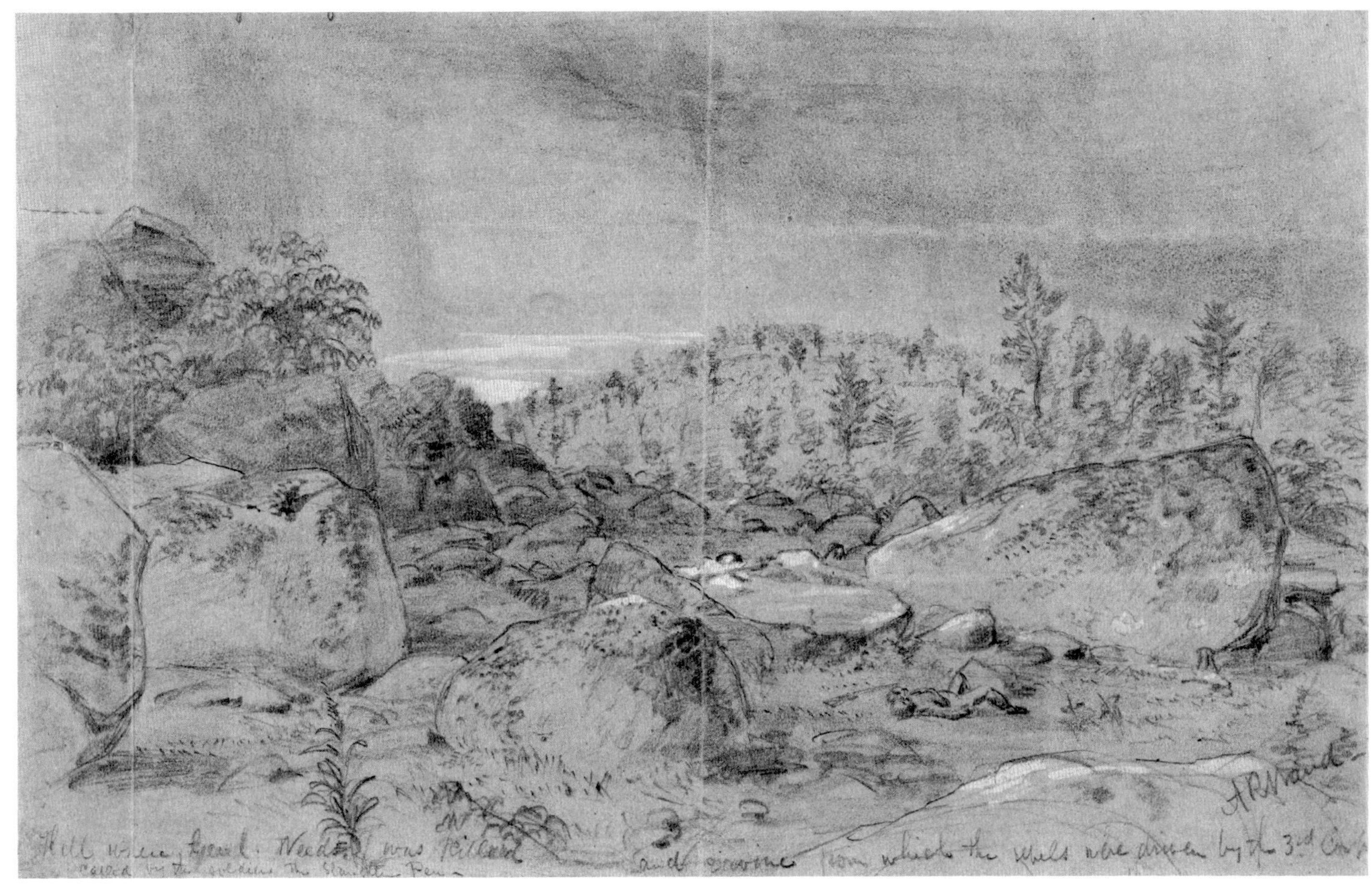

FIGURE 6.13. Waud's sketch of Devil's Den, the Slaughter Pen, and Little Round Top. Library of Congress.

sharpshooter. A likely scenario is that Waud and the Gardner crew encountered each other while the photographers were working with, and moving, the dead Confederate sharpshooter. They then had Waud, who had been sketching from a similar location, join the team to the east of the main mass of boulders for his portrait. It is somewhat disconcerting to consider that as Waud sat on the boulder that would later bear his name, gazing northeast towards the Valley of Death, he was surrounded in almost every direction by nearby decomposing corpses. Gardner photographed the "sniper" to the west of Waud's rock and several more dead bodies were less than a dozen yards to the south and southeast in the Slaughter Pen and along Plum Run.

The most intriguing aspect of this sketch is found in the lower right quadrant of the print where a dead soldier lies with a rifle musket strewn above his head. This combination of corpse, rifle, and boulders is reminiscent of

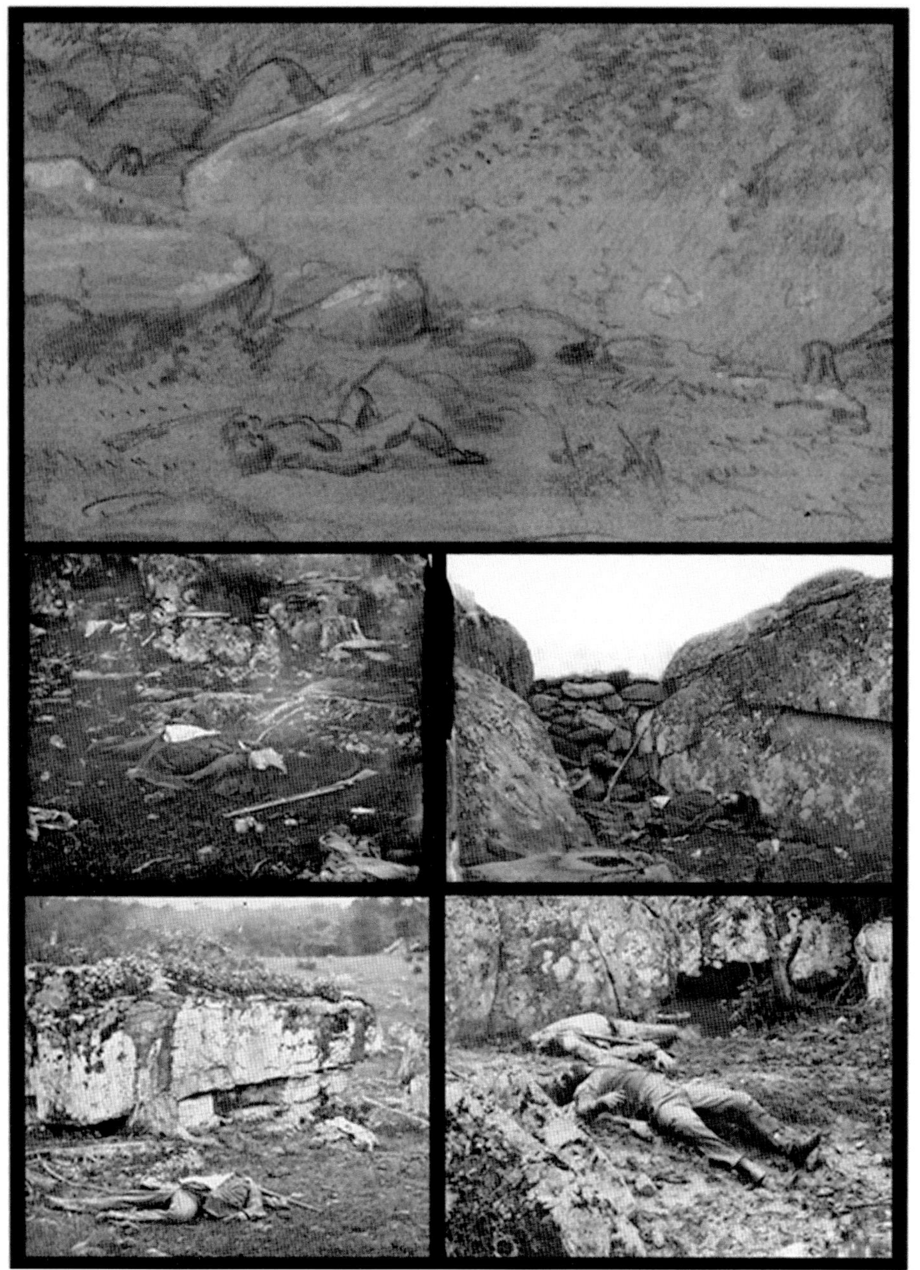

Gardner's collection of photographs of "A Sharpshooter's Last Sleep" and similar shots of nearby fallen soldiers (fig. 6.14).

Waud's fallen soldier has an orientation similar to Gardner's "sharpshooter" (6.14 center and bottom left), especially with respect to the placement of the rifle musket. The rocks, however, resemble Gardner's composed scene (6.14 center right). The elevated positioning of the soldier's knees best matches another Gardner shot (6.14 bottom right).

The inclusion of this soldier in the sketch raises another interesting set of questions regarding timing. We've already established that Gardner and his team were adding a prop rifle to the corpses they were photographing (chapter 5). It is unlikely that the photographers would have missed a corpse in such a prominent location as portrayed by Waud, so it is probable that Waud's dead soldier represents one of the dead in the Gardner series.[17] When, relative to the photographer's progress, did Waud begin his sketch? Was a rifle musket present? After all, there is a chance that Waud had already started sketching prior to the arrival of Gardner, and the rifle musket was actually present, lying above the fallen soldier's head. If so, Gardner may have photographed the unmanipulated scene for one of his first negatives, then later carried the musket (and body) to other locations.

Another series of questions: Had Waud sketched the dead Confederate *in situ*, or exactly where he had fallen? If so, Little Round Top and the Slaughter Pen would not have been visible in the background (fig. 6.15). Had Waud walked twenty or thirty yards to the east, both landscape features come into view and would appear as they did in his sketch. This would also have been true if Waud had been able to rise twenty-five or so feet in elevation.

FIGURE 6.14. The dead soldier in Waud's sketch (*top*) has characteristics found in several of the photographs of dead soldiers photographed by Gardner's team in the immediate vicinity of where the sketch was created. Library of Congress.

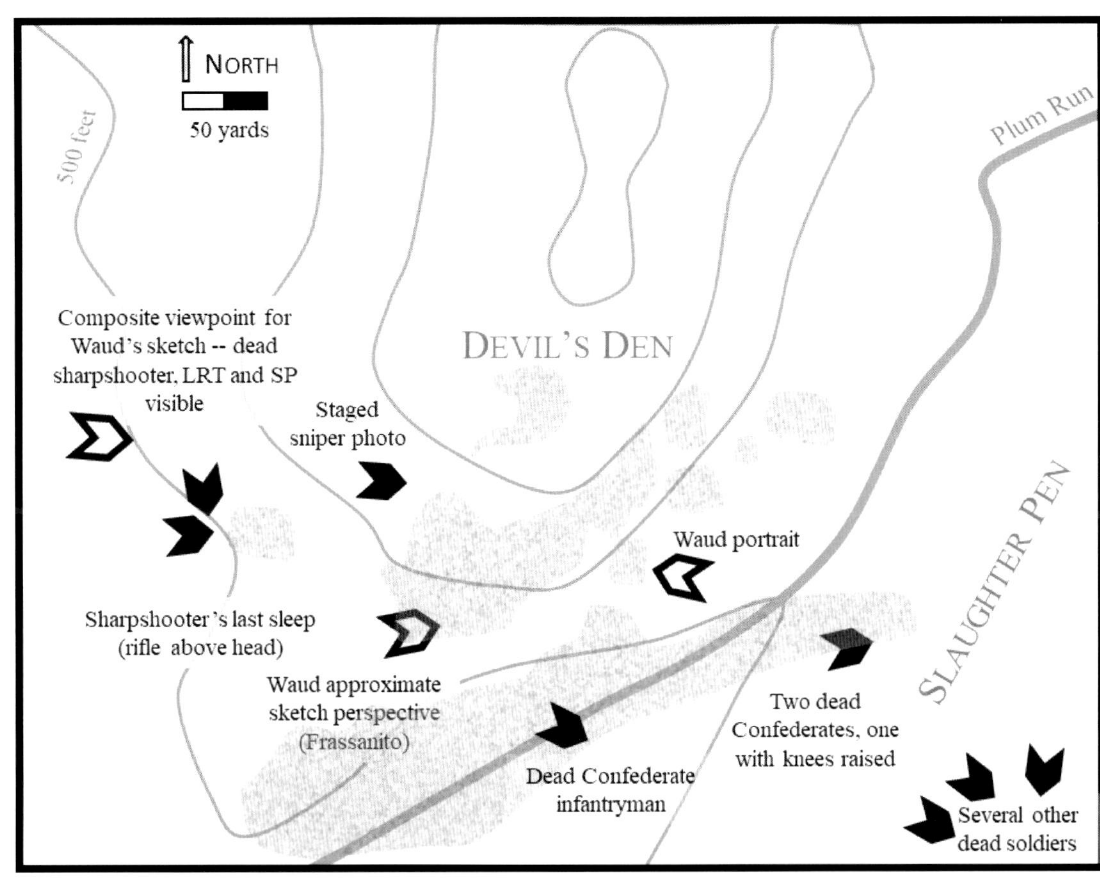

FIGURE 6.15. Relative positions of Gardner's photographs of dead soldiers and Waud's sketches. The location of Waud's portrait by Gardner et al. is also indicated, in between several corpses. Gray regions indicate approximate location of main boulder fields. LRT = Little Round Top; SP = Slaughter Pen.

Consider the topography of Devil's Den with respect to the perspective in this sketch. This drawing was composed from a viewpoint on the surface of the Earth that does not exist. The western side of Devil's Den slopes down away from Little Round Top and the Valley of Death. In other words, the farther the artist moved to the west, the more Little Round Top disappeared behind the boulders of the Den. The only way to incorporate both the dead Confederate and the site where Weed was killed on top of Little Round Top is to view this landscape from an elevated position, which is probably the vantage point Waud imagined when he composed this sketch. To create a more compelling view, one that would include the fallen soldier and Little Round Top, the landscape feature of interest, Waud created a composite of what he had observed, and sketched from an elevated viewpoint that does actually exist, albeit one to which he lacked access. His only other option would have been to drag the dead soldier to yet another, new, more sketch-worthy location, a tactic only his compatriots engaged in that day.

PART 3

THE DEVIL IN THE DETAILS

CHAPTER 7

Shedding Some Light on Exposure Times

Virtually all photographs from the frontlines or taken in camps included some degree of posing. In the previous two chapters we explored where this management of subject matter fell on our scale of manipulation, and how this introduction of artificial motionlessness compared with the work of sketch artists. This discussion probed the authenticity of the photographs and their importance as a tool for historians. Compared with composite photographs or the addition of props or dead bodies, this requirement for posing seems the most forgivable from a legitimacy perspective. Nevertheless, the prerequisite that the subject matter of a photograph remain completely stationary introduces an artificial stillness to the photographs that diminishes, however slightly, their authenticity.

Civil War historians and photographic experts disagree about the length of this motionless requirement, and there are many different opinions regarding the duration of time that was required for a negative to be exposed to light through the nineteenth-century camera lens (Tables 7.1–7.3).

There is quite a bit of difference between the estimated exposure times found in the literature, and the difference between an exposure time of one-tenth of a second and thirty seconds would have major implications for what could, and could not, be captured on glass. Also interesting is the difference between the most popular estimate put forth by historians, of two to three seconds, and the average of the estimates, over eight seconds. This latter, longer estimate is probably inflated in duration by authors who mistakenly included studio portraits in their estimate. Photographs taken indoors require a much longer duration, regardless of the amount of natural light funneled into the studio.

One area of critical reasoning that might shed some light on this question of exposure times are the photographs themselves. When people or animals are moving, how much action is actually recorded in the blurred images?

Start with a safe assumption: Adults, and especially soldiers, are disciplined enough to stand perfectly still for up to twenty or so seconds. For children, this would be more challenging, especially if they were in an uncomfortable or awkward pose. Animals have virtually no self-control or desire to freeze for a photographer.

Imagine a child sitting with his parents or other children as a photographer prepares the camera. How much does a child typically move in the span of a second? In ten or twenty seconds? A blur that extends for a few inches would suggest only a moment of movement, but in ten or twenty seconds a child might move to an entirely different location. Now imagine the same exercise with horses or cattle or a rambunctious dog.

There is one important rule to remember for these exercises: The more distant the moving subject, the less the blur across the negative. However, when the high-resolution negatives are magnified, the degree of movement becomes apparent and can again be used to estimate the duration of

Table 7.1 Estimated exposure times (i.e., "shutter speeds") for Civil War-era field cameras.

Duration	Source
A few seconds or even fractions of a second	Robert McNamara, "Why Are There No Combat Photographs from the Civil War?," ThoughtCo., September 29, 2017, https://www.thoughtco.com/combat-photographs-from-the-civil-war-1773718.
for several seconds	Department of Photographs, "Photography and the Civil War, 1861–65," in *Heilbrunn Timeline of Art History*, Metropolitan Museum of Art, October 1, 2004, http://www.metmuseum.org/toah/hd/phcw/hd_phcw.htm.
for several seconds	Ethan S. Rafuse, "Robert E. Lee and Traveller in Petersburg" in Lens of War: Exploring Iconic Photographs of the Civil War, ed. J. Matthew Gallman and Gary W. Gallagher (University of Georgia Press, 2015), 17–24.
for several seconds	"Taking Photographs during the Civil War," Civil War Glass Negatives and Related Prints Collection, Library of Congress, https://www.loc.gov/collections/civil-war-glass-negatives/articles-and-essays/taking-photographs-during-the-civil-war/.
for several seconds	Smithsonian Institution, Smithsonian Civil War: Inside the National Collection, ed. Neil Kagan, foreword Jon Meacham, introduction Michelle Delaney, photography Hugh Talman (Smithsonian Books, 2013).
2–3 seconds	"Photography in the Civil War," American Battlefield Trust, https://www.battlefields.org/learn/topics/photography-civil-war.
2–3 seconds	"Origins of Photojournalism," American Battlefield Trust, https://www.battlefields.org/learn/articles/origins-photojournalism.
2–3 seconds	Rebecca Beatrice Brooks, "Civil War Photography," Civil War Saga (blog), August 9, 2011, civilwarsaga.com.
2–3 seconds	Stephen L. Vaughn, ed., Encyclopedia of American Journalism, (Routledge, 2008).
at least 2–3 seconds	Lucie Monk Carter, "Point and Shoot," Country Roads Magazine, October 27, 2014, https://countryroadsmagazine.com/art-and-culture/history/point-and-shoot/.
1–10 seconds (for views)	A. S. Heath and A. H. Heath, Photography: A New Treatise, Theoretical and Practical, of the Processes and Manipulations on Paper, Dried and Wet: Glass, Collodion and Albumen (New York, 1855.)
2–10 seconds	"10 Facts about the Civil War," American Battlefield Trust, https://www.battlefields.org/learn/articles/civil-war-facts.
2–10 seconds	William A. Frassanito, Gettysburg: A Journey in Time (Charles Scribner's Sons, 1975).
5–10+ seconds	Lawrence Lee Hewitt, Port Hudson: The Most Significant Battlefield Photographs of the Civil War (University of Tennessee Press, 2021). The sign "+" indicates much, much longer for night photographs.
as long as 8 seconds	David Morgan, "The Civil War: The Birth of Photojournalism," Sunday Morning, CBS News, July 7, 2013, https://www.cbsnews.com/pictures/the-civil-war-the-birth-of-photojournalism/10/.
5–20 seconds	"Civil War Photographs," National Archives and Records Administration, https://www.archives.gov/research/still-pictures/civil-war.

Duration	Source
5–20 seconds	Lauren Letizia, "Photography and the Civil War: A Cultural Lens, Gettysburg Compiler (blog), April 4, 2022, https://gettysburgcompiler.org/2022/04/.
5–20 seconds	Rebecca Beatrice Brooks, "Civil War Photography," Civil War Saga (blog), August 9, 2011, civilwarsaga.com /civil- war-photography/.
as long as 10–30 seconds	"Photo Gallery: Civil War Photographs," Galleries, Lawrence Journal-World, February 12, 2011, https://www2.ljworld.com/photos/galleries/2011/feb/12/civil-war-photographs.
10–15 seconds	Noel G. Harrison, "Are These Photographs Our Earliest, Closest Equivalents of 'Movies' of Civil War Field Operations?," Mysteries and Conundrums (blog), https://npsfrsp.wordpress.com/2011/06/29/are-these-photographs-our-earliest-closest -equivalents-of-movies-of-civil-war-field-operations/.
10–15 seconds	N. G. Burgess, The Photograph and Ambrotype Manual: A Practical Treatise on the Art of Taking Pictures (1858).
5–30 seconds	George Sullivan, The Civil War at Sea (2001).
20 seconds–5 minutes	"Wet-Plate Photography," article supplement, "The Wizard of Photography" episode, American Experience, PBS, https://www.pbs.org/wgbh/americanexperience/features/eastman-wet-plate-photography/.
at least 30 seconds	James R. Arnold and Roberta Wiener, eds., American Civil War: The Essential Reference Guide (ABC-CLIO, 2011).

Duration	Source
1/10th second ("instantaneous" stereo) Several seconds (field photographs with relatively insensitive plates)	Keith F. Davis, "A Terrible Distinctness: Photography of the Civil War Era, 1861–1865" in The Origins of American Photography: From Daguerreotype to Dry-Plate, 1839–1885, eds. Hall Family Foundation and Nelson-Atkins Museum of Art (Yale University Press, 2007).
Fraction of a second (bright sunlight) Several seconds—minutes (cloudy or in shade)	Beaumont Newhall, The History of Photography: From 1839 to the Present (Museum of Modern Art, 1982).
A few seconds (sunny day) 10–30 seconds (cloudy)	Naomi Rosenblum, *A World History of Photography* (Abbeville Press, 1997).
3–6 seconds (bright spring/summer) 12–24 seconds (dull winter months)	T. Frederick Hardwich, A Manual of Photographic Chemistry, Including the Practice of the Collodion Process (London, 1858).

TABLE 7.3 Summary of exposure times: range, consensus, average

range of exposure estimates	1/10th – 30+ seconds
general consensus (most common estimate)	2–3 seconds
mean exposure time	~ 8 seconds

Note: These estimates only include purported "shutter speeds" for stereo cameras and field cameras that were taken on the road; no studio camera estimates were included in the data set (as described by the "experts"). Artificial or limited natural lighting in studios required much longer exposure times.

the exposure. In other words, if two slow-moving locomotives are photographed from different distances, the picture with the closer train will have more perceived blurring. However, when the distant train is inspected in a magnified view, the relative amount of blurring will be identical—the streaking will simply cover a smaller area on the negative. From a distance, the perceived motion of the "smaller" train is not as great.

Let us consider three images that depict motion, one from afar, one from close by, and one at a middle distance. For the intermediate image, figure 7.1, we are looking at a canal barge full of African American refugees and household belongings, floating in the burned-out shell of Richmond. The photograph was taken by Alexander Gardner at the end of the war, when seemingly everyone in America who owned a camera was descending on the devastated Confederate capital.

There are several different degrees of movement visible in the photograph, as indicated by the varying amounts of fuzziness or distortion at certain locations. The brick buildings in the background are perfectly in focus, as would be expected. So is the canal wall adjacent to the barge on the left. The barge itself isn't quite as sharp, and the distant end is clearer than the end of the boat closer to the camera. Several figures on the raised fan end of the barge are moving (fig. 7.2): The gentleman to the left is resting his arms on the stern deck of the boat, and shadows indicate he has rocked forward and back (his torso and arms remain stationary, providing a darker but slightly blurred image). In the background a small skiff sits with its tiller out of the water, and it appears to have drifted to the right a foot or two. Given all of these various degrees of apparent movement, which seems more realistic: an exposer time of one second or ten? Could all these people have remained nearly motionless—on a moving boat—for even five seconds? The movement by the rocking/leaning man and the drift of the skiff would also be more consistent, from a natural perspective, with a shutter speed of one or two seconds, rather than five or ten.

Of the three photographs studied here, the next distant image most clearly contains a subject that does not know a photographer is at work.

This photo depicts cavalry in the process of crossing a bridge over the North Anna River (figs. 7.3 and 7.4). This negative was taken by Timothy O'Sullivan on May 25, 1864.

A detailed examination of the crossing cavalry indicates a slight degree of movement, but individual mounts can clearly be deciphered. As such, their trodden movement slightly blurs their image from left to right, the direction of movement. Assuming they are crossing at a brisk walk, how much ground would a horse cover in five seconds? A few horse-lengths? The bridge is sharp and in focus, but the horses show a blurring equivalent to a foot or two of movement. Either this is the slowest moving mounted column of all time, or the exposure time couldn't have exceeded a second or two.

For the last, and most proximal photograph used in this shutter-speed study, we have another O'Sullivan negative, this time produced in the summer of 1862 (fig. 7.5). O'Sullivan photographed African Americans crossing the Rappahannock River, surrounded by US cavalry who are taking a break to water their horses. The horses are clearly not posing for the camera, and the degree of motion indicated by the blur of their drinking suggests a very short exposure time. Interestingly, the wagon in the photograph is motionless and perfectly sharp, a sign that the "refugees" stopped midstream, perhaps when asked to pose for the photograph.

In these three photographs the degree of cooperation with the subject matter varies. The cavalry crossing the bridge seem unaware of the camera operator's presence, perhaps because he is so far distant. The refugees in the wagon appear to have stopped their progress and (mostly) posed. On the canal boat, almost everyone seems to have ceased moving for a chance to be caught on film. In each image, the degree of movement and action clearly points to a shorter exposure time, one not exceeding three seconds.

Exposure times certainly change with ambient lighting conditions, but I would suggest that most combat, landscape, and camp photographs had a shutter speed of around one second. Those experts that place the range between five and twenty seconds may have been confusing field photography with studio photography. In the studio, the poorer lighting conditions would

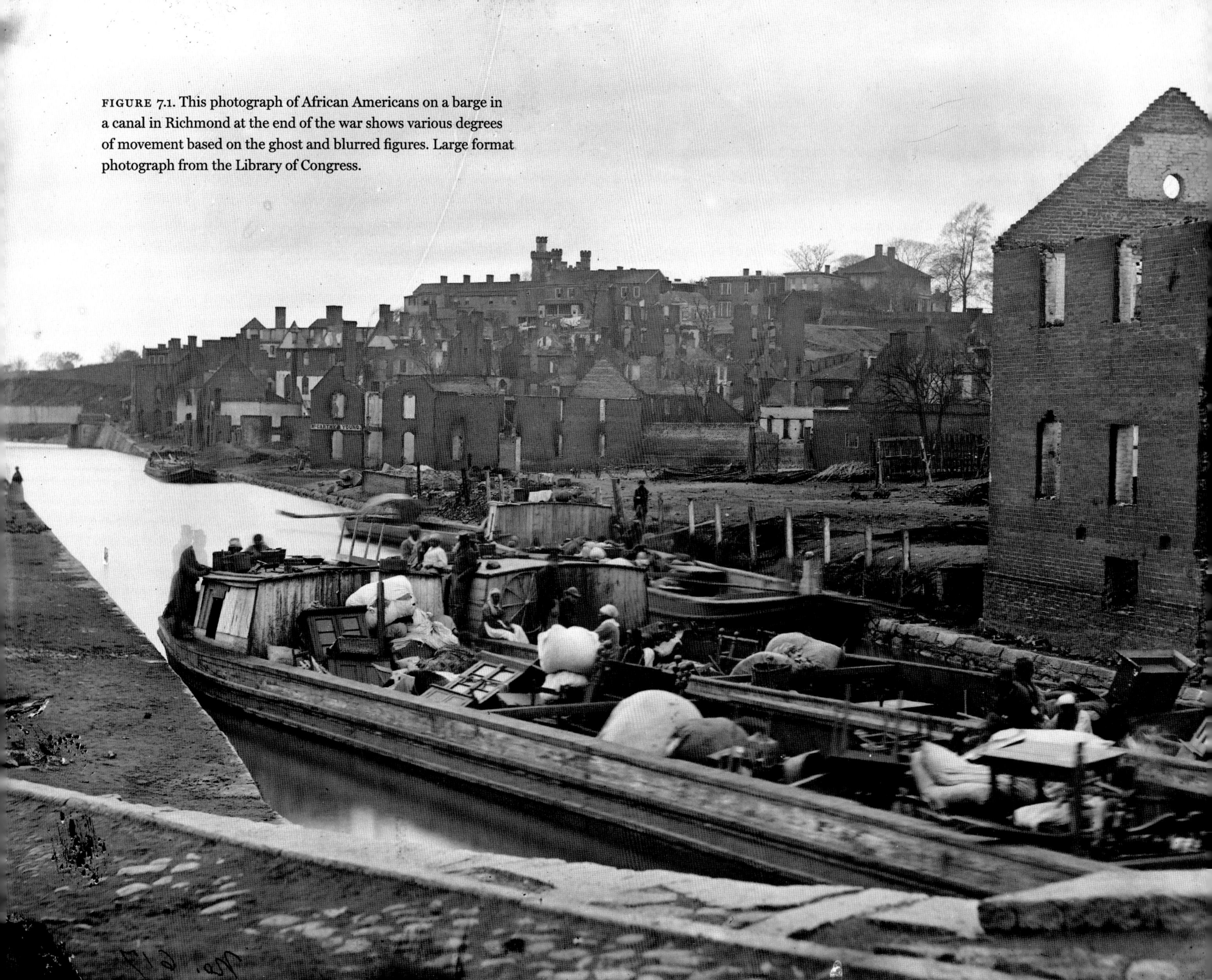

FIGURE 7.1. This photograph of African Americans on a barge in a canal in Richmond at the end of the war shows various degrees of movement based on the ghost and blurred figures. Large format photograph from the Library of Congress.

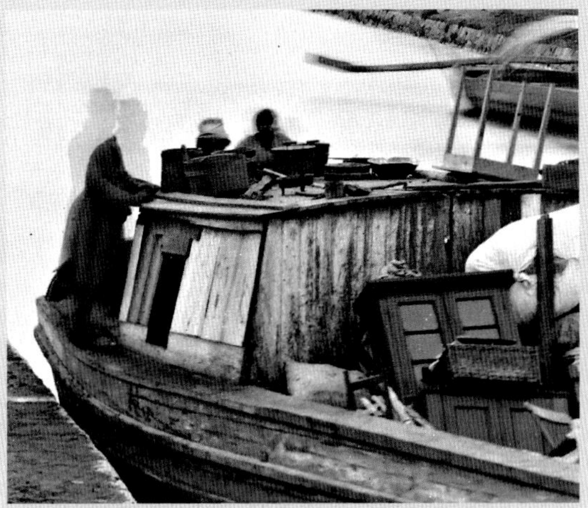

FIGURE 7.2. Movement apparent because of the ghost figure (*left*), who appears to be rocking forward and back. His torso and arms remain stationary, but his head and upper chest appear at two places at once. Note that the barge sits relatively motionless in the canal, allowing for a sharp picture. Detail from Library of Congress.

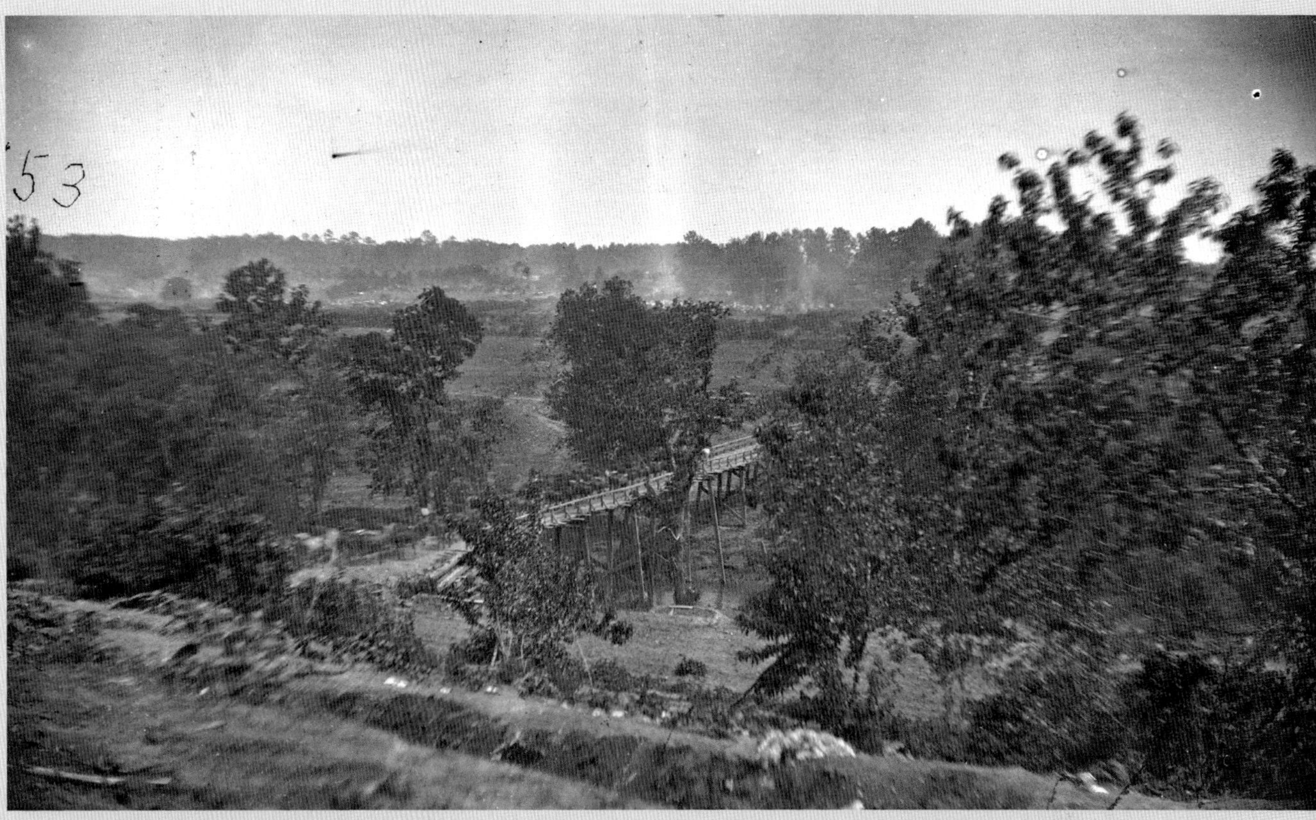

FIGURE 7.3. Cavalry cross the North Anna River. In this photograph, the movement is captured along a column that is clearly not posing for the camera while they are on the Chesterfield Bridge. Stereograph photograph from Library of Congress.

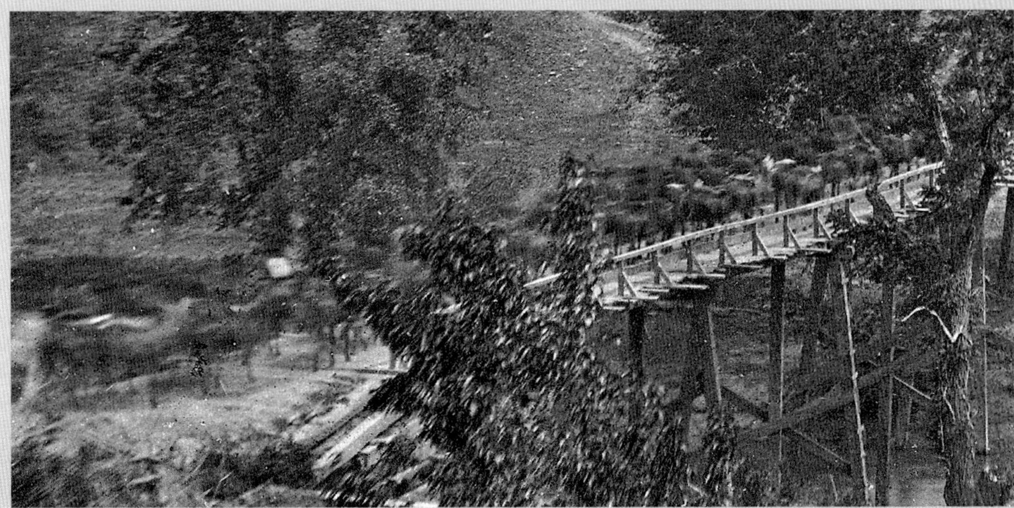

FIGURE 7.4. In this enlarged photograph, the cavalry horses are slightly blurred, but individual animals can clearly be differentiated. Stereograph photograph from Library of Congress.

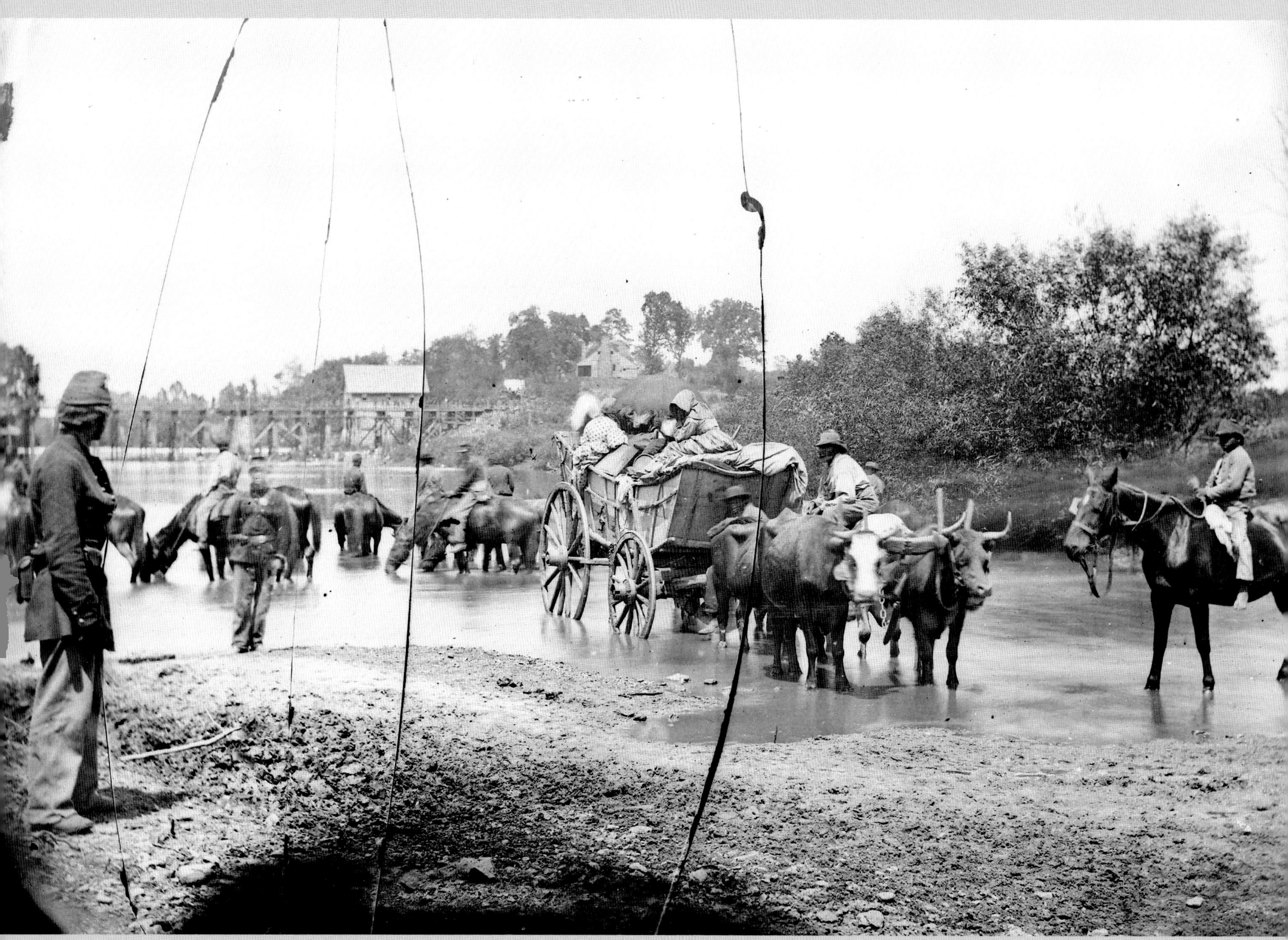

have necessitated a much longer exposure, and thus braces were often employed to aid a subject in remaining *perfectly* still. In the field, in contrast, a shutter speed estimate of more than ten seconds does not appear realistic for any of these photographs. Could a cavalry horse not walk many yards in ten seconds, rendering the image a completely blurred streak?

Stereoview versus Large-Format Cameras

One puzzling estimate of required exposure duration centers around the size of the negative. Some experts state that smaller negatives for stereoview cameras required shorter exposure times when compared to large-format cameras.[1] However, Civil War-era cameras had no aperture to control the amount of light hitting the negative. The exposure time would be dependent on the sensitivity of the film (negative) and on the amount of light available, but not the size of the negative.

If stereoview cameras had much faster shutter speeds than large format cameras, we should be able to detect this by examining and comparing their end products: There should, on average, be more sharpness and clarity on stereoview prints, especially when moving subjects are involved.

To quantify the degree of motion and estimate the exposure time for both types of cameras, one hundred photographs were selected at random from the collection of the Library of Congress and evaluated with respect to the degree of blurring and sharpness visible in each image (Table 7.4).

When the fifty large format and fifty stereoview negatives are compared, there is a very small indication that more blurring and ghost figures were present with the larger negatives (average 3.39) compared with the smaller side-by-side negatives (3.18). This suggests a very small increase in the

Opposite:
FIGURE 7.5. O'Sullivan's photograph of refugees crossing the Rappahannock River in August 1862. Library of Congress.

TABLE 7.4 The scale of sharpness used to compare stereoview cameras and large-format cameras to determine if one variety of camera had more blurred images and thus longer presumed exposure durations. Only photographs that were clearly not posed were used in this small study.

Rank	Description
1	Sharp: no detectable movement.
2	Slight blur: movement of only a few inches. Facial features and clothing details are blurry but discernable.
3	Movement greater than 6 inches based on length of complete blur. Humans and horses still recognizable as moving creatures.
4	Complete blurring and ghosts present. Humans may be transparent or appear in two different locations in the same frame.

exposure times for large format cameras compared with the stereoview variety, though a few factors could explain this slight difference. For example, the photographer may have been more inclined to use the large-format camera, with its higher resolution, for capturing landscape scenes or scenes of distant subjects. The stereoview camera may have been preferred for shots where the depth of field would be more interesting, and these often would be of subjects that were closer.

There might be several other factors that played a part in the choice of camera for a particular subject. The stereo camera was lighter and more portable compared with the large format eight-by-ten-inch variety. The negatives were also smaller and easier to prepare and handle. Stereoviews were also very popular.[2] Finally, the stereo camera offered a degree of flexibility the large-format camera could not—a stereoview could always be cut in half to produce a single print for enlargement, but a single eight-by-ten-inch print can never be viewed in three dimensions.

Casting More Light on Exposure Times

One further piece of evidence on the negatives regarding the shutter-speed debate can be found by considering moving, inanimate objects. Another common element of many of these wartime photographs gives an indication of movement and disturbance: a simple flag. Of course, this degree of movement is dependent on the strength of the disturbing force, the wind, but analysis of flags in sepia and a comparison to modern photographs of flags taken with varying exposure times can provide some parameters for shutter-speed duration.

Figure 7.6 presents the same American flag taken on a sunny day when the wind speed varied between five and ten miles per hour. Four photographs were taken of the flag using a shutter speed setting of one-tenth of a second. Another four photographs were taken with the shutter speed decreased to one-half second, one second, two seconds, and four seconds. As the exposure duration increases more and more blurring becomes apparent. At one-sixtieth or one-thirtieth of a second the flag appears frozen on the negative and no movement is apparent. At one-tenth of a second the tip of the flag often appears to show a slight amount of blurriness, indicating motion. This blurring becomes more apparent at one-half and one second. At exposure times beyond two seconds the gentle fluttering of the flag causes movement that isn't recorded on the negative—the waving flag is rendered invisible or a slight shadow because of the movement. The flag is a ghost.

Compare the relationship between shutter speed and image sharpness in figure 7.6 with five photographs of flags taken during the Civil War (fig. 7.7). Each blurred flag shows a combination between exposure duration and wind speed. The blurring increases from A to E, suggesting a faster shutter speed for the first two photographs (A and B) and a longer shutter speed or more flag movement for the others. Note that the degree of movement represented by the blurring flag has one large caveat: The most blurring may occur when the flag is moving the most relative to the background

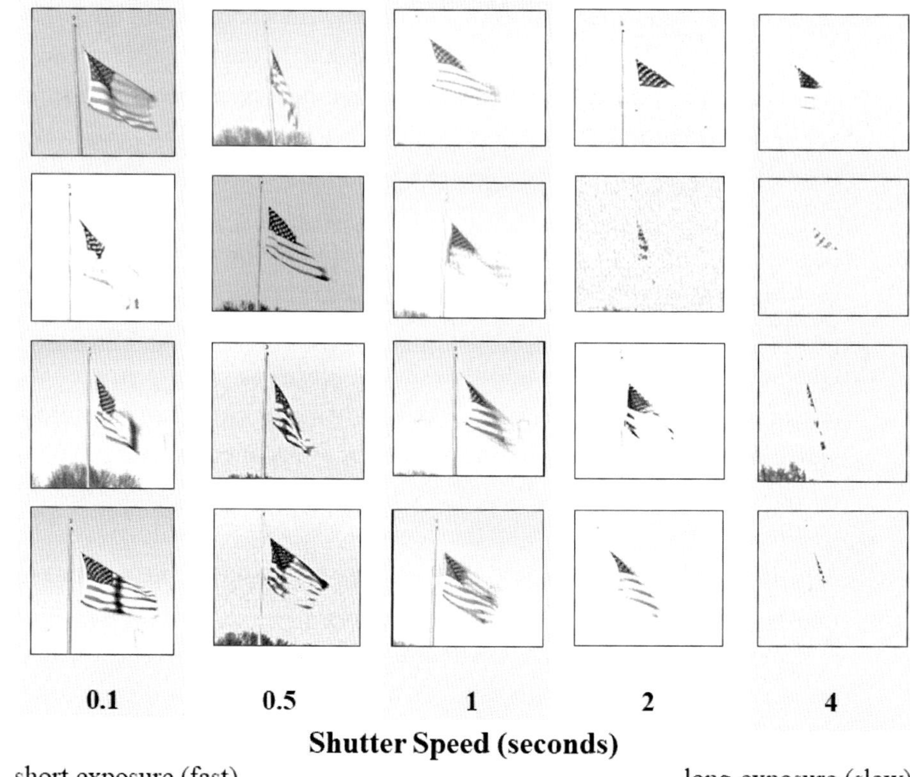

FIGURE 7.6. Four photographs of the same flag in a slight breeze, all photographed with a different shutter speed. Blurring becomes apparent between one-thirtieth and one-tenth of a second and the flag gets less and less distinct as the speed slows to longer than one or two seconds.

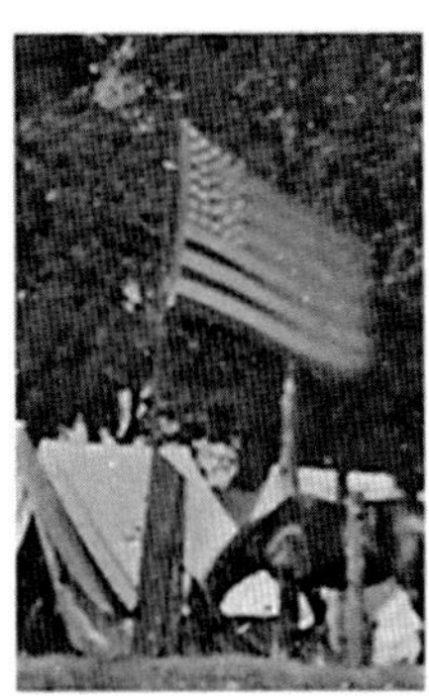 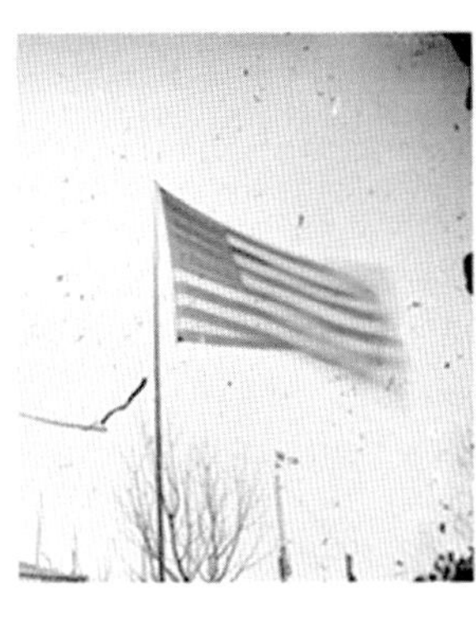 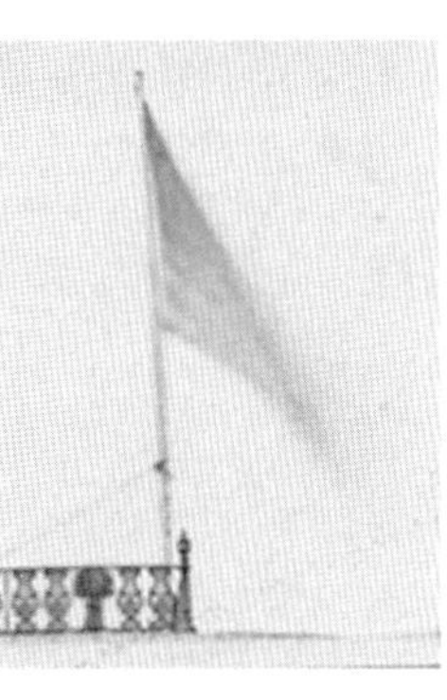 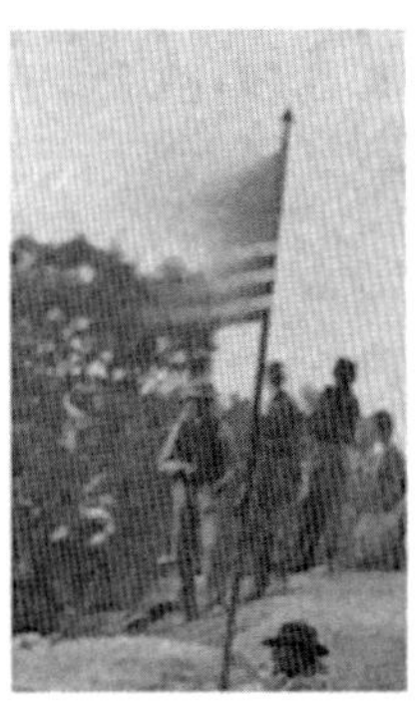 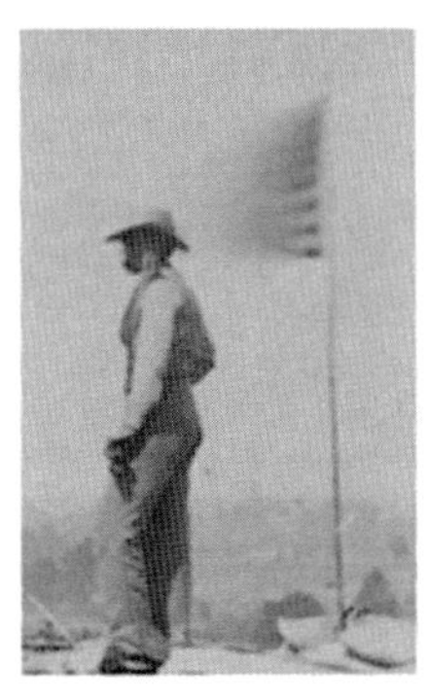

A.   B.   C.   D.   E.

FIGURE 7.7. Five flags photographed between 1862 and 1865, each indicating a different combination between wind movement and shutter speed variation. Taken collectively, they indicate an exposure time of between one-half and two seconds.

during a slight breeze or on a blustery day, where the cloth is flopping all around. At higher, consistent wind speeds the flag may straighten and flutter more rapidly but over a smaller area. This wind-straightened flag will show less blurring regardless of shutter speed.

Either way, comparison between the Civil War flags and the modern flags would suggest an exposure duration of between one-half and two seconds, based on a comparison of blurring in each set of images. This duration is entirely consistent with the photographs considered earlier of the refugees in barges or crossing a river and the mounted cavalry crossing the North Anna.

Finally, shutter speeds exceeding four or five seconds would have made capturing an image of a waving flag such as figure 7.7 (B) highly improbable. The traditional story explaining the failure of Civil War photographers to capture actual battle scenes points to lengthy exposure times and the prohibitively rapid movement during combat. A shutter speed of one-half or one second, in contrast, suggests that such scenes could have been recorded after all (especially on a sunny day). Perhaps the photographers just weren't willing to risk getting shot to get the shot.

CHAPTER 8

Resolution in the (High) Resolution

Some of the most intriguing photographs to emerge from the Civil War contain messages from the photographer to the viewer that transcend the obvious. Sometimes this is a particular look or facial expression by the subject, sometimes it is a message in the form of graffiti in the background. In all cases, it certainly wasn't an accident that the photograph contains more of a missive than first appears.

This chapter is dedicated to three examples of Civil war photographs that tell the viewer a great deal about the photographer's motivation for capturing a particular shot, and what the message was that the artist was sending through his composition. We start at the end of the war, in Richmond, Virginia. After Mathew Brady's field crew finished a lengthy and productive effort to photograph Grant's base of operations at City Point in April 1865, they decided to head north to document what was left of the former Confederate capital. At the same time, Robert E. Lee was making his way east from Appomattox, after just surrendering the Army of Northern Virginia in central Virginia.

Alexander Gardner also had a crew operating in the burned-out city at this time. At Gettysburg, two years earlier, Gardner and his team had arrived first at the war-torn town, capturing numerous images of the fallen in the field. They had also left the region long before Brady arrived, and all the bodies had been interred. Brady's tardiness cost him an opportunity to photograph any of the actual participants in the battle except for a few rebel prisoners. In Richmond this same scenario played out again, but with very different photographic results.

John Reekie, Gardner's representative behind the camera, arrived in the city days before Brady's team and completed his work by noon on April 15. While Brady & Co. began their work over the next few days, they discovered that their later arrival in the city had very fortuitous timing: news that the great, and now defeated, general had just arrived home. It took Brady less than a day to arrange a sitting with Lee. This unlikely scenario was possible because the war's most famous photographer used his reputation and connections to reach out to the wife of the war's most famous general.

Brady took six negatives of Lee during the one hour he was allotted (fig. 8.1). Of these photographs, all taken on the back porch of Lee's Franklin Street residence, two portray the general, his eldest son, and Colonel Walter Taylor.[1] Lee had lost his previous, more prestigious residence, the mansion at Arlington, when it was seized by the Federal government at the start of the war in response to Lee's decision to join the Confederacy. So it was here at Richmond that Lee would return after the surrender at Appomattox, and here where he would once again don the uniform he had worn at the McLean residence to meet with Grant. It was also here that Brady would take his last Civil War photograph.

The six photographs captured by Brady were well received at the time. The *Richmond Whig* declared "all were pronounced admiral pictures."[2]

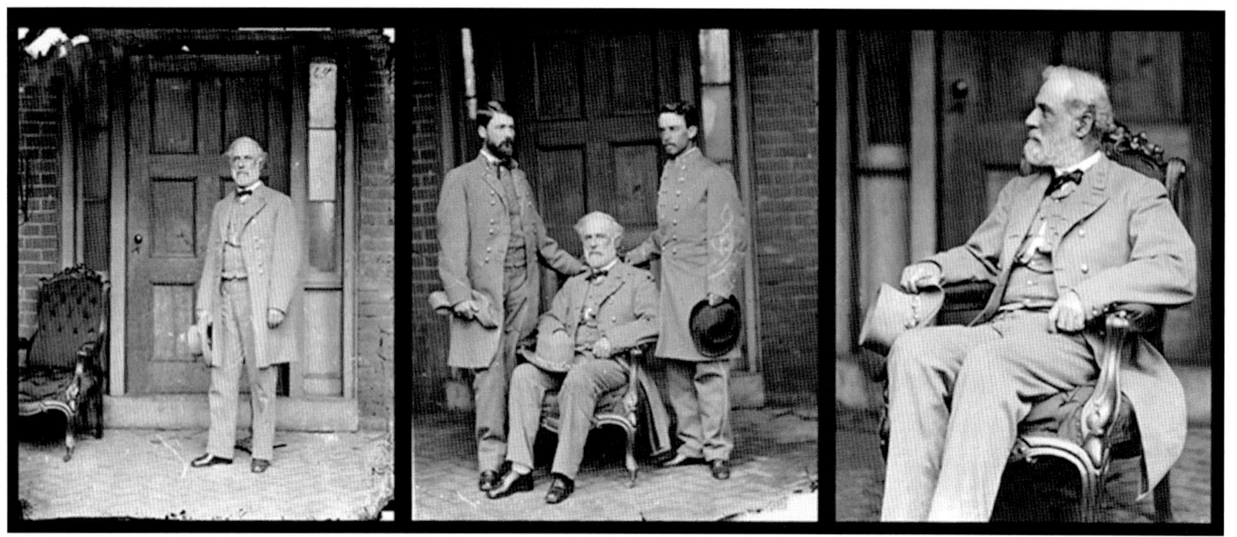

FIGURE 8.1. Three of the six photographs of Robert E. Lee that were taken by Mathew Brady and Company when the general returned to Richmond soon after the surrender at Appomattox. Note the position of Lee relative to the cross formed by the rail and mullion of the door behind him, especially in the middle picture. Library of Congress.

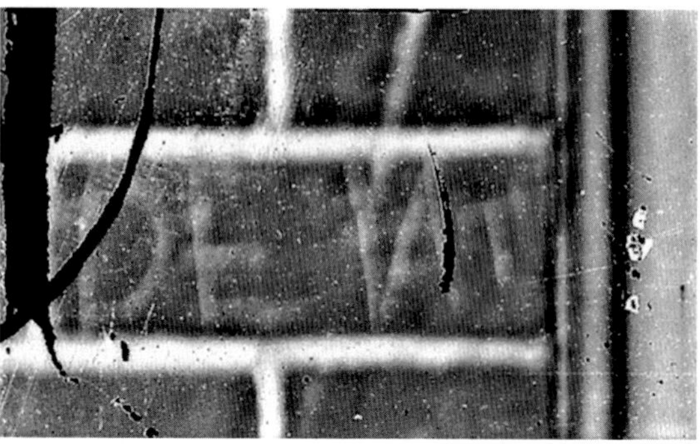

FIGURE 8.2. The word "DEVIL," carved into the brick surrounding the backdoor of Robert E. Lee's Richmond residence. The word appears five bricks above the unoccupied chair in the leftmost photograph in figure 8.1.

The New York Times correspondent commented two days later on the "splendid" portraits.[3] Praise for the photographs continues today. Jeff Rosenheim, in *Photography and the Civil War*, pronounced, "To many, Brady's pictures of Lee on his back porch, holding his hat, is one of the most reflective and thoughtful wartime portraits".[4] Joseph Glatthaar compared Lee's portrait to that of William Tecumseh Sherman's, in his essay for *Lens of War*.[5] Sherman's appearance: "stern, intense gaze, disheveled hair, and generally unmilitary appearance"; Lee's appearance: "Handsome, dignified, almost serene."

It is a wonder that Lee could have remained so serene considering that someone had clearly carved the word "DEVIL" into the bricks beside his back door (fig. 8.2).[6] Brady and his team, and Lee's son and his aide, couldn't have missed this condemnation, could they? The word is really only clear on one of the six portraits, but what was the inclusion of this graffiti meant to convey to the viewer of the image? Perhaps that postbellum life for Lee and his family might not be as restful, peaceful, and dignified as one might have expected?

On the other hand, the framing of Lee in the other photographs, with respect to the most Christian of symbols which appears either above or behind him, is hard to miss. Robert Wilson points out in *Military History Quarterly*, "One photograph in particular became iconic. In it, the hatless general's head is squarely centered in front of the crossed rails of a panel door, suggesting Christ on the cross to those for whom Lee would become a powerful symbol of the martyred South."[7] The viewer is left to ponder the mixed message in Brady's compositions— as he transitions from soldier to citizen, is Lee to be thought of as Christ or the Devil?

Ron Field offers insights into Brady's intentions. He pointed out, for the first time, that the same "DEVIL" brick is visible in some prints of the General and his aids, but the graffiti has been "scrubbed out." He bolsters his argument that Brady did not want this message conveyed with further evidence: "It was later discovered that the photographic wet plate including it [the photograph of Lee alone] had the instruction 'Do Not Use' scratched at the side."[8] Under this scenario, then, either the photographer or the subjects noticed the "DEVIL" after the first photograph had been taken. Realizing this photo contains a message that Brady & Co. didn't wish to convey, the negative is marked as unusable and the photographic team continues their work, either intentionally or insentiently framing Lee under or in front of a cross.

Whoever left this message for Lee, whether soldier or citizen, was clear in their expression. Brady's message with the door and cross panels is less so, but not by much. For an especially clear message, consider a photograph of the members of Company E of the 4th US Colored Infantry. William Morris Smith photographed these 27 men at Fort Lincoln in the northeastern quadrant of Washington DC (fig. 8.3).

This earthen fort was one of seven temporary structures constructed at the start of the war to protect the capital. The 4th US Colored Infantry would see extensive action as a member of the XVII and XXV Corps, fighting at Richmond and Petersburg and participating in the bloody capture of Fort Fisher. The most striking aspect of this photograph under magnification is the determination, and even defiance, in the soldiers' facial

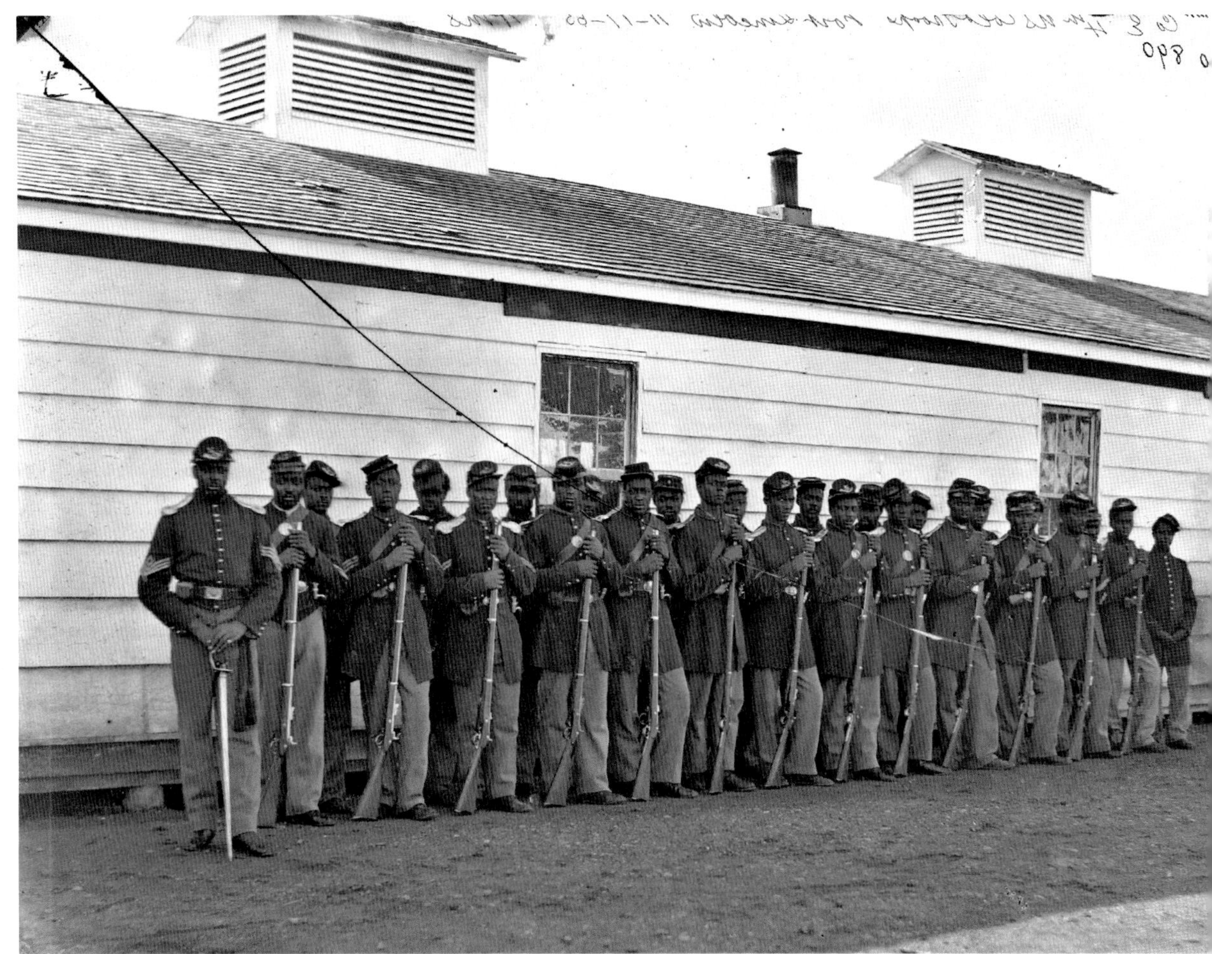

FIGURE 8.3. William Morris Smith's photograph of Company E of the 4th US Colored Infantry taken in Fort Lincoln, Washington DC. Library of Congress.

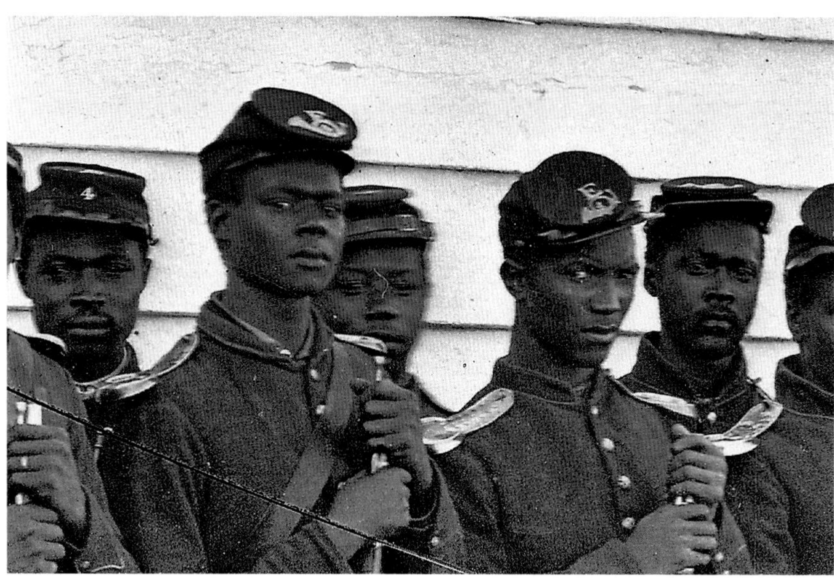

FIGURE 8.4. Detail from the center of figure 8.3. Do these look like unserious soldiers?

expressions (fig. 8.4). In *Exposing Slavery*, Matthew Fox-Amato used this "dignified" photograph as an example of how the portrayal of Black men changed over the course of the war, from "racial inferiors to, broadly speaking, resourceful and courageous figures, men who had even made important contributions to the nation in wartime."[9]

African American men were originally refused entry into the US Army during the first half of the war, in part because Lincoln was wary of offending the border states. This, of course, included Maryland. By the end of the war, many of the fortifications in Washington that were adjacent to Maryland were garrisoned by Black soldiers, including Fort Lincoln. This photograph was probably taken at the end of the war, during the time that the 4th was assigned to the northern defenses of the capital.

Interestingly, the location of this photograph, inside Fort Lincoln, would have a long and enduring role in the history of the fight for equality for African Americans. The fort was constructed for the Civil War, but a hundred years later it was a critical location in the fight for Civil Rights. In short, the neighborhood that grew up around the fort became a geographic symbol of the fight for social justice. *The Washington Post* described this legacy, "President Lyndon B. Johnson had hopes for Fort Lincoln to be a showcase for his Great Society Programs—Policy initiatives primarily aimed at abolishing inequality and establishing communities that would be racially and economically integrated."[10] One hundred and fifty years ago it was considered controversial to hand an African American an Enfield so he could guard the Maryland border at the fort. Today, this same portion of the capital is considered one of the most diverse areas of the city.[11]

William Morris Smith may or may not have been making a statement about the combat readiness of Company E and their potential usefulness in battle with his photograph recording the determination on the faces of the soldiers. George Barnard, in contrast, is abundantly clear about his message in his photograph of an African American soldier that was taken after the capture of Atlanta, Georgia.

The photograph, which was briefly discussed in chapter 2, poignantly portrays an African American soldier, sitting and reading a book, with his rifle musket resting against the front wall of a slave auction house (figs. 8.5 and 8.6). The incongruous message is hard to miss: a free, armed, and educated Black man, sitting below a large sign that reads "Auction and Negro Sales."[12]

Historian Stephen Berry from the University of Georgia wrote a fascinating essay about the sardonic nature of this photograph which he titled "The Book or the Gun."

He stated:

> We will probably never know his name, but we can certainly guess what it meant to him to be sitting in uniform, gun in hand and reading, outside an auction house that had just a few weeks before been actively engaging in buying and selling members of his race. I would love to believe that the photograph is candid. I would love to think that Barnard came around a corner and

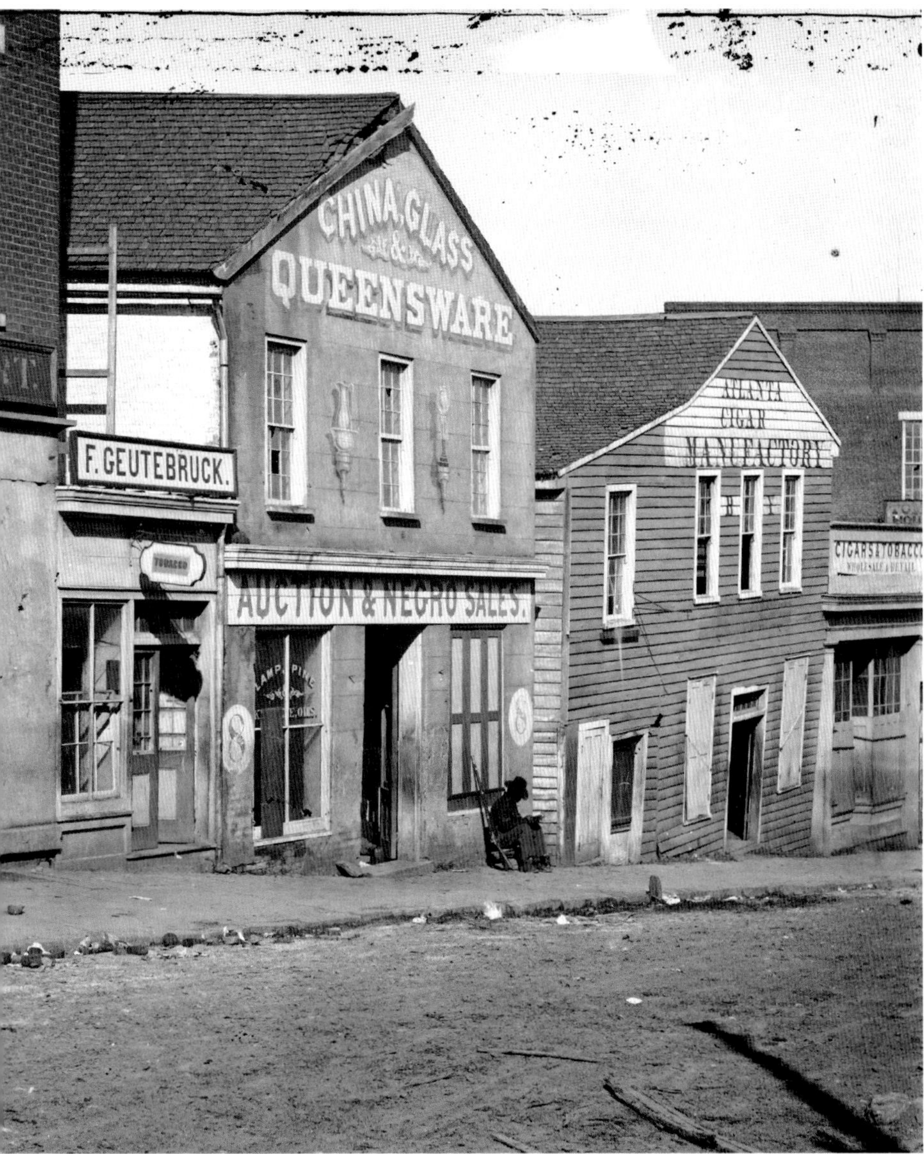

FIGURE 8.5. George M. Barnard's photograph of an African American soldier sitting and reading a book with his rifle musket resting beside him and a sign reading "AUCTION AND NEGRO SALES" hanging over his head. Library of Congress.

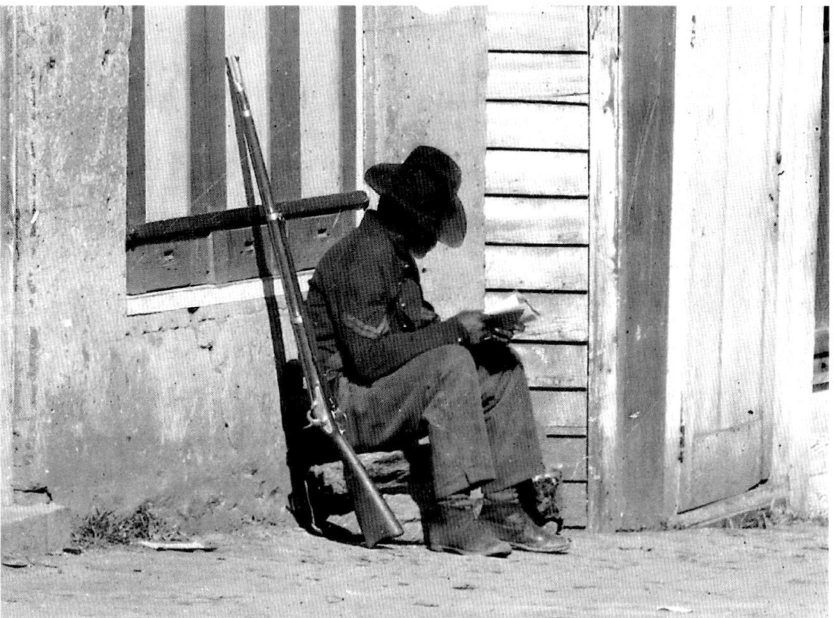

FIGURE 8.6. Detail of figure 8.5, showing the soldier's book and rifle musket.

found himself captivated by the scene as I am. For here is the whole of the war in a single tableau—a war fought so that men capable of thinking and reading and dreaming might never be sold as things.[13]

Berry is also highly suspicious of the authenticity of the image, pointing out that no United States Colored Troops, as they were called, participated in the Atlanta Campaign. Sherman didn't want them. What Sherman did want, however, was photographs of the city of Atlanta before he torched it. Thus, Barnard, the official army photographer for the Military Division of the Mississippi, was ordered to report downtown. Barnard was told that he had a few days to photograph anything of interest before the conflagration.

Berry's "historical instincts" that indicated this image was posed are supported by a second, less well-known photograph of the same street,

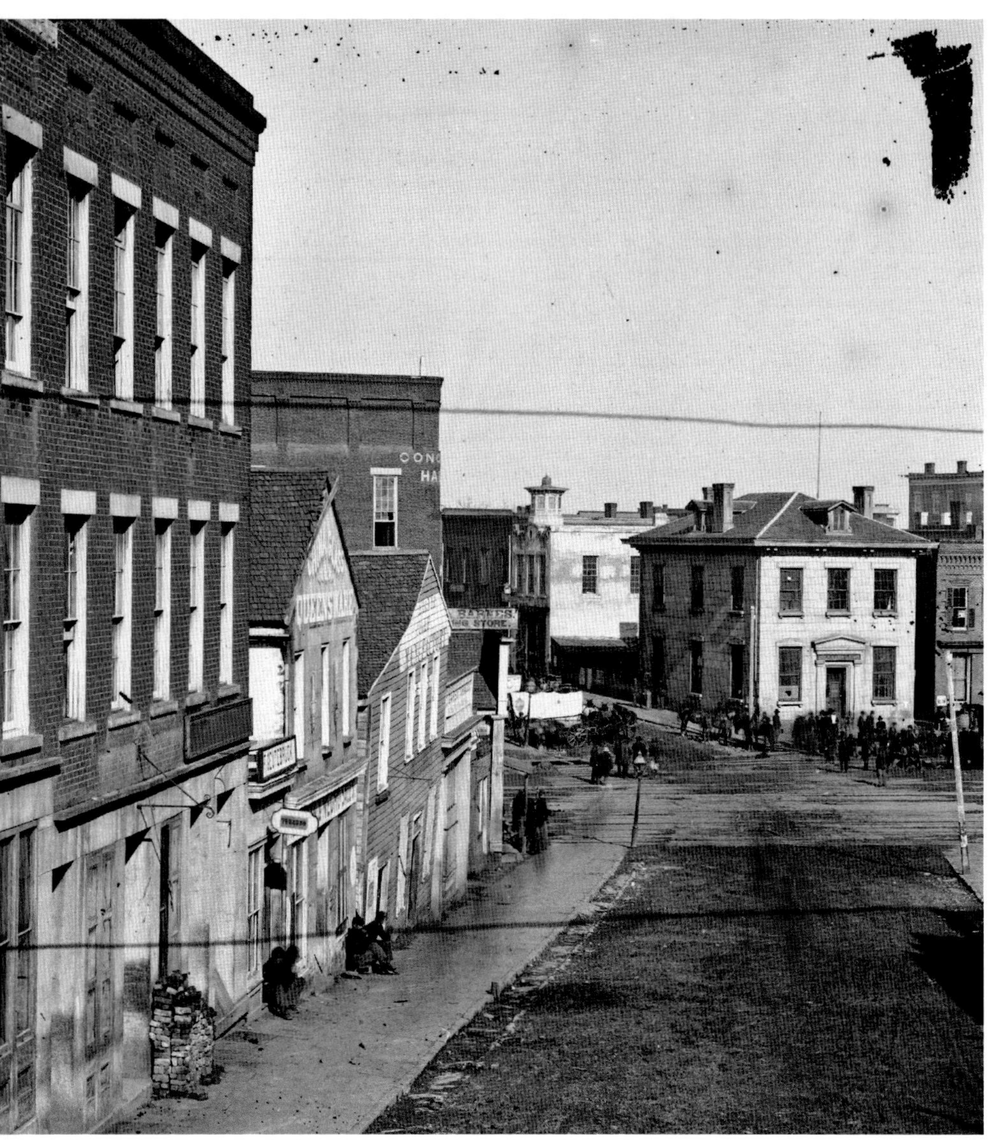

FIGURE 8.7. Another of George M. Barnard's photographs of Whitehall Street in Atlanta, probably taken earlier in the day than figure 8.5. Library of Congress.

taken from a slightly different angle (figs. 8.7 and 8.8). This image, with four soldiers sitting along the storefronts, was probably taken at an earlier point in time, as indicated by the subtle changes between the two negatives. In the photo with four soldiers present, there is a stack of bricks on the left side of the frame. In the "Book or Gun" image some of these bricks and stones have been scattered on the sidewalk and onto the edge of the street. There is also notably more trash in the street in the image with the seemingly solitary soldier. One could posit that the "single soldier" photograph might have come first, and then someone cleaned up the immediate area, but who would be tiding up a street in a city that was soon to be burned to the ground?

The most likely scenario is that Barnard photographed the group of soldiers resting along Whitehall Street. After considering the "Auction and Negro Sales" sign, he imaged just how compelling it would be if he had an African American soldier in the photograph. Or, perhaps even more intriguing, a Black soldier who was demonstrating a degree of discipline and education. The White soldiers in his first photograph were resting, possibly drinking and smoking and unarmed—not particularly soldierly. His African American soldier would be ready for battle if needed, and was passing time reading a book—a rather gentlemanly pursuit. To complete his photograph he needed three things: an African American in a uniform, a musket, and a book. All three were available nearby, as other photographs of Whitehall Street, likely taken the same day, show a wagon train stopped along the street. Perhaps a cook or teamster could be encouraged to pose along with some of the contents of the supply train.

In the end, Barnard's efforts to assemble a compelling image resemble those of Gardner at Gettysburg. He found an interesting location (slave auction house vs. sniper den), but one lacking a compelling human figure (four boring, unarmed soldiers or no soldier/corpse at all), so the photographer added to the human interest by adding a human (and Springfield rifle). The results were, in Barnard's case, a thought-provoking image asking viewers to contemplate the value of freedom and, in Gardner's case, a melancholy

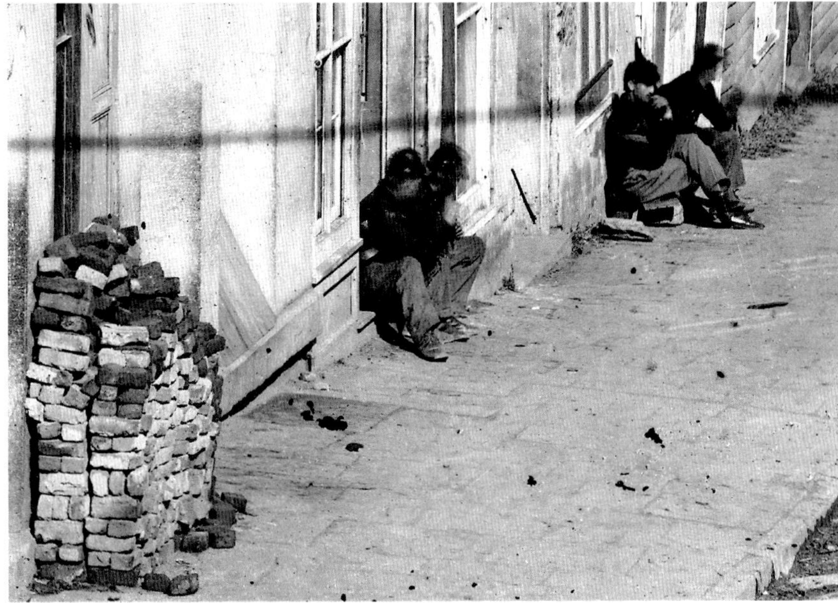

FIGURE 8.8. Detail of figure 8.7, showing four resting, seemingly unarmed Federal soldiers and the pile of brick that will become partially scattered in figure 8.5.

this unusual exclusion. At Antietam, the subject of her article, there were no Black men in uniform. In later engagements, where these men saw heavy combat, they served almost exclusively on the Federal side, meaning that their dead were usually buried before the enemy on battlefields controlled by the North.

This chapter largely focused on the motivations behind the photographers for capturing the images that they did, whether financial or seeking to send a more important societal message.[15] It is important not to forget the motivation of the men being photographed. As Deborah Willis summarized in her excellent study *The Black Civil War Soldier: A Visual History of Conflict and Citizenship*:

> From the earliest days of the war, black men strived to prove their worthiness as soldiers and fighters. A primary way to accomplish this was to stand in front of a camera and be photographed, to be depicted as men who had made a choice to be free. As soon as they were given their gear—from uniforms to forage caps to weapons—they posed for photographs, holding their weapons as if they were props that signified the future. Standing alone or in groups, they held flags, rifles, and banners and looked directly into the camera lens, sending a message of undeniable patriotism, commitment, and courage.[16]

statement about the loneliness of death in battle. Barnard portrayed the reason for the great fight, Gardner the cost. Both photographs demand a contemplation of a deeper meaning for the image, as long as you aren't distracted by a consideration of the authenticity of the image.

Of course, the greatest difference between Barnard's creation and Gardner's fraudulent sharpshooter image in the Devil's Den is the human subject. One is Federal, Black, and alive. The other is Confederate, White, and quite dead. Interestingly, as A. Maggie Hazard points out in *Civil War History*, not a single image of dead Black soldiers exists from the war.[14] More than 200,000 African American soldiers fought during the war, so it seems almost impossible that of all of the images of the dead in the field, not a single one contains a soldier of color. There are several reasons for

When the Library of Congress digitized its collection of Civil War negatives in an extremely high-resolution format, it made the details in the photographs available to most historians for the first time. Simple digital manipulation (to clarity, exposure, or contrast, not to content) and enlargement revealed aspects of these photos that had been overlooked through time. This portion of the text documented three, with an emphasis on the message being sent by the photographer to the viewer, whether intentional or not. Over the next several chapters similar details will reveal dissimilar topics ranging from the gruesomeness of combat to the frivolities associated with camp life, to the evolution of warfare and weapons during the war.

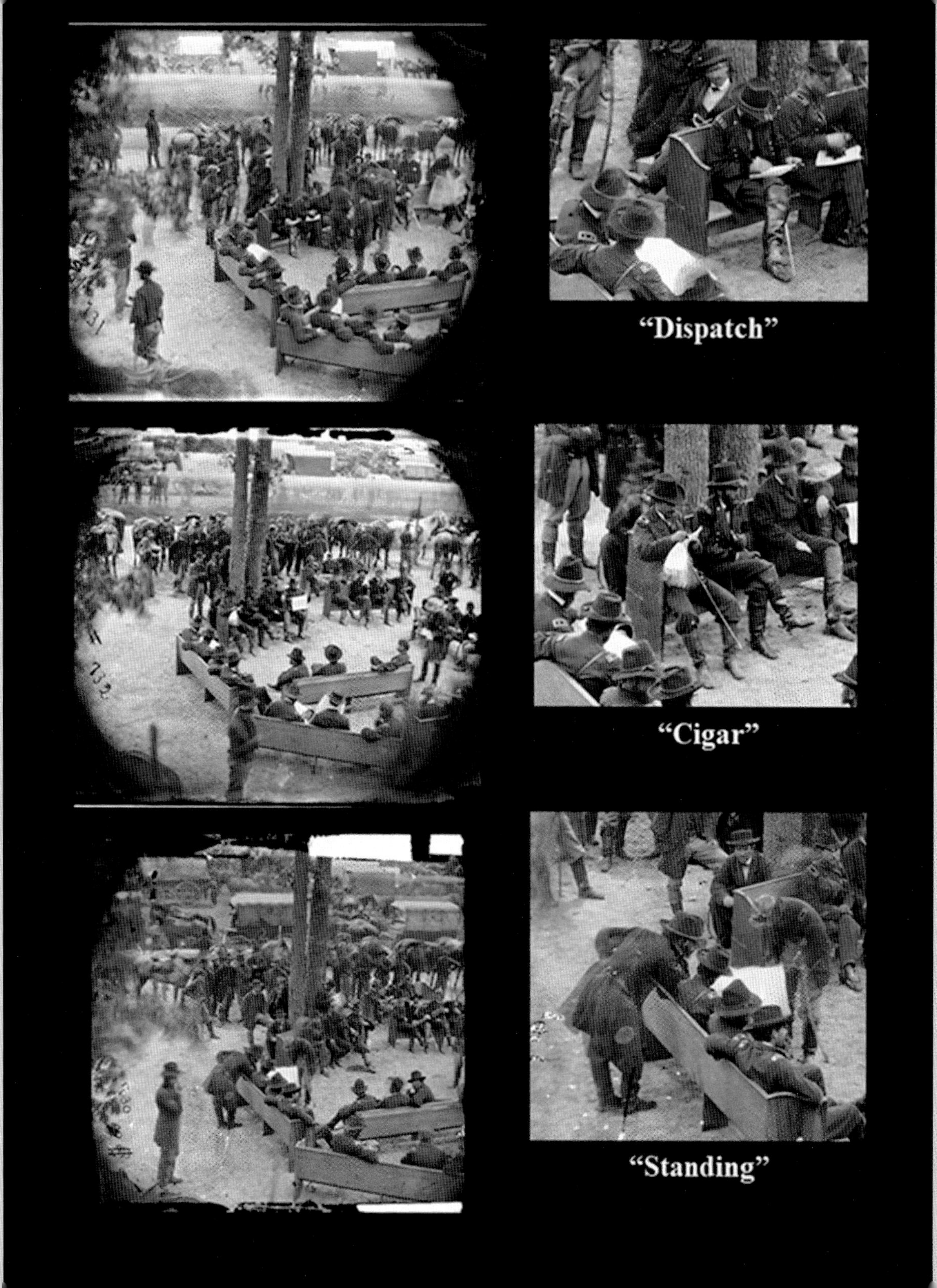

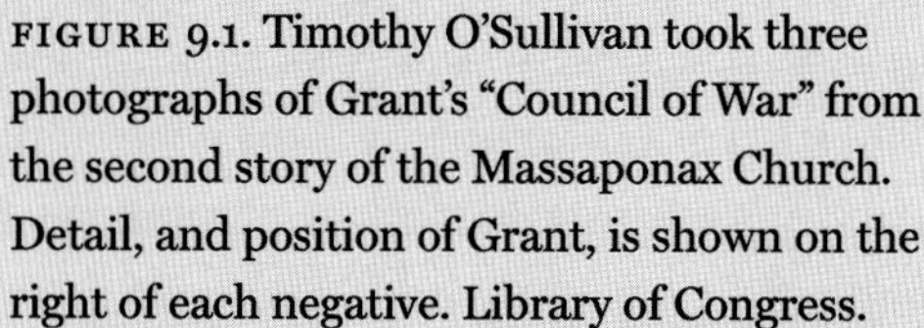

"Dispatch"

"Cigar"

"Standing"

FIGURE 9.1. Timothy O'Sullivan took three photographs of Grant's "Council of War" from the second story of the Massaponax Church. Detail, and position of Grant, is shown on the right of each negative. Library of Congress.

CHAPTER 9

Timing Is Everything

In chapter 3 we investigated how the rotation of the planet, and the resulting lengthening of shadows on the surface, could be used to sequence photographs. In this chapter we use a variety of forensic tools, and some critical reasoning, to place an even larger number of successive images into the proper context. Surprisingly, historians have struggled to place these photographs in proper order, despite the task appearing, at first consideration, to be a rather simple undertaking.

Perhaps the most famous of these series of three or more photographs, taken of the same subject matter from (relatively) the same position, was captured by Timothy O'Sullivan on May 21, 1864. This collection of four photographs includes Grant and his staff, sitting in church pews on the front lawn of the Massaponax Church.[1] O'Sullivan carried his bulky camera to the second story of the Baptist church to record his three negatives.

We will differentiate the three views using a descriptor of what the most famous person, Ulysses Grant, is doing in each scene (fig. 9.1). In one view Grant appears to be writing in a notebook or fashioning a dispatch or order of some type, and Meade sits at another pew, adjacent to Grant, studying a map. For the sake of simplicity, we'll refer to this negative as "Dispatch." In a second view, Meade is studying the map while Grant sits with his legs crossed, smoking a cigar; we'll refer to this photo as "Cigar." In a third view, Grant stands and joins Meade, deliberating about the map over his colleague's shoulder. We'll call this photograph "Standing."

So, in what sequence did O'Sullivan capture these three images? Shadows on the ground are nearly indecipherable, suggesting the photographs were taken around midday on (perhaps) an overcast day. In *Grant and Lee*, William Frassanito places the sequence as: "Standing," "Dispatch," and "Cigar." The author notes that this sequence matches the original negative numbers.[2] According to Fassanito's narrative, the sequence of photographs tells this story: Grant is standing behind Meade, presumably studying a campaign map, discussing strategy. When they are finished, Grant sits down to write a dispatch, almost certainly to Ambrose Burnside regarding the best routes of travel for the subordinate's IX Corps to take when withdrawing from the Spotsylvania battle line. After sending the dispatch, Grant sits back, crosses his legs, and lights his seemingly omnipresent cigar.[3] Photographic historian Bob Zeller agrees with this sequencing.[4]

William Davis and Wiley Bell, however, present a different order for the photographs in their comprehensive guide to the photographs of the Civil War.[5] They have "Cigar" as the first photograph taken in the series, followed by "Standing" and "Dispatch." In their scenario Grant is sitting, possibly listening to something being read by the gentleman who stands at the far right ("Cigar"), before he joins Meade to study the map ("Standing"), then proceeds to return to his seat to craft his dispatch.

Both arrangements of the photographs and resulting scenarios seem to make sense, but Frassanito's (and Zeller's) sequencing is bolstered by the

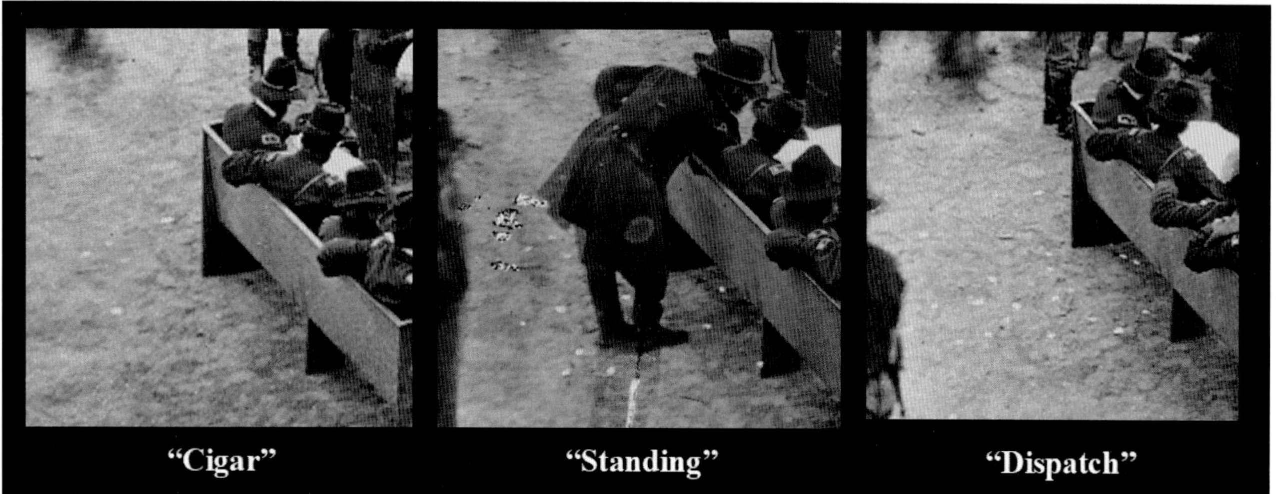

FIGURE 9.2. Entropy in nature tends to increase through time. Compare the relative amounts of trash or scrap paper at or behind Meade's seat in the pew. More litter equates to a later photograph, unless someone was cleaning up between shots.

numbering of the negatives. However, a few other details can be discovered under inspection at a great magnification that argue for a different order of events.

We'll use two well-known scientific phenomena to evaluate the series of photographs: gravity and entropy. The first concept is obvious—items fall towards the Earth. The second, entropy, is probably less familiar. Entropy is the measure of disorder in a system, and it tends to increase in nature. My office at the university where I teach was once orderly and neat; today, it looks like the "after" photograph in a "before and after" earthquake comparison. The same is true of the "Council of War" photographs, as the degree of disorder should grow to some respect between the first and last image.[6]

One key evidentiary aspect of the photographs that suggests a stage of entropy is the accumulation of trash and debris under the church pews. Another tracer that suggests timing is the movements of some of the soldiers and lower-ranking officers who can be followed between photos.

A careful inspection of the ground under and behind Meade's seat on the church pew reveals a change in the amount of litter that has collected—it almost looks as if Grant or someone seated had ripped up a piece of paper (fig. 9.2). No trash is present when Grant enjoys his cigar, but in the photograph where the General is standing behind Meade there is paper detritus on the ground. In the photograph where Grant is writing in his notebook or crafting his dispatch, the scraps of paper remain and are even more abundant. Unless someone was methodically cleaning up the church grounds (and escaped being captured in the negative), that leaves a sequence of "Cigar," "Standing," and "Dispatch."

Two soldiers in the photographs display actions that support this sequencing. The first is a young man who is prominently displaying a pistol on his hip, with his arm resting above the holster ("Standing"; far left of fig. 9.3). He, and the comrade standing beside him, are focused on the discussion between the generals. In another photograph, "Dispatch," this same soldier can be seen in a similar pose, standing several feet closer to the gathering of senior commanding officers. It makes more sense that he would be moving closer to his subject of interest through time, while consistently facing Grant and Meade, than the other way around. This leaves us with the "Standing" photograph having been created prior to "Dispatch."

Another soldier, perhaps a lieutenant colonel or major, appears to be joining Meade and Grant as they study the map ("Standing"), then standing idly by in proximity to our first human "tracer" ("Dispatch"). Perhaps this second soldier is waiting for Grant to finish his dispatch so that he might assure it finds its way to Burnside. Unfortunately, neither of these men can be found in "Smoking," allowing us to sequence only two of the three photographs ("Standing" before "Dispatch").

Finally, for a third confirmation of the proper order of the photographs, let's return to trash evidence. In two of the three photographs, the pew second farthest from the camera has four occupants, two of whom appear not to move very much (fig. 9.4). In the other photograph, this gentleman has moved, and the bench is unoccupied. In the first two photographs of the occupied seat there is no trash or debris under the pew, but the litterbug leaves something behind in the third photo, after this officer moves on ("Dispatch"). This leaves the photograph of Grant sitting, legs crossed

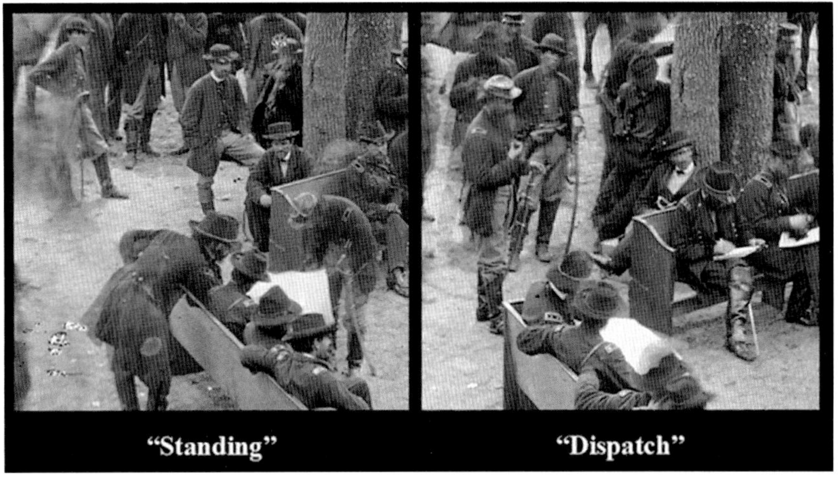

FIGURE 9.3. Two soldiers act as human tracers between these photographs. The first is in the back left of "Standing," and he moves closer to Grant and Meade in "Dispatch." The second is wearing a kepi and looking at the map upside down in "Standing," then appears to stand by, waiting for Grant to finish writing in "Dispatch."

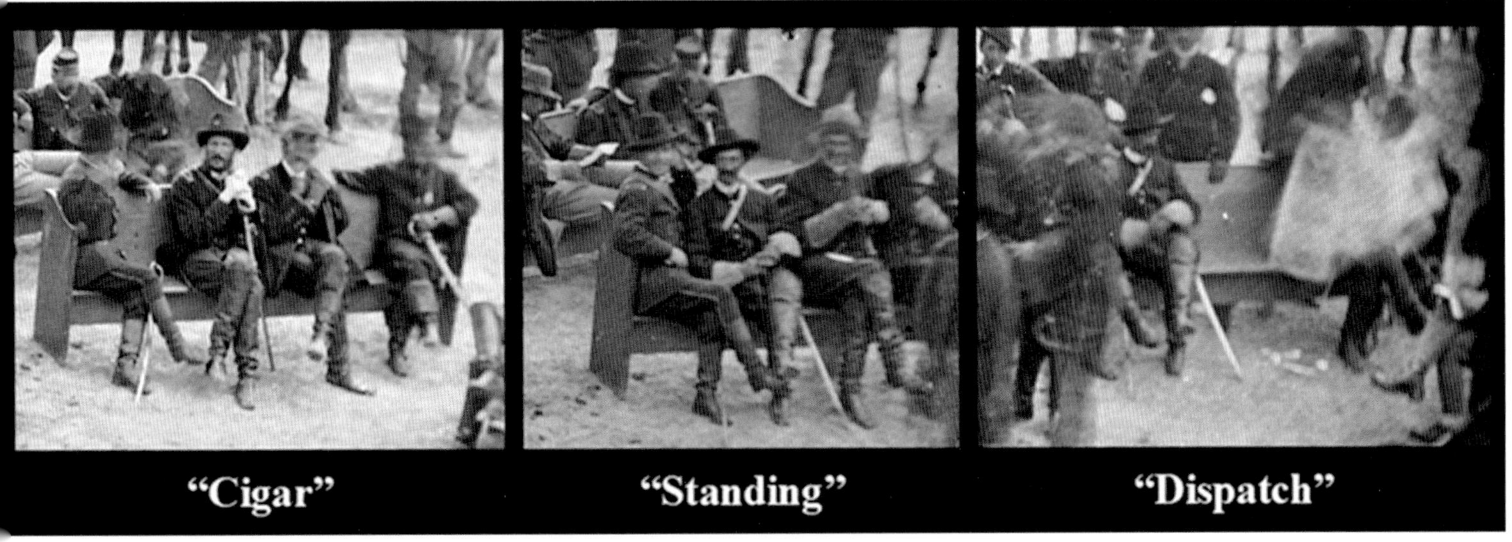

FIGURE 9.4. The back bench reveals two officers, seated to the left, one of whom appears not to move between the three photographs. The seat beside these men changes occupants before becoming vacant, with trash now deposited on the ground.

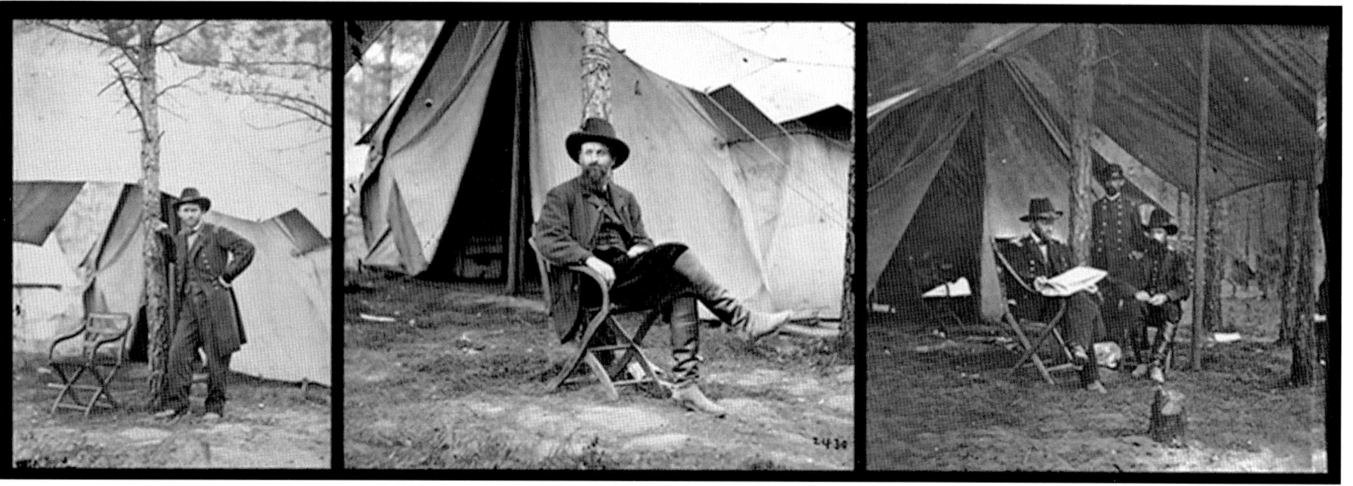

FIGURE 9.5. Brady's famous field portrait of Grant (*left*), Assistant Secretary of War Charles Dana (*center*), and Grant with Lieutenant Colonel Theodore Bowers and General John Rawlins (*right*). The same chair and tree appear in Grant and Dana's photographs.

and writing, as the clear final photograph in the series taken by O'Sullivan that day.

This sequencing, then, leaves this story as told by the three photographs. As O'Sullivan completes the setup of his bulky camera on the second story of the church, Grant sits smoking a cigar with Charles A. Dana, the Assistant Secretary of War, to his immediate left. Dana sits between Grant and General John A. Rawlins, who is Grant's Chief of Staff. Meade sits on an adjacent pew, facing away from the camera, studying a map with Lieutenant Colonel Cyrus B. Comstock, Grant's aide-de-camp.

After the first photograph was taken, Grant joins Meade and Comstock, and an unknown Captain in a kepi, to discuss potential travel routes for Burnside (or some other unknown matter). The second photograph is taken. Having finished the discussion, Grant returns to his seat to craft his dispatch as the kepi Captain waits nearby.

Three weeks later Grant and Dana would again be photographed together, this time by Brady & Co., at his headquarters tent at Cold Harbor (fig. 9.5). That same day Brady would also photograph Grant alone, in what might be the photographer's most famous field portrait.[7] Dana would also get a field portrait, in front of the same tent and tree, and sitting on the same chair that appears in the more famous photo of the more famous general.[8]

Another series of field photographs, also taken at Cold Harbor, could not be more dissimilar from those taken of Dana and Grant. These ghastly images show an African American burial party on the same battleground, working to inter or reinter corpses that had been left to rot in the elements. While it was Brady who would photograph the men responsible for planning the fight, it was John Reekie who would photograph the tragic results of their decisions.

Of all the most popular photographs from books (chapter 2), Reekie's photograph "Collecting Remains of Dead on Battlefield of Cold Harbor after the War" ranks in a tie for #7. Others found in 28 percent of all books are Gibson's view of the field hospital at Savage's Station, Barnard's photo of the remains of an ordnance train detonation and cheval de frise along the perimeter defenses of Atlanta (fig. 2.1). Reekie's Cold Harbor photograph is also extremely popular online, tying *A Harvest of Death* as the most common on websites.

Reekie captured at least three images of these scattered skeletal remains in April, 1865. The first of the views, fig. 9.6, shows the dead bodies before the burial crew arrived, and the location provided for the view is "Battlefield of Gaines' Mill, VA." For the second and third views (figs. 9.7 and 9.8), the location is described as "Cold Harbor, VA." This change in location might still be accurate, as the two battlegrounds overlap for the 1862 and 1864 fights (the primary combat at Gaines' Mill was just to the south of the majority of the fighting at Cold Harbor, but troop movements, and certainly casualties, occurred on many of the same fields).

In the first photograph, sans burial crew, we see five skulls and a portion of a rib cage, and perhaps most disturbingly, an articulated leg, complete with pant leg and boot. Close examination of one of the skulls that is farthest from the camera reveals a second boot and set of ribs. Two of the skulls, at the far left and far right, show signs of massive trauma, with the top of the cranium dispatched or with two distinct piercings.

In the second photograph (fig. 9.7), the African American burial crew has commenced with their dreadful work and started digging graves. Three men are present, one in a dark cap who is standing in a newly excavated grave. Five skulls lie above a collection of human debris on a stretcher, while a sixth skull remains in the background on the grass, behind an artfully placed shovel. An articulated leg and boot (from the first photograph?) hangs from the center of the stretcher, perfectly centered between the shovel and a canteen.

In the third photograph (fig. 9.8), the burial crew has expanded in number to five men, and five skulls remain on the stretcher. The sixth skull, which had been lying on the ground surrounded by tufts of grass, has mysteriously disappeared. One would think that this skull might have been added to the collection, but it has not. The man in the dark cap who had been working in the grave is now sitting directly behind the skull-laden stretcher, the camera slightly repositioned to align his head with the skulls of the dead. It is no wonder this gross, and engrossing, photograph has been reprinted so many times in the past.

Careful inspection of the two men in the background may explain the disappearing skull. The man on the left is holding a shovel, and this might be the same shovel that was previously resting against the stretcher. The other man appears to be lifting a skull or some other round object. Perhaps these two walked over to the stretcher between photographs and collected the digging tool and nearby previously uncollected skull.

There are a few reasons the camera was repositioned a few feet to the left between the second and third shot. Shifting the camera might have been necessary to include the two men working to the right. It also allows the head of the living man to better align with those of the dead and creates an interesting symmetry and orientation between the men at work and the man posing with the collected remains.

Despite studying the three views in great magnification, detail, and sharpened resolution, there are no specifics of the human detritus from the first view that can be matched to either of the other two images. This is, in part, because the first image isn't quite as sharp as the other two. The background tree line and topography also do not match between the first image and the second and third. Nevertheless, when all three views are studied in three dimensions (stereoviews), it is clear that they were all captured on a similar part of the battlefield. There is a distinct drop off (topographic low or swale) in the background of all three photographs, suggesting they may all have been taken along the same ridgeline or hilltop.

One possible scenario is that Reeckie came upon the first scene with human wreckage and skulls scattered across the field and took a picture. He then waited as these remains were gathered on the stretcher and transported to another nearby scene with additional relics (and the mystery skull), where he photographed the grisly stretcher and a portion of the burial crew to take a second photograph. Finally, he repositioned his camera slightly to the left and asked a member of the burial crew to pose with the stretcher for his third shot.

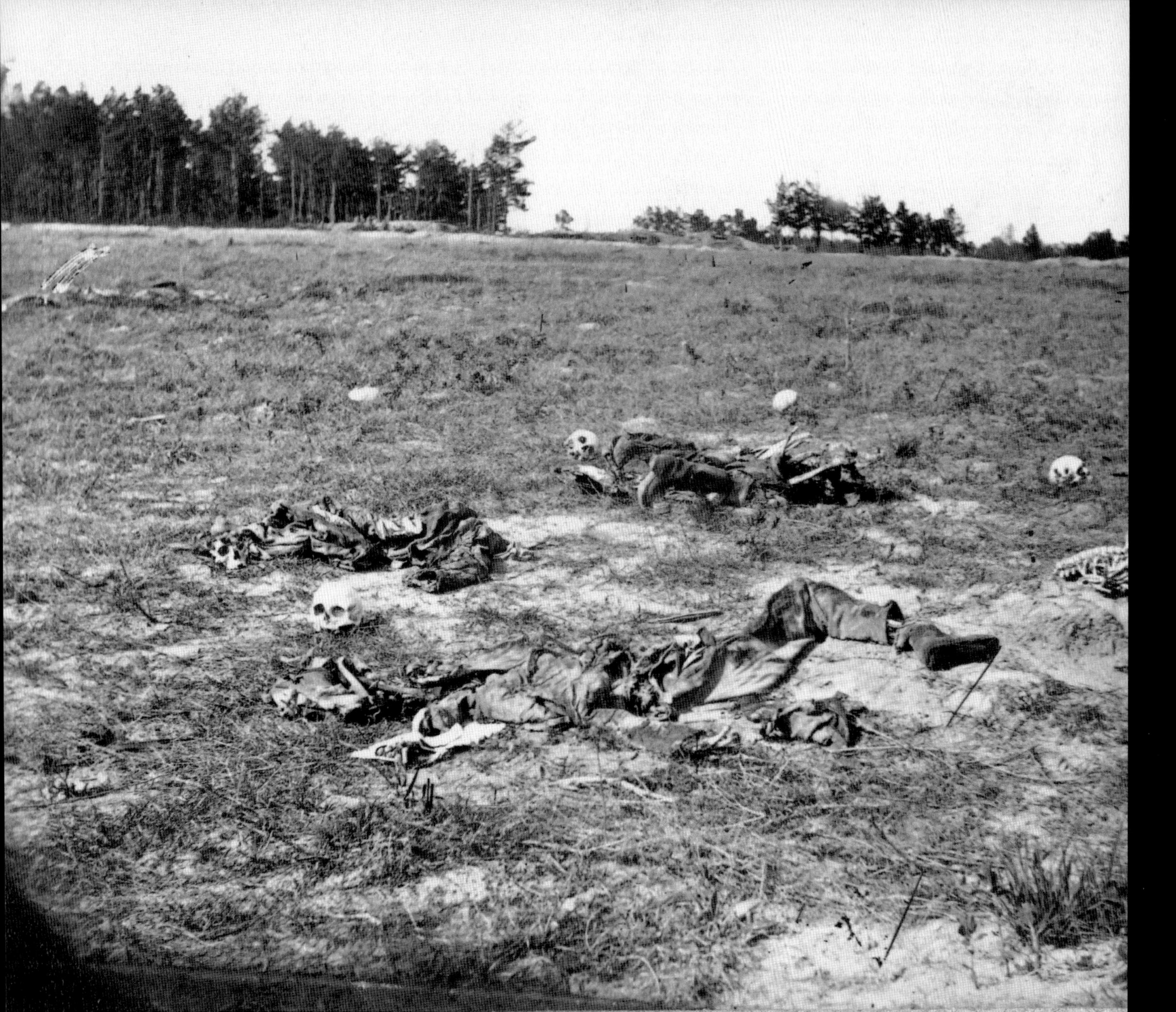

FIGURE 9.6. John Reekie's first photograph of the dead of Cold Harbor, awaiting burial (or reburial). This photograph was probably taken in mid-April 1865, ten months after Brady's portraits of Grant and Dana. Library of Congress.

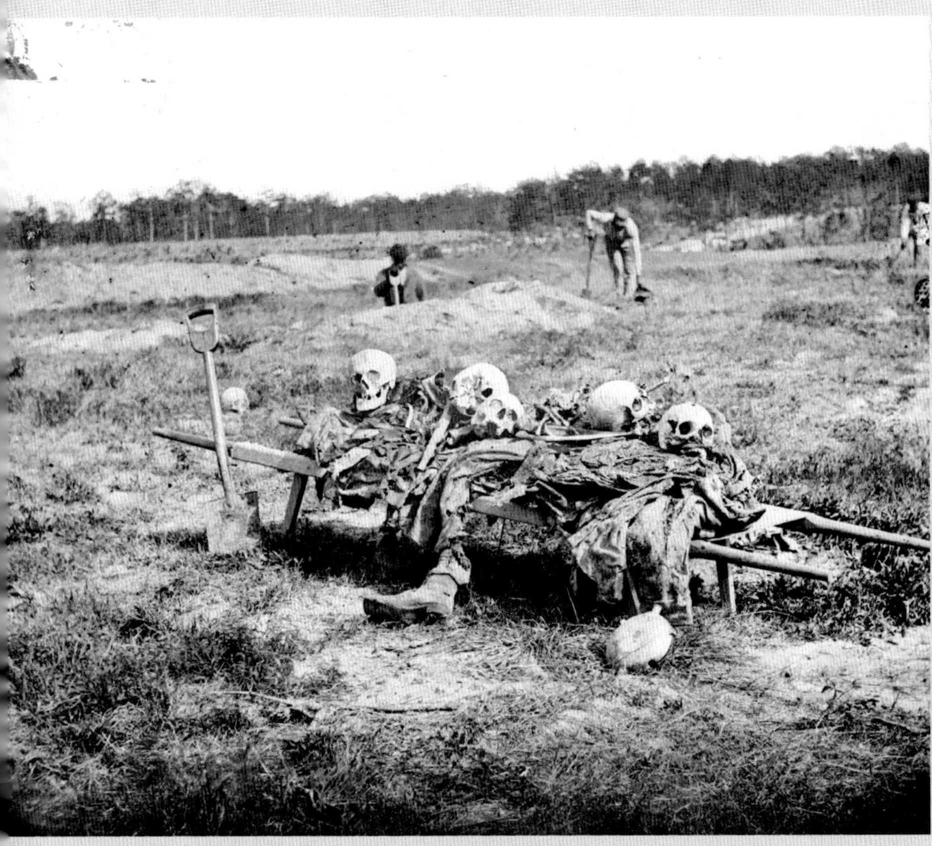

FIGURE 9.7. Reekie's second shot shows the burial crew at work. Note skull behind the shovel on the left, lying on the ground. Library of Congress.

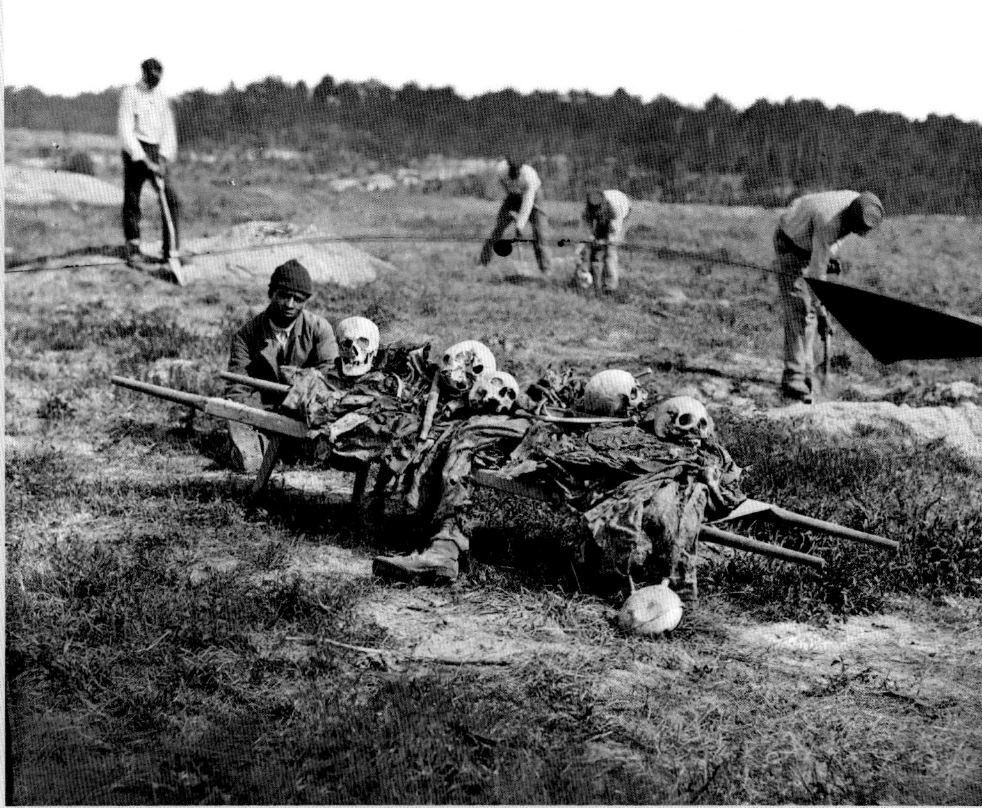

FIGURE 9.8. The third photograph in this series is both the most posed, and also the most compelling. Library of Congress.

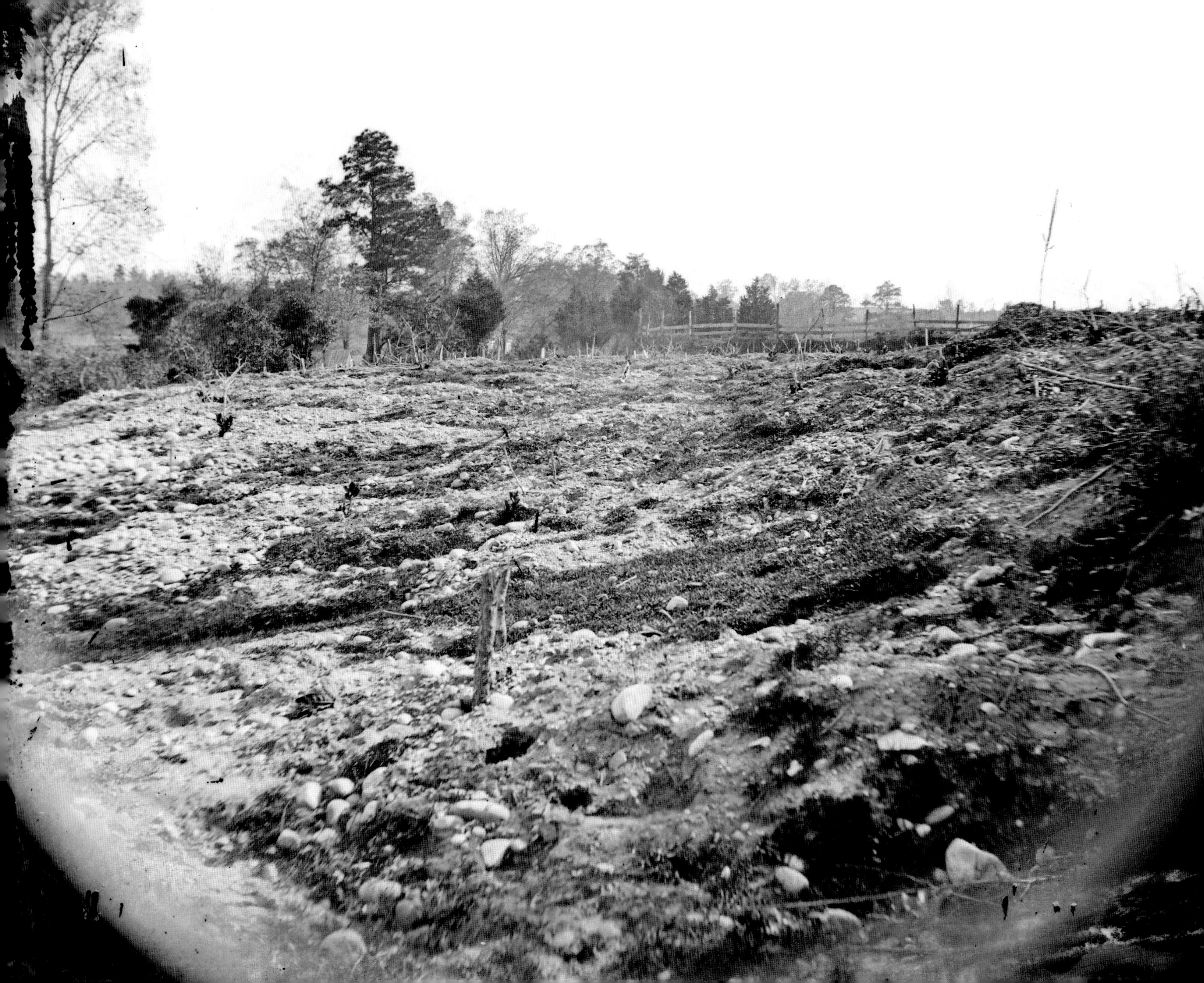

The overlapping Gaines' Mill and Cold Harbor battlefields have relatively flat terrain interrupted by gently undulating stream valleys. One of these streams may be present in the extreme lower left of the first photograph. Both landscapes are generally underlain by sands and clays, and these are the sediments we see in all three photographs. There are portions of the battlefield, especially in the northern sector (Cold Harbor) which sit above Pliocene gravels and sands.[9] Very large cobbles, and even small boulders, can be seen in at least one Cold Harbor terrain study (fig. 9.9). Because such stones are absent from the three skeleton photographs (note the piles of soil from the excavation of the graves), it is safe to say these photographs were captured on the southern portion of the Cold Harbor or Gaines' Mill battlegrounds, where the sand and silt of the Chesapeake Group of strata is generally bereft of anything larger than gravel.[10] The switching of locations between descriptions for the three photographs may, in hindsight, be significant, and may provide details about where the bodies were eventually being interred.

In the next chapter we revisit geology as a tool for understanding the Civil War. Frassanito famously used geological clues on the Gettysburg Battlefield to locate the site of many of Gardner's photographs on the Rose Farm. Geology also had an important relationship with the terrain and tactics of the war, and these become especially apparent when viewing the landscape images of the time.

Opposite:
FIGURE 9.9. This photograph is captioned "Cold Harbor, Va. View of the battlefield." Large cobbles and small boulders are unusual on a Coastal Plain battlefield, and probably indicate a fluvial (river) source. Library of Congress.

CHAPTER 10

A Photographic Chronology of a Colossal Waste of Time

US General Benjamin Butler was a big fan of "unconventional" strategies. When he heard about the results of a terrific explosion of an ordnance barge at City Point—an accidental blast big enough to damage the wharf and several other ships—he decided to build his own ship-bomb for use against the sandy parapet of Fort Fisher in North Carolina. The experiment did nothing other than waste an enormous quantity of black powder, as the ship exploded in a piece-meal fashion too far away from the fort to do any damage. When he returned north to Virginia, he would continue to attempt to use technological solutions to solve tactical problems.

Butler's campaigning along the James River in Virginia was becoming something of an embarrassment. As Grant relentlessly pushed south during his costly, but largely successful, Overland Campaign, Butler found himself in southeastern Virginia, trapped along a large meander in the James River. The one clear advantage he had over the Confederates in the region was the availability of heavy, mobile, water-borne firepower. Nevertheless, by the summer of 1864 the rebels had constructed many substantially fortified batteries that overlooked the river from the bluffs along the south bank.

Grant had faced a similar situation at Vicksburg a year earlier. The Federal navy was looking for a way to avoid the heavy artillery on the cliffs above the Mississippi River, guns that could drop heavy shells onto the vulnerable decks of the US vessels as they plowed upriver. These batteries couldn't simply be overwhelmed with firepower because, in many cases,

they were too high above the river to be reached by the heavy artillery of the Federal boats. After all, shipboard artillery is designed to shoot at targets on the horizon, not one hundred feet in elevation.

In a creative attempt to neutralize the Confederate guns at Vicksburg, US engineers decided to simply move the entire river out of range. A canal was to be cut across the neck of the peninsula opposite Vicksburg, so that the ships could avoid sailing through the vulnerable meander under the bluffs of the city. This bypass would straighten the course of the great river far enough away from Vicksburg so that the batteries would be rendered useless for defense and the city would lose its strategic value.

In early 1862, a similar canal project on the Mississippi had proven successful, allowing Federal forces to bypass the rebel fortifications at Island Number 10, after which they quickly captured New Madrid, Missouri. Nevertheless, cutting through the De Soto Peninsula across from Vicksburg would prove much more difficult and time consuming. After months of hard labor, a combination of thick, cohesive clay and loose layers of easily erodible sand, with unpredictable river fluctuations, and new, repositioned long-range Confederate artillery rendered the project more trouble than any promised value, and Grant looked to other experiments along the river to help him capture the Citadel of the South.

A year later and 750 miles to the east along the James River in Virginia, however, the situation appeared differently to Grant and Butler. Here, the surveys by the Federal engineer Peter Michie indicated the well-fortified rebel-held meander could be bypassed with a canal that was only 170 yards long.[1] He proposed to dig the entire canal while leaving bulkheads at either end, which could later be blown apart with mines.[2] This would allow US vessels a sudden new path upriver to Richmond, needing only to bypass a few batteries and the guns in Drewry's Bluff to reach the capital.

For the project to be successful, the engineers and construction crews would need a full understanding of the geology of the proposed path, and their failure to fully comprehend this relatively new science would ultimately determine the fate of the entire canal project.

This chapter, and the chapter that follows, use the photographs of the Civil War to document how a specific science—in this case sedimentary geology—influenced the tactics and outcome of the war. In the next chapter we turn from sand and silt to flesh and gore, with a documentation of forensic medicine, and specifically mechanical trauma. In both cases, the science cannot wholly be understood without visual images of the subject matter, whether in layers of sediment or shattered skin and tissue.

Boondoggles and Bomb Blasts: The Construction of Dutch Gap Canal

When Grant and his engineers constructed a large number of tunnels and mines towards and under the Confederate defensive lines at Vicksburg and Petersburg they took full advantage of the nature of the cohesive strata of the region. Vicksburg's loess, a weakly cemented silt, could be excavated easily and tunnels needed little structural support or revetting. Citizens of the city, threatened by falling artillery, cut caves into the sediment to create protected underground dwellings, with little need for bracing. Petersburg's sediments were more varied, with tough clay layers being more difficult to excavate than softer sand layers, but in tunnels the clay wasn't as

vulnerable to collapse as was the weaker sand.[3] In all cases, the tunnels and mines could be constructed covertly, hiding the engineering project from the enemy in the subsurface.

Not so with canals. Along the James River, the project that would eventually be dubbed the Dutch Gap Canal (earlier Dutch engineers had attempted a similar project for the sake of easier navigation of the river), would be under constant fire from the enemy.[4] By the end of the project, more than 20,000 shells, almost exclusively from mortars, would fall in or around the canal.[5] Some historians claim that the fall and explosion of one of these shells represents one of the earliest true "combat" photographs ever taken.[6]

The construction of the canal began on August 9, 1864, and within a week rebel shells began to fall on the construction site. The excavation began along the eastern, downriver side of the meander and worked its way west (fig. 10.1). Around 1,500 men, including a significant contingent of African American troops and local, recently freedmen, worked tirelessly in the miserable heat and unrelenting insects to dig through the sand, silt, and clay.

The initial excavation into the sediments was done by teams of men with shovels, dumping the sand, silt, gravel, and cobbles into two-wheeled horsedrawn wagons. This early excavation would have been deceptively easy because of the nature of the sediment in the upper, non-cohesive layers.

Dutch Gap Canal was cut through two distinct units of sediment. These strata (layers of sediment) are different with respect to their sedimentology. The upper, younger units, represent sediments deposited by rivers and streams during the last ice age, probably placed between 20,000 and 10,000 years ago. These units are usually unconsolidated and are easy to excavate and move. For the most part, explosives and blasting would be unnecessary.[7] Below these layers is the Potomac Formation, which dates to the early Cretaceous Period. That means that there is a contact between units, found about halfway up the canal wall, that represents a time of erosion and non-deposition in the sediments of more than one hundred million years.[8] This erosional contact is not subtle, because there is a distinct

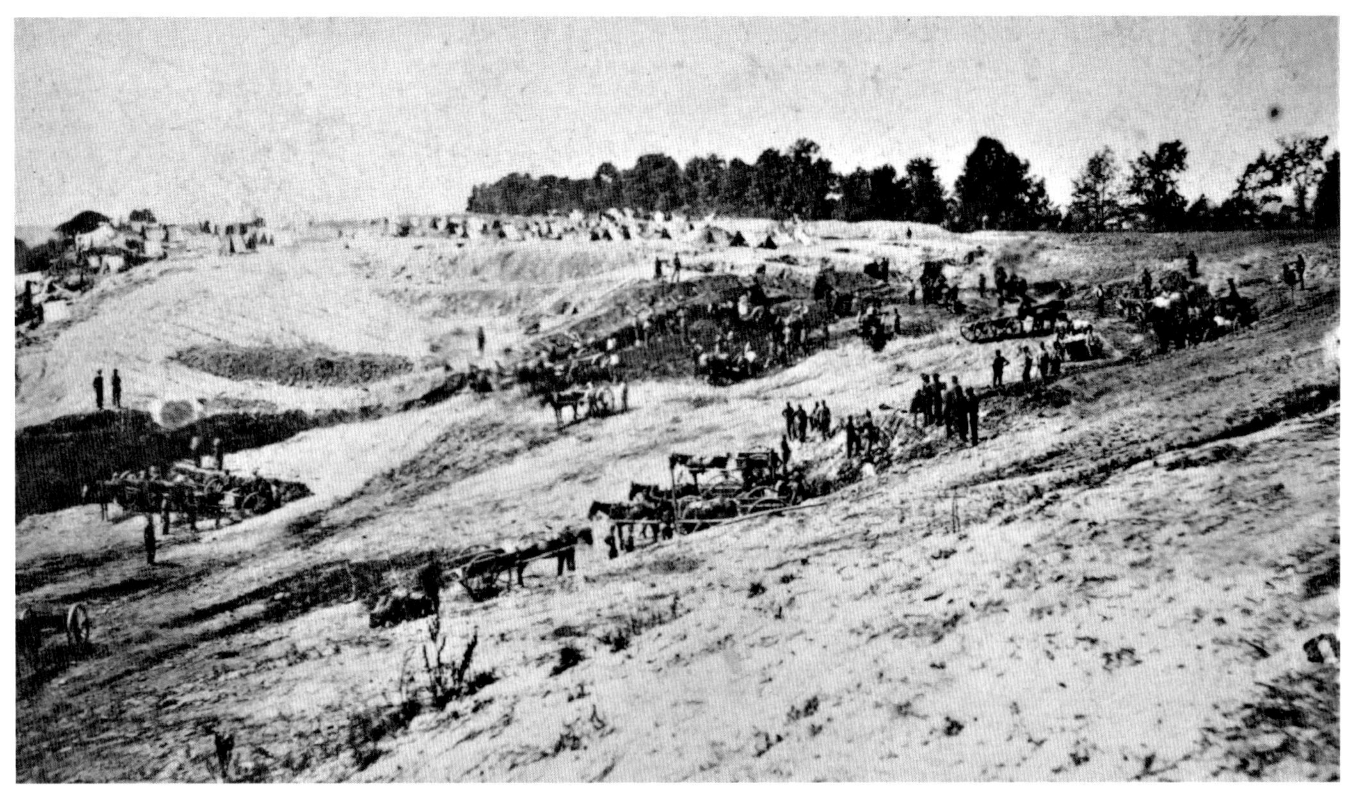

FIGURE 10.1. Around thirty photographs have been identified of the construction and completion of the Dutch Gap Canal. This may be the earliest, showing the initial excavation into the upper Pleistocene units of sand and gravel along the eastern extent of the river's meander. Library of Congress.

layer of cobbles and small boulders directly above the clay layers of the Potomac. This contact also marks a delineation of easy excavation and more difficult and exhausting digging.

By September of 1864 about half of the canal had been excavated by Butler's men. During the next month several photographers would dare to venture to the site, attempting to capture negatives and avoid Confederate shells. Among them were John Reekie, who was working for Alexander Gardner, and Andrew Russell and his crew. The E. & H.T. Anthony Company of New York also had several photographers taking uncredited photographs of the site. William Frassanito suggests many of these twenty-three photographs were taken by Russell or Egbert Fowx.[9] Note that Brady & Co. are absent from this collection.

During October the work also slowed in the canal, in large part because Confederate mortars had been brought to within 300 yards of the project. In response, a bombproof was constructed above the primary steam pump, with sandbags and earth used for protection (fig. 10.2). The digging was divided between sediments that were above river (sea) level and those that were below the water line. Men with shovels worked on the former while a steam dredge was used for the lower, tougher strata.

Eventually, after the stream dredge was brought in to facilitate the men

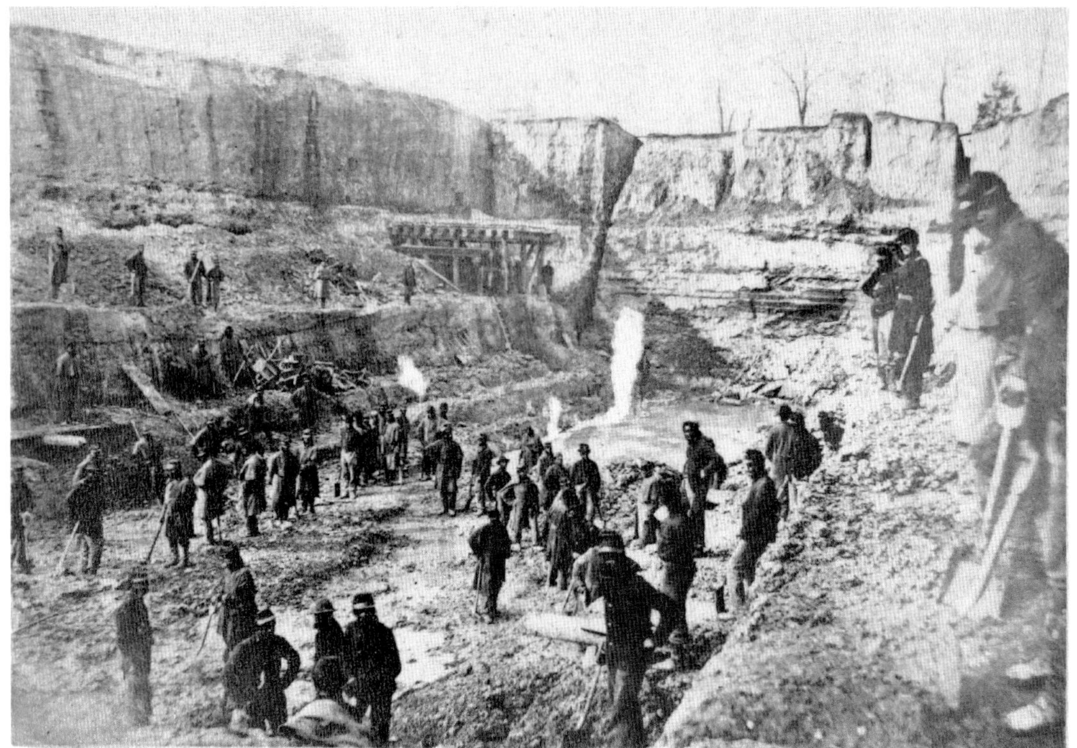

FIGURE 10.2. George Ennis's photograph of early work on the project shows the bombproof for the steam pump and water is absent from the bed of the canal. Note the vertical cuts in the far wall of the strata and the stair-step nature of the excavation, removing five or six feet of sediment at a time. Library of Congress.

with shovels, railroad tracks were laid along the southern side of the canal to aid with removing the sedimentary debris and make the project more efficient. Both the dredge boat (left, blurry) and railroad car (left in the background) can be seen in figure 10.3.

Several photographs were taken in early- and mid-November from this perspective and each shows some interesting differences in the work along the far wall of the canal. One of the more controversial aspects of this series of photographs is the possible inclusion of a mortar shell explosion. Bob Zeller describes the controversy in his book *The Civil War in Depth: History in 3-D* in a subsection titled "The Case for Northern Combat Photography."[10] He describes the caption on the back of "an obscure and unpublished Civil war photograph of Dutch Gap Canal in December 1864." The card reads "The mist arising against the bank is caused by a Rebel shell, which exploded just as this view was being photographed." A nearly identical photograph, with the same soldiers present, is provided as figure 10.4.

Zeller states that "the photograph becomes more intriguing when compared with an 1882 drawing and written account in 'Anthony's Photographic Bulletin' of a photographer under fire at Dutch Gap." The sketch shows a photographer in the approximate location where this photograph was taken from, with a ten-inch shell exploding nearby. The text was written by photographer Andrew Russell, who is describing a colleague's attempt to take a photograph while under bombardment. When the shell lands nearby, the photographer is spared and immediately relocates into the new

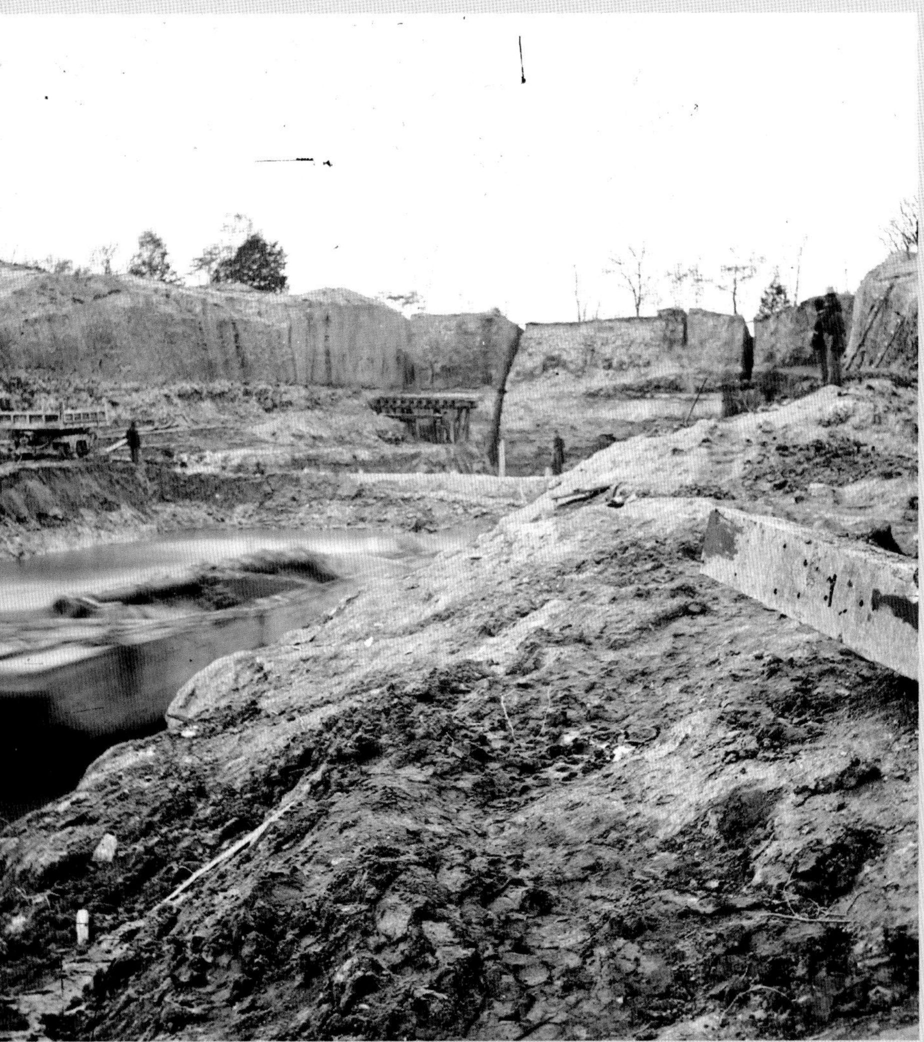

FIGURE 10.3. Many photographs were taken of the canal project in November 1864. Note that water is now present in the canal bed where the dredge is operating. Library of Congress.

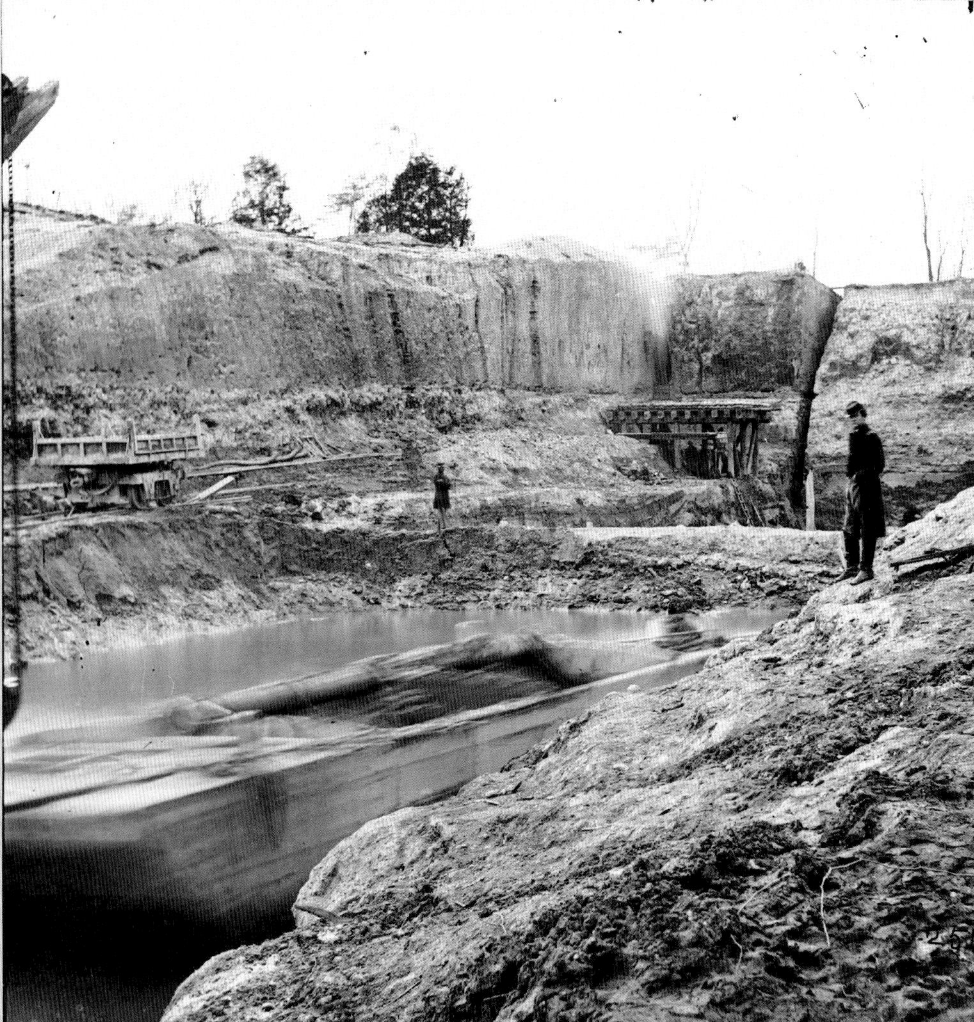

FIGURE 10.4. This image is nearly identical to the image presented in Zeller's book, with the same officer standing to the right and another soldier in the center of the photograph, standing on a ridge of dirt that runs perpendicular to the axis of the canal. The primary difference between the photographs are the movement of the boat and the location of the "mist." In Zeller's previously unpublished photograph the mist has drifted behind the officer on the right. Library of Congress.

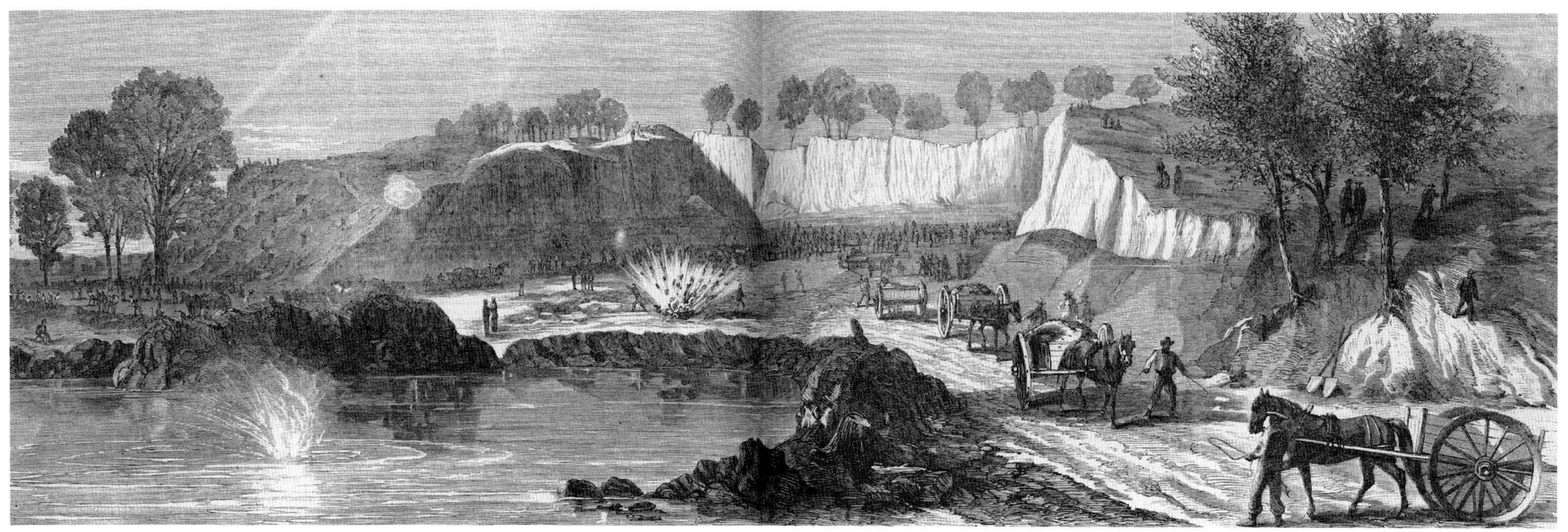

FIGURE 10.5. William Waud's sketch/engraving of Dutch Gap Canal from the November 5, 1864, edition of *Harper's Weekly*. Note the two impacting mortar shells. *Harper's Weekly*, vol. 8, 1864, HathiTrust.

crater. When asked about this curious move, he responds "Two shots never fell in the same place." This story, however, places the shell burst on the outside of the canal, at the position of the photographer, and not in the construction site, as supposedly portrayed in the photograph. Zeller notes this, "The account does not precisely jibe with the photograph."[11]

Perhaps the caption writer for the photograph were inspired by another sketch, this one by William Waud (fig. 10.5). Here we have shells exploding in the water in the canal (and later, on Thanksgiving Day, a shell did damage the dredge working in this area) and between several soldiers in the canal bed.

The "mist" that represents a shell impact in the photograph is probably steam from the steam pump, and not an explosion of a shell. This can be confirmed by analyzing several of the photographs that were captured this day, all taken from a proximal location. The "mist" is present in several of them, indicating either a great degree of mortar fire is landing in the canal (and none of the soldiers seem to care) or there is a secondary source of water vapor and dust—the steam pump.

Figure 10.6 is another image taken around the same time, with steam present from the far canal wall. The officer at right has moved a few steps farther from the canal.

Photographers continued working in the canal into November 1864, even as progress on the canal slowed. Eventually, the novelty of the project must have diminished, because the next set of photographs does not appear until April 1865. Figure 10.7, also taken in November, provides enough resolution to discuss some of the more interesting aspects of the geology of the canal path.

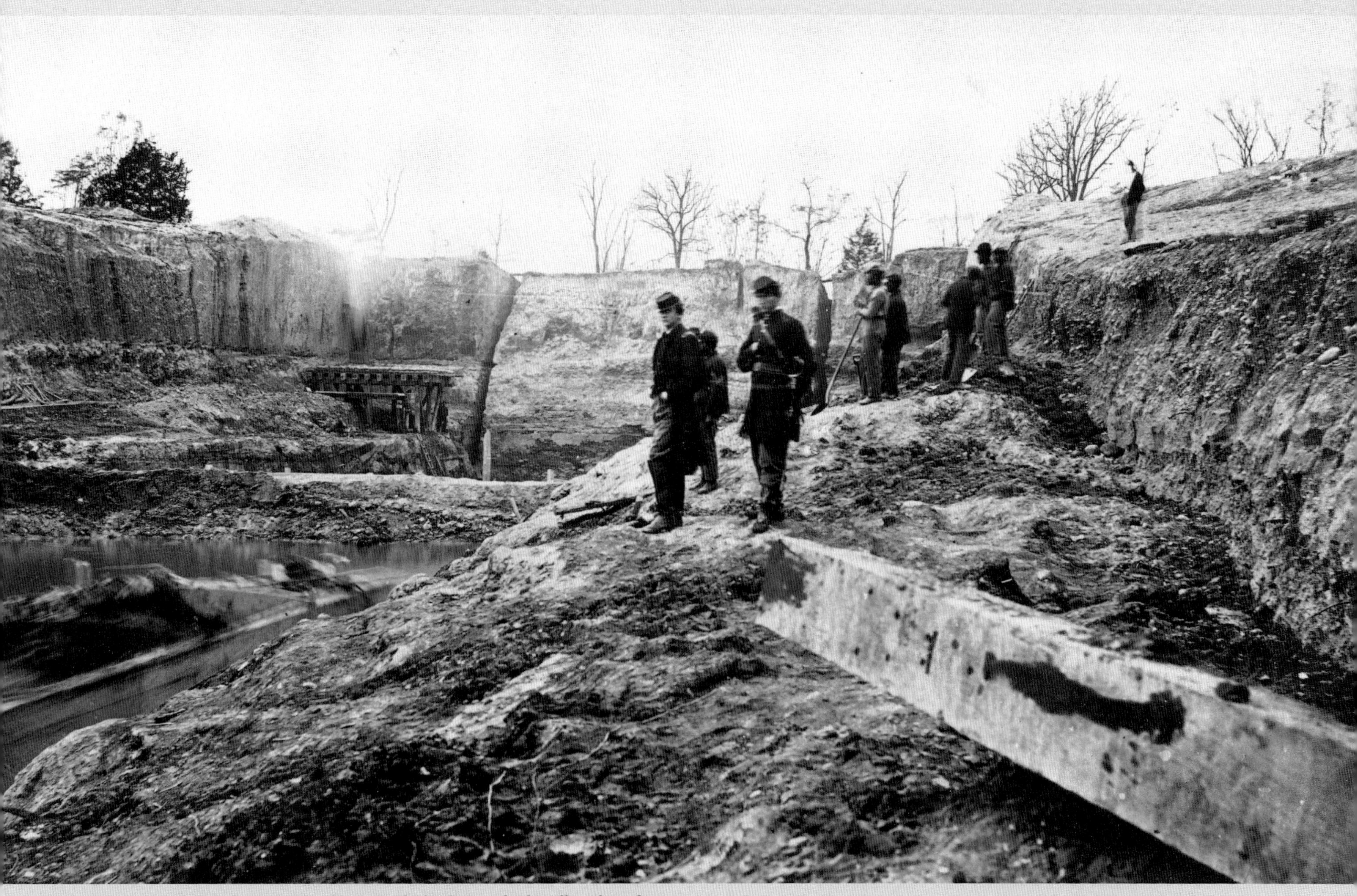

FIGURE 10.6. Another photograph with mist in the background. The officer from figure 10.5 remains, striking a similar pose to the earlier image but at a new location. Library of Congress.

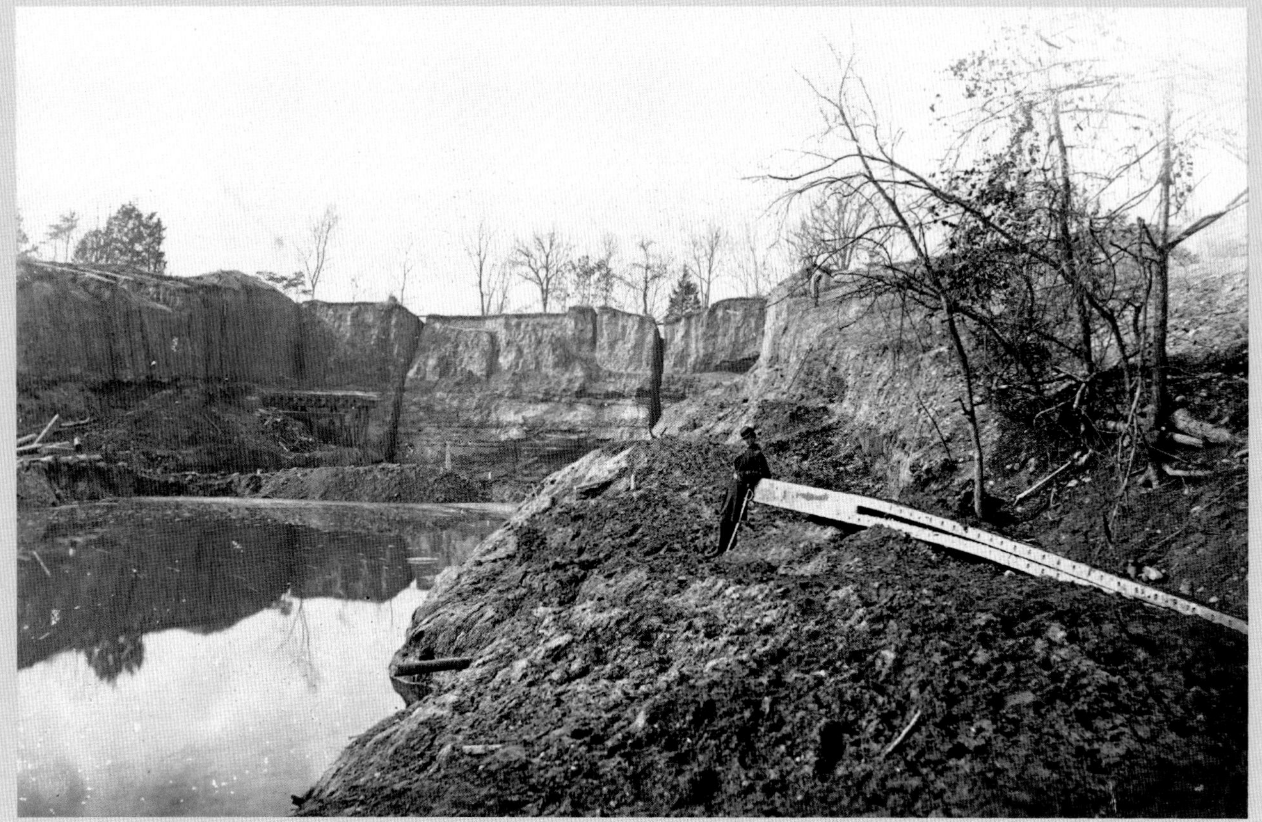

FIGURE 10.7. This photograph was taken a few weeks after figures 10.4 and 10.6, but from a similar perspective. A magnified version of this photograph is used to discuss the geology of the canal pathway. Library of Congress.

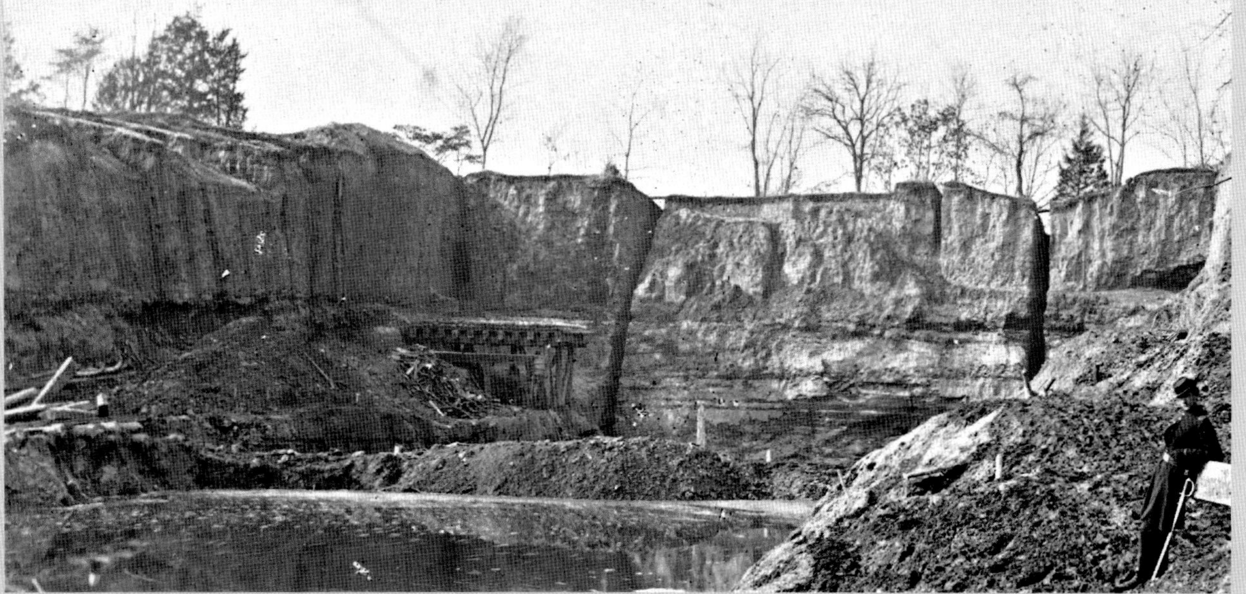

FIGURE 10.8. An enlarged view from figure 10.7 shows the geology of the canal walls. Note the distinct contact between the Potomac Formation (*bottom*) and the overlying sands and gravels from the Pleistocene Epoch, traversing horizontally across the canal just above the sandbags that cover the bombproof. Library of Congress.

The different strata present in the walls of the canal become apparent in an enlarged view of figure 10.7 (fig. 10.8).

The contact between the underlying Potomac Formation and the Pleistocene sands and gravels can be traced across the walls of the entire project. The contact is found just above the sandbags on the bombproof above the steam pump. The contact is especially apparent on the left-hand side of the photograph, where it appears as a dark horizontal line. Excavation above this line was easier than in the cohesive, clay rich strata of the Potomac.

The very hardest sediment to dig out is located just below the bomb-proof structure and it can be traced the entire way along the left wall where it is also found under the railroad ties. This layer of almost pure clay is also apparent in many other of the later photographs and it would have been very difficult to extract without a mechanical dredge. Clay is both cohesive (sticks to itself) and adhesive (sticks to everything else), so even after it is dug out it will cling to a shovel or pick, making excavation and transportation exasperating. When it gets wet, in a canal for example, it also becomes dangerously slippery. Almost any other type of sediment would be preferable for excavation.

There are two large vertical cuts to the far wall. Between these two cuts the horizontal bedding of several prominent clay layers can also be seen as they have a darker, smoother appearance compared with the clay and gravel. Strata with a large amount of clay are difficult to extract, as was seen with the famous Federal tunnel into the Crater at Petersburg. However, once it is extracted the remaining clay is usually cohesive enough that it will form vertical walls and tunnels or pits cut into it won't need as much structural reinforcement to avoid collapsing. This is why US soldiers were able to dig effective subterranean shelters into the sides of the canal sediments for protection from enemy artillery fire (fig. 10.9).

This analysis of the layers of sediment in the canal provides a good opportunity to revisit how science, and in this case stratigraphy (the study of layered rock) can enhance both the context of an old photograph and provide historical insights. For example, the sequencing of sand and gravel above clay suggests that Federal sappers underestimated the difficulty of completing this project. At first, the younger sediments would have been easy to dig through and remove, but when the older clay layers were encountered, they proved especially resistant to excavation. They did, however, allow for the construction of effective bombproofs along the canal walls.

These bombproofs were cut into the eastern side of the meander cliffs to avoid the Confederate artillery fire from the south and southwest. They are also visible on the left side of William Waud's action sketch of the canal (fig. 10.10), and the sketch illustrates the location of the bombproofs relative to the open face of the canal walls. Similar dwellings were seen at Vicksburg, when US soldiers carved protected areas out of the mildly cohesive silt (loess) along their lines, forming "Prairie Dog villages" (fig. 2.1, bottom center).[12]

When exposed in a cross section like a canal wall, sedimentary strata take on the striped appearance of an upright bar code, with layer after layer of varying thickness and shade. The addition of vertical cuts and fixed anthropogenic structures makes matching perspectives between a series of photographs relatively simple. Figures 10.11—10.14 show the progression of the canal work from October 1864 until April 1865. The canal was blown open in the intervening January, but with only limited success. A faulty fuse and wet powder were partly to blame, as was the nature of the geology. The clay-rich layer at the base of the canal largely negated much of the power of the explosion of the mine in the coffer wall, causing the sediment to fall back into place in the canal bed. Had the detonation been set off in sediment from higher in the strata, like the Pleistocene sands and gravels, the effect would have been much greater. Instead, the cohesive mud of the Potomac Formation limited the spread of the sediment. Only ships with a very shallow draft could traverse the new and narrow waterway and these could only do so under the barrels of new Confederate artillery that had been brought in to rake the west end of the canal. Thus the "boondoggle,"

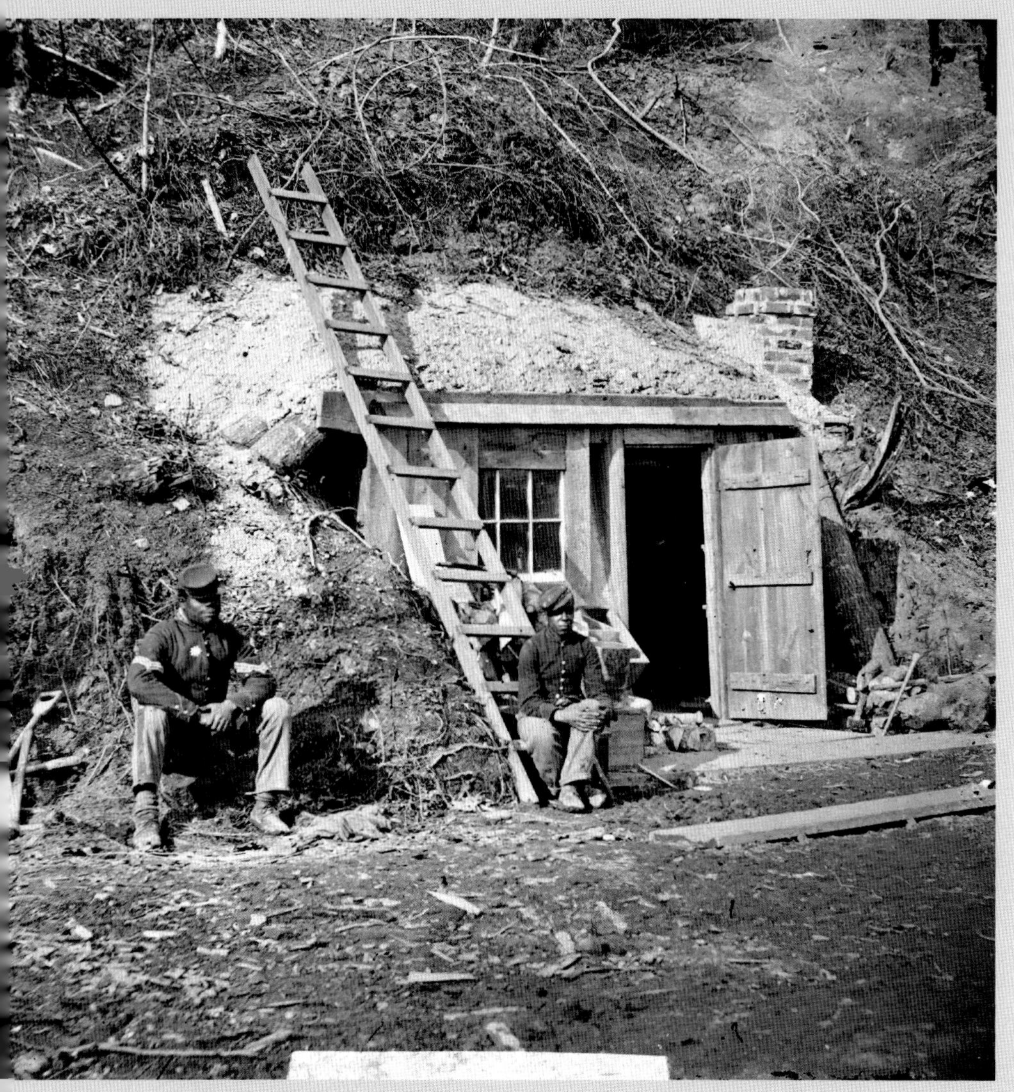

FIGURE 10.9. Two African American soldiers pose in front of a bombproof at Dutch Gap Canal in late 1864. Library of Congress.

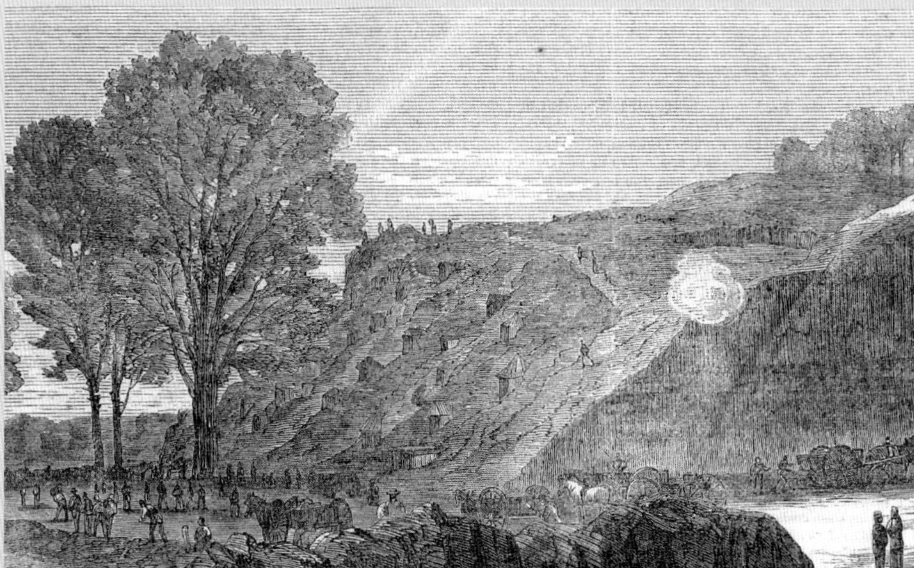

FIGURE 10.10. Detail from figure 10.5 showing the bombproof residences carved into the sand, silt and (mostly) clay sediments of the bluffs of the James River. The open digging of the canal is to the right, the James would be to the left. Library of Congress.

as the canal wasted a tremendous amount of manpower and never allowed the passage of a single military vessel until after the war was over.

There are several items that appear in each of the figures included in figure 10.11 that allow the precise perspective of each individual photograph to be determined. The first, indicated with the letter "L," is a series of ladders that were used to reach the next higher level of the canal. The number of ladders and exact location change over the months, but for the most part they remain in the same general position on the right of each photograph. The second fixed item does not move at all and is a bit of a mystery. It appears to be a broken portion of a wheelbarrow or wagon or possibly part of a hitch. It is indicated in each photograph with the letter "W" to help orient the viewer. A third fixed item appears approximately one-third of the way through the series, just as water is advancing into the canal. This item, designated with an "M," is probably some sort of anchoring system or mooring for boats (or a dredge) in the canal. Similar structures show up late in the series and appear to be used in this manner. With these three tracers identified in each photograph, the viewer can better appreciate the progress of the digging of the canal through time.

The proper sequencing of the photographs, including several that were taken within a month of each other, can be accomplished by using the progress of the canal and the appearance and disappearance of the fixed tracers in each photograph. Notice, for example, the wagon fragment ("W") is found in ten of the first eleven photographs, but it disappears in the final shot. The mooring ("M"), in contrast, is present in the final eight photographs, but not in the first three (no need for a mooring until the canal water has advanced to this point). The ladders ("L") along the right side of the canal were needed through the first seven photographs but are absent from the final four.

Figure 10.15 illustrates one portion of the far wall/bulkhead through time, documenting the results of the January 1865 explosion to open the canal. Vertical cuts through this portion of the dam, in a direction parallel to the axis of the canal, demonstrate that the blast that was designed to open

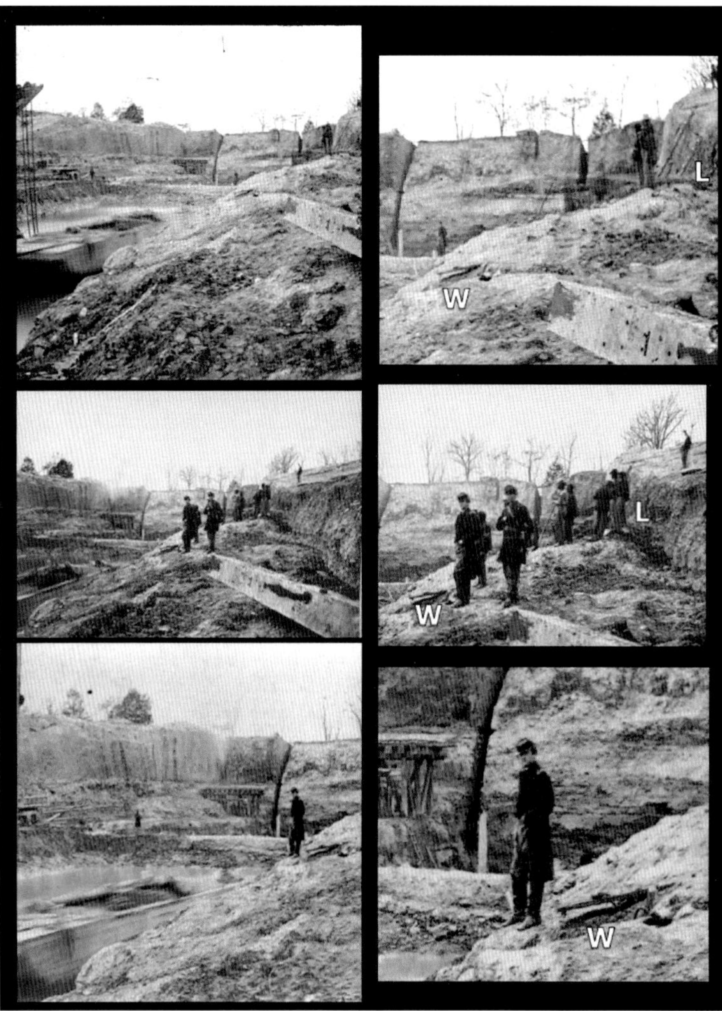

FIGURE 10.11. Dutch Gap Canal in late fall 1864. Each of these views is taken from approximately the same perspective. Detail of each photograph (*right*) shows stationary items that demonstrate the photographs are taken from approximately the same location. Note the solitary, upright shovel (*top right, between "W" and "L"*), which is then used as a prop in the second photograph (*second photograph, right*). Library of Congress.

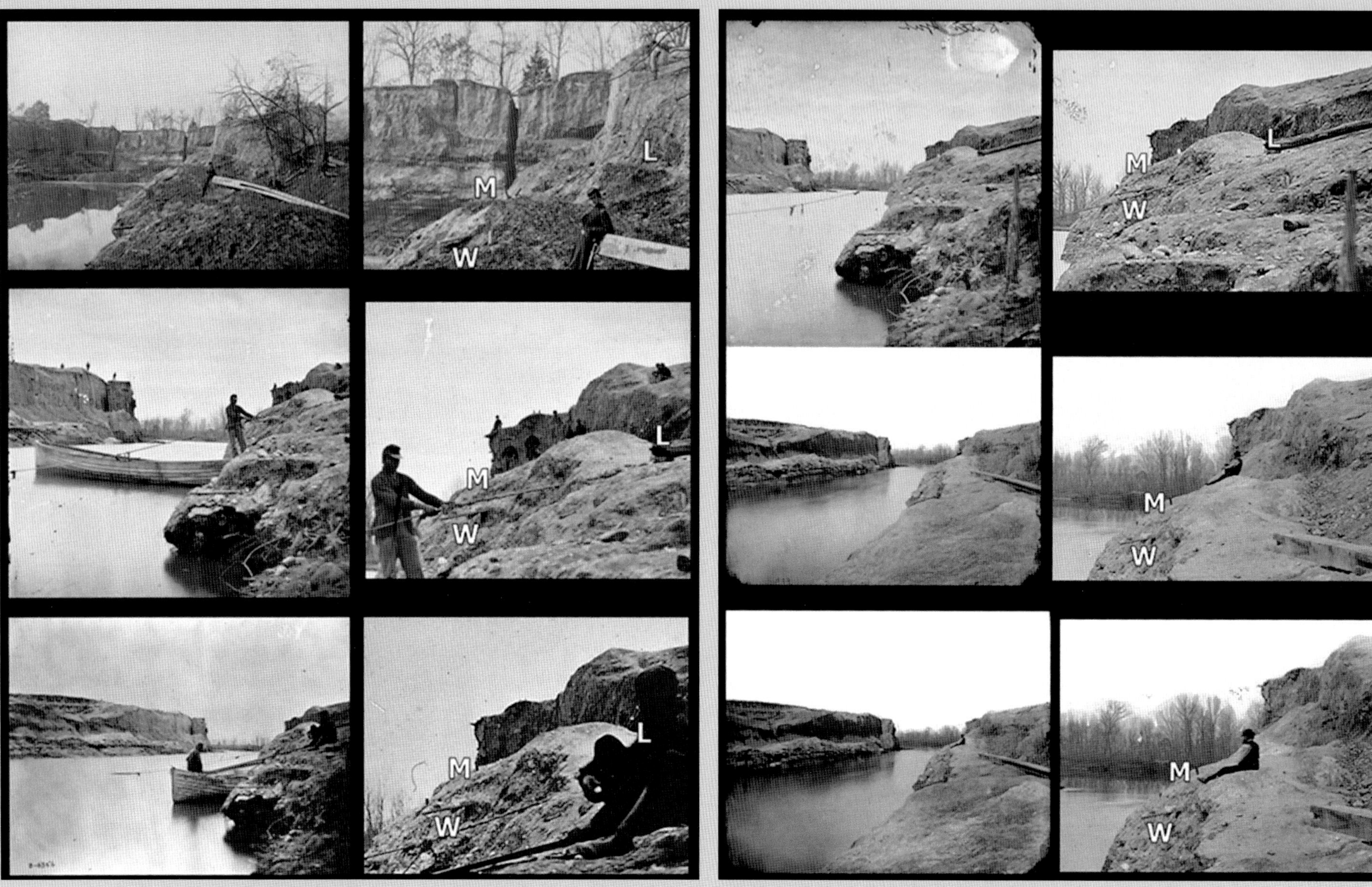

FIGURE 10.12. Progression of Dutch Gap Canal from November 1864 (*top*) to April 1865 (*middle, bottom*), during which the canal path was unsuccessfully blasted open. Note that the wagon "W," ladder "L," and mooring "M" are visible in each image even though they were taken several months apart. Library of Congress.

FIGURE 10.13. Three more views of Dutch Gap Canal from April 1865. Sequencing of these three photographs is possible because of the removal of the ladders (*right side of photograph, present in top view, absent in subsequent views*). Library of Congress.

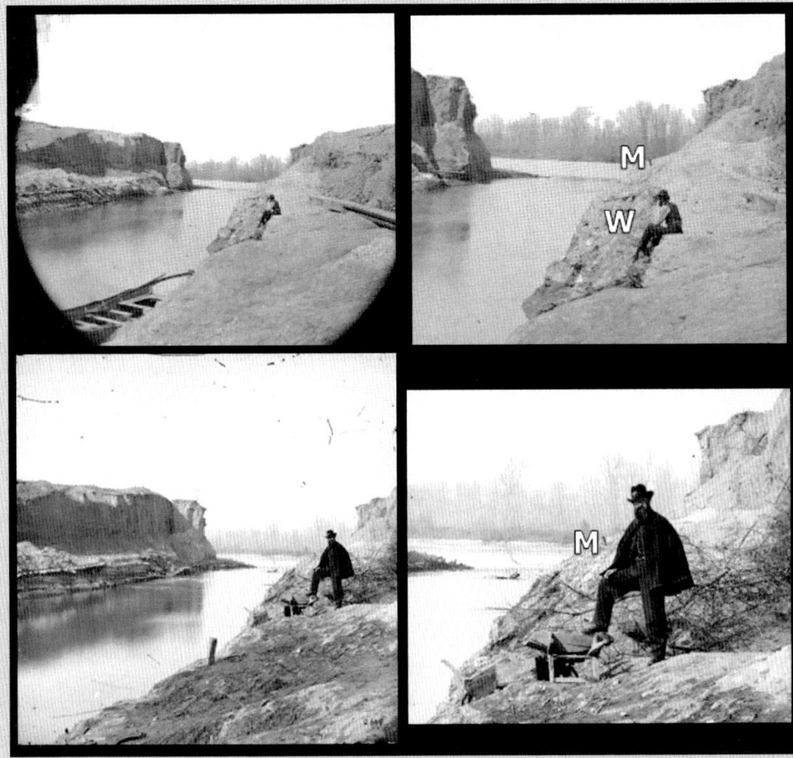

FIGURE 10.14. Two final views of Dutch Gap Canal from the spring of 1865. Note that only the mooring remains in the final shot. Library of Congress.

the canal was intended to remove this portion of the sedimentary strata as well. After the canal was "completed," this unstable portion of the canal wall continued to erode and would eventually crumble into the James.

The two groupings of photographs, one taken in October and November of 1864 and a second taken in April 1865, are divided in figure 10.15 between images 6 and 7. This lapse in time also includes the date of the explosion under the western bulkhead to attempt to open the canal in January 1865. This blast wasn't powerful enough to dislodge the clay-rich sediment of the Potomac Formation and completely alter the path of the James River through the canal, but it was strong enough to create vertical seismic fractures in what was left of the western wall (fig. 10.16). From a geological perspective, an enlarged view of figure 10.15 (image 9) indicates several interesting features that helped determine the fate of the project.

The original width of the planned canal was intended to be wider than that which was produced by the explosion of the mines. The vertical cut that is so prominent in figures 10.15 and 10.16 was the intended edge of the canal after the bulkheads were blasted, but this didn't materialize with the weakened, clay-muffled blast. Instead, a portion of the final bulkhead remained upright, if vertically fractured. To a geologist, this blast and removal of sediment is reminiscent of a meteorite impact. Immediately after a large impact the crater that is formed (the "transient crater") is deep with a sharp, vertical perimeter. Shortly thereafter, the crater begins to transition into a shallower crater with more gently sloping walls because of slumping along the overly steep crater walls. The same is true with the Dutch Gap Canal: the remaining fractured block that the soldier in figure 10.16 is standing on would soon begin to slump towards the canal, requiring additional dredging to remove the material from the canal bed. The rate of this erosion would also be increased by the vertical fractures (planes of weakness) in the block of sediment. In most circumstances this mass wasting would be increased by the rapid erosion of the James River along the base of the canal walls, but the cohesive clay at the water's edge probably minimized this additional potential catalyst.

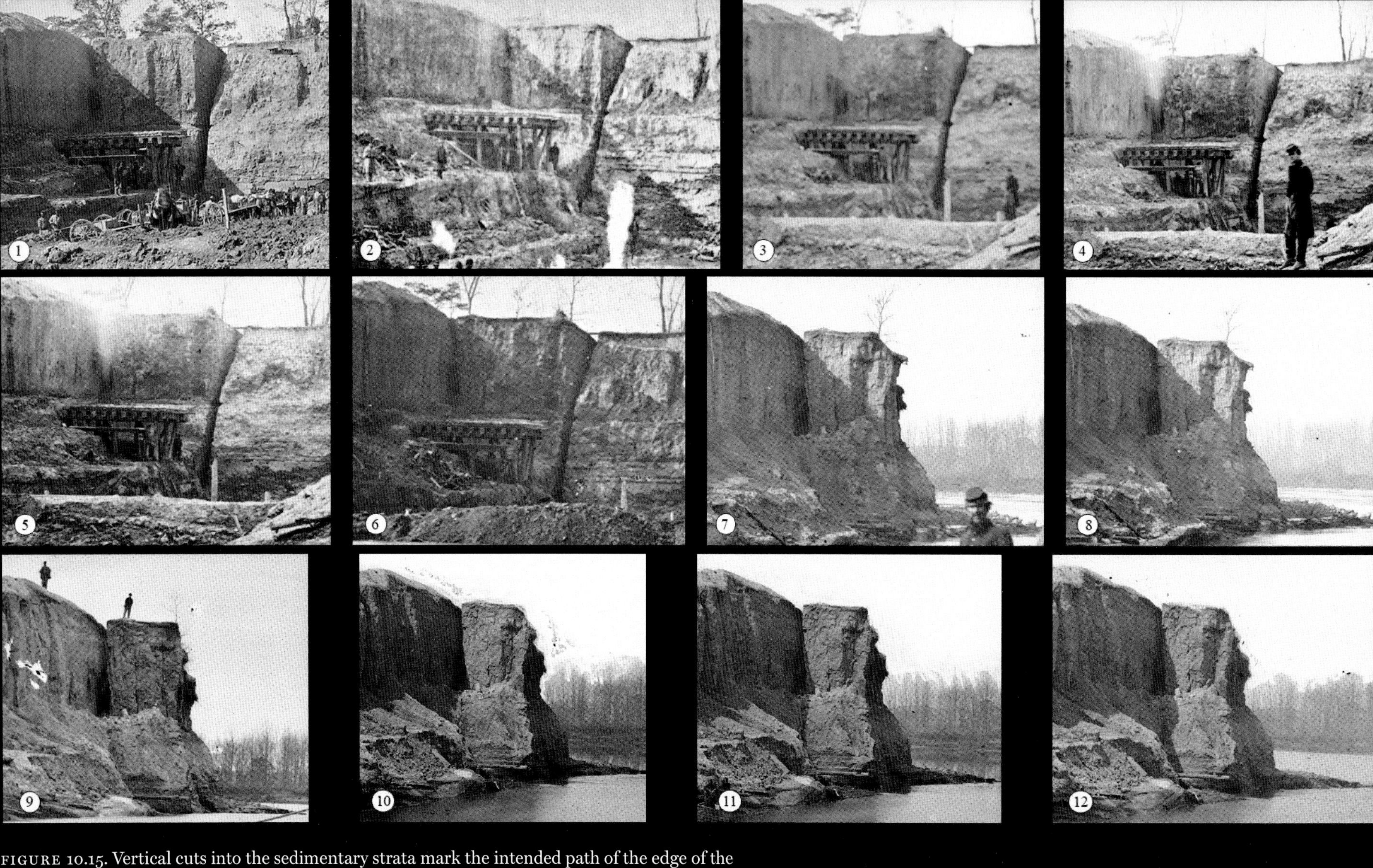

FIGURE 10.15. Vertical cuts into the sedimentary strata mark the intended path of the edge of the canal. The inadequate power of the black powder explosion, likely compressed and suppressed by the cohesive nature of the clay at the bottom of the canal, resulted in a failure to dislodge the leftmost layers of sediment in the bulkhead. Eventually, weathering, erosion, and gravity would cause this material to disintegrate into the river below. Library of Congress.

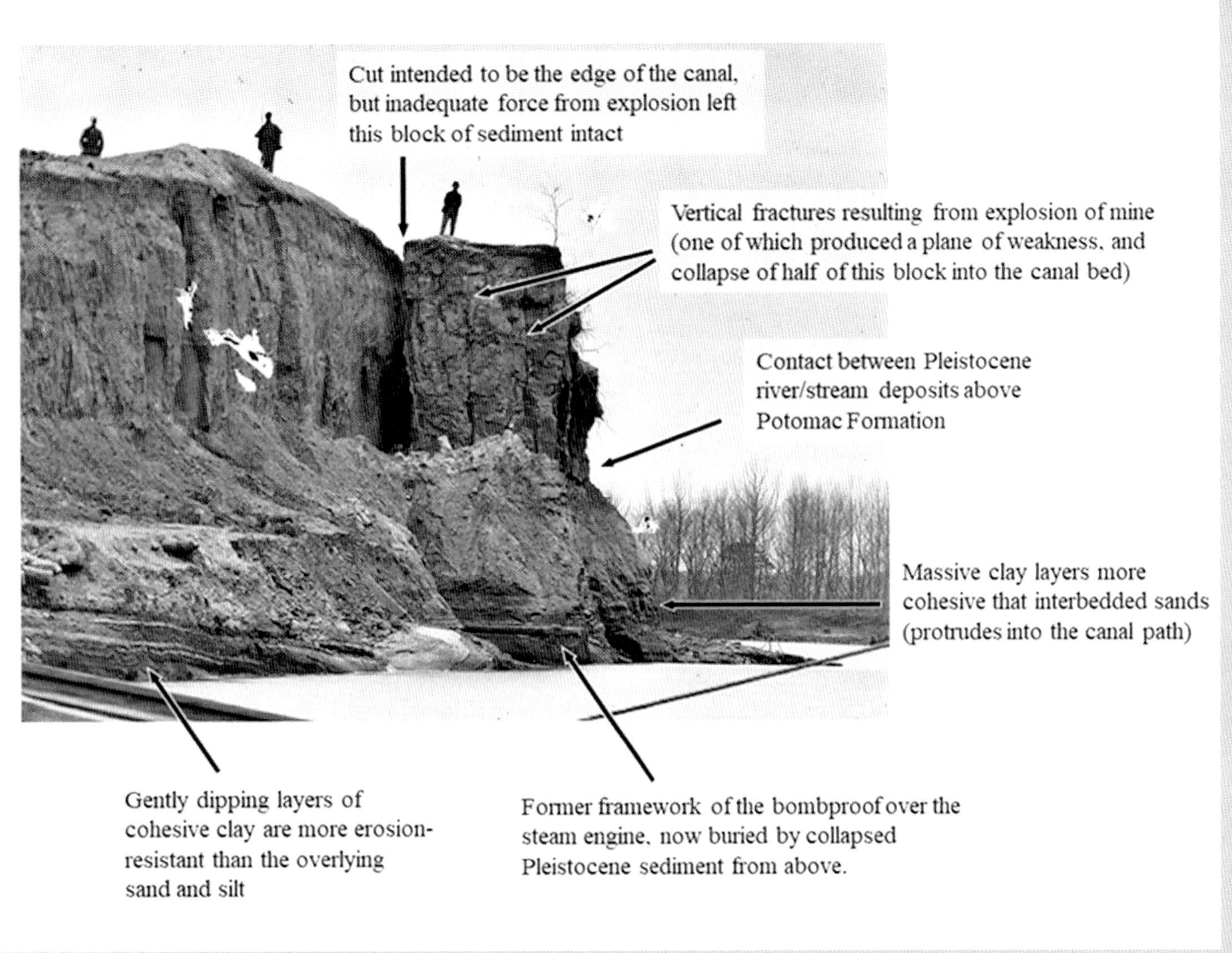

FIGURE 10.16. The sedimentology and stratigraphy of the material that the Dutch Gap Canal was excavated through helped to assure the worthlessness of the endeavor, from a tactical perspective. Library of Congress.

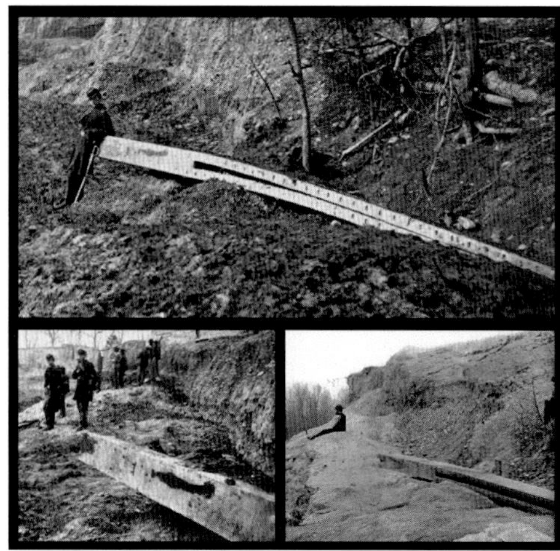

FIGURE 10.17. The mystery apparatus is clearly some type of mechanical device. It appears in at least six of the photographs of the canal, always discarded in the same approximate location. While it is always found in the same general position along the northern edge of the canal wall, it does change orientation slightly between November 1864 and April 1865. Library of Congress.

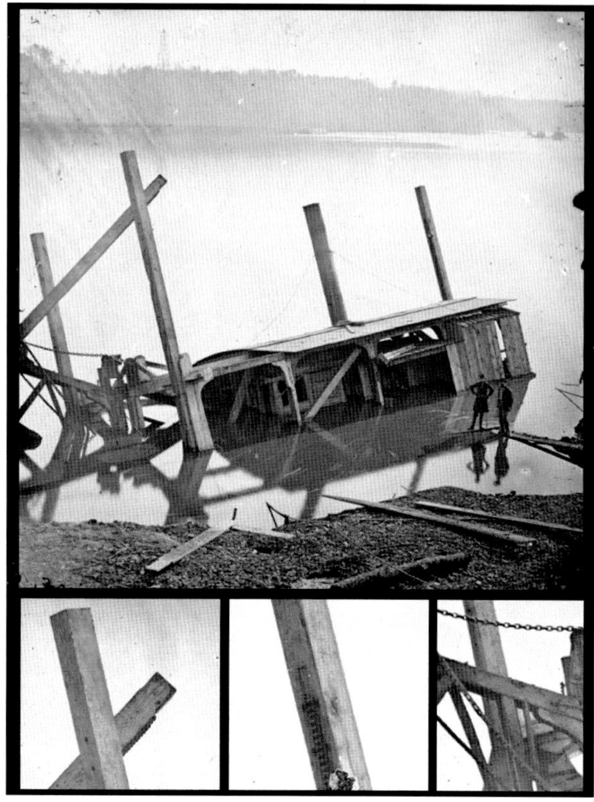

FIGURE 10.18. One half of a stereo pair titled "James River, Va. Butler's dredge-boat, sunk by a Confederate shell on Thanksgiving Day, 1864." Metal grooves are attached to the wooden posts in the left and center detail, and a split in the post is evident in the right detail. One "leg" or support of the dredge appears to be missing (*right corner*). Note the observation tower across the river. Library of Congress.

Two final curiosities arise from this series of photographs. First, what is the unusual apparatus that is seen on the right of so many of the photographs? It is clearly part of a mechanical device that has calibration on one side and metal ridges or teeth on another (fig. 10.17).

Careful inspection of all the photographs taken from the Dutch Gap region reveals an interesting image of the wrecked dredge from the canal. Two parts of this dredge boat, probably used for stabilization and to determine water and digging depth, show a similar shape and configuration (fig. 10.18).

A second question that arises from these series of photographs is where the camera was positioned, and why this position was chosen for 75 percent of the photographs taken of the interior of the canal. The canal digging commenced along the eastern bend of the meander peninsula and worked towards the west. Hand digging was used along the western wall, and the canal was deepened below the water line in the clay with mechanical dredges. The popular camera position (fig. 10.19) was located along the northeastern extension of the canal, where the work first commenced. This location provided a moderately high perspective of the digging and offered two advantages for the photographers. First, it was as far as possible from Confederate artillery. Second, based on the orientation of the canal and the direction of digging, it allowed the opposite wall of the canal to often be free of shadows and exposed to direct sunlight during most of the day, even during the late fall and early spring. This was important at a time when exposures were difficult to calibrate. Note that in several of the later photographs the developer of the photographs used darkroom manipulation to eliminate the sky above the canal's walls—this is especially evident when studying the trees on the opposite side of the canal (see, e.g., fig. 10.15, image 10).

This camera position also offers two other more subtle advantages for the photographer. First, positioning the camera on the opposite side of the canal at a similar location would have been too close to the rail line that was being used to transport overburden. This might have provided an obstruction or, if the rail cars were in action, vibration that would have ruined the negatives. A second advantage of the selected position is related to sedimentary geology. This elevation along the canal wall probably coincides with the contact between the overlying Pleistocene sands and gravels and the underlying clay-rich Potomac Formation. For a camera with a large tripod, the latter material would be much more preferable for a stable shooting position.

After the war, there were two dissimilar, yet positive, outcomes to Butler's boondoggle, one related to transportation and one to, of all things, paleontology. The canal did make travel up the James River more efficient, in a small way helping Richmond recover financially after the war. The construction of the canal, and the excavation into the Potomac Formation, also revealed a new fossil locality that produced some *extremely* old plant fossils. One of these, *Potomacapnos apeleutheron* dates to the Early Cretaceous (125 million years ago), and is one of the earliest forms of flowering plants ever discovered in North America. The genus and species names, *Potomacapnos apeleutheron*, also have an interesting significance. The generic designation obviously delineates the geologic formation where the fossil was discovered, but the latter, *apeleutheron* was selected to honor the men whose relentless labor created the canal—"apeleutheron" is the Greek term for freedmen.

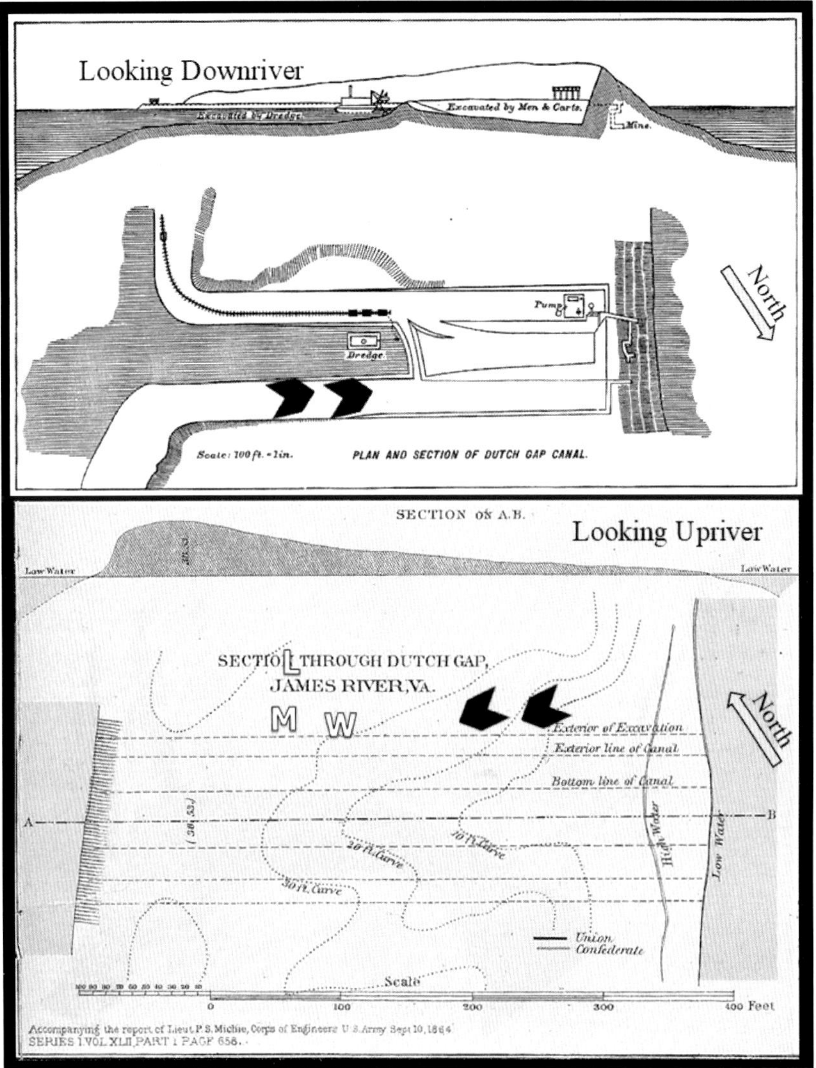

FIGURE 10.19. Most of the photographs of the interior of the Dutch Gap Canal were taken from the same relative position on the northeastern side of the works. This location, indicated with two arrows, provided a flat, slightly elevated position to capture the progress of the work. "W," "M," and "W" are the location of fixed references seen in figures 10.11–10.14 (details). Library of Congress.

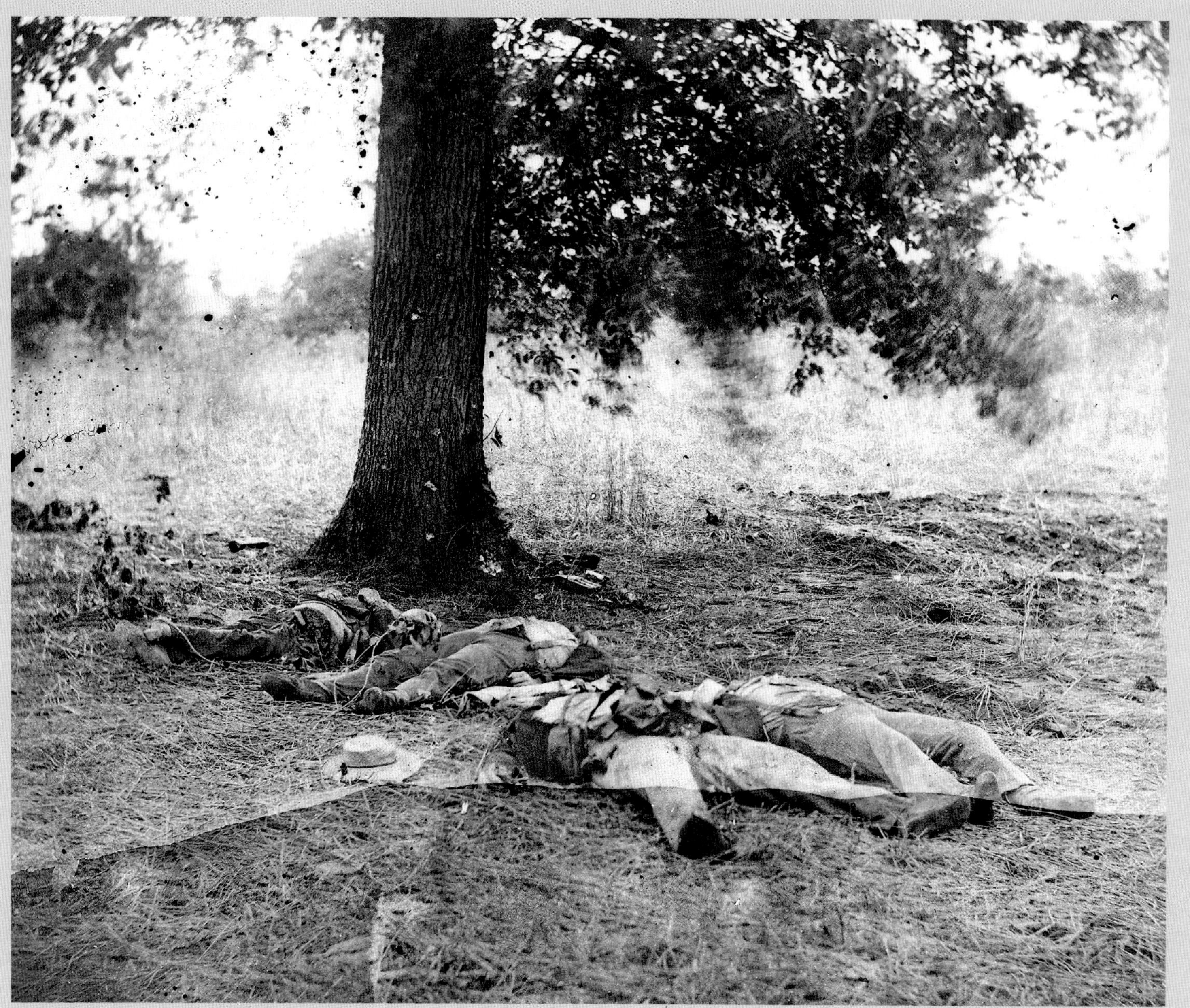

FIGURE 11.1. The dead soldier to the far left has a massive lower torso wound that is similar to that suffered by his comrade who died on a nearby field. This photograph was taken by Timothy O'Sullivan under the direction of Alexander Gardner. Library of Congress.

CHAPTER 11

Photographing Damnation and Hell

The most graphic image from our top twenty-five list of most popular photographs was undoubtedly Gardner's picture of a gut-torn Confederate soldier on the Rose Farm at Gettysburg (fig. 2.1; detail in 11.2, below). Timothy O'Sullivan captured this image two or three days after the battle ended and Alexander Gardner gave it the caption "War, effect of a Shell on a Confederate soldier at Battle of Gettysburg" in his September 1863 catalog. The implied cause of death is strongly supported by compositional elements of the gruesome photograph, complete with an artillery shell and the massive, gaping abdominal wound produced by the bolt.[1]

Alan Trachtenberg suggests that Gardner's own camera betrayed him when composing this photograph:

> The Civil War camera disclosed debris strewn about, weary men, slovenly uniforms—soldiers not as heroes but as soldiers. The very advantage of the camera suggested a liability. What the photograph depicted originated, as everyone understood, in the world itself, not in the imagination—even if objects must be moved to realize the photographer's intention. This becomes a liability when the staging of scenes, even scenes of death, suggests the photographer's desire to satisfy a need (his own and his audience's) for order, even that of theatricality.[2]

The orientation of the dead and the amount of battlefield debris randomly scattered across the fighting ground in *A Harvest of Death* suggests authenticity; in Gardner's photograph of the eviscerated rebel, everything is proportional and appears too neatly composed.

William Frassanito argued persuasively that this horrifying injury was produced by a combination of battle wound and later feasting by wild hogs.[3] He produced two lines of reasoning to support his hypothesis, including a postwar account by a Federal soldier who had been wounded during the second day's fighting at Gettysburg, after which he spent a night fighting off "stray hogs" of "enormous size."[4] As a second piece of evidence of predation by pigs, Frassanito pointed to a second photograph of dead Confederates awaiting burial on the same fields (fig. 11.1). The soldier on the left has a similar gaping wound to the lower abdomen.

Suppose for the moment that Gardner's captions were correct (the second destroyed corpse was also described as the product of US artillery fire). Had the wounds been created by an artillery bolt (solid shot), we would expect to see a mangled wound with strips of torn flesh. Had the wound been created by an exploding shell, the torso would have been blasted apart, with flesh showing signs of tearing as it expanded or was blown to pieces. The photographs indicate neither scenario was the likely cause of the massive wound. Instead, the flesh appears as if it has been carefully trimmed, almost in a systematic manner (fig. 11.2). The gouged appearance of the wound suggests predation by creatures with relatively small, but non-serrated teeth (this isn't a "clean" cut or slice into flesh like a shark might produce).

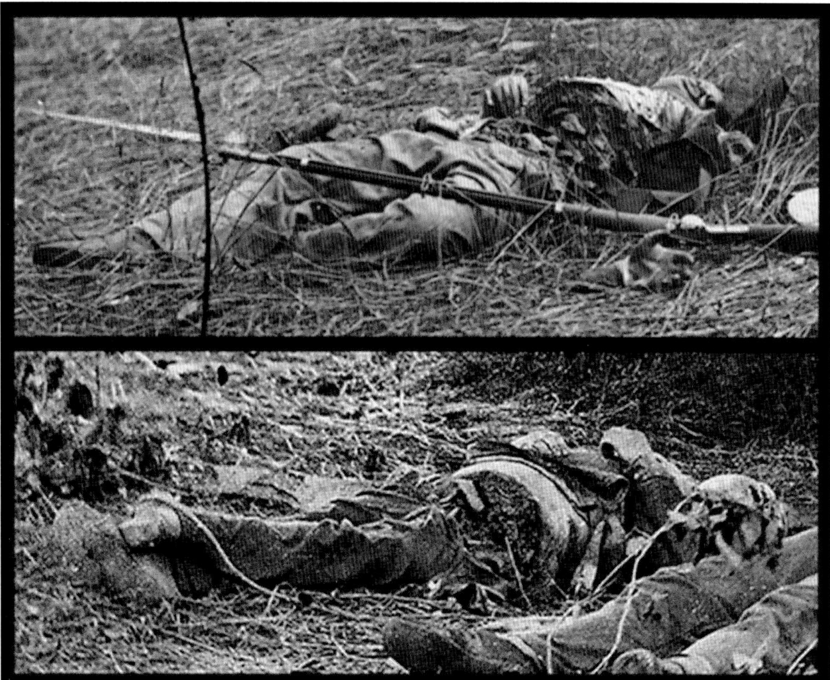

FIGURE 11.2. A comparison of the lower-abdomen wounds to two men who were (presumably) found only a short distance from each other on the southern Gettysburg Battlefield. At an initial glance they might be mistaken for the same corpse, who has been gathered for burial in the second photograph, however, only one of the bodies still has both arms intact. Library of Congress.

Note that of the hundred or so "combat" photographs that were studied for this book, including all those reproduced herein, these are the only two pictures showing this type of wound. None of the photographs of the dead at Spotsylvania, Antietam, or Petersburg have such a large and gaping wound. All of these battles had significant casualties caused by artillery, but no similar wounds were created; nonetheless, not all of these battlegrounds had roving hogs on the field immediately after the sun set on the day of battle, a horrifying spectacle reported at Gettysburg.[5]

Wound Forensics at Petersburg

Frassanito believed that the disembowel and dismembered soldier at Gettysburg was "unquestionably the most gruesome photograph of a battlefield corpse to be recorded during the entire war."[6] Much of the rest of this chapter is dedicated to assessing, and perhaps challenging, this statement. Some of the photographs by Thomas Roche in the trenches of Petersburg, for example, are just as disturbing and graphic—the primary difference is that they have not been reproduced in the literature as often and the viewer must look a bit more closely to see the dreadful gore.

Regardless of these photographers' photojournalistic motives, there was clearly an economic motivation for taking many of the photographs of the dead. Shocking and disturbing photographs garner attention, as Gardner learned after his photographs of the dead at Antietam were displayed at Brady's New York City gallery.[7] It is no wonder then that when he and O'Sullivan and Gibson arrived at Gettysburg, they did not seek out key battle sites or landmarks, they focused on the dead in the field. And, if groups of dead soldiers had proven popular with the general public, what would happen if their negatives showed both the horror of war and the true carnage? His photograph of the dead Confederate with the isolated hand and missing arm might have been taken from any angle, but he and O'Sullivan specifically chose the perspective that drew attention to the massive wound. He then composed the rest of the photograph—artillery shell, hand, canteen, and rifle with bayonet—to complete his composite.

Thomas Roche's photographs from the trenches of Petersburg are every bit as graphic, if not more so. No photographs exist from the Petersburg front lines for the second half of 1864 or the winter and early spring of 1865. As Grant's siege line extended to the west, the photographers didn't really have any safe place to set up their tripod and camera. Sniper fire and cold weather do not work well with the slow wet emulsion process for procuring negatives.[8]

During the first week of April 1865, Roche was at City Point with fellow photographer Andrew Russell when he caught word that the Federal forces were preparing a massive attack across the Confederate lines. He immediately started west in hopes of arriving on a fresh battlefield, and he was successful.

Roche and his assistant must have worked at a very high rate of productivity on April 3 as they raced the Federal burial crews in the trenches, because they produced twenty-two negatives of the dead where they had fallen. Of all the most gruesome images captured by the photographers, one stands apart as to the terrible wound inflicted upon the unfortunate soldier (fig. 11.3). A magnified view of the top of this man's head reveals the cause of his instantaneous death: the top of his skull has essentially been removed by a Minié ball or artillery fragment. A pistol round or bayonet thrust simply would not have had the energy necessary to cause this magnitude of damage.

A magnified view of the terrible wound reveals a few disturbing details (fig. 11.4). At the bottom of the enlarged view on the left, what appears to be a tuft of hair, and corresponding skull fragment, is lying in the mud. The size and shape of this dark object appears to match the gaping hole in the skull. If this is in fact the ejected portion of the man's skull, one must consider the possibility that Roche or his assistant placed the object closer to the dead man's head in a manner similar to what Gardner et al. are suspected to have done with the hand of the disgorged rebel at Gettysburg.

The greatly magnified view (fig. 11.4, right) shows that the skull was not simply fragmented with a portion ejected; instead, the edges of the skull do not align as it has been so traumatically damaged that the outer portions of the cranium no longer join together. The rear fracture (towards the back of the head) appears to correspond to the coronal suture, an area that runs from ear-to-ear on the skull that connects the two rearward parietal bones to the frontal bone of the skull. This suture allows the skull to expand and grow in young children and also represents an area of inherent structural weakness.

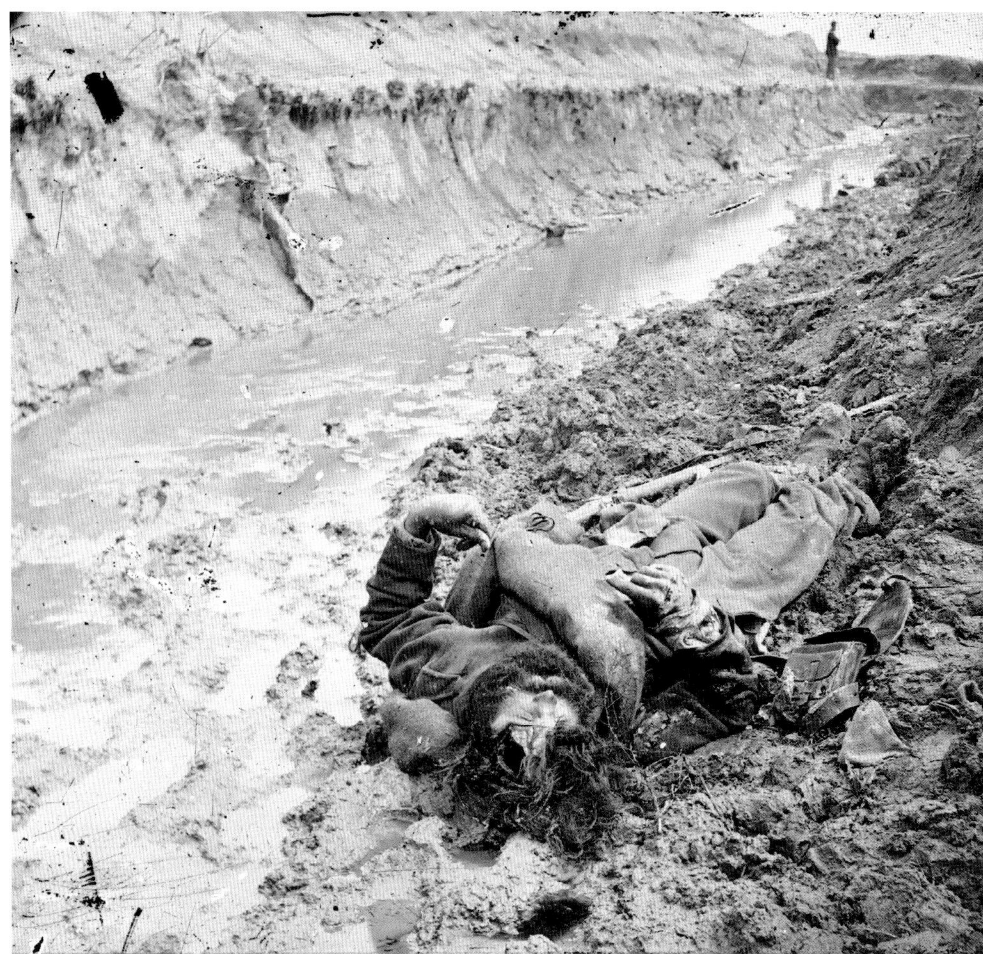

FIGURE 11.3. This dead Confederate infantryman suffered a ghastly wound to the forehead. Thomas Roche took this photograph on April 3, 1865, the day after the Confederates retreated through Petersburg. Library of Congress.

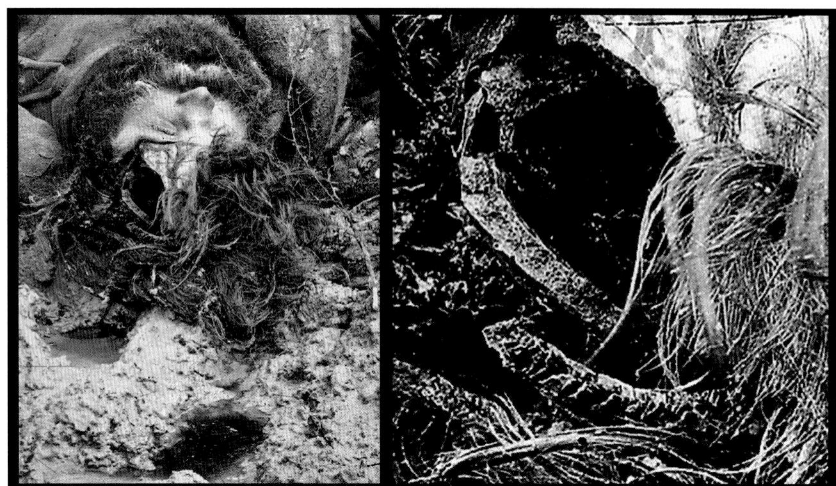

FIGURE 11.4. Two enlargements of the dead soldier's head from figure 11.4 reveal the exposed and fractured skull. In the image to the left, this oval fragment at the bottom of the detail may be the displaced skull fragment. Library of Congress.

The extreme enlargement also reveals the spongy diploë bone material (as seen by the small holes or pores on the surface of the skull fractures). This type of bone material fills in between the more compact and harder outer and inner layers of skull bone, and in conjunction all three layers offer a greater degree of protection from impact—with the exception being an artillery round.

The magnitude of the wound assures that this man died instantaneously and suffered little. In stark contrast to this is the mortally wounded Confederate in figure 11.5. Here we see one of the worst of all types of wounds, a shot or slice to the abdomen that exposes or spills the intestines but probably doesn't bring immediate death. Injured and in great pain, as his posture suggests, he suffered for some time before succumbing to the shock and loss of blood. Of all the death studies to emerge from the Civil War, this is the most disturbing and disheartening: A disemboweled soldier, lying barefoot in the slop of the muddy trenches, has his innards

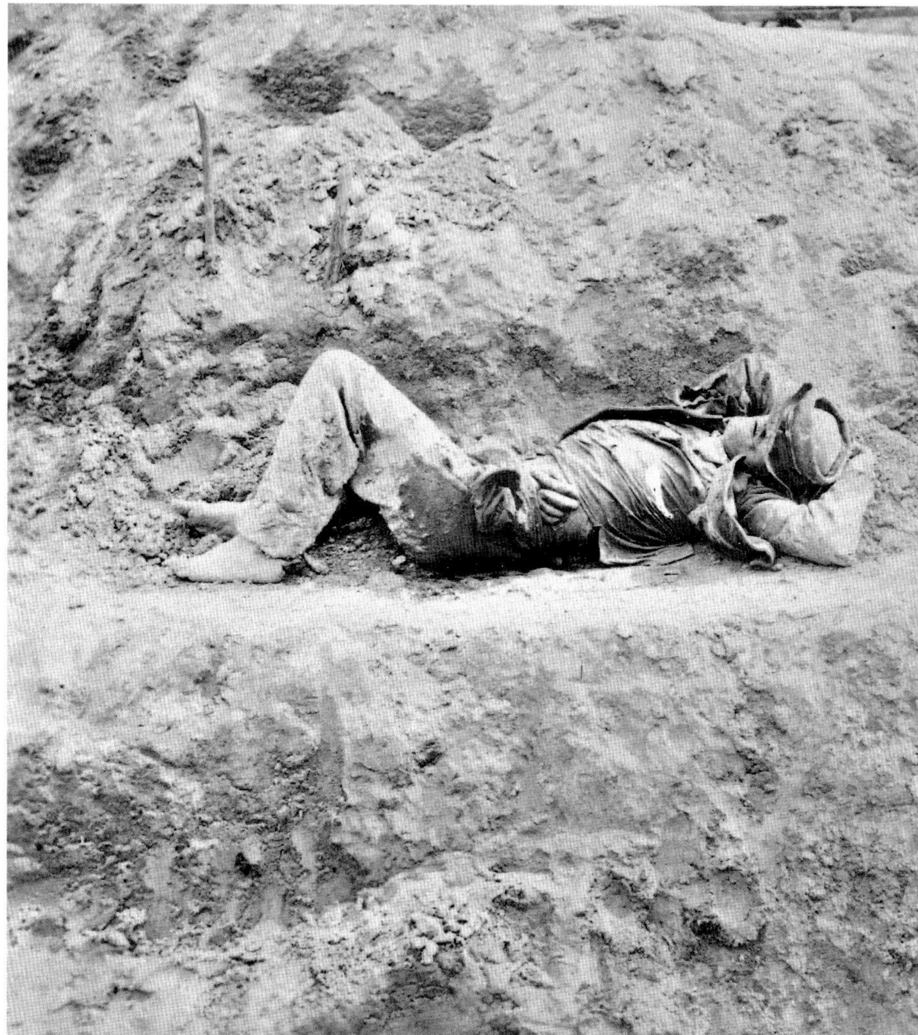

FIGURE 11.5. This Confederate suffered a wound to the lower torso that left his intestines exposed. Library of Congress.

 CHAPTER 11

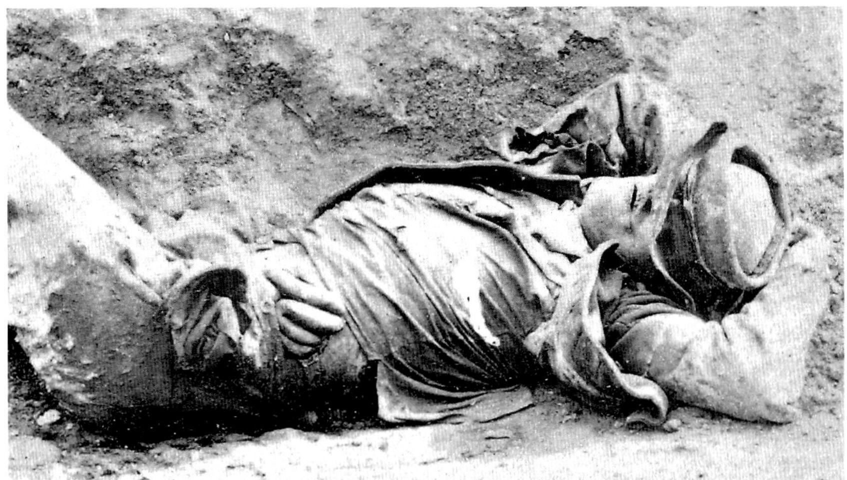

FIGURE 11.6. Compare this abdominal wound to the two photographed by Gardner and his team at Gettysburg (fig. 11.2). Library of Congress.

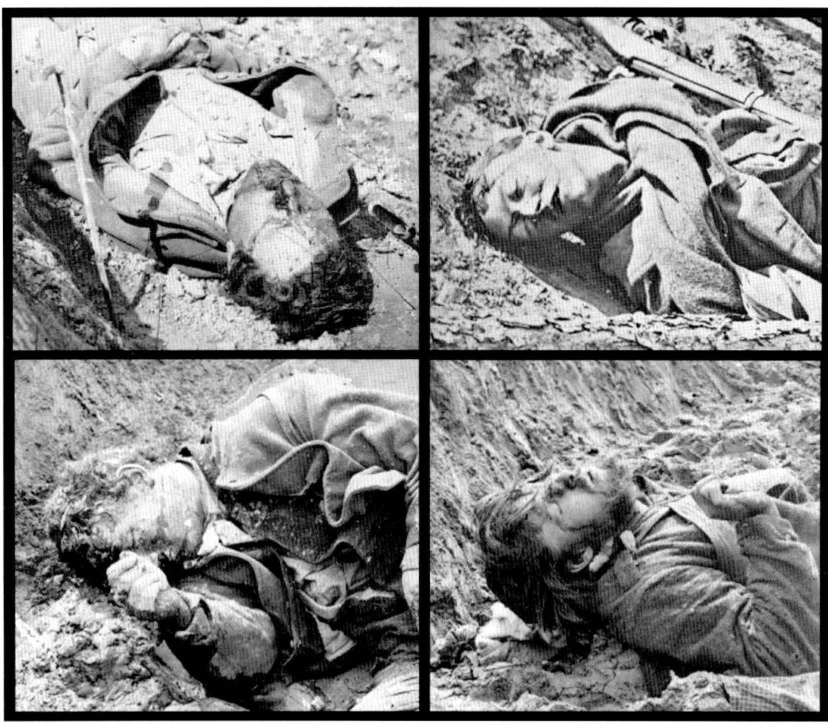

FIGURE 11.7. Of the twenty-two photographs of dead soldiers taken by Thomas Roche at Petersburg, eight show evidence of bleeding from the mouth and nose. The photograph in the upper right was one of the twenty-five most popular photographs to emerge from the Civil War. Library of Congress.

exposed as he slowly dies, all while knowing the cause that he fights for is clearly already lost.

It is hard to imagine how the hat on this poor soldier stayed on top of his head as he suffered with the wound. A magnified view (fig. 11.6) clearly shows the pooled blood around the fissure that exposes his small intestine. The nature of this wound to his lower torso, when compared with those photographed at Gettysburg by Gardner and his crew (fig. 11.2), seems to bolster the argument that the dead at Gettysburg were fed upon by feral hogs.

Many of the dead photographed at Petersburg show evidence of bleeding from the nose and mouth, suggesting a head or upper torso wound (fig. 11.7). There are two ways of calculating what percentage of the dead suffered from this type of wound. If we concentrate only on the photographs where the dead soldier's face is clearly visible, around 50 percent of the images show evidence of head or upper torso injury. If we concentrate on the entire collection, there is blood present on the faces of eight soldiers, and the other fourteen photographs show no evidence of blood on the face, although in many cases the face is obscured. This leaves us with between 35 and 50 percent of the soldiers in the trenches dying of upper body wounds.

This is a seemingly very high figure, considering that most statistical compilations of Civil War wounds state that upwards of 75 percent of all wounds are to the extremities, with only around 10 percent occurring to the head or neck. One might be tempted to surmise that the unusually high number of cases of head and neck trauma at Petersburg is the result of the nature of the fighting—combat in trenches often results in wounds

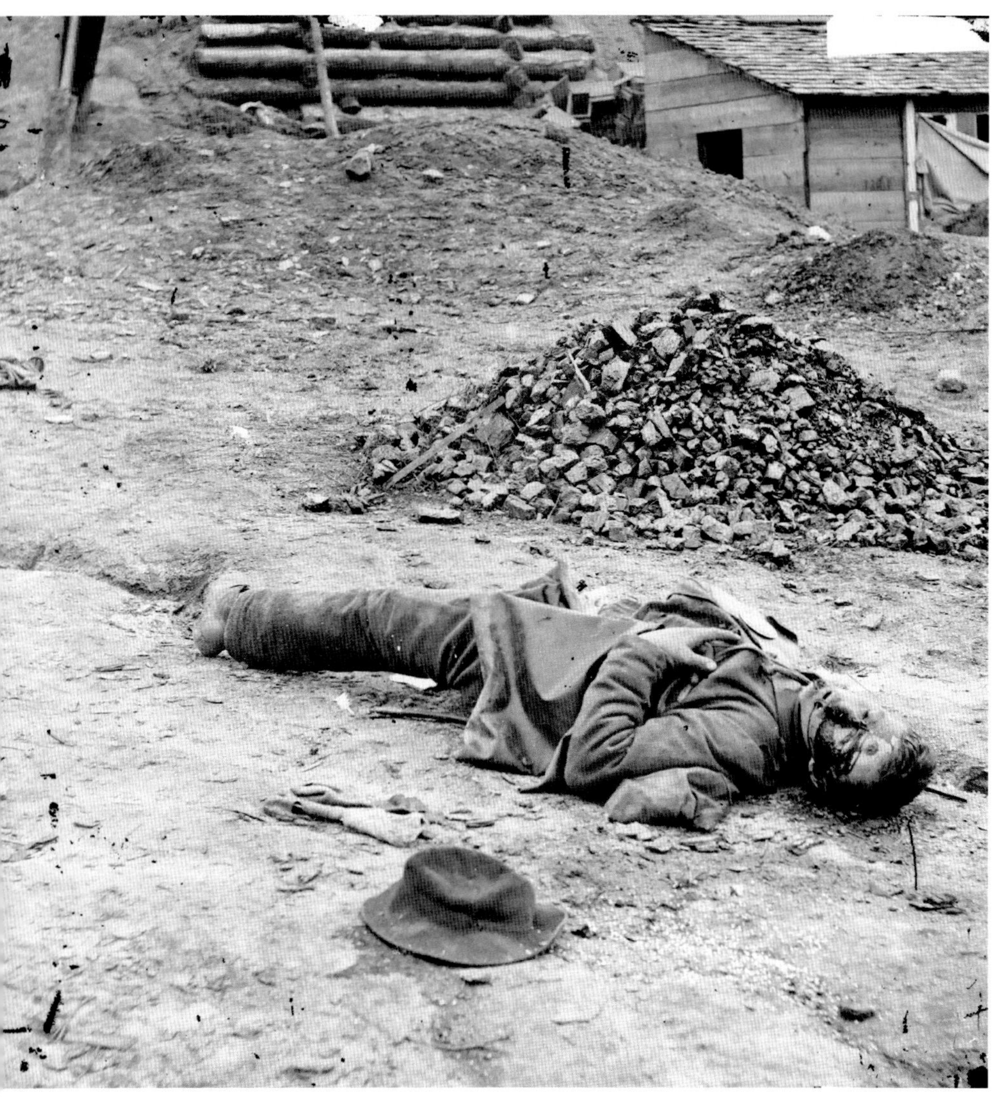

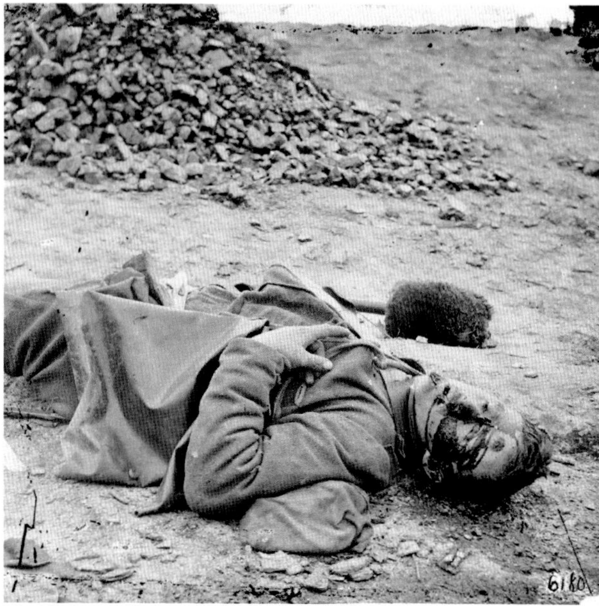

FIGURE 11.8. A dead rebel soldier, killed on April 2, 1865, and photographed by Thomas Roche the next day. Library of Congress.

to the head and upper chest because that is all that is exposed to the enemy behind earthen parapets.

A more likely explanation is the nature of the wounds themselves. During the Second World War, two medical officers published a statistical breakdown of Civil War wounds and, importantly, divided the data into mortal wounds and those that were more superficial (or at least not fatal). Their findings found that "head, neck, and face" wounds are much less common than those to the upper and lower extremities (11 percent versus greater than 70 percent). However, when an unfortunate soldier is hit in the head, neck, or face, he is much more likely to die from his wounds. For fatal wounds, 42 percent occur to the head and neck and 51 percent impact the torso; less than 10 percent of arm or leg wounds prove fatal.[9]

The bloody faces in the trenches of Petersburg are probably a combination of the nature of the fighting and the wound selection that proved fatal.[10] Note, interestingly, that the soldier who suffered the most drastic of the wounds, with the top of his head removed, showed no evidence of bleeding from the mouth or nose.[11]

Roche was especially interested in one of the dead soldiers who had blood on his face, as suggested by the number of photographs he captured. This dead man was, according to Roche's caption, "A Rebel soldier killed in the trenches before Petersburgh. The spots and marks on his face, are blood issuing from his mouth and nose. The wound is in the head, caused by a fragment of shell" (fig. 11.8).

In a second photograph, we learn that this generic "soldier" was also an artilleryman, as suggested by Roche's caption and the artillery sponge next to his body (fig. 11.9).

Of the three photographs that Roche took the time to compose and develop of this dead soldier, one is especially interesting because it also contains another dead artilleryman (fig. 11.10). Why Roche took two other photographs of the same dead soldier, before including the other unusually dressed artilleryman is a mystery.

Roche describes both men as "Rebel artillery soldiers" and explains the prominent "US" on the Confederate soldier's cartridge box by stating "The one in the foreground has U.S. belts on, probably taken from a Union soldier prisoner."

Roche is telling quite a story with these three photographs. First, our soldier is just "a soldier" before the artillery sponge is added. Next, he is joined by another dead soldier, and the presence of this corpse is proof that African Americans were fighting and dying for the Confederacy in the trenches of Petersburg. Except that they clearly were not; proof that this photograph is entirely fraudulent is not hard to find, because the same African American "soldier" can be seen walking around Petersburg in later photographs (fig. 11.11). Also, we can be certain that these photographs of the living African American young man were taken "later," because Roche wouldn't have had access to downtown Petersburg until after April 3.

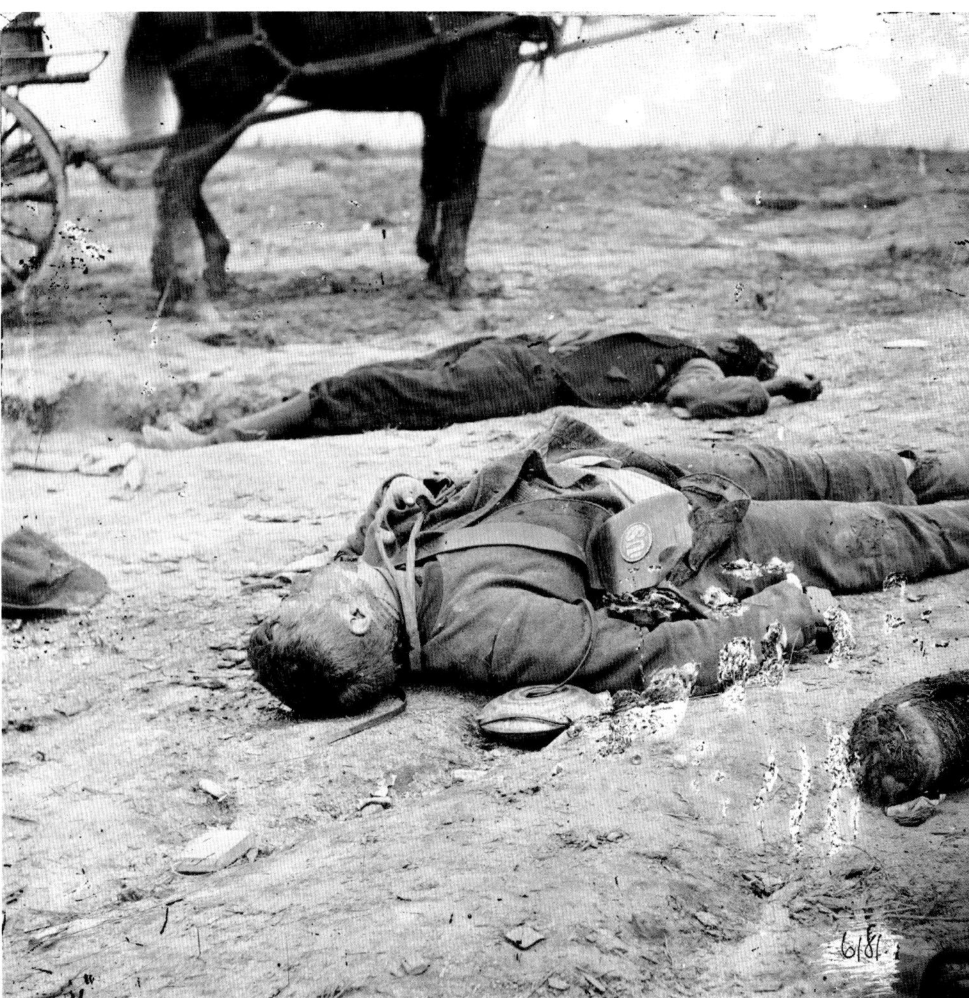

FIGURE 11.10. Photographed from a different angle, the dead "artilleryman" now has a "dead" neighbor, another presumed artilleryman who also happens to be an African American serving the rebel defenses. Library of Congress.

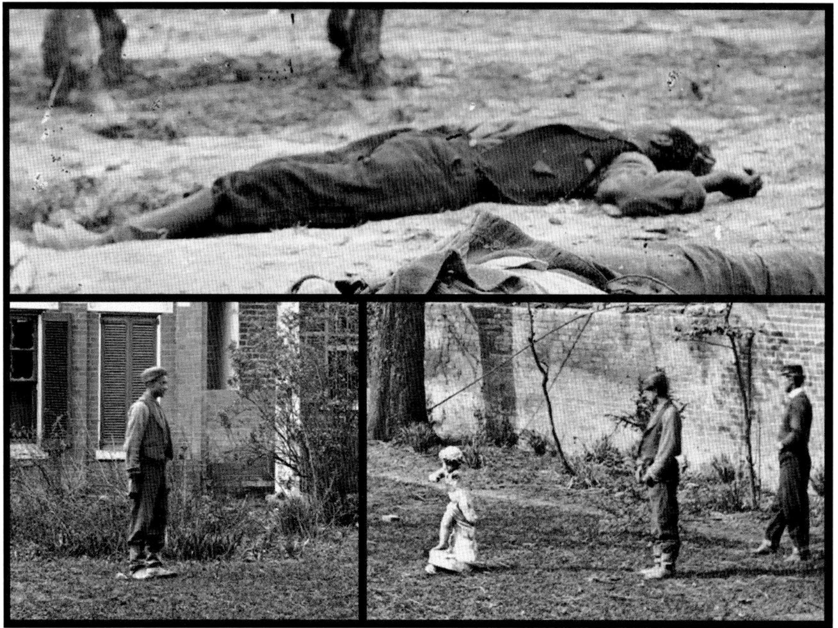

This is a story we have seen before. Roche found a dead soldier and took a picture. Then he added the broken sponge to suggest he was an artilleryman, making the image slightly more compelling. Then he added his field attendant to complete the composition, including modifying the caption to explain why the rebel was using Federal equipment.[12] So, even with ample carnage present in the form of a dozen fresh dead corpses strewn in the mud of the Petersburg trenches, Roche was still compelled to manipulate the scene with added props and even a fake "cadaver."[13]

For his non-posed, presumably unmanipulated death scenes, one final question arises about Roche's *modus operandi* on April 3: how deliberate were his efforts to maximize the gory content of the scenes? In other words, did he photograph his disemboweled and nearly decapitated subjects from an angle that would maximize the horror and ghastliness of the terrible wounds?

Gardner had certainly done exactly this at Gettysburg with his eviscerated lone corpse on the Rose Farm, shooting from a direction that looks directly into the underside of the gaping wound and empty shoulder socket (after, of course, adding a shell, disarticulated hand, and bayonetted rifle). Was Roche composing his photographs in a similar manner? If so, his motives would be twofold: The gore would convey to the general public just how far their visualization of what death in the trenches was from reality and secondly, the horrifying pictures would sell.[14]

Proof that photographing the dead was profitable is not hard to find: Just look at the price of the stereograms themselves. Images of important landscapes, buildings, or camp scenes sold for twenty-five cents, while those containing dead bodies usually sold for fifty cents. The angry owners of *The War Photograph and Exhibition Company* went so far as to scold their customers on the back of their photographs with a message to those seeking "CHEAP war views," "A gentleman living near Watkin's Glen, New York, wrote to us that he thought 30 cents each, too high a price for the stereoscopic war views, as he could buy views of Watkin's Glen for $1.50 per dozen." The Hartford, Connecticut, publisher responded that the only way their view of the Sunken Lane at Antietam and the views of Watkin's Glen would ever sell for a comparable price would be if the Glen were "wiped off the face of the earth" and that only one negative of the Glen existed and the photograph of the Glen would need to grow in popularity so that "all the people of this country were as much interested in a view of Watkin's Glen as they are in seeing the real scenes of our great war." They ended their annoyed rant with a note that "when we change the price of these war views, it will be to double it; they will never be any cheaper than now."[15]

The price of these photographs was relatively high regardless of content. Note that thirty to fifty cents in 1864 is the equivalent of six to twelve dollars (in 2026) for a single view. That is the equivalent of picking up

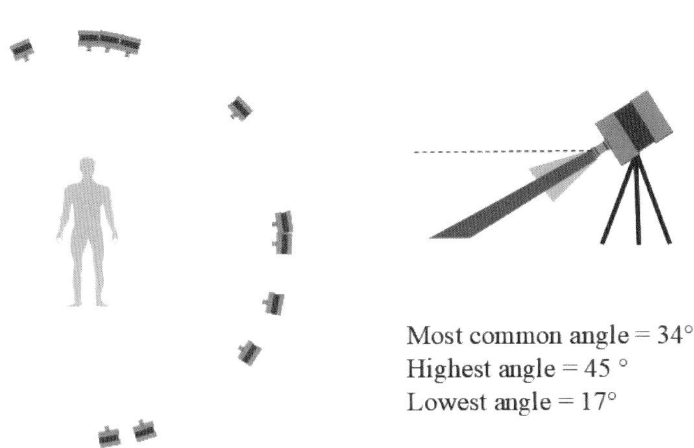

FIGURE 11.12. Orientation of camera with respect to a solitary fallen soldier (*left*) and angle of camera position relative to the horizon for each of the twelve photographs of dead soldiers. Multiple photographs (large format, stereoview) of the same subject from the same perspective were treated as a single photographic viewpoint.

a magazine at a bookstore, indicating that building a collection of prints from the war would represent a significant financial investment.

Returning to the photographic analysis: Figure 11.12 uses a rose diagram to illustrate the various perspectives for photographs that Gardner, O'Sullivan, and Gibson chose to use when encountering solitary dead soldiers at Antietam, Gettysburg, and Spotsylvania. Most of these photographs were captured at Gettysburg in the Devil's Den and Rose Farm region. Note that an unusual number of these photographs were taken from

a direction that would show the left side of the corpse. The right half of the diagram (fig. 11.12) shows the most common angle from which the photographers took the photograph relative to the horizon (5 degrees would indicate a camera orientation almost parallel with the body and ground—shooting towards the horizon, 70 degrees would indicate a shot from above). The range of camera positions for these photographs is relatively small, falling between 17 degrees and 45 degrees. This is because the tripod for the camera in each instance appears to have been on the ground beside the body, never on an elevated position or in a depression.

We would expect that if Gardner, O'Sullivan, and Gibson found twelve dead bodies on a battlefield that they would photograph around six from the left side and somewhere around six from the right. Perhaps four or five from one perspective, and seven or eight from the other. But in this case, eleven of the twelve photographs were taken from between 350 degrees and 175 degrees, with only one photograph offering the perspective of the other hemisphere. If the photographic position were chosen randomly, there is only a 0.3 percent chance of this type of orientation. Why might this be so?

Half of the photographs of the dead in this small data set were killed in and around Devil's Den. They are Confederate soldiers who were certainly killed on July 2, during Longstreet's assault on the left of the Federal line. As such, they would likely have been taking at least some degree of cover behind the giant diabase boulders of the Den. As a result, if they had been killed where they were fighting, we would expect to find their corpse beside a large outcrop, and it is difficult to get a camera and tripod onto such a rock. This might explain the orientation of so many of the photographs, facing towards the boulders and not photographed from above, on the boulder, but it also would require the dead man to have fallen with his right side facing the rocks.[16] Also, we know that for at least one of these photographs the body was carried to the location so the orientation of the corpse was predetermined by the photographer.

For about three-quarters of the solitary death studies, the exact position on the modern battlefield can be established, largely because of the exposed geology. For these, every single shot of the dead at Gettysburg was taken looking towards either the east or south (eight of eight). At Antietam, both shots were taken from the opposite direction, looking towards the west. The most likely explanation for this unusual consistency of orientation would involve the lighting for the scene and the position of the sun and time of day. At Gettysburg, for example, it is easier to take a photograph towards the east in the afternoon and early evening because the sun will be behind you. Morning photography in the Devil's Den is difficult if looking towards the east because of the shadows produced by the large boulders and glare from the sun. The same is true in the afternoon if looking towards the west.

So, back to Roche in the trenches at Petersburg. Does the orientation of his camera hint at any motives or other parameters that would explain an unusual frequency of camera perspectives? Figure 11.13 displays the rose diagram for Roche's work, indicated a nearly random positioning for his camera.

Roche was taking photographs from every orientation relative to his individual fallen soldiers. It is also apparent that he was taking his photographs from a larger and more inconsistent range of vertical orientations. Studying the photographs themselves reveals why: Roche varies the location of his tripod between three surface positions throughout the entirety of the collection of photographs, switching between the top of the parapet, the banquette tread, and the bottom of the muddy trench.[17] The determination of which of these three positions seems to be a trade-off between the composition of the subject and position of the body and the need for a stable (not muddy) position for the tripod legs. For several of the fallen soldiers it appears Roche was changing positions to capture multiple views of the same man from different vertical perspectives. He also took at least one shot of a soldier who was on the banquette tread from a position where his camera was in the bottom of the trench (fig. 11.5). His favored position,

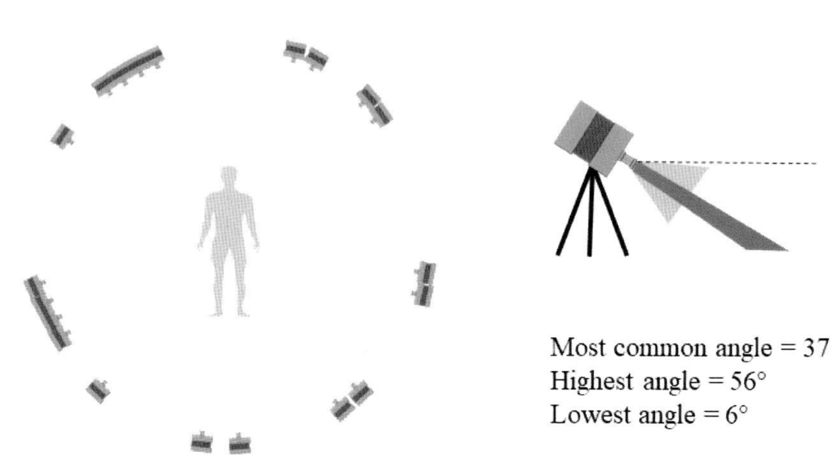

FIGURE 11.13. Orientation of camera with respect to a solitary fallen soldiers as photographed by Thomas Roche at Petersburg. Note the much larger range of vertical camera perspectives when compared to the work from the earlier battlefields.

however, remained to position his camera on the more solid ground above the trenches, peering into their grim contents from above.

For all these photographs of the dead, the photographers seemed to have established three patterns. First, if the soldier's face was visible, they took the photograph from an angle where we can see his lifeless (or bloated) expression. Second, if a wound is visible, they chose to position the camera to best detail the horridness of the injury. Third, if they saw any battle debris lying around nearby, they added it to the picture to maximize compositional interest and add to the story their negative was telling. This could include a hat, musket, bayonet, artillery accoutrement, or a field assistant.

Andrew Russell recounted the significance of Roche's work in the trenches of Petersburg in an article he wrote seventeen years after the

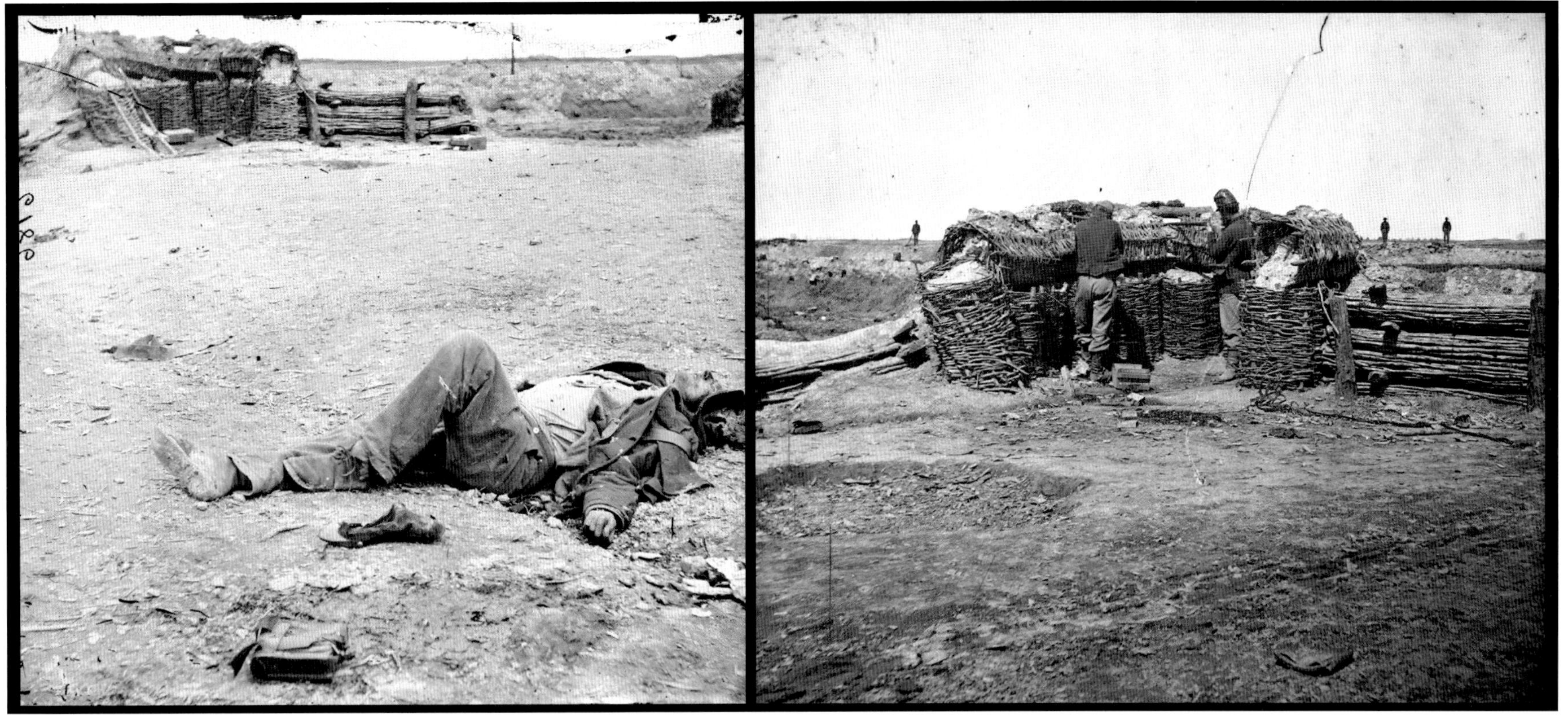

FIGURE 11.14. One of the twenty-two photographs of dead soldiers taken by Roche on April 3 (*left*), and a second photograph from the same general location taken by Roche or Russell later the same day.

event, "I found Mr. Roche on the ramparts with scores of negatives taken where the harvest of death had indeed been gathered—pictures that will in truth teach coming generations that war is a terrible reality."[18] While it is certainly true that Roche's negatives taught future generations about the terrible nature of death in combat, the degree of manipulation in these images questions the use of the term "reality."

Russell wrote of joining Roche in Fort Damnation after the latter had finished taking his twenty-two death studies. He may have even been behind the camera for another set of fabricated "action" scenes that were photographed later that same day (fig. 11.14).

Note the timber wall and gabion reinforced shooting position in the background of figure 11.14 (left). This wall and gabion collection can be identified in a series of photographs taken the same day. In figure 11.14 (right) the same position is now occupied with skirmishers, pretending to load their Springfields and fire at the enemy only around one hundred yards distant. We can be sure that photographs were taken within a few

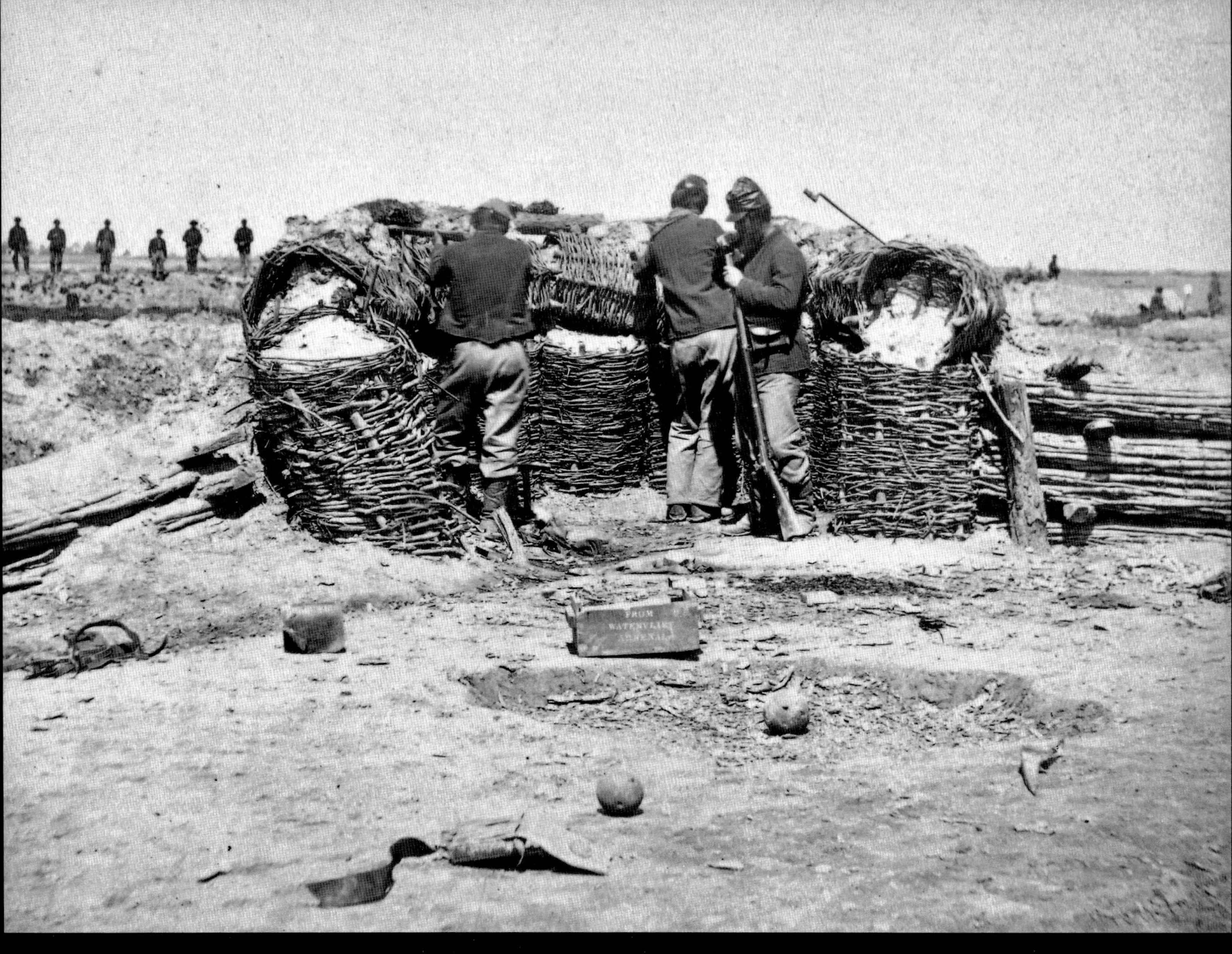

FIGURE 11.15. Thomas Roche's photograph of a "Union picket line." Note the bayonet stuck into the top of the spilled gabion on the right. Library of Congress.

hours of each other, because Russell wrote of Roche finishing his work in Fort Damnation (Fort Mahone) and Fort Hell (Fort Sedgwick) before racing to take more negatives in the now unoccupied city of Petersburg. He was apparently in a rush to photograph his not-dead assistant walking around downtown in the backyards of damaged houses.

One possible scenario for this group of photographs would explain the presence of several rifle muskets in the background of the death scene, propped against the gabions (fig. 11.14 left). Perhaps these belonged to the men who were busy burying the Confederate corpses. When they were finished with their loathsome task, including interring the man in the photograph, they took time to pose for multiple photographs of themselves pretending to be engaging the enemy. We know they had a shovel, because it appears in one of the "combat" scenes, materializing magically next to the ammunition crate.

One final illustration brings us full circle back to Roger Fenton and the addition of cannon balls to a composition. Figure 11.15 shows the exact same position, with the same men, but now there are ammunition chests, bayonets, and cannon balls strewn around during the heat of battle.

A viewer can only assume that Roche and his photographic colleagues never considered that their collection of photographs might actually be viewed *collectively*, where their devious craftsmanship is so apparent it raises a new question about whether a photographer with deceitful intentions can also capture a historically important negative.

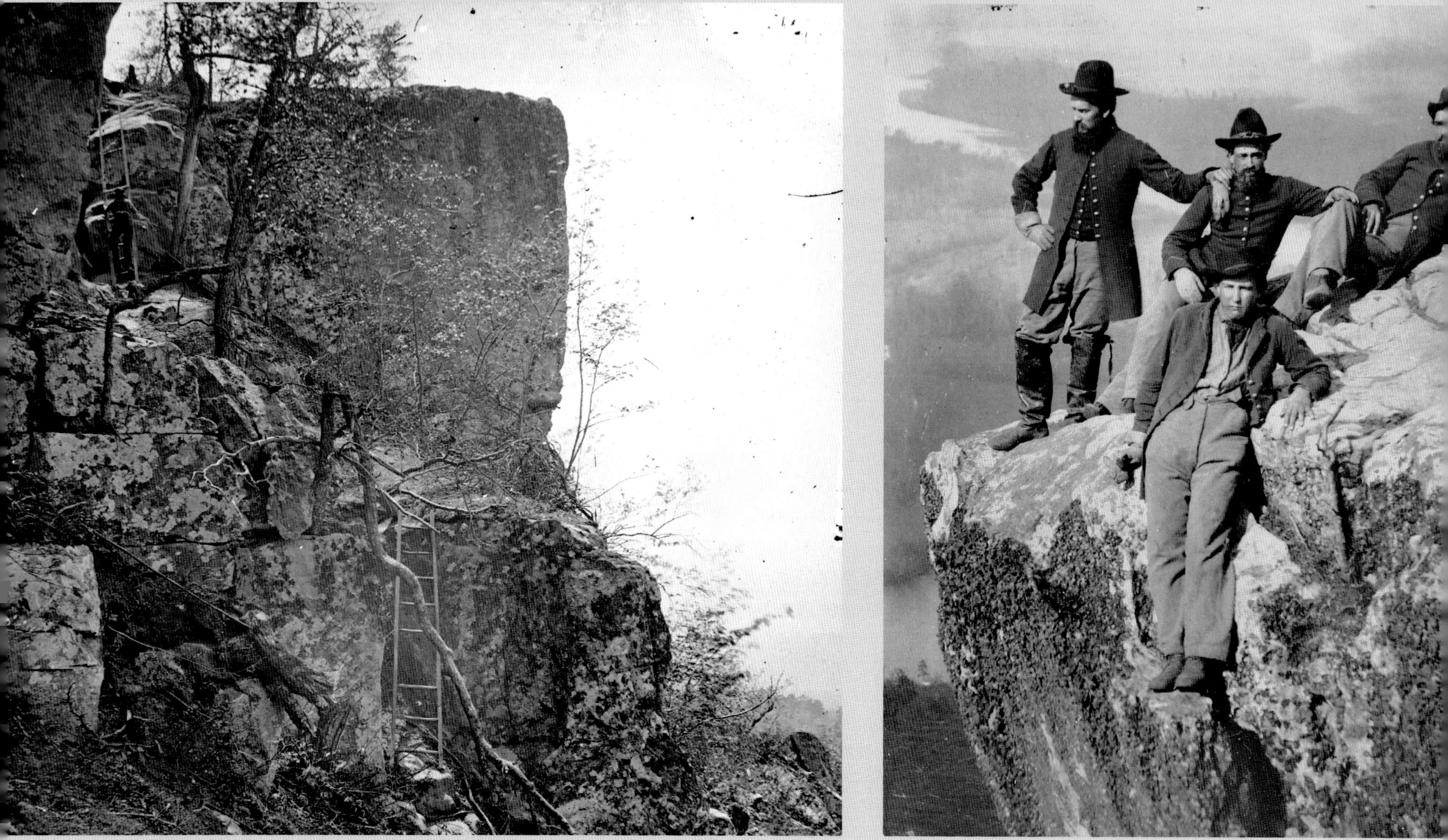

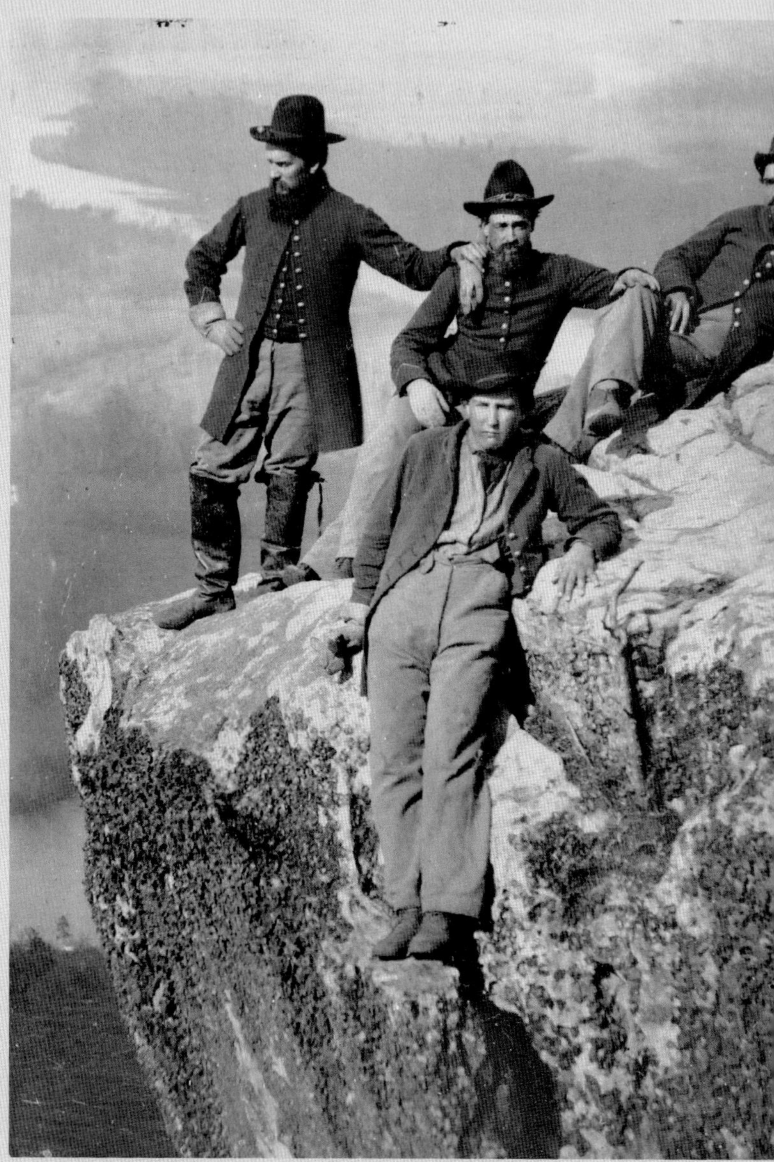

FIGURE 12.1. Thick, hard sandstone caps Lookout Mountain, Tennessee. Softer rock, found below the lower ladder, is less resistant to erosion, producing cliffs that were extremely popular with photographers from the region (*left*). Four (ill-advised) members of the 78th Pennsylvania pose in this photograph by Royan Linn (*right*). Library of Congress.

CONCLUSION

The Significance of Science and Sepia

Unanswered Questions and Future Work

Two chapters of this book explored specific scientific disciplines through the lenses of Civil War cameras. Chapter 10 focused on the construction of the Dutch Gap Canal and explored the stratigraphy and sedimentology of the construction site with respect to the difficulty of excavation and ultimate failure of the strategy. This collection of photographs and sketches demonstrates the effectiveness of using a combination of media to more completely understand a historical event. The photographs of Reekie, Russell, and Fowx provide the detail and resolution to see individual layers of sediment or particular excavation techniques necessary to understand and imagine the scope of the engineering undertaking, but the sketch by William Waud better illustrates the challenge of this endeavor while under artillery fire. This same theme runs throughout all the combinations of battlefield photographs and their corresponding sketches: The fighting around Devil's Den at Gettysburg or the Sunken Lane at Antietam, or even the Crater at Petersburg, is best interpreted by studying the photographs of the site (or aftermath) for details about the landscape and soldiers, while appreciating the sketches produced by the artists who were on site at the time of the historic event.

Chapter 11 also focused on a specific scientific discipline, forensic pathology, to explore the motives of the photographers for capturing the maximum volume of gore on a negative. No other series of photographs approached Thomas Roche's collection from the trenches of Petersburg with respect to the horrors of death and the inglorious sacrifice made by these men on the battlefield. There are certainly other scientific fields and subjects that could be explored using the photographs that were produced during the war. For example, the Dutch Gap Canal was excavated through sedimentary strata, but other types of geology determined everything from the lay of the land to the sources of drinking water.

The first battlefield that comes to mind when considering Civil War geology is Gettysburg and more has been written about both the history and geology of this battlefield than all other battlegrounds combined. The reason for this overwhelming attention is simple: The dramatically outcropping rocks produce a battlefield landscape unlike any other and it is easy to imagine how the rocks affected the fighting.[1]

Despite this inordinate amount of attention, there are many other battlefields where the geology, and its influence on the combat in the area, are easy to understand through period photographs. Lookout Mountain, overlooking Chattanooga, Tennessee, has rather simple geology that led to rather difficult terrain (fig. 12.1). Here, hard sandstones cap the mountain, resisting weathering and erosion, while softer limestones are found below, producing precarious cliffs. The resulting dramatic and photogenic location proved to be a favorite of photographers and led to the site being the most photographed battle location of the war.

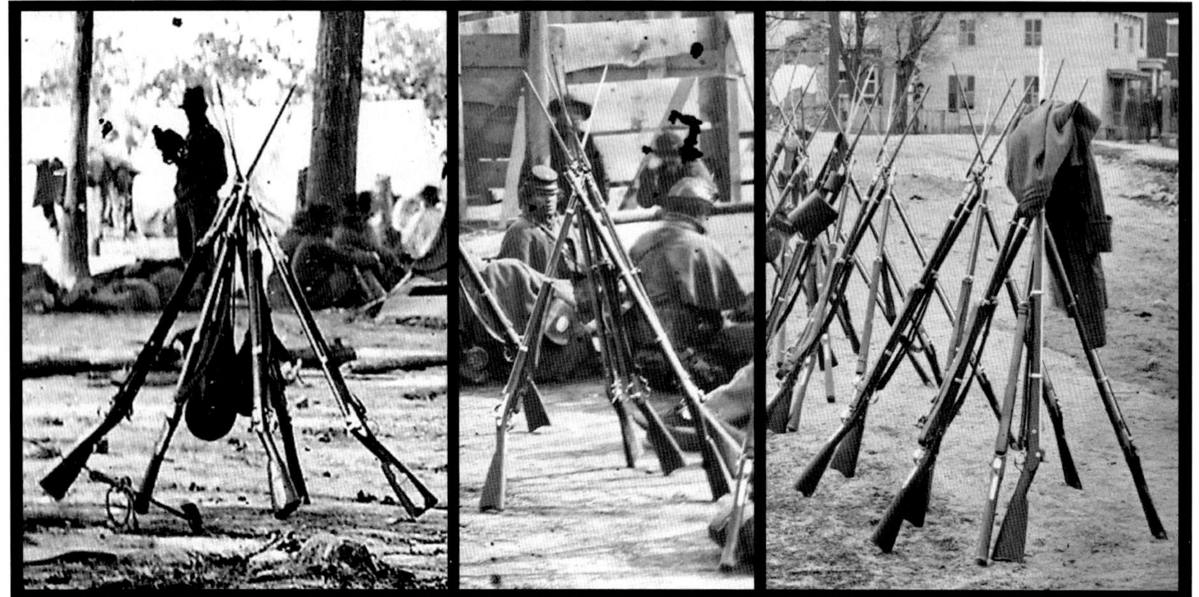

FIGURE 12.2. Comparison of longarms from June 1862 at Fair Oaks (*left*), February 1863 at Aquia Creek Landing (*center*), and April 1865 at Petersburg (*right*). As the war lasted into the third and fourth years, obsolete weapons like Model 1841 Mississippi rifles (*left*) began to disappear from the negatives to be replaced by more modern rifle muskets. Library of Congress.

Antietam is another battlefield where geology played a major role in the fighting and tactics and is well captured on glass negatives. The morning phase of the battle, for example, was fought over the Conococheague Limestone, a rock unit that weathers in a consistent manner, producing a flat or gently undulating landscape (see fig. 2.6 or 2.8, or Gardner's photograph of the dead arranged for burial [fig. 2.1, bottom right]). In contrast, the second and third phases of the great battle were fought above the Elbrook Formation, a combination of dolostones and shales that weathers into a more rolling terrain (fig. 2.11 or see any of the many photographs of the Lower [Burnside's] Bridge). Thus, combat took place at a slightly longer range during the opening phase of the battle on flatter terrain, and during the afternoon and evening portion of the battle the rolling hills meant that men encountered each other at shorter distances but had more cover and concealment.

Another scientific approach to the Civil War using photographs could explore the evolution of technology between 1861 and 1865. This branch of military science would use the photographs to document the change in weapons and tactics by the fighting men and explore the perceived growing advantages in weapons and materiel by the Northern armies.

Consider, for example, the shift in small-arms firepower for Federal infantry between the Battle of Fair Oaks (1862), Chancellorsville (1863), and Petersburg (1865). During the Peninsula Campaign, at least a fraction of Federal soldiers were carrying obsolete 1841 Mississippi rifles, while two or three years later the soldiers have seemingly fresh-from-the-factory Model 1861 or 1863 Springfield rifle muskets (fig. 12.2).

Brady, Gardner, and other photographers took many portraits of soldiers in the field (camp), often posing alone or in small groups. Photographs of officers relaxing in camp are especially common. In most of these photographs their weapons are often visible, including rifles and sabers. One gun that is surprisingly absent from nearly all of these photographs is the common revolver, and this deficiency is especially surprising considering how many of these pictures feature officers. One of the exceptions is a particularly photogenic, and oft photographed, Federal officer (fig. 12.3).

A companion discussion to the narrative about the evolution of weapons and firepower during the Civil War might concentrate on their true effectiveness in combat. Many historians have argued that the rifle musket was a weapon that transformed the nature of combat on the battlefield and rendered tactics from former conflicts entirely obsolete. Others have argued that it represented only a small (if any) improvement over the weapons that came before, in large part because of the slow rate of fire and the low muzzle velocity and resulting high, parabolic trajectory of the bullet. If the rifle musket was revolutionary, one might wonder why the six soldiers in figure 12.4 didn't simply select a rifle musket when heading off to combat, instead finding it necessary to arm themselves with more than twenty-five supplemental weapons!

From top left to bottom right, these men are each armed with three, four, four, five, and five weapons, providing them with more than seventy-five rapid shots in combat. In reality, of course, most photographic studios probably had prop weapons that the soldiers could select from, and these folks got a little carried away, with silly results. The soldier in the upper left has only three weapons, suggesting that he might be under-gunned, but the fact that he is picking his teeth with a bowie knife indicates that his attitude should probably be counted as a fourth weapon.

Other areas of exploration in this collection of priceless black-and-white artifacts might include medical sciences (photographs of amputations exist from several field hospitals and studies of bullet wounds are abundant), architecture, logistics, or engineering (Andrew Russell, in particular, dedicated many large-format negatives to photographing railroads and bridges).

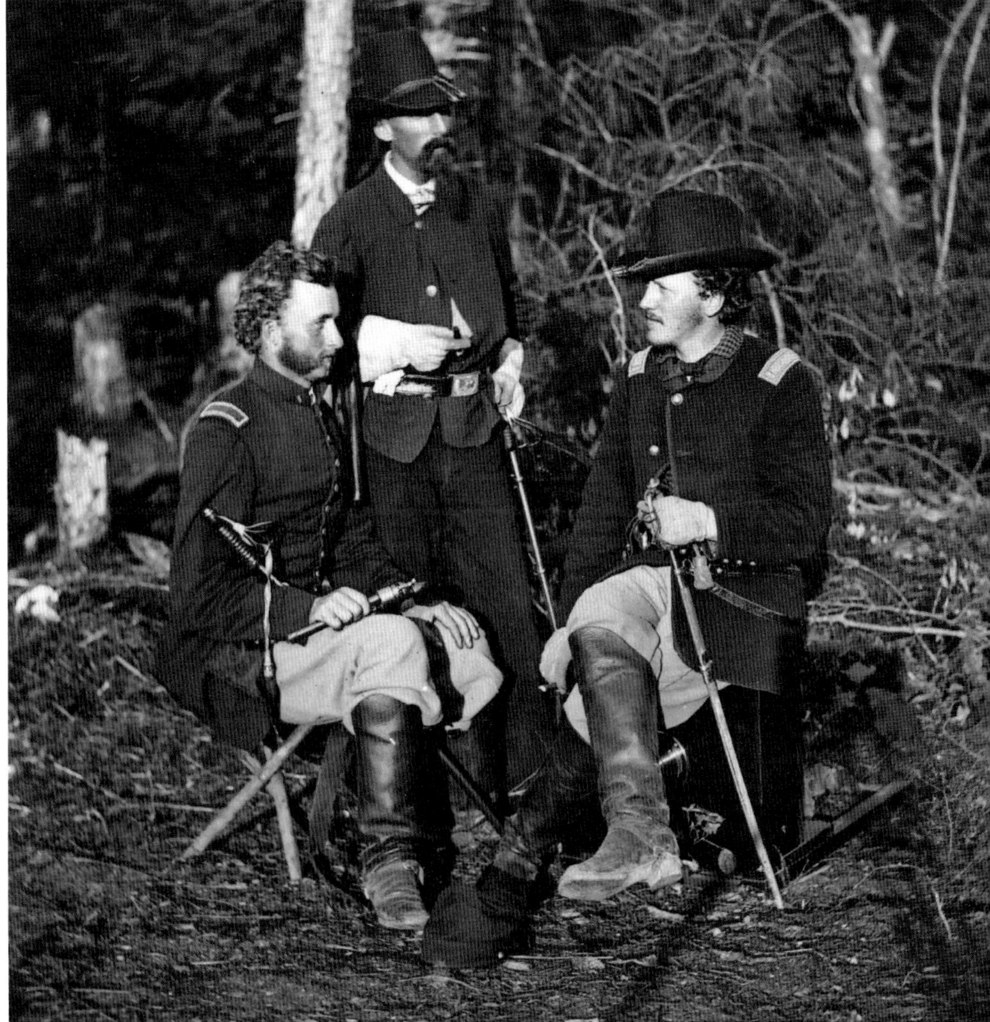

FIGURE 12.3. A rare field photograph of an officer with a pistol. In this case it a young George Custer with a Model 1851 Colt pistol, the second most popular sidearm from the war. Note the shadow of the photographer's camera and tripod in the right bottom quarter of the negative. Library of Congress.

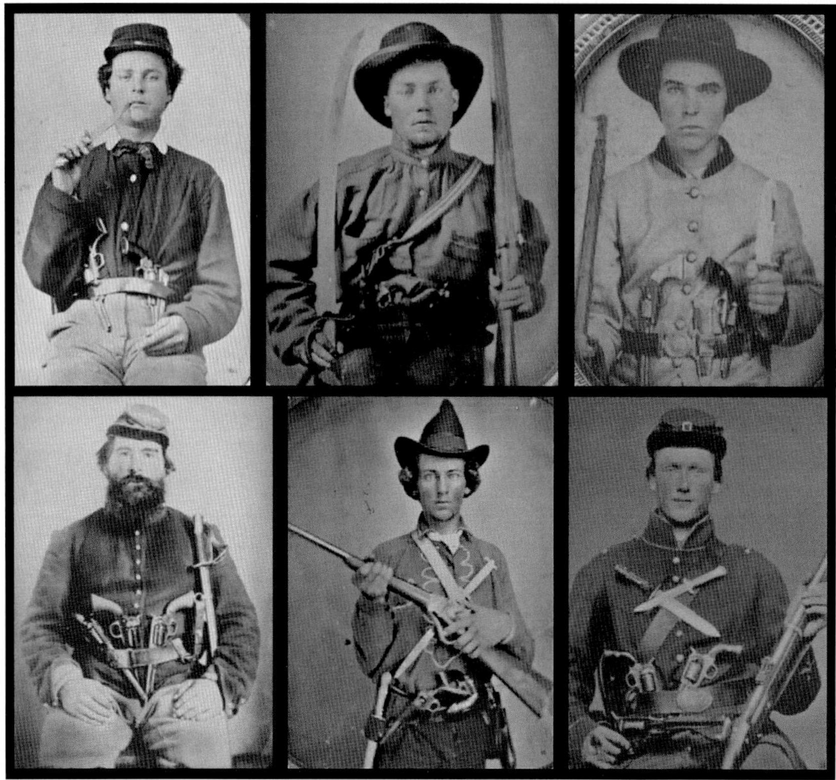

FIGURE 12.4. If the rifle musket was such a game changer in combat, why did so many soldiers seek to arm themselves with all forms of backup weapons?

These photographs would also provide an excellent resource for the study of environmental sciences and landscape degradation and change. Construction of earthworks, plank roads, and campfires required an endless supply of lumber that was devastating to a local environment, as was the waste from hundreds of thousands of men and their horses, mules, and cattle in the field. Photographs from different physiographic regions like Atlanta, Nashville, and Petersburg could provide insights into the effects of masses of humans at conflict on the land.

Civil War Photographic Superlatives

This book began with a ranking of the most popular photographs to emerge from the Civil War ("The Hierarchy of Historical Preeminence"). It seems only fitting that it should end with a discussion of the most important photographers and photographs from the period. Here we will drift away from the strict accounting in chapter 2 to a bit more opinion, but judgement and argument based on countless hours poring over these negatives with a more complete understanding and consideration of the degree of manipulation presented in many of the images.

Our superlatives will include four categories: most important photograph, most important photographer, least recognized "combat" photograph, and least important photograph (or perhaps most manipulated photograph). All consideration for these awards will contemplate the photographs or photographers' contribution to Civil War history and how the image and creator influenced our understanding of the past. As always, these are photographs that were taken in the field, action or "combat" shots of battlefields and participants during conflict, not portraits of famous people.

All of Gardner and Gibson's work at Antietam should be nominated for the "most important picture award," if for no other reason than they were the first photographers to successfully bring the horrors of the battlefield back from the front lines. As an additional bonus, there is no evidence of manipulation of the photographs. Several of our top twenty-five most popular photographs fall into this category and are worthy of consideration, including their shot of the fallen Confederate soldiers along the Hagerstown Pike, the dead soldiers arranged in a large "V" formation in preparation for burial, the massed dead bodies in the Bloody Lane, and the corpses and dead horses strewn in front of the Dunker Church. There is also the highly artistic shot of a lone grave under a large, leafless tree produced at the same time. Collectively, these shots represent more than a quarter of the most popular photographs to appear in books from the last 150 years, and they continue to be popular today.

Many of Gibson and Gardner's photographs from September 19, 1862, share a commanding sense of composition and artistry, especially with respect to perspective. When viewed together, their structuring of the negatives of the Bloody Lane, Hagerstown Pike, and dead arranged for burial is striking. In all three photographs, the direction of your attention is forced, following fence, ditch, and (always) bodies. Even the Dunker Church shot shares this orientation, with the eye drawn from corpses to caisson to stark building.

Clearly any of these prints might be considered the most important Civil War photograph. The poignant lone grave under a highly contrasted, sprawling tree, for example, was chosen for the compelling cover on William Frassanito's book on Antietam.

Gardner and Gibson (and O'Sullivan) also captured many popular photographs nine months later at Gettysburg. The problem with nominating any of these shots as the "most important" is that each one of the photographs has some degree of concern regarding either staging, the addition of props, a misleading caption, or mystery location. The *Harvest of Death* is certainly a popular photograph and an incredibly engrossing and heartbreaking composition, but doesn't it lose some degree of historical importance because we are unsure where, exactly, the photograph was taken?[2] The application of science and critical reasoning has not diminished the importance or iconic nature of these photographs, but the new context provided, whether from the repeated use of props or the staging of scenes, suggests their significance is lessened when they are considered from a photojournalism perspective. This collection has drifted from truth towards art, a shift Gardner's Antietam series never suffered.

For years the fallen sharpshooter in Devil's Den was the most popular photograph to appear in print, until it was unveiled as a contrivance. After this, the photographs inclusion in books diminished and it was nearly always identified as fraudulent. Gardner's photograph of the disemboweled soldier on the Rose Farm just barely made the top twenty-five most popular list and while it is certainly shocking, it is unworthy of further

consideration for "most important" because of the degree of staging present and the apparent lack of complete authenticity.

The most popular photograph from the Civil War, Brady & Co.'s *Three Confederate Prisoners* (fig. 2.2) is a strong contender. It shows real fighting men, in uniform, only days after a battle. They are, however, clearly posing and are photographed in a location that wasn't especially compelling (but at least it was on the battlefield of the first day's fight). Perhaps it is no wonder that this photograph is most popular in books, but much less so in more contemporary magazines, websites, and videos.

Unlike Mathew "The Eye of History" Brady, Samuel Cooley was not a particularly well-known photographer. Nevertheless, in December of 1864 he took a photograph that precisely defines one of the great values of Civil War negatives (fig. 12.5). This photograph of Fort Sanders in Knoxville, Tennessee, is of special value to historians because it is one of only a few from the battlefield, showing the desolate, stripped landscape before the earthen fortification. Today, this area is completely overrun with houses and sprawl from the city, leaving no trace of the history that took place here. Without Cooley's photograph, it would be much more difficult to imagine Longstreet's futile struggle to capture the fort.[3]

Unfortunately, Cooley's photograph doesn't include a human element, rendering slightly less intriguing despite the important documentation of the historical landscape. George Barnard took a similar photograph at around the same time that does include two historical figures (fig. 12.6). On the left is Colonel Orlando M. Poe, General Burnside's chief engineer for the XXIII Corps, who participated in the battle. Poe's design of a successful defensive scheme for the city, including Fort Sanders, led Major General William Sherman to select him as his chief engineer a year later. Poe is conversing in this photograph with one of his engineering assistants, Colonel Orville E. Babcock, who would also rise in reputation after this overwhelming Federal victory.

The only thing missing from Cooley and Barnard's photographs is a sense of immediacy. These photographs could have been taken a few days

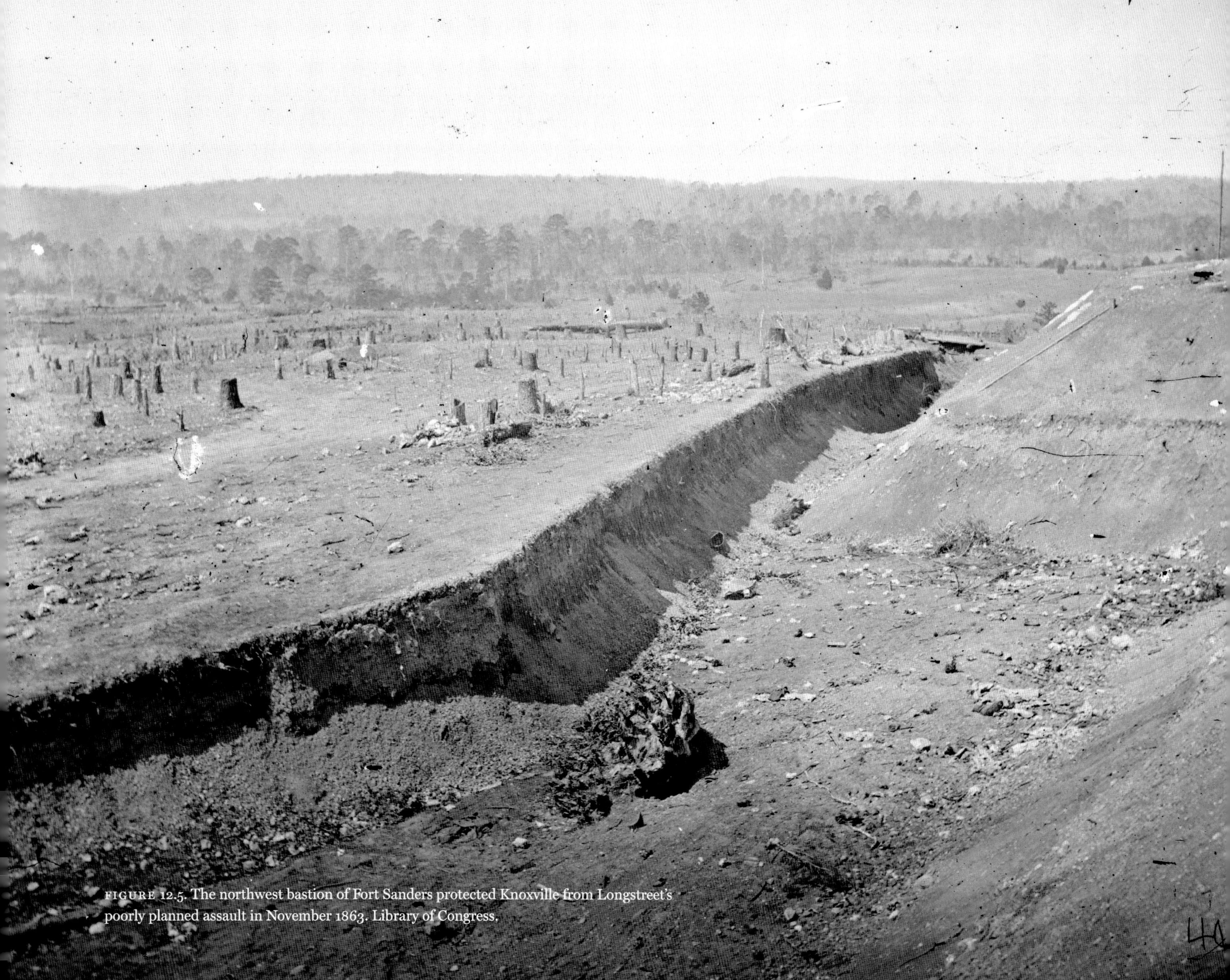

FIGURE 12.5. The northwest bastion of Fort Sanders protected Knoxville from Longstreet's poorly planned assault in November 1863. Library of Congress.

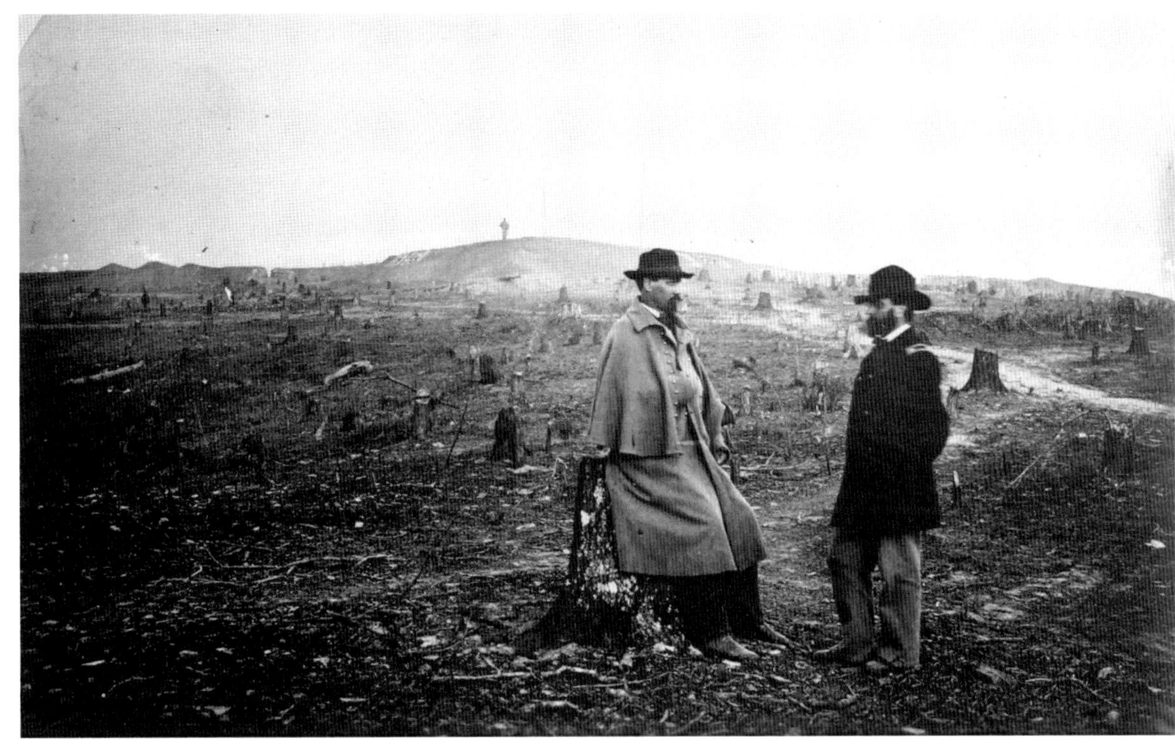

FIGURE 12.6. Two of Burnside's most important engineers converse in front of their masterfully designed Fort Sanders. The Confederates would lose more than eight hundred men trying to capture this earthen structure, while the Federals would suffer only thirteen casualties. Library of Congress.

after the battle or a few months. They provide critical information about the design of the fort and the local terrain (both of which have been plowed under and built over), but don't relay the desperation of the struggle because the post-battle detritus has largely disappeared, and the dead have long since been buried.

That leaves one final photograph that meets all the following important criteria (in no particular order): 1) it shows an actual battlefield, where there had been fighting (very!) recently; 2) it shows dead soldiers in uniform where they had fallen; 3) it shows the actual weapons they were using (not props), and it provides insights into how they were fighting (e.g., cover and concealment or fieldworks). This photograph is, as you might have deduced, Andrew Russell's negative of the Stone Wall at Fredericksburg

after US forces overran the position on May 3, 1864 (fig. 2.5). This photograph, the third most popular in our earlier survey, includes dead men who fell in combat only hours before, and certainly represents the quickest any camera was brought to a battle site during the Civil War. As a result, we are seeing the immediate aftermath of battle, not like at Antietam (weapons gathered, bodies transported and collected for burial) or Gettysburg (bloated bodies with prop weapons). Even at Petersburg a year later, Roche had difficulty finding more than one or two bodies together where they had fallen in the trenches, and the lack of any landmarks renders the discovery of many of their locations impossible. Here, Russell has captured the dead Confederates slumped into the ditch behind the famous Stone Wall below Marye's Heights, one of the strongest defensive positions from the entire

Civil War (and one that was fought over more than once). He has photographed such an important site without manipulation, complete with the fallen who fought and died there.[4]

Even the details in this photograph are intriguing, with cups, canteens, bayonets, and clothing scattered across the landscape. Russell also created a composition reminiscent of the perception of depth created by Gardner and Gibson at Antietam: The road, ditch, stone wall, and bodies all draw the eye to a convergence point on the horizon. One final aspect of this photograph that makes it so historically compelling is that we know exactly where it was taken, and we can visit the site today, along with a copy of the print, to study how the landscape has (or hasn't) changed through time.

As far as the most important photographer from the Civil War, our history books have already decided. There can be only one "Father of Photojournalism," and the award has already been given to Mathew Brady.[5] This is, of course, despite the fact that Brady took few of the photographs credited to his name, or at least his company's name. In support of Brady's nomination as the most important Civil War photographer is the volume of work produced by Brady & Co. and their image from Gettysburg that proved to be the most popular photograph in our survey. Interestingly, none of the photographs where Brady himself appears made the list of the top twenty-five most popular. The closest any of his "self-portraits" got was probably one of the many landscape shots at Gettysburg, where he appears in front of Little Round Top or the field where General Reynolds fell.

Brady's onetime employee, and then direct competitor, Alexander Gardner, can make a strong case for most important photographer (fig. 12.7). His partnership at Antietam and team at Gettysburg captured dozens of exceedingly important photographs, although it is arguable that the collection from the former, a collection free of fraud, might be more important to history. Nevertheless, no other photographer is associated with as many photographs from our twenty-five most popular than Gardner.[6]

Along that same line of reasoning, we arrive at Timothy O'Sullivan. O'Sullivan was working with Gardner at Gettysburg, so his work is well represented in the top twenty-five list. He was also present at more battlefields than any other photographer, covering Cedar Mountain (with Brady), Gettysburg, Spotsylvania, Petersburg, Fort Fisher, and Appomattox. He even traveled to places as far ranging as Fairfax Courthouse in Virginia and Charleston and Savannah.

If Gardner had been asked to candidly provide his opinion about the Civil War's most important photographer (photographer, not developer or publisher), his answer might surprise. Consider, again, his choice for his famous *Sketch Book*: Gardner chose fifteen of his own photographs for inclusion in his masterwork, but *forty-four* of O'Sullivan's taking. Even Gardner's own talented brother merited only ten pictures. So, when Gardner chose what he considered the most important photographs associated with his studio, he selected more photographs from O'Sullivan than his colleagues Barnard, Gibson, Reekie, Wood, Knox, and Pywell *combined*.

O'Sullivan also worked in collaboration with both Brady and Gardner, certainly picking up artistic techniques from both. His photograph *A Harvest of Death* and his highly detailed photographs of the newly captured Fort Fisher reveal interesting artistic touches.[7] His photographs of the newly captured Fort Pulaski in Georgia aren't as detailed or clear, but they are important in the study of how military firepower had recently changed.[8] Overall, it seems that O'Sullivan's camera documented all types of important historical events and sites, from all types of battlegrounds and geographic locations, building a strong resume—even when compared with Brady and Gardner—that he was the most important photographer from the Civil War.

Finally, two last awards for Civil War photographs, not based on popularity or importance, but on obscurity and ridiculousness. Throughout this text the definition of a "combat" photograph has been rather nebulous, in part because photographs of actual battle action don't exist. "Combat photographs" conveys the idea that the photograph was either taken soon after combat, relates directly to the men in or around a battle, or depicts the aftermath of fighting. Nearly all the combat photographs from the Civil

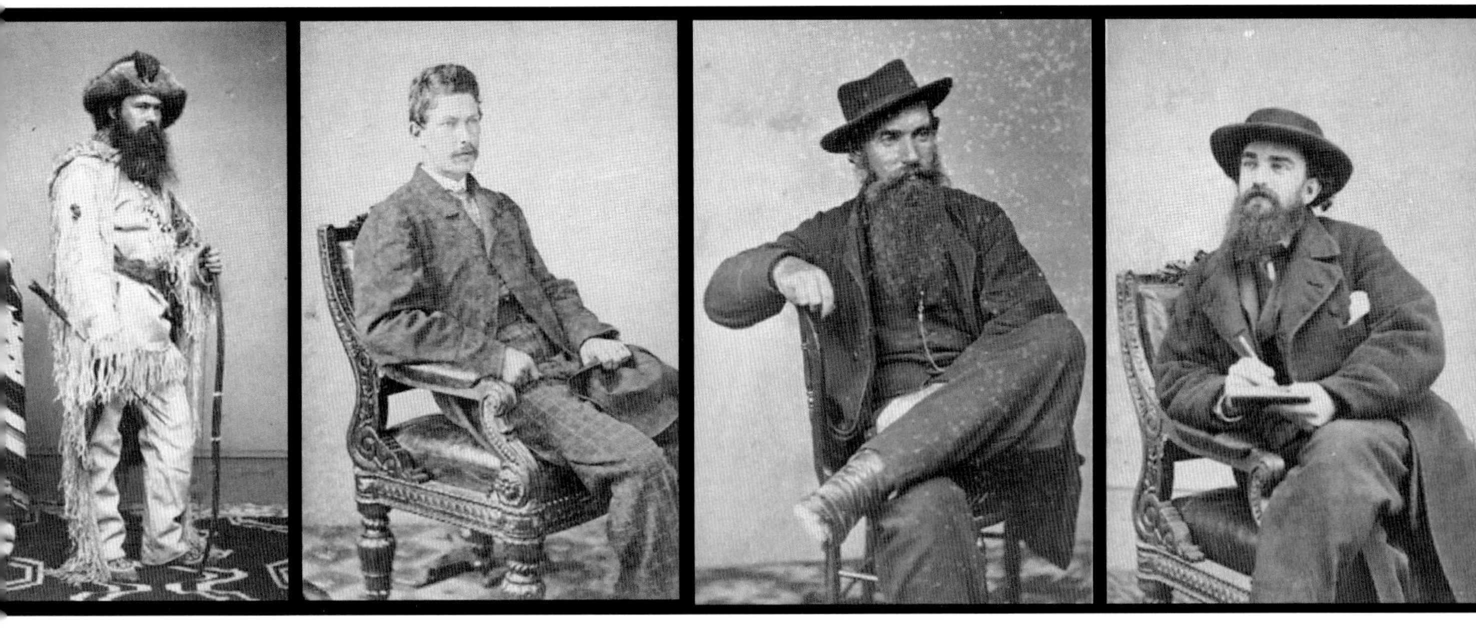

FIGURE 12.7. Costumes, colleagues, and competition: Alexander Gardner's contribution to Civil War photography went far beyond his field photographs. In addition to photographing Abraham Lincoln on many occasions, he also found time to take self-portraits (in Brady's studio, early in the war, *left*) and photographs of Timothy O'Sullivan, his own brother James, and sketch artist Alfred Waud. National Portrait Gallery and Library of Congress.

War have been reprinted over the years in various outlets and they continue to be featured online and in magazines. Many also found their way onto our list of the most popular photographs. One, however, stands out while remaining in obscurity. This photograph has also been used in publications as a landscape study, without recognizing that there is a corpse in the image (fig. 12.8).

James Gibson and Timothy O'Sullivan were working together on July 6, alternating shots as they worked their way across Devil's Den, Little Round Top, and the Valley of Death. The apparent landscape photograph depicting the Valley and Round Top also contains a dead body, which can be seen when viewed under magnification (fig. 12.9). James Gibson also captured this dead man on glass, from a slightly different and higher perspective (figs. 12.10 and 12.11).

Gibson may have chosen to include the two living men to draw the viewer's attention to this portion of the photograph, so that the corpse might be more readily noticed. It might also be that these men were part of a burial party and were growing anxious for Gibson and O'Sullivan to finish their work.[9] Note that, as with 95 percent of the other photographs of solitary dead soldiers at Gettysburg, the left side of the dead man's body is being photographed. Even from this far distance, both photographers chose to shoot from approximately 160 degrees.

Perhaps this photograph might have been more widely reproduced had the body been more prominently featured, as with the rest of the photographs Gardner and his crew took only a short walk to the south in and around Devil's Den. One final shot, which represents the most absurd image from the Civil War, does make dead soldiers the main focal point of

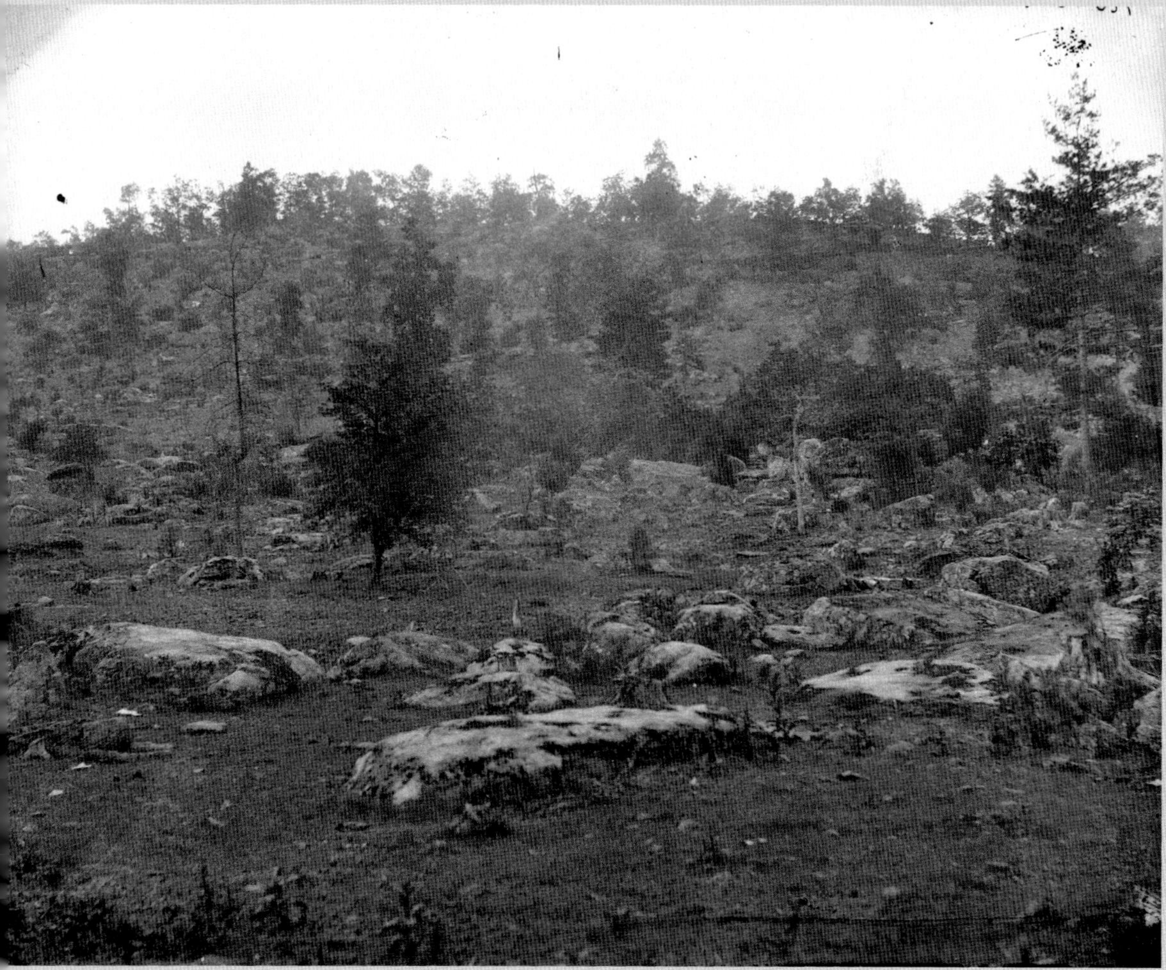

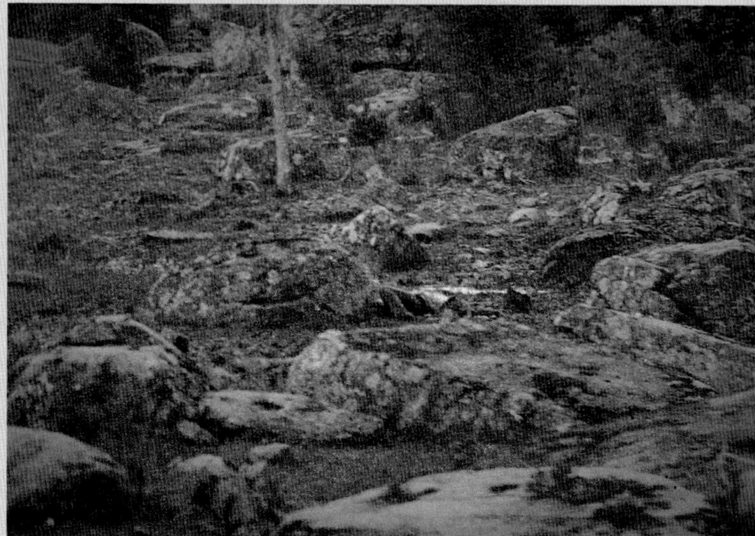

FIGURE 12.9. A much-magnified view of O'Sullivan's photograph reveals a corpse, lying to the right of the large spherical boulder in the center of the image.

FIGURE 12.8. Little Round Top, as photographed by Timothy O'Sullivan only a few days after the fighting for this hill had ended. Many viewers of this photograph over the years have not realized that there is a dead man in the lower right quadrant (see fig. 12.9). Library of Congress.

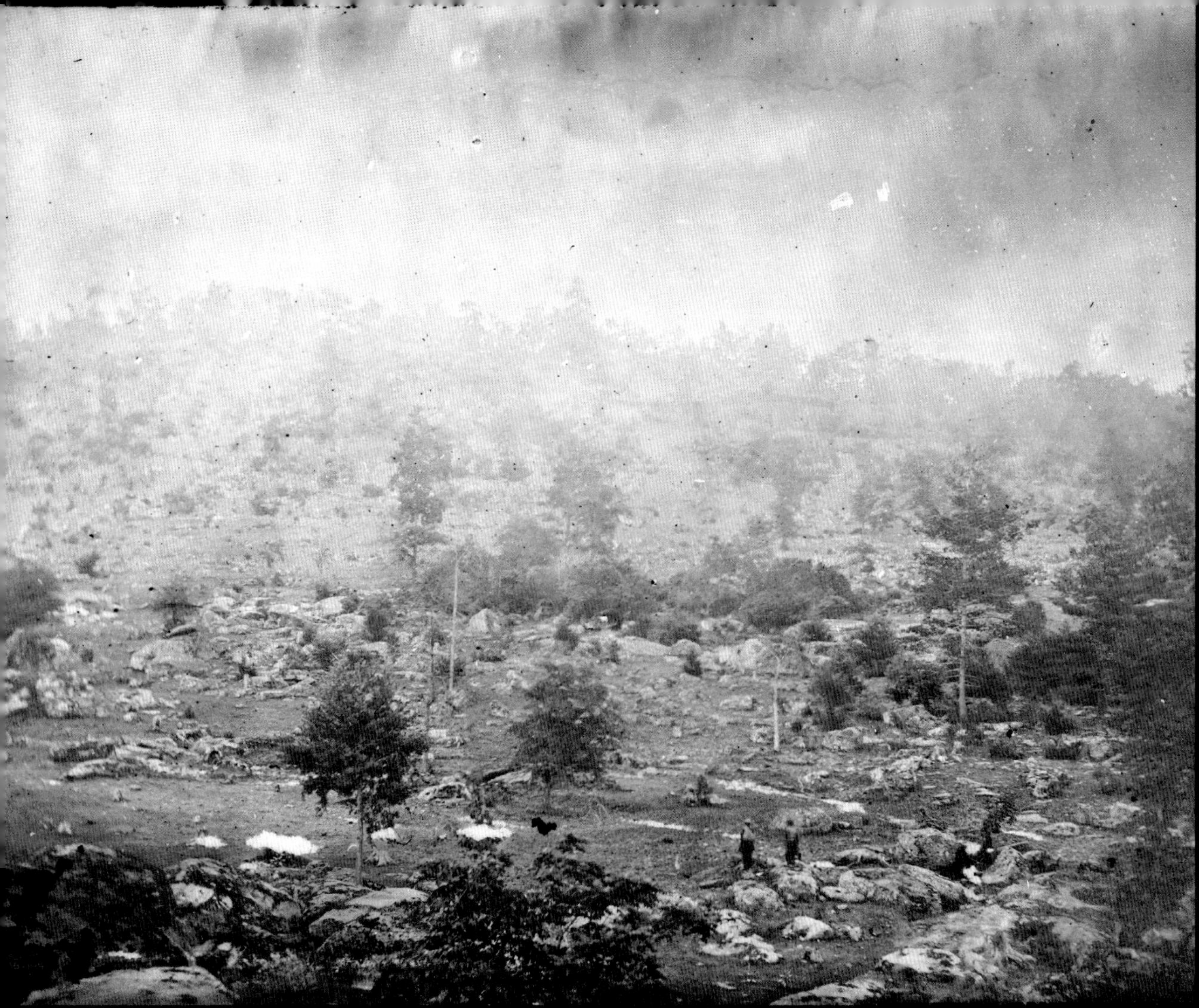

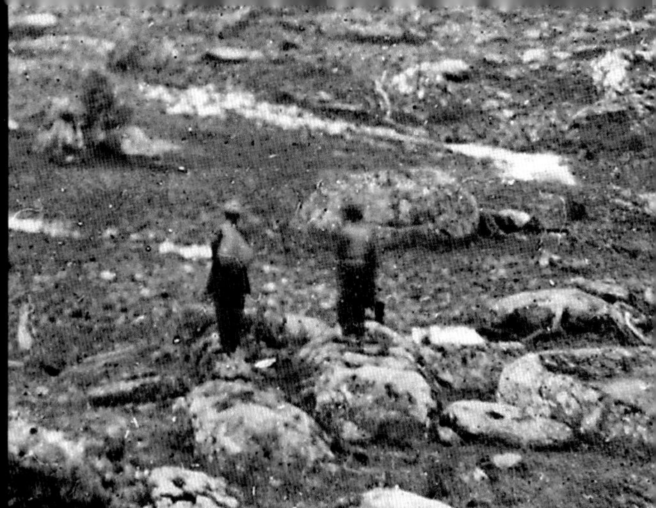

FIGURE 12.11. Detail from Gibson's negative shows the same dead soldier wearing dark pants and a light shirt. The corpse lies to the right of a large boulder, with the dead man's left knee bent and slightly elevated.

FIGURE 12.10. James Gibson's photograph of the same landscape may have been taken a few minutes after Gibson's. The same fallen soldier can be spotted in the lower right quadrant where two men approach. Library of Congress.

the photograph and it, too, rekindles some of the ludicrous photographic strategies Gardner would employ in the Den.

Figure 12.12 is a fine study of the gabion-supported parapets and traverses found in Fort Sedgwick, and the elaborateness of the architecture found in these earthworks. This photograph from Petersburg would never be considered as one of our more important "combat" images, however, because it is lacking a human element.[10]

When Andrew Russell and Thomas Roche discovered this viewpoint, they must have been struck by the confounding array of crisscrossing lines representing the sides and tops of the parapets, and the serrated teeth of the fraise and branching abatis jutting out at contradictory angles. All that was missing was a few of the dead bodies they had witnessed earlier that morning, but these bodies were likely all interred at this point later in the day.

Roche, of course, knew what to do to improve the solemnity of the scene: He needed a few bodies, whether alive or dead. His field assistant/teamster was still around (and extant), so he could be one "cadaver." He didn't have another assistant for a second dead body, but with Russell present, he now had a new photographer. Thus, in figure 12.13, Roche is captured on a negative for the second time at Petersburg.

A detail of figure 12.13 makes it clear what the photographer was up to and the degrees he would go to in order to capture the perfect shot. The dead soldier to the left is clearly the same young man that was posing in figures 11.10 and 11.11. The dead soldier on the right looks to have suffered a very gentle death and he, too, is familiar (fig. 1.3). When compared with the portrait of Thomas Roche in front of the headquarters of Fort Sedgwick, only yards away, it becomes clear that Roche has posed himself as a dead rebel, killed in action (fig. 12.14).

Without Roche to operate the camera for this photograph, and one of his assistants playing the part of his dead compatriot, it seems a likely scenario that Andrew Russell took over the operation of the camera. That leaves us with Russell, who took arguably the most important photograph of the Civil War along the Stone Wall at Fredericksburg, as the creator of the

most ludicrous photograph from the war. It also leaves Roche, the "photojournalist" responsible for producing the most gruesome set of Civil War scenes of the mortally wounded, as the *subject* of the war's silliest scene. What better way to summarize, in three photographs taken by— or including— two lesser-known photographers, the main argument of this book: Without critical analysis and the resulting context, most of these iconic photographs are not what they seem. As a result, this context, whether in terms of manipulation or motivation, is critical to using the pictures as a historical tool.

This photograph brings us back full circle to the discussion of the value of photographs compared with sketches and the nature and role of Civil War photographers as journalists. Certainly, no argument exists that Roche was taking himself completely seriously as a journalist while recording his negatives at Petersburg during the last weeks of the war. After running low on corpses to photograph in the trenches, he began to add props and assistants to his compositions and even created a self-portrait of sorts. These later photographs certainly suggest artistry, rather than photojournalism. Instead, the image only offers to document what the trenches and gabions of the front line looked like, along with the photographic team's affinity for plaid.

Perhaps Russell himself summarized the work of the photographers well when he described Roche's work at Petersburg, "Many were the records he preserved that day that will last while history endures, to relate the eventful story of a victory sorely won."[11] A "sorely won" victory indeed, as Roche and his assistant apparently gave their lives in the quest for these enduring records.

So, in the end we look at this magnificent collection of black-and-white images, a direct link to a war from more than 150 years ago, as a fascinating source of information. This information is best viewed with an eye towards context and skepticism, however, as much of what is conveyed in sepia has been crafted in some manner. Gardner added props. So did O'Sullivan, although not as consistently or blatantly.[12] Brady was fanatical about appearing in his own shots, and was not averse to posing a soldier

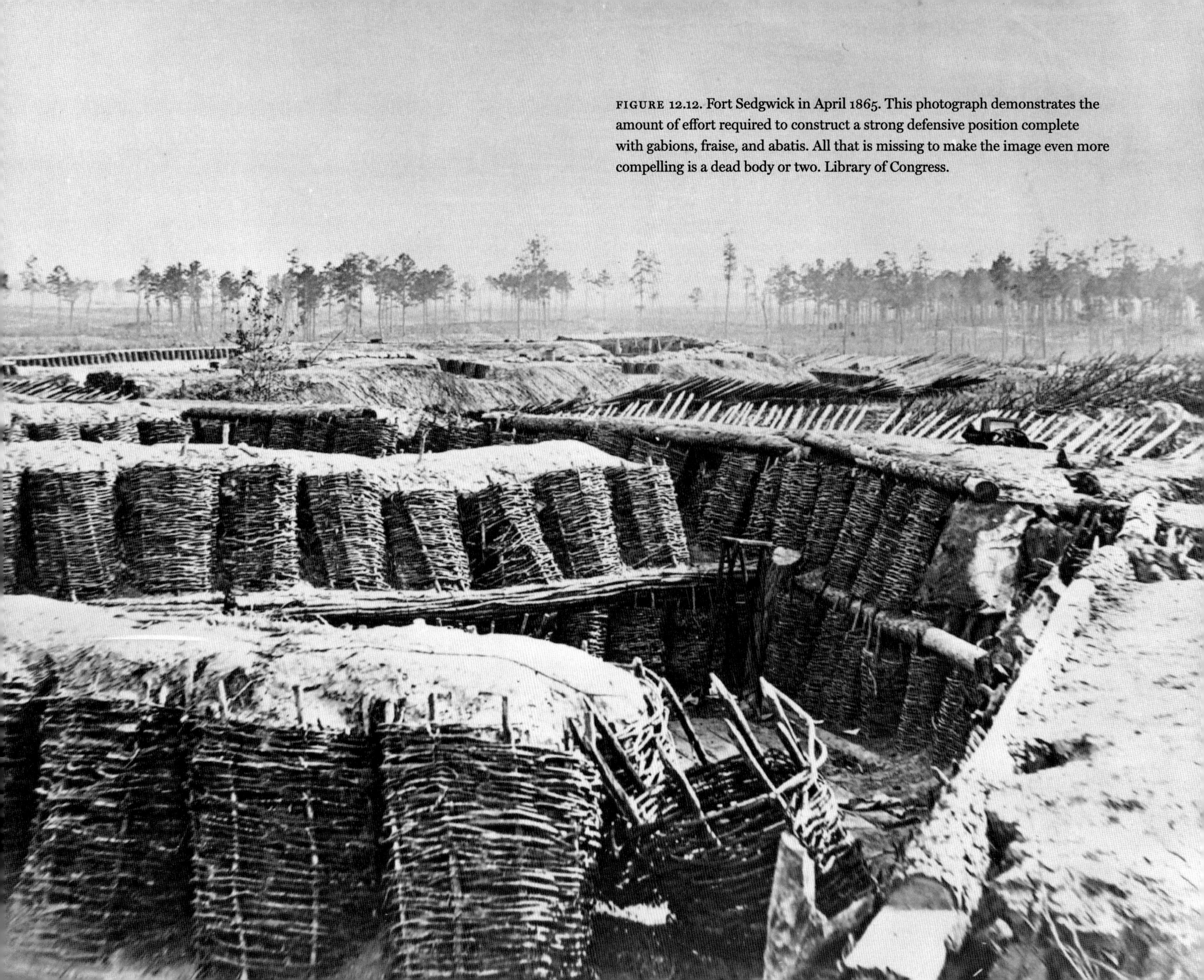

FIGURE 12.12. Fort Sedgwick in April 1865. This photograph demonstrates the amount of effort required to construct a strong defensive position complete with gabions, fraise, and abatis. All that is missing to make the image even more compelling is a dead body or two. Library of Congress.

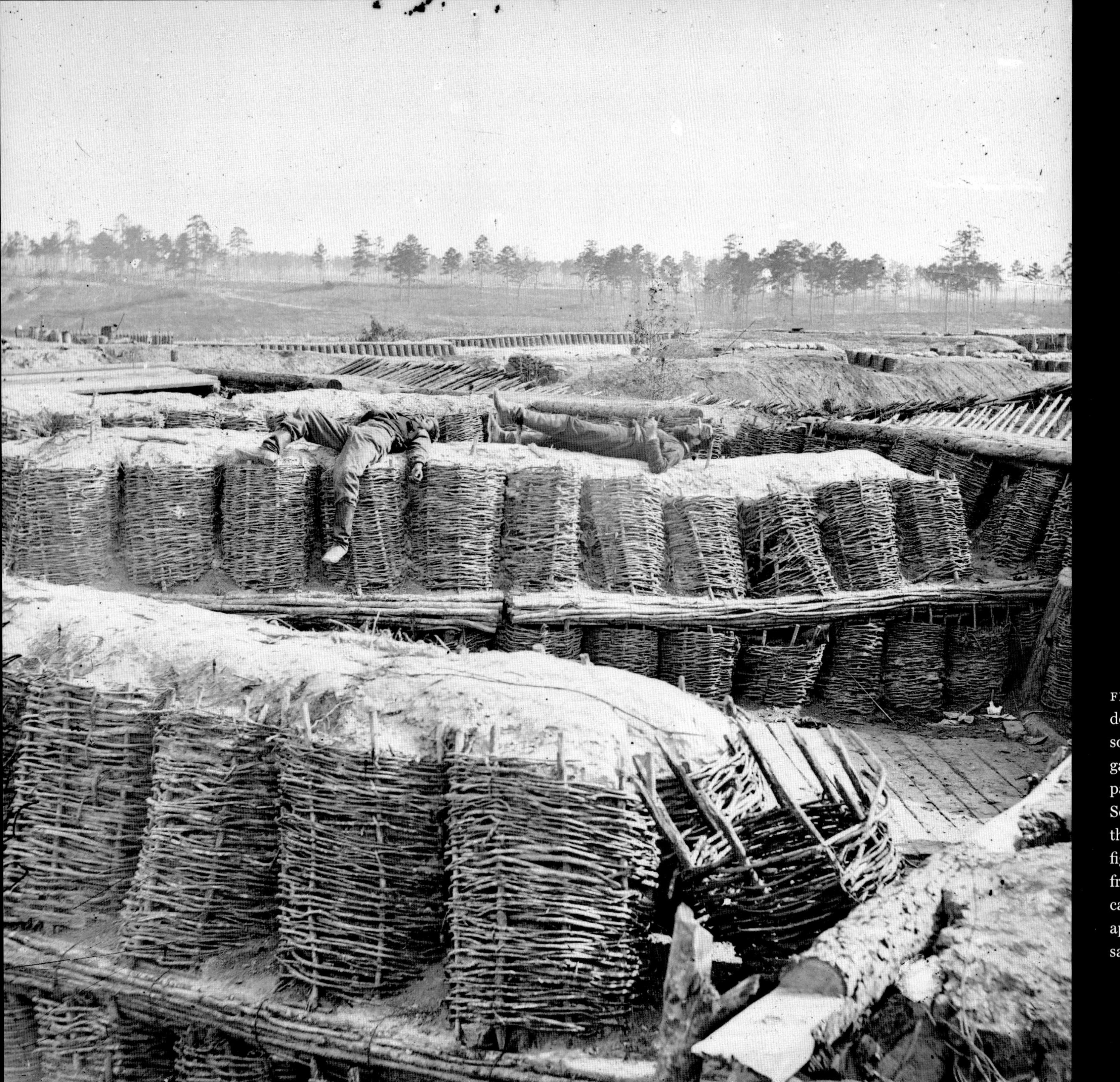

FIGURE 12.13. Two dead Confederate soldiers killed on the gabion-supported parapet of Fort Sedgwick. Compare this figure with figure 12.12, taken from the identical camera position at approximately the same time.

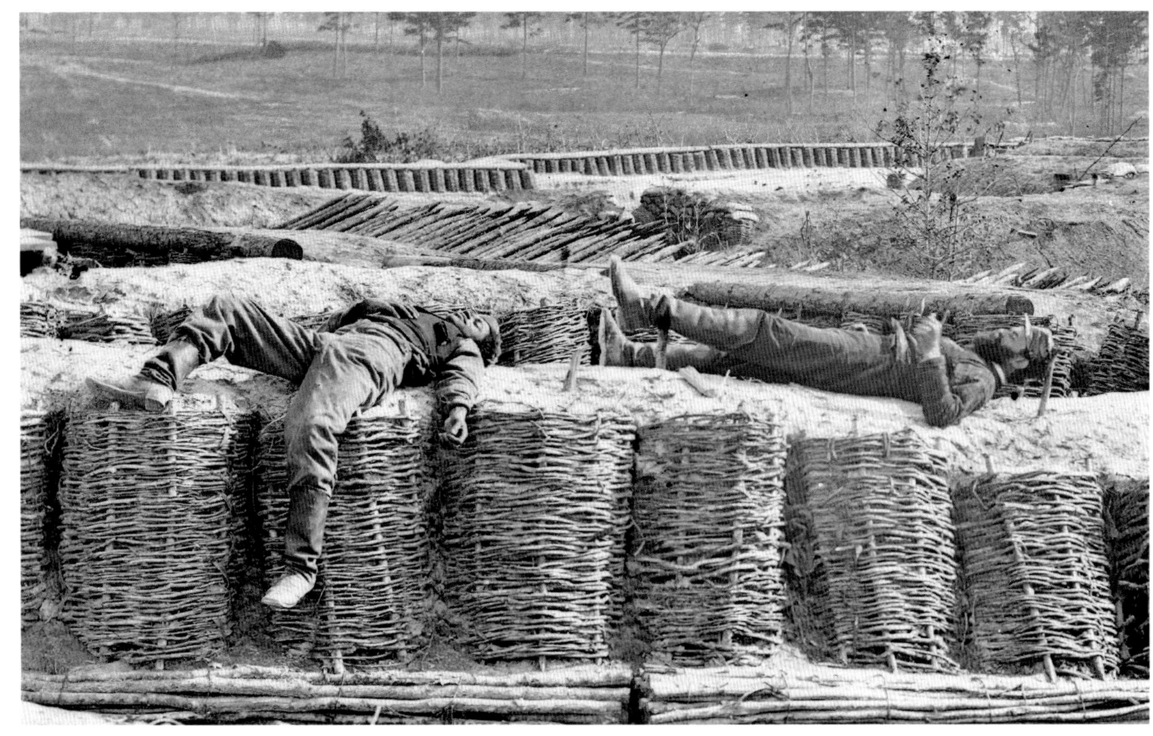

or assistant as a corpse. Roche was a respected photographer, whether dead or alive, and his twice reincarnated assistant must have been good at his job as well.

Where these photographs excel as a historical resource is in their details, which is why it is even more beneficial that the Library of Congress has such an exemplary collection of extremely high-resolution photographs available to the public. Roche may have been playing fast and loose with the rules of photojournalism at Petersburg, but his photographs are unrivaled in showing what the living and fighting conditions were really like for the soldiers who lived, fought, and died there. How long must the written description of the misery of mud in the trenches be to match one or two of Roche's three-dimensional photographs of the slop? And certainly, the sketch artists of the day, no matter how talented, could not match the detail of the images on glass.

Civil War photographs, especially when viewed in their intended stereographic fashion, are a truly marvelous way to travel through time and imagine the battlegrounds of the Civil War. This text is dedicated to providing context to this journey, and to document that this collection of images was created by men whose artistic license and desire to sell photographs occasionally overwhelmed their pretensions as photojournalists. Despite this, there is no comparable manner for which a skeptical viewer can recreate and reimagine the battlefield landscape during this time, to appreciate what the men experienced and what the landscape looked like after the battle moved elsewhere.

APPENDIX A

Data for selection of the "most popular" photograph in books published between 1912 and 2022. Results for books, magazines, websites, and online videos are presented in appendix B.

The Photographs

Book	Author	Publication Date	Virginia Soldiers (Booth?)	Field Hospital at Savage's Station	Union Soldiers Sitting above Camp	Antietam "V" Arranged for Burial	Antietam: Hagerstown Pike	Antietam: Bloody Lane	Antietam: Tree and Grave	Antietam: Dunker Church and Dead	Quaker Gun	Dead at Corinth	Fredericksburg: Destruction	Refugees Cross River	Fredericksburg: Dead at the Stonewall	Gettysburg: Three Rebels	Gettysburg: Sharpshooter's Last Sleep	Gettysburg: Harvest of Death (Union)	Gettysburg Harvest of Death (Rose Farm)	Gettysburg: Disembowed	Vicksburg Prarie Dog Villiage	Union Soldiers Waiting: Two Officers Standing	Spotsylvania: Alsops Clenched	Spotsylvania: Alsops Breastworks	Cold Harbor: Skeletal Remains	Atlanta: Detonation Damage	Atlanta: Chevaul de Frise	Petersburg: Dead Soldier (Two Rifles)	Petersburg: Dead Soldier with Artillery Swab	Petersburg: Dead Soldiers among Chevaul de Frise
Mathew Brady's Illust. History of the C.W.	Lossing	1912		X			X	X	X	X		X	X			X	X	X	X	X		X			X	X	X	X		
American Heritage	Catton	1960	X	X	X		X			X	X			X	X	X	X		X			X		X		X	X	X		
The Civil War: Nat. Geographic	Jordan	1969					X																							
Civil War Battles	Johnson and McLaughlin	1977		X			X											X					X							
Bruce Catton's America	Jensen	1979															X										X			
Civil War Quiz and Fact Book	Gragg	1985			X						X				X															
An Illustraed History of the Civil War	Humble	1987	X	X	X					X					X	X														X
Battle Cry of Freedom	McPherson	1988																							X	X				
A Pictoral History of the Civil War	Barnes	1988						X								X											X			
Distant Thunder	Abell and Pohanka	1988								X																				
Commanders of the Civil War	Davis	1989																									X			
Civil War Day by Day	Bishop et al.	1990												X	X	X	X	X				X								
The Civil War: An Aerial Portrait	Abell and Pohanka	1990																			X									
The Civil War	Ward	1991	X	X		X	X	X	X	X					X	X	X	X			X	X			X	X	X		X	
A Civil War Photographic History	Schindler	1991																X				X			X		X			
The Civil War	Roth	1992		X			X			X					X	X	X	X	X			X	X	X						
The Civil War Album	Robotham	1992						X				X			X	X		X				X								
The Complete Civil War	Kacher	1992						X																						
Battle Maps of the Civil War	O'Shea	1992																							X					
The Civil War Almanac	Bowman	1993						X							X	X	X	X				X								
The Atlas of the Civil War	McPherson	1994					X	X							X	X			X				X		X	X	X			
Civil War Curiosities	Garrison	1994									X																			
American Battlefields	Cobb	1995																				X								
More Civil War Curiosities	Garrison	1995					X																							
Landscapes of the Civil War	Sullivan	1995													X											X	X			
Illustrated Atlas of the Civil War	Time Life	1996					X	X		X								X								X	X			X
Ken Burns's The Civil War	Toplin	1996	X													X														
The Blue and the Gray	Gratham	1997		X											X	X	X	X				X							X	
The Civil War in Depth	Zeller	1997		X	X	X	X	X	X	X					X	X								X	X					
Civil War: Complete Photographic History	Davis and Wiley	2000	X		X		X	X	X	X	X	X	X		X	X	X	X	X	X		X	X	X		X	X		X	
The Civil War in Depth Volume 2	Zeller	2000					X										X						X		X					
Civil War Dictionary	Garrison	2001			X			X										X			X									
The Civil War	Gallegher et al.	2003						X					X	X												X	X			
Battles of the Civil War	Davis	2003					X	X	X				X		X											X				
Fields of Honor	Bearss	2006			X			X	X	X			X			X		X				X								
The Civil War	Sutherland and Carnwell	2007		X											X	X		X								X	X			
The Civil War Day by Day	Katcher	2007		X											X			X												
Battle Cry of Freedom Illustrated	McPherson	2008		X				X		X		X				X		X				X					X			
Atlas of the Civil War	Kagan and Hyslop	2009	X	X	X		X	X	X	X					X			X					X			X	X		X	
The Untold Civl War	Robertson	2011						X	X						X	X									X	X	X			
The Civil War Years	Denney	2011		X		X																								
The Civil War: A Visual History	Smithsonian	2011	X		X				X	X						X		X				X			X	X	X			
The Civil War: Volume 1	Bauernfeind	2013		X		X										X			X	X										
Mathew Brady's First Manassas	Hogge	2013				X										X										X				
The Civil War in 500 Photos	Time Life	2015		X	X	X	X			X					X	X		X				X			X	X		X		
Lens of War	Gallman and Gallagher	2015		X															X	X	X	X				X	X			
Legends and Lies: The Civil War	Fisher	2017																								X	X			
Silent Witness	Field	2017	X	X				X	X	X			X									X	X	X			X			
Remembering the Civil War	Barton and Kupfer	2020						X																			X			
A Short History of the Civil War	Anderson	2020						X										X			X									
50																													
TOTAL:			8	14	12	7	17	16	10	16	7	6	5	3	18	21	12	19	11	6	9	15	9	6	14	14	14	5	3	3
PERCENT:			16	28	24	14	34	32	20	32	14	12	10	6	36	42	24	38	22	12	18	30	18	12	28	28	28	10	6	6

APPENDIX B

The results of the "most popular" contest for books, magazines, websites, and online videos. All values are percentages.

The Photographs

Media	Virginia Soldiers (Booth?)	Field Hospital at Savage's Station	Union Soldiers Sitting above Camp	Antietam "V" Arranged for Burial	Antietam: Hagerstown Pike	Antietam: Bloody Lane	Antietam: Tree and Grave	Antietam: Dunker Church and Dead	Quaker Gun	Dead at Corinth	Fredericksburg: Destruction	Refugees Cross River	Fredericksburg: Dead at the Stonewall	Gettysburg: Three Rebels	Gettysburg: Sharpshooter's Last Sleep	Gettysburg: Harvest of Death (Union)	Gettysburg Harvest of Death (Rose Farm)	Gettysburg: Disembowed	Vicksburg Prarie Dog Villiage	Union Soldiers Waiting: Two Officers Standing	Spotsylvania: Alsops Clenched	Spotsylvania: Alsops Breastworks	Cold Harbor: Skeletal Remains	Atlanta: Detonation Damage	Atlanta: Chevaul de Frise	Petersburg: Dead Soldier (Two Rifles)	Petersburg: Dead Soldier with Artillery Swab	Petersburg: Dead Soldiers among Chevaul de Frise
BOOKS	16	28	24	14	34	32	20	32	14	12	10	6	36	42	24	38	22	12	18	30	18	12	28	28	28	10	6	6
MAGAZINES	0	2	0	4	6	0	8	10	2	0	0	0	0	2	4	6	0	0	2	0	0	2	0	2	0	0	0	0
WEBSITES	2	8	2	0	18	6	6	24	0	0	0	0	12	16	16	28	4	6	4	28	2	6	28	0	0	6	10	0
ONLINE VIDEO	4	14	2	18	22	28	12	18	2	4	4	4	14	12	38	32	30	8	8	2	8	16	20	12	8	18	6	4

NOTES

Preface

1. Lawrence Lee Hewitt, *Port Hudson: The Most Significant Battlefield Photographs from the Civil War* (University of Tennessee Press, 2021), 392. Hewitt's book won the Book of the Year award in 2021 from Civil War Books and Authors (www.cwba.blogspot.com/2021/).

2. Hewitt, *Port Hudson*, xxxi.

3. *Lens of War* contains several photographs that some historians might classify as less than "iconic," and it was published six years before *Port Hudson* gained so much attention for the photographs from that site. Had the dates of publication been reversed between the two photographic books, it is certainly possible that at least one Port Hudson image might have made it into *Lens of War*.

4. Hewitt, *Port Hudson*, xxvii

Chapter 1. The Photographers and Their Photocraft

1. *The New York Times* warmly (and ostentatiously) praised the authenticity of Brady's work: "faithful as is everything that comes from the studio of the Sun" (July 21, 1862).

2. Keith Davis writes of the reputation of Civil War photographers, "It is difficult now to grasp fully the ways in which Civil War photographs were appreciated in their own time. The inherent truthfulness of the camera's transparent, minutely detailed descriptiveness was universally accepted." Keith F. Davis, "'A Terrible Distinctness': Photography of the Civil War Era," in *Photography in Nineteenth-Century America*, ed. Martha A. Sandweiss (Harry N. Abrams, 1991), 170.

3. Mary Panzer (*Mathew Brady and the Image of History*) summarizes the primary difference in the work produced by the great photographers: "Brady's photographs allowed viewers to see the war through the eyes of their loved ones. Gardner's, by contrast, revealed the world that those soldiers would never see" (110).

4. This point is even more important considering the new ways in which Civil War photographs are being used by historians. Cecily Zander (Pennsylvania State University) describes this new approach in a book review: "In recent years, scholars have argued that photographs are more than objects—they are sites of memory and can be read for information about the past in the same manner as letters in an archive or a diary hidden in the attic." But how is this interpretation changed if the author of the letter or diary has a documented history of manipulating the truth? *The Civil War Monitor*, posted March 3, 2021, accessed November 1, 2024; https://www.civilwarmonitor.com/willis-the-black-civil-war-soldier-2021/.

5. Davis, "A Terrible Distinctness," 135.

6. An entire photographic volume could be written about Civil War dogs. Images of high-ranking officers in camp with their dogs at their feet were extremely popular. Matthew Fox-Amato brings to light a more sordid nature of some of these poses, as many other images contain a "contraband" in an identical position and orientation, sitting on the ground below the white officers. As he states, "Written evidence suggests the visual equation of African Americans and dogs actually reflected the widespread racial perception that northern whites held." Matthew Fox-Amato, *Exposing Slavery: Photography, Human Bondage, and the Birth of Modern Visual Politics in America* (Oxford University Press, 2019), 190, 343.

7. While A. Maggie Hazard explored the financial incentives behind photographing the dead, Matthew Fox-Amato discusses a similarly unwholesome relationship between photographs of tortured and scarred slaves and their popularity: "These photographs transformed the long-standing antislavery practice of oral witnessing into one of visual witnessing. . . . Fugitive testimony now came as a marketable photographic commodity." Fox-Amato, *Exposing Slavery*, 178.

8. Veterans returning to Devil's Den, as well as local advertisers, chiseled graffiti into the boulders. Later, the Federal Government removed this work, further scarring the boulders. This "anthropogenic weathering" can be used to approximate the date when many of the early images were captured.

9. Civil War photography has other links to science as well. For example, in the realm of materials research, Captain Thomas Rodman, designer of famous cannons for the Ordnance Department, used photographs to document the changes to iron under varying degrees of tensile strength. These photographs of the resulting fractures helped improve the guns' durability and reliability. Davis, "A Terrible Distinctness," 156. Photographs were also important references in the medical sciences, with different types of wounds illustrating potential clinical solutions.

10. Keith Davis describes the chronology of this contrast: "Most typically, Civil War photographs have been considered simple, unimpeachable bits of visual fact and used as mere adjuncts to historical texts. In more recent years these same images have been regarded by some photographic historians as autonomous works of 'art' most revealing of the medium's inherently 'fictional' nature and the self-expressive subjectivities of 'artists.'" Davis, "A Terrible Distinctness," 131.

11. Historian William Frassanito states, "Because Brady's firm was just one of many larger establishments and did not bother to credit individual cameramen, the Civil War period term, 'Photographed by Brady,' cannot be interpreted by modern historians as signifying anything more than the fact that the camera was operated by someone in Brady's employ." William Frassanito, *Grant and Lee: The Virginia Campaigns, 1864–1865* (Thomas Publications, 1996), 191.

12. Caleb Crain, "How Soon It May Be Too Late," *The New York Time*, August 4, 2013, https://www.nytimes.com/2013/08/04/books/review/mathew-brady-by-robert-wilson.html.

13. Large-format cameras produced larger, more detailed, one-dimensional prints. Stereoviews or stereographs produced two smaller negatives that when viewed together produced a three-dimensional image when viewed through a stereoviewer. The larger prints are especially dramatic because of the detail they include, while the stereoviews give the viewer a sense of actually traveling to the spot of the photograph.

14. Keith Davis writes of this hypocrisy when Mathew Brady signed a contract with the Edward A. Anthony Company: "Ironically, while Brady never gave individual credit to his own photographers, he insisted that all views that the Anthonys published from his negatives bear the 'Brady & Co.' imprint." Davis, "A Terrible Distinctness," 138.

15. Frassanito comments "Failing eyesight had long precluded him from operating a camera, and the famous photographer's role at Gettysburg was essentially that of a supervisor." William Frassanito, *Gettysburg: A Journey in Time* (Thomas Publications, 1975), 38.

16. Ron Field, *Silent Witness: The Civil War Through Photography and Its Photographers* (Osprey, 2017).

17. In 2026 US dollars, Brady would have received approximately $750,000 for his negatives.

18. "Father of Journalism" attribution from James D. Horan: *Mathew Brady: Historian with a Camera* (Bonanza Books, 1955).

19. Enlargers were not used during this early time in photographic processing: Most photographs were contact prints, with the negative being the identical size as the resulting print.

20. A. Maggie Hazard, "Marketing the Dead of Antietam: Photographs of Death as a Cultural Commodity," *Civil War History* 69, no. 1 (2023): 20.

21. When the stereoviews of these negatives were later sold by Brady, they carried the title "Brady Album Gallery." When the stereoviews were later sold by Gardner, they were labeled "From Gardner's Gallery" and "Negative by Alex. Gardner."

22. Davis, "A Terrible Distinctness," 139. These photographs were expensive, as $1.50 in 1863 is equivalent to more than $35 in 2026, and the stereographs cost more than $12 per print.

23. Gardner's choices for inclusion in his *Sketch Book* show a strong bias towards the Eastern Theater of war. Anthony Lee reasons "Photographers focused almost entirely on developments on the East Coast, within reach of the major chemical and glass plate suppliers in New York and Philadelphia. . . . His [Gardner's]

decision to stay close to his base is the single reason the geographic spread of the *Photographic Sketch Book* is so limited." Anthony W. Lee and Elizabeth Young, eds., *On Alexander Gardner's* Photographic Sketch Book *of the Civil War* (University of California Press, 2007), 23.

24. Alan Trachtenberg also points out that Gardner (and Barnard) were competing with themselves when presenting these books to a popular audience, as many Americans and war veterans had already seen the same images as more affordable stereographs or newspaper reproductions. Alan Trachtenberg, *Reading American Photographs: Images as History Mathew Brady to Walker Evans* (Hill and Wang, 1989), 95.

25. Keith Davis argues against the notion that this project or George Barnard's volume *Photographic Views of Sherman's Campaign* were economic failures: "The consistently repeated 'fact' that these publications were commercial failures is highly questionable. Both works were conceived as luxurious, limited-edition items with edition sizes fairly closely matched to the number of actual buyers. In the absence of evidence to the contrary (such as advertisements for either volume being 'remaindered' at drastic discount), it is likely that these enterprises were, in fact, a commercially successful." Davis, "A Terrible Distinctness," 168.

26. Department of Photographs, "Photography and the Civil War, 1861–65," in *Heilbrunn Timeline of Art History*, Metropolitan Museum of Art, October 1, 2004, http://www.metmuseum.org/toah/hd/phcw/hd_phcw.htm.

27. It is also certainly possible that atmospheric conditions, not improved skill with the camera, played a role in the quality and clarity of the photographs.

28. This opinion is from Frassanito, *Grant and Lee*, 22.

29. Perhaps the greatest advocate of Barnard's work was the brilliant US Army quartermaster-general Montgomery Meigs, who specifically requested the photographer for documentation of his department's great efforts in preparing for the Atlanta Campaign. Later, Meigs would also use the photographic talents of Andrew Russell, Jacob Coonley, Thomas Roche, and Samuel Cooley in all theaters of the war.

30. Field, *Silent Witness*, 215.

31. A third, if lesser-known album of Civil War photographs was created by Andrew Russell. It was intended to accompany General Herman Haupt's instruction manual titled *Photographs Illustrative of Operations in Construction and Transportation* (1863). Trachtenberg, *Reading American Photographs*, 107.

32. Barnard's book weighed twenty pounds and sold for $100. Garner's *Sketch Book*, in contrast, contained 39 more prints and cost $150. In 2026 currency, these books were selling for two or three *thousand* dollars.

33. Davis, "A Terrible Distinctness," 165.

34. *How to Make Photographs: A Manual for Amateurs*, 1883.

35. The number of surviving photographs of the USS *Monitor*, when compared with its Confederate foe, clearly demonstrates the bias of Civil War photography towards northern subjects.

36. Gibson paid $10,000 for the half-share according to Waldsmith. Thomas Waldsmith, "James F. Gibson," *Stereo World* 2, no. 6, Jan–Feb 1976, 1–5.

37. "Whipped Peter," also known as "The Scourged Back" or "Gordon," was not the only image seized upon by abolitionists. Another earlier photograph is described by Matthew Fox-Amato in *Exposing Slavery*: Jonathan Walker, a White tradesman, failed in his attempt to help seven slaves escape from Florida to the Bahamas. A judge decided that as part of his punishment he was to have his hand branded with "SS," for "slave stealer." When Walker later returned to New England, a small daguerreotype was created to, in Fox-Amato's words, "dramatize Walker's recent suffering." The print was soon converted to an engraving and appeared in books, newspapers, and pamphlets. In short, "In the mid-1840s, *The Branded Hand* revealed to abolitionists how they could use the daguerrean process for politics." Fox-Amato, *Exposing Slavery*, 116, 117.

38. Lawrence Lee Hewitt, *Port Hudson: The Most Significant Battlefield Photographs from the Civil War* (University of Tennessee Press, 2021), 62–63. Hewitt also notes that McPherson created the first compositional print and the first photograph to be captured outdoors at night.

39. Hewitt, *Port Hudson*, 13.

40. Davis, "A Terrible Distinctness," 164.

41. Anthony and Company, the producer of the prints of this series, unfortunately only attributed one of the dozen or more photographs taken this day.

42. It is also important to remember that the popularity of a particular photograph (or photographer) can also influence how history is interpreted. For example, Keith Davis points out that the 13-inch mortar *Dictator* "remains well known to us through several impressive photographs made in the summer of 1864," even though it saw very limited combat and was placed into storage soon after it appeared at

Petersburg. Without the photographs, Davis notes, "the *Dictator* would most likely have remained an obscure military footnote." Davis, "A Terrible Distinctness," 135.

43. Keith Davis notes that there were important campaigns and entire geographic regions that were completely missed during the Civil War, including General Philip Sheridan's Shenandoah operation. Davis, "A Terrible Distinctness."

44. Gardner may have been photographed inadvertently by one of his assistants while working on his famous *A Harvest of Death* series at Gettysburg. He doesn't appear to be posing when he is caught standing on the very fringe of one of the negatives. This is explored more in the next chapter.

Chapter 2. The Hierarchy of Historical Preeminence

1. Stephen Berry, "The Book or the Gun?," in *Lens of War*, eds. J. Matthew Gallman and Gary W. Gallagher (University of Georgia Press, 2015), 214–21.

2. Lawrence Lee Hewitt, *Port Hudson: The Most Significant Battlefield Photographs from the Civil War* (University of Tennessee Press, 2021).

3. According to Hewitt more than two thousand photographs were taken on Lookout Mountain alone.

4. Hewitt, *Port Hudson*, xxxi.

5. Hewitt, *Port Hudson*, xxx.

6. Hewitt states that this list might include Port Hudson: "McPherson and Oliver had an opportunity to safely photograph corpses between the lines during the siege of Port Hudson, but opted not to, possibly because they all wore blue uniforms." Hewitt, *Port Hudson*, xxxi.

7. These are the books you would commonly find at Barnes & Noble, Books-A-Million, or a National Battlefield bookshop.

8. Note that all photographs and sketches in this book are from the Library of Congress collection (unless otherwise noted). Other figures, maps, and charts are the author's own creation.

9. Both William Frassanito (*Gettysburg: A Journey in Time*, 1975) and Brooks Simpson (Gallman and Gallagher, *Lens of War*, 2015) provide the July 15 for the day that Brady and his assistants were working on Seminary Ridge and the battlefield of the first day's fighting at Gettysburg.

10. Frassanito, *Gettysburg*, 71.

11. Brooks D. Simpson, "Three Confederates at Gettysburg," in Gallman and Gallagher, *Lens of War*, 87.

12. William Frassanito, of course, was responsible for demonstrating that these two sets of images are of the same group of fallen US soldiers in his groundbreaking 1975 book *Gettysburg: A Journey in Time*.

13. Chapter 4 is dedicated to using science to investigate the location of these photographs on the Gettysburg Battlefield.

14. William A. Frassanito, *Early Photography at Gettysburg* (Thomas Publications, 1995), 315.

15. Earl Hess notes that this photograph is even more interesting because the Federal army would yield this position by the end of the day. Earl Hess, "Andrew J. Russell and the Stone Wall at Fredericksburg" in Gallman and Gallagher, *Lens of War*, 87.

16. Portions of this Stone Wall also have an earthen embankment on the opposite side (facing the attacking Federals), similar to the piled sod along the split-rail breastworks behind Brady's three captured Confederates. The purpose of the additional piled earth was to reduce visibility to the enemy and offer protection against incoming artillery fire.

17. Frassanito suggests that this may be because these were the first set of corpses that the photographers encountered on the battlefield. William Frassanito, *Antietam: The Photographic Legacy of America's Bloodiest Day* (Thomas Publications, 1978).

18. A full 122 or 123 rails appear to be in place; only 3 or 4 have fallen.

19. Careful examination of the fence across the pike in the photographs reveals that six or seven entire segments between posts have been dismantled.

20. A. Maggie Hazard recently wrote an interesting study about the merchandising of Gardner's photographs for *Civil War History*, which paid particular attention to this image. She noted that Gardner and E. & H. T. Anthony offered an "even more gruesome," enhanced version of this print, where a technician had added red paint to the face of the only dead soldier whose face is visible to the camera. This bright trickle of blood emerges from his mouth and flows down his cheek, in stark contrast to the rest of the sepia image. A. Maggie Hazard, "Marketing 'The Dead of Antietam': Photographs of Death as a Cultural Commodity," *Civil War History* 69, no. 1 (March 2023): 9–41.

21. Frassanito, *Antietam*, 206.

22. This is why a second defensive line was added on the higher ground to the south behind the Sunken Road to support the position.

23. The orientation of these photographs, used to determine the southern and northern side of the Bloody Lane, follow the reasoning from William Frassanito's work presented in *Antietam*.

24. I spent an entire chapter of *Myths of the Civil War* documenting and debunking the "density of death/human carpet" trope. If all of the killed-in-action from the entire battle of Antietam from both armies were collected and dragged them to the cornfield, you still could not cover the ground adequately to create this grisly, if imaginative, carpet of death. Scott Hippensteel, *Myths of the Civil War: The Fact, Fiction, and Science Behind the Civil War's Most-Told Stories* (Stackpole Books, 2021).

Chapter 3. Photographic Forensics

1. Ben McGrath, "The Professor of Baseball," *The New Yorker*, July 14, 2003. https://www.newyorker.com/magazine/2003/07/14/the-professor-of-baseball.

2. Bill James, *The Bill James Baseball Abstract, 1984* (Ballentine Books, 1994).

3. William Frassanito, *Early Photography at Gettysburg* (Thomas Publications, 1995), x.

4. Errol Morris, "The Best Books on Photography and Reality," interview by Eve Gerber, Five Books, September 30, 2011, https://fivebooks.com/best-books/errol-morris-on-photography-and-reality/.

5. Garry Adelman, the Director of History and Education at the American Battlefield Trust, explained this phenomenon to Ned Jilton III in the July 8, 2022, edition of *The Times News* (Kingsport, TN): https://www.timesnews.net/living/do-civil-war-photographs-match-today-s-digital-images-in-showing-details/article_3281d122-c14b-11ea-b1b5-0fcc76112510.html.

6. William Frassanito, *Gettysburg: A Journey in Time* (Thomas Publications, 1975), 228.

7. G. R. Dunning and J. P. Hodych, "U/Pb zircon and baddeleyite ages for the palisades and Gettysburg sills of the northeastern United States: Implications for the age of the Triassic/Jurassic boundary," *Geology* 18 (1990:) 795–98.

8. Weathering is the physical breakdown of a rock, whether mechanical, chemical, or biological in nature. Erosion is the transport and removal of these weathered components.

9. Unfortunately, even some of these hard rock tracers have been lost at Gettysburg through the years. An effort to create a narrow-gauge railroad trackway around and through the Slaughter Pen and Valley of Death destroyed many boulders through blasting and excavation.

10. Chris E. Fonvielle Jr., *Fort Fisher 1865: The Photographs of T. H. O'Sullivan* (Slap Dash Publishing, 2011).

11. Repairing this wall would have been required to offer protection from a Confederate attack from the north. Wilmington, North Carolina, was still in Confederate hands at this stage of the war and was located 15 miles upriver to the north.

12. The camera was also repositioned slightly, complicating the estimation of a time duration using shadow length.

13. "In experienced hands," according to Anthony Lee, "a single, usable picture took thirty minutes to obtain." Lee and Young, *On Alexander Gardner's Photographic Sketch Book*, 22.

14. Capturing wet-emulsion negatives along the brilliant, sandy, wind-blown coast of the Carolinas certainly presented an especially large number of challenges and complications.

Chapter 4. Harvest of Confusion

1. This gorier photograph barely snuck into the top twenty in our earlier popularity contest. Perhaps authors and editors found it too disturbing for most general interest history books.

2. It is not surprising that Gardner, Gibson, and O'Sullivan apparently failed to take a single photograph of either the first day's or third day's battlefields. Arriving so soon after the battle, local guides may not have been able to provide any context as to what had occurred during the very recent fighting. What might be more surprising is that when Brady and his team arrived almost two weeks later, they still did not take a single photograph of the fields of Pickett's Charge.

3. William Frassanito, *Gettysburg: A Journey in Time* (Thomas Publications, 1975), 225.

4. William Frassanito, *Early Photography at Gettysburg* (Thomas Publications, 1995).

5. Frassanito, *Early Photography at Gettysburg*, 315.

6. Gary Adelman, the vice president of the Center for Civil War Photography, began to post a standardized reply titled "Plea for Patience with all things Harvest of Death" in response to the frequency of online claims of a "conclusive" discovery.

7. Has this colorization been scientifically tested? Have modern black and white images of, say, reenactors in historically accurate garb been recolorized to make sure they match? Proper scientific testing would require a modern scene with soldiers in gray, butternut, and blue to be photographed using Civil War era cameras, and then the sepia prints could be recolorized to see if the process properly identifies the correct shades.

8. Warren, the hero of Little Round Top, was creating a high-resolution topographic map with a four-foot contour interval, all based on an elevation data point near the cemetery, more than a mile from the proposed photographic site. The Elliott map is known to be fairly accurate for the northern part of the battlefield, less so for the southern.

9. Quote from page 32.

10. Note that McPherson's Ridge, from a geological standpoint, should be one of the more gently sloping ridges around Gettysburg as it is underlain by sandstones and shales (unlike Seminary and Cemetery Ridges, which are composed of harder igneous rock).

11. Patrick Brennan, "A Harvest of Death," *The Civil War Monitor* 12, no. 1 (Spring 2022): 35.

12. Brennan, "A Harvest of Death," 40.

13. Or perhaps within 24 hours, at best, of the shooting of the *Harvest* series. The travels of Gardner's team around the Gettysburg Battlefield are a contentious subject that is still debated today.

14. Brennan, "A Harvest of Death," 40.

15. LIDAR, an initialism for "Light Detecting and Ranging" is a remote sensing tool that uses pulsed lasers to measure variable distances (ranges). This aerial tool can map the surface of the Earth in great detail, removing the influence of vegetation to better understand the topography. In doing so, it provides a map of the Earth's solid surface—perfect for analyzing a modern forested area to see if the slope matched that of an area that was farmland in the 1860s.

16. This criterion assumes that the photographic team probably wouldn't have wanted to pack up and move their camera/tripod/darkroom wagon any more than necessary when pressed for time. It would be more efficient to take as many photographs as possible in a single geographical area (e.g., Devil's Den or the Rose Farm) before spending the time to pack up and move elsewhere.

17. An excellent overview of the history of changes to the battlefield can be found in Jennifer Murray, *On a Great Battlefield: The Making, Management, and Memory of Gettysburg National Military Park, 1933–2013* (University of Tennessee Press, 2014).

Chapter 5. The Scale of Manipulation

1. Quote from Amazon.com product description (December 12, 2022), https://www.amazon.com/Historic-Photos-Gettysburg-John-Salmon/dp/1596523239.

2. Jennifer Murray, *On a Great Battlefield: The Making, Management, and Memory of Gettysburg National Military Park, 1933–2013* (University of Tennessee Press, 2014).

3. William McPherson did capture one image of US sharpshooters operating behind hogsheads that were piled into a huge mound at Port Hudson. Although taken from a distance, these men do appear to be engaged with the enemy (although the number of sharpshooters is unclear, and the enemy remains unseen). See commentary for figures 17 and 18 in Hewitt's *Port Hudson* for a more complete discussion and detailed examination of these men in "combat." Lawrence Lee Hewitt, *Port Hudson: The Most Significant Battlefield Photographs from the Civil War* (University of Tennessee Press, 2021).

4. Alan Trachtenberg blamed the lengthy time to set up a photograph for the absence of "combat" photographs: "the process required that the camera be planted, the lens focused, the plate coated, exposed, and developed while still wet, all within precious moments at the scene of the 'view' to be made. Not surprisingly, few signs of actual battle appear in any Civil War pictures." Alan Trachtenberg, *Reading American Photographs: Images as History Mathew Brady to Walker Evans* (Hill and Wang, 1989), 72.

5. This was difficult to explain to small children and horses, who often appear blurred.

6. Or was this much light needed? See chapter 7.

7. At this same level of inauthenticity, we might include George Barnard's use of combination printing to "add majestic cloudscapes to otherwise blank skies in his landscape views." Keith F. Davis, "'A Terrible Distinctness': Photography of the Civil War Era," in *Photography in Nineteenth-Century America*, ed. Martha A. Sandweiss (Harry N. Abrams, 1991), 171.

8. Some historians might argue that Cook's photograph of Federal ironclads firing at Charleston Harbor or McPherson's photograph of Federal sharpshooters at Port Hudson are just as, or perhaps, even more valuable because they portray men actually engaged with the enemy. I would counter that these images were captured from such a great distance that the nature of the engagement is usually rendered as a minute blur, at best.

9. Chapter 7 of this book delves deeper into the lowest level of our scale of manipulation—the posing of subjects required by the slow shutter speeds of the cameras. The analysis yields some surprising results about the probable exposure durations required for most photographs from the era, especially those shot outdoors when the weather was agreeable.

10. In both cases the rifle is very easy to miss, because it is hidden in the details. For figure 5.3, image 2, it is almost certainly the same rifle that appears with the dead Confederate "sharpshooters" that were found nearly five hundred yards away.

11. This collection of random photographs acts as a "control group" for the test involving the missing ramrod. Effectively, it serves as a baseline for comparison.

12. This isn't surprising, because a rifle musket without a ramrod is essentially no better a weapon than a nine-pound club; if we believe that these photographs are completely authentic, this may explain why the Confederates lost the battle: All of their soldiers were armed with useless guns.

13. An alternate hypothesis might be that all these Confederates were killed because they were armed with an inoperable rifle. Those must have been some poorly trained soldiers.

14. Manipulated images also had influences on writing outside of the non-fiction realm. For example, according to Trachtenberg, Stephen Crane used reproduced photographs from the Civil War for reference and inspiration when composing the 1895 novel *The Red Badge of Courage*. Trachtenberg also noted that Harold Frederic, a contemporary novelist, thought that consulting Civil War photographs gave Crane better grounds to depict what his fictional subject actually witnessed, rather than what all his background reading had told him he should expect to see. Trachtenberg, *Reading American Photographs*, 78.

15. In a brief study of the captions and descriptions in *Home of a Rebel Sharpshooter*, I found that 100 percent of the time the image was not recognized as manipulated in books published prior to William Frassanito's 1975 book, *Gettysburg: A Journey in Time*. After 1975, it was noted that the image was staged in approximately 80 percent of the time.

16. Davis, "A Terrible Distinctness," 171.

17. Trachtenberg, *Reading American Photographs*, 83.

Chapter 6. Artistry and Authenticity: The Photographer versus the Sketch Artist

1. Although these authentic photographs, even when viewed as purely historical archives, were often critiqued by the public for their artistic value: "To a degree only partially understood today, Civil War photographs represented a seamless integration of art and information. It should not strike us as curious therefore that what would appear to be purely 'documentary' photographs were evaluated, at least in part, on aesthetic grounds." Keith F. Davis, "'A Terrible Distinctness': Photography of the Civil War Era," in *Photography in Nineteenth-Century America*, ed. Martha A. Sandweiss (Harry N. Abrams, 1991), 171.

2. Perhaps "combat" or "action" isn't the correct modifier. Mathew Brady divided his photographs into a grouping he termed "war-scenes," which seems equally descriptive and appropriate.

3. When sketches and photographs were included in the newspapers of the day, both lost detail in the engraving process. For the photographs, this is a critical problem because it robs them of their advantage of seeming authenticity. Keith Davis explains "The endless detail of the photograph—its appearance of factual transparency—was impossible to convey in a manually rendered image, and the content of

the original image was inevitably simplified." For Gardner's *Dead at Antietam* photographs-turned-lithographs, specifically: "In the pages of *Harper's Weekly* these images were moving, but not shocking." Davis, "A Terrible Distinctness," 150, 152.

4. Sketch artists also had an advantage in speed when it came to getting their works published quickly in newspapers. Keith Davis relates that after the Battle of Antietam, sketches were appearing in *Harper's Weekly* at the same time the battle was being announced (two-and-a-half-week delay), while photographs would not appear as engravings until after five weeks. This same lengthy delay in photographic processing and conversion for newsprint also occurred after Gettysburg. Davis, "A Terrible Distinctness," 148.

5. Anthony Lee points out that Gardner himself commented on the question of photographic authenticity in the preface to his own book. When pointing out the differences between his photographic book, and others based on sketches, he addresses the potential differences in authenticity between his prose that accompanies each photograph and the sepia images themselves: "Verbal representations of such places, or scenes, may or man not have the merit of accuracy, but photographic presentments of them will be accepted by posterity with an undoubting faith." Gardner's abuse of the scale of manipulation suggests a bit of skepticism should be brought by posterity to their "undoubting faith." His team's actions of adding props and moving corpses demonstrates the false advertising of this statement. Lee and Young, *On Alexander Gardner's* Photographic Sketch Book, 35–36.

6. Frederick Ray, *Our Special Artist: Alfred R. Waud's Civil War* (Stackpole Books, 1994), 27.

7. With this distinction in mind, isn't it interesting that Gardner chose to name his 1866 compendium *Sketch Book*? It is as if he is claiming the instantaneousness of the sketch artists with the authenticity promised by his detailed photographs.

8. Theodore R. Davis, "How a Battle is Sketched," *St. Nicholas* 16 (1889), 661–68.

9. A. B. Paine, *Th. Nast: His Period and His Pictures* (The Pyne Press, 1904), 7.

10. Photographs also had to go through the engraving process to be reproduced in newsprint and these secondary artist/technicians often deleted details or combined photographs into elaborate composites. There was, of course, no mention in the caption of this manipulation.

11. This test of authenticity *might* also translate to the artist's battle scenes, although this cannot be tested because of the absence of a true combat photograph to serve as a control.

12. William A. Frassanito, *Early Photography at Gettysburg* (Thomas Publications, 1995), 103.

13. The Library of Congress' title for this photograph includes "July 3rd," although the painting probably represents the scene on the Round Top from a day earlier.

14. The value of Brady's terrain studies such as this to the popular viewer (e.g., newspaper readers) is summarized by Mary Panzer: "These nearly empty landscapes provided a screen on which they could project a private vision of the battle." Mary Panzer, *Mathew Brady and the Image of History* (Smithsonian Books, 1997), 109.

15. When the details of this sketch are compared to the painting of Paul Philippoteaux's 1884 *The Battle of Gettysburg* (better known as the Gettysburg Cyclorama), the details, immediacy, and importance of Waud's sketch are illuminated. For example, Philippoteaux was working from photographs of the landscape that were taken almost twenty years after the battle had ended: His depiction of the Codori farm, at the center of his massive artwork, contains additions and outbuildings not present in 1863. Waud's sketch shows the buildings more accurately, in the proper configuration.

16. Anthony Lee explores the relationships between sketch artists and photographers in detail. He also details the advantages and disadvantages of the images created by both types of documentarians. An individual photograph took more than half an hour to produce, and only one could be produced at a time. Photographs also required a logistically challenging amount of equipment and chemicals that needed replenished often. Artists could work on several sketches at a time, filling in details later. They also only needed a pad and pencil, making them much more mobile and more likely to capture first-person views of action scenes. Lee and Young, *On Alexander Gardner's* Photographic Sketch Book.

17. Gardner and his team took multiple photographs of one dead soldier, from different angles, then ignored completely another nearby corpse, deciding, I suppose, not to sacrifice even a single glass plate.

Chapter 7. Shedding Some Light on Exposure Times

1. See, for example, Mary Paul, "The Mystery Man Who Took the Pictures: Civil War Photojournalists Associated with Mathew Brady's Gallery from 1861–1865," in *A Press Divided: Newspaper Coverage of the Civil War*, ed. David B. Sachsman (Routledge, 2014), 189–215.

2. As Keith Davis notes, "The sales potential of these photographs varied in roughly inverse proportions to their retail cost (and size)." Keith F. Davis, "'A Terrible Distinctness': Photography of the Civil War Era," in *Photography in Nineteenth-Century America*, ed. Martha A. Sandweiss (Harry N. Abrams, 1991), 142.

Chapter 8. Resolution in the (High) Resolution

1. Taylor was an aide to Lee. After the war he was elected to the Virginia General Assembly.

2. *The Richmond Whig*, April 21, 1865.

3. J. R. Hamilton, *The New York Times*, April 23, 1865.

4. Jeff Rosenheim, *Photography and the American Civil War* (Metropolitan Museum of Art, 2013), 221.

5. Joseph Glatthaar, "The Peculiar Genius of William Tecumseh Sherman," in *Lens of War*, eds. J. Matthew Gallman and Gary W. Gallagher (University of Georgia Press, 2015), 59–66.

6. Michael D. Gorman, "Lee the 'Devil' Discovered at Image of War Seminar," *Battlefield Photographer* 3, no. 1, (February 2006): 1.

7. Robert Wilson, "Dignity in Defeat: Mathew Brady's Photographs of Robert E. Lee," HistoryNet, October 31, 2013, https://www.historynet.com/dignity-in-defeat-mathew-bradys-photos-of-robert-e-lee/.

8. Ron Field, *Silent Witness: The Civil War Through Photography and Its Photographers* (Osprey, 2017), 287.

9. Fox-Amato, *Exposing Slavery*, 208.

10. Nina Zafar, *The Washington Post*, December 2, 2020. "In DC, Affordable Fort Lincoln still Evokes Its Great Society Origins."

11. The neighborhood reviews website Niche gives Fort Lincoln an A+ for "Diversity." https://www.niche.com/places-to-live/n/fort-lincoln-washington-dc/.

12. Contrast this image with those captured in the 1845 and 1863 of "The Branded Hand" and "Whipped Peter." Matthew Fox-Amato (*Exposing Slavery*) raises an interesting question about why "damage photography," in his words, wasn't used more effectively by abolitionists in the years between these two photographs.

13. Stephen Berry, "The Book or the Gun?," in *Lens of War*, eds. J. Matthew Gallman and Gary W. Gallagher (University of Georgia Press, 2015), 216.

14. A. Maggie Hazard, "Marketing the Dead of Antietam: Photographs of Death as a Cultural Commodity," *Civil War History* 69, no. 1 (2023): 20.

15. Keith Davis reminds us, "Civil War photographs stem from a complex range of individual motivations, including a sense of contemporary history, patriotism, adventure, and professional or social prestige. However, entrepreneurship and the simple need to earn a living dominate all other concerns." Keith F. Davis, "'A Terrible Distinctness': Photography of the Civil War Era," in *Photography in Nineteenth-Century America*, ed. Martha A. Sandweiss (Harry N. Abrams, 1991), 131.

16. Deborah Willis, *The Black Civil War Soldier: A Visual History of Conflict and Citizenship* (New York University Press, 2021), 26.

Chapter 9. Timing is Everything

1. One additional photograph was taken by O'Sullivan at the church, but from a completely different viewpoint.

2. Frassanito presented the photos in reverse sequence in his book "for ease of discussion, since 10a ["Standing"] is the most visually revealing of the three." William A. Frassanito, *Grant and Lee: The Virginia Campaigns, 1864–1865* (Macmillan Publishing Company, 1983), 121.

3. Frassanito points out that only one dispatch was sent on May 21, the day these photographs were taken, to the commander of the IX Corps, Burnside.

4. Bob Zeller, *The Civil War in Depth: History in 3-D* (Chronical Books, 1979).

5. William C. Davis and Wiley Bell, *Photographic History of the Civil War: Vicksburg to Appomattox* (Black Dog and Leventhal Publishers, 1994).

6. We witnessed this in the previous chapter as well, with the scattered bricks and trash along the street where "The Book or the Gun" was photographed in Atlanta.

7. This book focuses on photographs other than portraits. However, if portraits were included in our study and discussion of popularity, this field photograph of Grant at Cold Harbor would be at the top of the list for most reproduced pictures from the war.

8. Brady was undoubtedly present for these photographs as he appears, unsurprisingly, in one shot, posing next to Ambrose Burnside.

9. The Pliocene Epoch lasted from between two and five million years ago.

10. The Fredericksburg Battlefield is also underlain by the Chesapeake Group. The formations that comprise this group, including the Choptank and Calvert Formations, are durable enough to form high ground yet soft enough to be excavated for gun pits or protected artillery positions—excellent defensive terrain.

Chapter 10. A Photographic Chronology of a Colossal Waste of Time

1. Peter S. Michie, "Account of the Dutch Gap Canal as Prepared by P. S. Michie, Engineer in Charge of the Work," in *Battles and Leaders of the Civil War*, vol. 4, ed. Frank Leslie (Century Co., 1865), 575.

2. Or at least at one end, so that when the bulkheads were violently removed with explosives, the canal would suddenly be available to US monitors and ironclads, providing a degree of surprise along the river.

3. When tunneling under the Confederate lines at Petersburg prior to the Battle of the Crater, the Federal sappers had great difficulty working with marl, a clay-rich layer that was exhausting to remove. Eventually, they redirected their mine to stay in the sandier strata.

4. Earl J. Hess, *In the Trenches at Petersburg: Field Fortifications and Confederate Defeat* (University of North Carolina Press, 2009).

5. Rifled artillery from Confederate batteries had too shallow of a trajectory to successfully fall into the canal. The higher parabolic path of the mortar shells allowed them to rise above the ridges along the river and fall into the open, deep canal path.

6. Bob Zeller dedicated a page in his book *The Civil War in Depth* (1997) to discussing "The Case for Northern Combat Photography." He displays a previously unpublished photograph from Dutch Gap Canal that caries the caption "The mist arising against the bank is caused by a rebel shell, which exploded just as this view was being photographed." Zeller, *The Civil War in Depth*, 68.

7. With proper bulldozers and dump trucks, a large construction company or the Army Corps of Engineers could cut a canal through this Pleistocene material in a matter of a week or two. The underlying layers would take substantially longer.

8. William Morris Fontaine, "The Potomac Formation in Virginia," *Department of the Interior Bulletin of the United States Geological Survey*, no. 145 (1896): 151.

9. William A. Frassanito. *Grant and Lee: The Virginia Campaigns, 1864–1865* (Macmillan Publishing Company, 1983).

10. Less than a year earlier George Cook photographed ironclads exchanging gunfire with Fort Moultrie in Charleston Harbor (fig. 1.5), certainly the first example of "action" or "combat" photography from the war.

11. Bob Zeller, *The Civil War in Depth: History in 3-D* (Chronicle Books, 1997), 68.

12. One of the more famous photographs from the Vicksburg battlefield of the Shirley House made the list of the twenty-five most popular photographs from the war.

Chapter 11. Photographing Damnation and Hell

1. This Gardner photograph follows a compositional pattern similar to those discussed earlier about his work at Antietam. The first location the eye is drawn to on so many of his photographs is in the lower right. The eye is then drawn upwards and to the left, either down the Hagerstown Turnpike, along the Bloody Lane, or, in this case, from the dismembered hand, following the rifle musket across the horrific wound to the bolt that was the cause of death.

2. Alan Trachtenberg, *Reading American Photographs: Images as History Mathew Brady to Walker Evans* (Hill and Wang, 1989), 83

3. William A. Frassanito, *Early Photography at Gettysburg* (Thomas Publications, 1995), 336–41.

4. This account by Lt. Berzila Inman of Company F of the 188th Pennsylvania Regiment was recounted in 1888. John Smith, *History of the Corn Exchange Regiment, 118th Pennsylvania Volunteers* (Philadelphia, 1888).

5. There are reports from the Antietam Battlefield that hogs and birds did feed on the dead, but only after they had been buried in shallow graves and a combination of burrowing and erosion exposed their flesh to the scavengers.

6. Frassanito, *Early Photography at Gettysburg*, 337

7. The March 2023 volume of *Civil War History* contains an interesting article written by A. Maggie Hazard about the financial incentives for photographing the dead on the battlefield. She points out "that people in the nineteenth century had a very different attachment to death than we do today—one that highlighted a kind of reverence for the life lived, the process of death, and the maintaining of a physical connection to those who had passed on. The collection of a lock of hair or other memento from the body of the deceased for placement in a locket to be worn or incorporated into a wall hanging points to a society much closer to the experience of death than most twenty-first century viewers are." Additionally, she posits about their popularity, "The photographs presented such a different view of war death than was previously understood and were so detailed that they suggested the possibility of 'finding' a loved one among the carnage. As such, the cultural familiarity with death and the existing postmortem photographic industry that Brady and Gardner banked on for their success only added to the images' impact when they were presented for sale." A. Maggie Hazard, "Marketing the Dead of Antietam: Photographs of Death as a Cultural Commodity," *Civil War History* 69, no. 1 (2023): 21–22.

8. These "snipers" were, in reality, sharpshooters and designated riflemen taking long-distance shots. The "sniper", as we think of the role today, didn't really exist during the Civil War.

9. B. Noland Carter and Michael E. DeBakey, "Current Observations on War Wounds of the Chest," *Journal of Thoracic Surgery* 13, n. 4 (1944): 271–93.

10. One additional complicating factor is the rate of successful recovery from a wound to the extremities: Gangrene and primitive medical procedures in field hospitals certainly led to more superficial wounds turning into mortal wounds during the Civil War when compared to later conflicts.

11. The instantaneous nature of this wound would not have allowed for blood to circulate, and his nose and mouth are both elevated as he lies on his back.

12. David Lowe and Philip Shiman suggest this young man was a teamster. Lowe and Shiman, "Substitute for a Corpse," *Civil War Times*, Dec. 2010, 41.

13. The hat and artillery sponge both move, and there is a Minié ball present in figure 11.8 beside the canteen, perhaps to hint at the irony of an artilleryman cut down by small arms fire.

14. Gore sells. This is still true today, with the worldwide box office from the *Saw* movie franchise at $1.1 billion and rising. https://www.the-numbers.com/movies/franchise/Saw#tab=summary.

15. This entire warning from the company can be found on the back of a number of stereoviews available in the Library of Congress collection. For example, the "Sunken Road" at Antietam has an entire "1861—Photographic History—1865" summary. See https://www.loc.gov/resource/stereo.2s02696/.

16. This isn't entirely unrealistic: If the soldier is shot in the front, with the bullet coming from across the boulder field, he would be expected to fall backwards, with his feet and right side closest to the rocky formations.

17. The banquette tread is the flat area directly behind the interior crest of the parapet where infantrymen would stand to fire over the defensive fortification.

18. As recounted in Frassanito, *Grant and Lee*, 337.

Conclusion. The Significance of Science and Sepia

1. The rocks under the Manassas battlefields are identical in age, composition, and depositional environment, but do not crop out as strikingly.

2. And Gardner certainly didn't do anything to help with this situation with his multiple descriptive captions that were full of inaccuracies.

3. Lawrence Hewitt raised just this question: "Beyond quantity, diversity, and uniqueness, should images of hallowed ground that has since been irreparably altered rank higher [in significance] than well-preserved landscapes? A visitor to Gettysburg or Antietam can view the topography much as the soldiers did. That is not the case for urban Atlanta and Nashville, or victims of nature such as Battery Wagner, Fort Fisher, and Port Hudson." Lawrence Lee Hewitt, *Port Hudson: The Most Significant Battlefield Photographs from the Civil War* (University of Tennessee Press, 2021), xxxi.

4. Although one might argue that the positioning of the rifle muskets suggested that they were prepared for salvage if the Confederates pushed to recapture the position.

5. According to the National Archives, to historian James Horan (*Mathew Brady: Historian with a Camera*), and to Wikipedia.

6. Gardner's photographs from Antietam and Gettysburg were also probably

competing with each other with respect to overall popularity. For example, for a general history of the Civil War a publisher might select a photograph or two from each battle, so that only one of Gardner's important photographs from Antietam might be included. For Russell's photograph of the Stone Wall at Fredericksburg, in contrast, there really isn't any direct competition.

7. And the one detracting element from *Harvest* is the misleading captions provided by Gardner, something that shouldn't be held against the person who captured the actual negative.

8. Fort Pulaski was devastated by long-range, land-based heavy rifled artillery fire.

9. The photographers also never photographed a closer image of this body, perhaps because it was already in the process of being interred.

10. And, just like Cooley and Barnard's photographs of the earthworks at Knoxville, this fortification would eventually be lost to urban sprawl.

11. Ron Field, *Silent Witness: The Civil War Through Photography and Its Photographers* (Osprey, 2017), 279

12. See O'Sullivan's collection of dead Confederate soldiers at Spotsylvania, where an Enfield rifle begins to move between different dead bodies.

INDEX

props, 32, 75–76, 121,171; added to
    photographs, x, 3, 103, 163,
    176, 192n5; artillery swabs and
    sponges, 80–81, 157–58, 195n13;
    rifles, ix, 39, 76–81, 97, 196n12;
    studio, 167–68
Pywell, William, 10, 17, 172

Quartermaster Corps, 11, 14
Quinby, G.J., 15

radiometric dating, 47
Rawlins, John, 126
Reekie, John, 8–10, 165, 172; biography,
    14; at Cold Harbor, 126–31; at
    Dutch Gap Canal, 135; at Rich-
    mond, 115
resolution, 76, 127, 138, 165; compari-
    son of glass plates to 35 mm film,
    46; digital, 4; high, 6, 9, 12, 30,
    46–47, 52, 54, 103, 111, 121, 179
Reynolds, John, 47, 57, 91–94, 172;
    Avenue, 59
Richmond, Virginia, 13, 14, 115–17, 134,
    149; photographed after burning,
    9, 108, 115
Roche, Thomas, 80, 187n29; biography,
    12–13; at City Point, 12, 153; at
    Dutch Gap Canal, 12; at Peters-
    burg, 152–58, 160–63, 165, 171,
    176–79
Rodes, Robert, 28, 40
Russell, Andrew, 11–12, 15, 165, 167,
    187n31; biography, 11; at City

Point, 153; at Dutch Gap Canal,
    135–36; at Fredericksburg, 24, 27,
    32–34, 171–72, 176; at Petersburg,
    160–63, 176; *Photographs Illus-
    trative of Operations in Construc-
    tion and Transportation*, 187n31

Sabine, USS, 88–89
Savannah, Georgia, 11, 14, 172
Scott, Winfield, 7
self-timers, camera, 5
shadows, as timekeepers, 52, 54–55,
    107, 123
Sherman, William, 11, 12, 14, 87,
    116–19, 169
shutter speeds, 14, 75, 103–5, 191n9;
    comparison of camera types,
    111–12; length, 103–7; studio cam-
    eras, 103, 106–7, 111; summary,
    106; testing, 112–13
Sleeper, J. Henry, 86
Smith, William Morris, 17, 117–18
South Mountain, Maryland, 15
Spotsylvania Court House, Virginia,
    9–10, 16, 24, 152, 159, 196n12;
    battlefield, 24, 123, 172
St. Augustine, Florida, 14
stratigraphy, 141, 147, 165
Survey of the 100th Meridian, 10

Taylor, Walter, 115, 193n1
Tipton, William, 17, 73
Tyson, Charles, 17
Tyson, Isaac, 17

Union Pacific Railroad, 11
United States Army Department of the
    South, 14
United States Geological Exploration
    of the 40th Parallel, 10
United States Geological Survey, 10
United States Military Railroad, 11
United States Tank Corps, 69

Valley and Ridge Physiographic Prov-
    ince, 49
Vicksburg, Mississippi, 133–134, 141,
    194n12
Virginia, CSS, 13
Vizetelly, Frank, 87

War Photograph and Exhibition Com-
    pany, The, 158
Warren, Gouverneur, 58–59, 190n8
Waud, Alfred, 85–86, 173; comparison
    of sketches to photographs, 88–94;
    at Gettysburg, 96–99, 192n15
Waud, William, 87, 165; at Dutch Gap
    Canal, 138, 141
weapons, ix, 76, 121, 167, 171, 186n9;
    change during the Civil War, 5,
    121, 166; salvaged, 34, 195n4
weathering, 30, 48–49, 61, 69, 146, 165;
    anthropogenic, 5, 186n8; defined,
    189n8; spheroidal, 48
Weaver, Peter, 74, 79–80
Wheeler, George, 10
"Whipped Peter," photograph, 15,
    187n37, 193n12

Whitney, Edward, 16, 17
Wood, John, 10, 13
Woodbury, David, 10; biography, 16

Yorktown, Virginia, 13, 17